Ryan D. Collman
The Apostle to the Foreskin

Beihefte zur Zeitschrift
für die neutestamentliche
Wissenschaft

Edited by
Knut Backhaus, Matthias Konradt, Judith Lieu,
Laura Nasrallah, Jens Schröter, and Gregory E. Sterling

Volume 259

Ryan D. Collman

The Apostle to the Foreskin

Circumcision in the Letters of Paul

DE GRUYTER

ISBN 978-3-11-162799-1
e-ISBN (PDF) 978-3-11-098172-8
e-ISBN (EPUB) 978-3-11-098178-0
ISSN 0171-6441

Library of Congress Control Number: 2022923376

Bibliographic Information published by the Deutsche Nationalbibliothek
The Deutsche Nationalbibliothek lists this publication in the Deutsche Nationalbibliografie;
Detailed bibliographic data are available in the Internet at http://dnb.dnb.de.

© 2024 Walter de Gruyter GmbH, Berlin/Boston
This volume is text- and page-identical with the hardback published in 2023.

www.degruyter.com

"Why are we doing this again?" my wife asked me, not for the first time, on the night of the seventh day of our second son's life.

— Michael Chabon, "The Cut"

Contents

Acknowledgments —— 1

Copyright Permissions —— 3

Abbreviations —— 4

1 Introduction
 Paul: A Circumcised Apostle —— 5
1.1 Introducing Paul and Circumcision —— 5
1.2 Paul and Circumcision via "Paul and Judaism" —— 7
1.2.1 An Emerging Paradigm —— 9
1.3 Recent Contributions —— 11
1.4 Circumcision, Foreskin, and Paul's Ethnic Map —— 16
1.5 Method —— 18
1.6 Outline —— 20

2 Keeping the Commandments of God
 Circumcision in 1 Corinthians —— 22
2.1 Introduction —— 22
2.2 Paul's Rule in All the Assemblies and the Language of Calling —— 23
2.3 Circumcision and Foreskin as Callings —— 26
2.3.1 Epispasm and Jewish Identity —— 30
2.3.2 Circumcision and Non-Jews —— 32
2.3.3 An Objection: "When you were gentiles..." (1 Cor 12:2) —— 34
2.4 Circumcision and Foreskin as Nothing —— 36
2.4.1 Rhetorical Negation and Comparison —— 38
2.5 Circumcision and Keeping the Commandments of God —— 41
2.6 Conclusion —— 45

3 Do You Not Hear the Law?
 Circumcision in Galatians —— 47
3.1 Introduction —— 47
3.2 Galatians 2 —— 48
3.2.1 The Apostolic Consensus on Gentile Circumcision —— 49
3.2.2 "Not even Titus was Compelled to be Circumcised" —— 50
3.2.3 The Antioch Incident —— 52

3.3	The Presenting Issue: Gentile Circumcision —— 55
3.3.1	Why Does Paul Oppose Circumcision in Galatians? Some Prominent Proposals —— 56
3.3.2	Critiquing Previous Proposals —— 60
3.4	Paul and the Allegory of the Enslaved Woman and the Free Woman: Galatians 4:21–5:1 —— 63
3.4.1	Competing Mothers, Missions, and Offspring —— 66
3.4.2	Where is Circumcision? —— 69
3.5	Sonship via *Pneuma*, Not Circumcision —— 76
3.6	Pruning Circumcised Gentiles in Christ: Galatians 5:2–4 —— 80
3.6.1	Schweitzer, *Pneuma*, and *die Todsünden* —— 81
3.6.2	Circumcision and the Whole Law —— 86
3.7	Are Circumcision and Foreskin Actually Nothing? Galatians 5:6 and 6:15 —— 92
3.7.1	Galatians 5:6 —— 93
3.7.2	Galatians 6:15 —— 95
3.8	Paul: Proclaimer of Circumcision? Galatians 5:11 —— 99
3.8.1	Prevailing Perspectives —— 100
3.8.2	A New Proposal —— 108
3.9	"Cutting Off" The Agitators: Galatians 5:12 —— 112
3.9.1	Galatians 5:12 and Castration —— 113
3.9.2	Galatians 5:12 and Exclusion —— 116
3.10	Identifying the Agitators: Galatians 6:12–13 —— 119
3.11	Conclusion —— 123

4 We Are the Circumcision
Circumcision in Philippians —— 125

4.1	Introduction —— 125
4.2	The Dogs —— 127
4.2.1	The Deconstruction of an Ideological Tale: Dogs in Ancient Jewish Sources and the Gospels —— 128
4.2.2	A New Proposal: An Overlooked Meaning of κύων —— 131
4.3	The Wicked Workers —— 134
4.4	The Mutilation —— 136
4.5	Further Identifying the Opponents: Philippians 3:18–19 —— 140
4.6	"We are the Circumcision!" —— 142
4.6.1	Paul's Pristine Pedigree —— 145
4.7	Conclusion —— 146

5		The God of the Circumcision and the Foreskin Circumcision in Romans —— 148
5.1		Introduction —— 148
5.1.1		Reading Romans —— 149
5.1.2		Romans and the Diatribe —— 151
5.2		Paul and An Interlocutor: Romans 2:17 —— 153
5.2.1		Identifying the So-Called Jew —— 154
5.2.2		Indicting the So-Called Jew —— 157
5.3		Circumcision and the So-Called Jew: Romans 2:25–29 —— 160
5.3.1		Circumcision as Foreskin and Foreskin as Circumcision —— 162
5.3.2		Heart Circumcision and the Jew in Secret —— 169
5.4		The Benefit of Circumcision: Romans 3:1–2 —— 177
5.5		The God of the Circumcision and the Foreskin: Romans 3:29–30 —— 180
5.5.1		The One God of Jews and the Nations —— 180
5.6		Abraham's Faithful Foreskin: Romans 4:9–12 —— 183
5.6.1		Reckoning *Dikaiosynē* to Abraham: Not "When?" but "How?" —— 185
5.6.2		Foregrounding the Forefather's Foreskin: An Epispasmic Reading of Romans 4:9–12 —— 187
5.7		The Messiah as Agent of the Circumcision: Romans 15:8 —— 190
5.8		Conclusion —— 195
6		Conclusion Paul: The Apostle to the Foreskin —— 197
6.1		Re-reading Paul and Circumcision —— 197
6.2		Early Christian Circumcision Polemics —— 198
6.3		Paul and the Polemicists —— 201
6.4		Conclusion: The Apostle to the Foreskin —— 202

Bibliography —— 203
   Primary Sources —— 203
   Secondary Sources —— 205

Index of Names —— 224

Index of Subjects —— 229

Ancient Sources —— 231

Acknowledgments

This project would not have been possible without the help and encouragement of numerous individuals. This book is a revised version of my PhD thesis, which was completed under the supervision of Matthew Novenson at the University of Edinburgh. First and foremost, I must thank Matt for his excellent supervision, guidance, and encouragement while I was working on this project. Matt is a champion of his students, and I'm truly grateful for the opportunity to have worked with him since my arrival in Edinburgh in 2015.

Many of my colleagues at New College served as voices of encouragement and critique throughout the production of this work. Special thanks go to the past and present members of the Novenson cohort: Bernardo Cho, J. Thomas Hewitt, Benj Petroelje, Daniel Jackson, Sydney Tooth, Brian Bunnell, Patrick McMurray, Sofanit Abebe, Alex Muir, and Manse Rim. The final year of my PhD was completed during the COVID-19 pandemic, and I would also like to express gratitude to my writing group, the COVID Collective, for providing me with the scholarly community that helped see this project to completion. Our weekly Zoom meetings and ongoing chat were a bright spot in a dark year. The COVID Collective is comprised of Isaac Soon, Grace Emmett, and Logan Williams. Belonging to both the Novenson cohort and Covid Collective are Matthew Sharp and Charles Cisco. I am particularly grateful for their friendships and for the hours of conversations we have shared over countless cups of coffee and pints these past handful of years. Since completing my PhD, Emily Gathergood and Alexi Chantziantoniou have also become consistent voices of scholarly encouragement and friendship. Not only have all of these colleagues influenced this book and me as a scholar, but many of their families have provided my family with a great community in Scotland. Special thanks go out to Josh and Lindsay Bruce who became our extended family during our first few years in Edinburgh.

Portions of this research were presented in various scholarly settings: The New College Biblical Studies Seminar, the University of Nottingham Biblical Research Seminar, and the annual meetings of the British New Testament Society and the Society of Biblical Literature. Thanks to all who interacted with my work in these venues. I was also fortunate enough to participate in the Expert Meeting on Male Circumcision at the University of Oslo (9–11 May 2019), which was organized by Karin Neutel. I am particularly thankful for the group of scholars that attended this meeting and the valuable feedback they gave me. I must also extend my gratitude to my examiners, Philippa Townsend and Paula Fredriksen, for giving me a stimulating viva in a collegial atmosphere. Both Philippa's and Paula's ongoing support of my scholarship has been invaluable. The anonymous reviewer for

De Gruyter offered insightful feedback that improved many aspects of this book. My editors at De Gruyter, Aaron Sanborn-Overby and Alice Meroz, have been helpful at every step in the publication of this book and are due many thanks.

Lastly, I would like to thank all of the family members who have served as ongoing sources of support and encouragement throughout the completion of this project. Thanks to my father and mother for each instilling a love of learning in me in their own ways. Very special thanks go to my mom who has supported me in every way imaginable. I could not have made it this far without her. My children, Islay and Isaac, have been constant sources of joy over the past few years. Though they may not be aware of it now, they have both sacrificed much throughout their early years of life. I am grateful for their unconditional love. The person most deserving of gratitude is my wife, Lauren. This project would not have been possible without her continued sacrifice, support, and willingness to leave everything behind and start fresh in Edinburgh. It is hard work to complete a PhD, but it is much more difficult to be partners with someone completing a PhD. This book is as much a product of her sacrifice as it is my research. I dedicate it to her.

Copyright Permissions

Portions of this book have previously appeared in *New Testament Studies* and *Journal of the Jesus Movement in its Jewish Setting*. They have been reproduced here in modified form with permission.

Ryan D. Collman, "Beware the Dogs! The Phallic Epithet in Phil 3.2," *NTS* 67 (2021): 105–20. Reprinted with permission.

Ryan D. Collman, "Just A Flesh Wound? Reassessing Paul's Supposed Indifference Toward Circumcision and Foreskin in 1 Cor 7:19, Gal 5:6, and 6:15," *JJMJS* 8 (2021): 30–52. Reprinted with permission under a Creative Commons Attribution License: https://creativecommons.org/licenses/by/4.0/

Abbreviations

All abbreviations conform to those prescribed in *The SBL Handbook of Style: For Biblical Studies and Related Disciplines*, ed. Billie Jean Collins, Bob Buller, and John F. Kutsko, 2nd ed. (Atlanta: SBL Press, 2014). For abbreviations not found in *The SBL Handbook of Style*, see Siegfried M. Schwertner, *IATG³: Internationales Abkürzungsverzeichnis für Theologie und Grenzgebiete*, 3rd ed. (Berlin: de Gruyter, 2014).

1 Introduction
Paul: A Circumcised Apostle

[Jesus'] disciples said to him, "Is circumcision beneficial or not?" He said to them, "If it were beneficial, their father would beget them already circumcised from their mother.[1] Rather, the true circumcision in spirit has become completely profitable." (Gos. Thom. 53 [Lambdin])

1.1 Introducing Paul and Circumcision

While these words almost certainly do not go back to the mouth of the historical Jesus of Nazareth,[2] many find them to be at home in the theology of the apostle Paul. For example, Gerd Lüdemann comments, "Like Paul (Rom. 2.25–29; 1 Cor. 7.7–19 [sic]; Gal. 6.5 [sic]; Phil. 3.3), this verse understands circumcision in the metaphorical sense and thus provides a further argument against the benefits of circumcision."[3] In the same vein, Joshua Jipp and Michael Thate note, "Paul redefines circumcision and Judaism in such a way that the literal is transcended by the spiritual; that is, circumcision is not of the flesh but is rather a process worked by the Spirit on the heart....Like Paul, [in the Gospel of Thomas] true circumcision is not of the flesh but is altogether located in the metaphorical and spiritual realm."[4]

These remarks represent a fairly standard reading of Paul and circumcision that has been prevalent for centuries.[5] This common understanding of how Paul

---

[1] This argument against circumcision is also made by Justin (*Dial.* 19.3) and the Judaean governor, Tineius Rufus (according to Midr. Tanḥ., *Tazria* 7 [Buber]).

[2] Simon Gathercole, *The Gospel of Thomas: Introduction and Commentary*, TENTS 11 (Leiden: Brill, 2014), 420.

[3] Gerd Lüdemann, *Jesus After 2000 Years: What He Really Said and Did*, trans. John Bowden (London: SCM, 2000), 616.

[4] Joshua W. Jipp and Michael J. Thate, "*Dating* Thomas: Logion 53 as a Test Case for Dating the Gospel of Thomas within an Early Christian Trajectory," *BBR* 20 (2010): 237–56, at 248–49. Jipp and Thate do cite Rom 3:1–2, correctly noting that Paul still affirms the validity of circumcision as God's covenantal sign for Israel. This, however, is overshadowed by their emphasis on Paul's redefinition, allegorization, and spiritualization of circumcision. See also, Gathercole, *Gospel of Thomas*, 420–22.

[5] See, e.g., Justin, *Dial.* 19.3; 92.3–4: John Chrysostom, *Hom. Gal.* 5; Thomas Aquinas, *Comm. Rom.* §240–45; Martin Luther, *A Commentary on the Galatians* (Chester: Jones & Crane, 1796), 326–31; Ferdinand Christian Baur, *Paul the Apostle of Jesus Christ*, 2 vols. (London: Williams & Norgate, 1873) 1:208; 322; Rudolf Bultmann, *Theology of the New Testament*, trans. Kendrick Grobel, 2 vols. (New York: Scribner's Sons, 1951), 263–64, 340–41; Peter Richardson, *Israel in the Apostolic Church*,

speaks about circumcision makes a handful of claims. First, Paul denies the benefit and value of physical circumcision.⁶ Second, Paul redefines what constitutes proper circumcision and who it applies to. Third, spiritual circumcision makes physical circumcision redundant or obsolete. Lastly, like Thomas' Jesus, Paul's negative evaluation of circumcision occurs irrespective of ethnic concerns. While individual interpreters' readings are nuanced in their assessment of Paul's discourse on circumcision, these are the commonly shared ideas that one typically encounters in scholarly discussions of Paul and circumcision.

In this book, I argue that Paul held none of these views about circumcision. Through a comprehensive examination of every instance of circumcision language in Paul's epistles, I make the case that he upholds the practice and value of circumcision for Jews. He does not redefine it, replace it, declare its irrelevance, or expand its application to non-Jews—metaphorically or otherwise. Paul's rejection of circumcision for non-Jews does not indicate any repudiation of the practice for his fellow Jews. For example, in Phil 3:3, Paul's statement, "We are the circumcision," does not refer to "Christians" as the "true circumcision"—a phrase that does not occur in Paul's writings or the New Testament—but simply refers to Paul and Timothy, the Jewish authors of the letter (Phil 1:1). Or in Rom 2:28–29, when Paul speaks about circumcision of the heart, he does not do so to describe a universal circumcision available to his gentile audience or to devalue physical circumcision, but to describe the necessity of heart-circumcision for physically circumcised Jews. Or in 1 Cor 7:17–19, Paul does not view circumcision and foreskin as things of indifference, but as important ethnic and social categories that have ongoing implications for how Jews and non-Jews in the assembly are to live.

Crucial for this investigation is Paul's self-identification as an apostle to the nations (e.g., Rom 1:5; 11:13–14; Gal 1:15–16; 2:7–9). It is within the context of his epistles written to foreskinned non-Jews that we find all of Paul's words on circumcision. Hence the title of this work, *The Apostle to the Foreskin: Circumcision in the*

SNTSMS 10 (Cambridge: Cambridge University Press, 1969), 115; Ernst Käsemann, *An die Römer*, 4th ed., HNT 8a (Tübingen: Mohr Siebeck, 1980), 68–69; E. P. Sanders, *Paul, the Law, and the Jewish People* (Philadelphia: Fortress, 1983), 102–3; Heikki Räisänen, *Paul and the Law*, WUNT 29 (Tubingen: Mohr Siebeck, 1983), 76, 258; Thomas R. Schreiner, "The Abolition and Fulfillment of the Law in Paul," *JSNT* 35 (1989): 47–74; Daniel Boyarin, *A Radical Jew: Paul and the Politics of Identity* (Berkeley: University of California Press, 2004), 80–82, 93–94; John M. G. Barclay, "Paul, the Gift and the Battle Over Gentile Circumcision: Revisiting the Logic of Galatians," *ABR* 58, (2010): 36–56; Nina E. Livesey, *Circumcision as a Malleable Symbol*, WUNT 2/295 (Tübingen: Mohr Siebeck, 2010), 77–122.

6 Rom 3:1–2 is Paul's clearest statement against this position. Some individuals, however, assert that this positive statement is more about the place of Jews in salvation history (e.g., Jipp and Thate, "*Dating* Thomas," 249).

Letters of Paul. This title—I think—captures the physical and ethnic binary that frames Paul's discourse on circumcision.

1.2 Paul and Circumcision via "Paul and Judaism"

Scholarly treatments of Paul and circumcision are often determined by how one views Paul's relationship to Judaism.[7] The centuries-long, prevailing perspective in Pauline studies is that Paul abandoned Judaism, which included a rejection of the necessity of physical circumcision.[8] The justification given for Paul's conversion out of Judaism often mirrors one's justification for Paul's abrogation of physical circumcision. For the majority of the nineteenth and twentieth centuries, Paul's rejection of Judaism and circumcision was thought to be a product of his rejection of the supposed legalism and exclusivity of Judaism, and his conversion to universalistic, law-free Christianity.[9] For example, Rudolf Bultmann writes, "Paul's struggle in Galatia against the Law as the way to salvation is simultaneously a struggle against the ritual and cultic rules, particularly against circumcision and the Jewish festivals."[10] By positioning legalistic Judaism as law-free Christianity's foil, it was easy to justify Paul's rejection of physical circumcision within the context of his rejection of the legalism of Judaism.

While some scholars in the twentieth century began to question the validity of the characterization of Judaism as legalistic[11]—and thus, Paul's relationship to it[12]

---

[7] For a concise overview of scholarship on Paul's relationship to Judaism, see Magnus Zetterholm, "Paul within Judaism: The State of the Questions," in *Paul within Judaism: Restoring the First-Century Context to the Apostle*, ed. Mark D. Nanos and Magnus Zetterholm (Minneapolis: Fortress, 2015), 31–51. For a fuller treatment of this topic, see Magnus Zetterholm, *Approaches to Paul: A Student's Guide to Recent Scholarship* (Minneapolis: Fortress, 2009).
[8] Similarly, Paul's writings that discuss circumcision are used as evidence to demonstrate that his thinking was not compatible with Judaism. Citing Gal 5:12 and Phil 3:2, Räisänen notes that Paul's words are no longer representative of "a genuinely Jewish stance" (*Paul and the Law*, 258). Cf. idem, "Galatians 2.16 and Paul's Break with Judaism," *NTS* 31 (1985): 543–53.
[9] On the problematic nature of the terminology of universalism and particularism, see Anders Runesson, "Particularistic Judaism and Universalistic Christianity? Some Critical Remarks on Terminology and Theology," *ST* 53 (2000): 55–75.
[10] Bultmann, *Theology of the New Testament*, 1:341. Similarly, F. C. Baur asserted that Paul "emancipated Christianity from Judaism, by freeing it from circumcision, the outward sign of subjection which Judaism wished to impose on it as the necessary condition of salvation" (*Paul*, 1:322).
[11] E.g., George Foot Moore, "Christian Writers on Judaism," *HTR* 14 (1921): 197–254.
[12] E.g., C. G. Montefiore, *Judaism and St. Paul: Two Essays* (London: Goschen, 1914); Johannes Munck, *Paul and the Salvation of Mankind*, trans. Frank Clarke (London: SCM, 1959); Krister Stendahl, *Paul Among Jews and Gentiles, and Other Essays* (Philadelphia: Fortress, 1976).

—it was not until the publication of E. P. Sanders' *Paul and Palestinian Judaism* in 1977—and the subsequent birth of the so-called "New Perspective on Paul"—that perspectives on Paul's relationship to Judaism began to shift more broadly. As scholars adopted Sanders' revised view of Judaism as a religion of grace, they began to rethink the question of Paul and circumcision.[13] Most notably, James Dunn and N. T. Wright argued that Paul rejected the necessity of physical circumcision because of the ethnocentrism and exclusivism of Judaism, not because of its supposed legalism.[14] On their readings, circumcision and other works of the law functioned as Jewish badges of covenant membership that divided Jews from non-Jews. As Wright puts it, "They were determinative for showing who was a part of the people dividing lines between Jews and gentiles, and have no place in the *ekklēsia.*"[15] Since—on this reading—the people of God have now been redefined through *pistis* directed toward the Messiah, Paul can dispense with the ongoing validity of these Jewish identifying marks, of which circumcision is chief.

Despite the fact that the majority of interpreters assert that Paul no longer found physical circumcision to be of value for those who followed the Messiah, many note that circumcision continued to have metaphorical and symbolic value for Paul.[16] Due to the perceived negative assessment of Judaism in Paul's writings, his positive employment of circumcision leads many interpreters to conclude that he is redefining or reinterpreting circumcision.[17] On this type of reading, Paul transforms what it means to be circumcised and what the category of "the circumcision" refers to. Here, scholars appeal to Rom 2:28–29 to argue that Paul spiritualizes—and thus universalizes—circumcision by noting "true circumcision" is of the heart. Furthermore, Phil 3:3 is used to demonstrate that the Christian church has replaced Jews as "the circumcision." On these readings, Paul reappropriates and Christianizes circumcision for the church.

---

[13] For a critique of Sanders and his use of the category of grace, see Jonathan A. Linebaugh, *God, Grace, and Righteousness in Wisdom of Solomon and Paul's Letter to the Romans: Texts in Conversation*, NovTSup 152 (Leiden: Brill, 2013), 6–13; John M. G. Barclay, *Paul and the Gift* (Grand Rapids: Eerdmans, 2015), 151–58.

[14] James D. G. Dunn, *The New Perspective on Paul*, rev. ed. (Grand Rapids: Eerdmans, 2008); N. T. Wright, *Paul and the Faithfulness of God*, 2 vols. (Minneapolis: Fortress, 2013).

[15] Wright, *Paul*, 1136.

[16] For a recent treatment of circumcision as a metaphor in Paul's thought, see Ralph Bisschops, "Metaphor in Religious Transformation: 'Circumcision of the Heart' in Paul of Tarsus," in *Religion, Language, and the Human Mind*, ed. Paul Chilton and Monika Kopytowska (New York: Oxford University Press, 2018), 294–329. On the distinction between physical and metaphorical circumcision in Rom 2:28–29, Bisschops notes, "The fact that he needed circumcision as a metaphor to abrogate genital circumcision is puzzling in itself. He introduces a supreme Jewish value to abolish it" (316).

[17] For my rebuttal of this perspective, see my discussions of Phil 3:3 and Rom 2:28–29.

1.2.1 An Emerging Paradigm

The primary point of departure between this project and the majority of previous treatments of Paul and circumcision—and thus one of the main contributions of this work—is how I understand Paul's relationship to Judaism. I make the argument of this book within the context of the emerging Paul within Judaism *Schule*.[18] Simply put, the guiding assumption of this perspective is that "the writing and community building of the apostle Paul took place *within* late Second Temple Judaism, *within* which he remained a representative after his change of conviction about Jesus being the Messiah (Christ)."[19] To put it another way, Paul's acknowledgment that Jesus was the Messiah[20]—and his subsequent call to be the apostle to the nations—did not constitute an abandonment of his ancestral traditions (or his ethnic identity), but was simply its own expression of Judaism within a sea of other expressions (e.g., Pharisaic Judaism, Qumran Judaism, Enochic Judaism, etc.).[21] Or to state it more succinctly, Paul was not a Christian.[22]

---

[18] For an overview of the Paul within Judaism movement, see Nanos and Zetterholm, *Paul within Judaism*. See also, Kathy Ehrensperger, "Die ›Paul within Judaism‹-Perspektive. Eine Übersicht," *EvT* 80 (2020): 455–64.
[19] Mark D. Nanos, "Introduction," in Nanos and Zetterholm, *Paul within Judaism*, 1–29, at 9 (emphasis original). See also, Paula Fredriksen, "What Does It Mean to See Paul 'within Judaism'?" *JBL* 141 (2022): 359–80.
[20] On Paul's designation of Jesus as the Messiah, see Matthew V. Novenson, *Christ among the Messiahs: Christ Language in Paul and Messiah Language in Ancient Judaism* (New York: Oxford University Press, 2012).
[21] On this, see Matthew V. Novenson, "Did Paul Abandon Either Judaism or Monotheism?" in *The New Cambridge Companion to St Paul*, ed. Bruce W. Longenecker (Cambridge: Cambridge University Press, 2020), 239–59. See also Anders Runesson, "The Question of Terminology: The Architecture of Contemporary Discussions on Paul," in Nanos and Zetterholm, *Paul within Judaism*, 59–68, esp. 67–68; Anders Runesson and Daniel M. Gurtner, "Introduction: The Location of the Matthew-within-Judaism Perspective in Past and Present Research," in *Matthew within Judaism: Israel and the Nations in the First Gospel*, ed. Anders Runesson and Daniel M. Gurtner, ECL 27 (Atlanta: SBL Press, 2020), 1–6. Mark Nanos and Anders Runesson have coined the term "Apostolic Judaism" as a way to refer to the early Jesus movement as an expression of ancient Judaism. On this, see Anders Runesson, "Inventing Christian Identity: Paul, Ignatius, and Theodosius I," in *Exploring Early Christian Identity*, ed. Bengt Holmberg, WUNT 226 (Tübingen: Mohr Siebeck, 2008), 72–74.
[22] Here, I refer to the provocative title of Pamela Eisenbaum's book: *Paul Was Not a Christian: The Original Message of a Misunderstood Apostle* (New York: HarperOne, 2009). On the invention of the terms "Christian" and "Christianity," see Anders Runesson, "Inventing Christian Identity," 59–92; Philippa Townsend, "Who Were the First Christians? Jews, Gentiles and the *Christianoi*," in *Heresy and Identity in Late Antiquity*, ed. Eduard Iricinschi and Holger M. Zellentin, TSAJ 119 (Tübingen: Mohr Siebeck, 2008), 212–230. On the current debate surrounding the usefulness of the category of "Jewish Christianity" in the first century and beyond, see the discussions in Annette Yoshiko

Like most deities in antiquity, Paul's god is an ethnic god; he was Jewish.[23] As Paula Fredriksen notes, unlike other gods and their peoples, the Jews claimed that their god "was *also* the universal god, the highest god, the supreme god. Even odder was the claim of some Jews of apocalyptic bent: the Jewish god, they said, would ultimately be worshiped by ethnic others, both human and divine."[24] Paul believes that through the work of the Messiah, the time has come for non-Jews to worship Israel's god. It is within this eschatological context that Paul receives his call to the nations, to call them to worship the god of Israel through his Messiah Jesus.[25] But in this call and mission he is adamant that they remain the ethnic other—that they remain distinct from Jews (Rom 11:13–24).[26]

With this as a starting point, we can begin to read Paul's discussion of circumcision afresh. If Paul remained a Jew who lived Jewishly, and was writing to non-Jewish audiences, we need to interpret his statements about circumcision and foreskin within that specific context. Interpreters have been too quick to universalize Paul's every word, when in actuality his epistles were written to very specific groups of people for very specific reasons. To be sure, I am not the first person to read Paul in this manner and explore his usage of circumcision language.[27] This is, however, the first comprehensive treatment of circumcision in Paul's epistles from this perspective. It should also be noted that while I situate this work within the Paul within Judaism movement, I do not write this volume as a means of converting others to this perspective. This book is simply my reading of Paul's discourses on circumcision and foreskin. If one finds merit in my treat-

---

Reed, *Jewish-Christianity and the History of Judaism*, TSAJ 171 (Tübingen: Mohr Siebeck, 2018); Matt Jackson-McCabe, *Jewish Christianity: The Making of the Christianity-Judaism Divide*, AYBRL (New Haven: Yale University Press, 2020).

23 The premier treatment of this concept is Paula Fredriksen, "How Jewish Is God? Divine Ethnicity in Paul's Theology," *JBL* 137 (2018): 193–212. Contra John M. G. Barclay, "An Identity Received from God: The Theological Configuration of Paul's Kinship Discourse," *EC* 8 (2017): 354–72, at 369.

24 Fredriksen, "How Jewish is God?" 194 (emphasis original).

25 On Paul's "calling," rather than his "conversion," see the classic treatments of Munck (*Paul and the Salvation*, 11–35) and Stendahl ("Call Rather Than Conversion" in *Paul Among Jews*, 7–23). For an overview of the debate surrounding this distinction, see Paula Fredriksen, "Paul the 'Convert'?" in *The Oxford Handbook of Pauline Studies*, ed. Matthew V. Novenson and R. Barry Matlock (Oxford: Oxford University Press, 2022) 31–53.

26 There are, however, some key Pauline texts that have traditionally been interpreted as indicating that Paul abolished ethnic distinctions (e.g., Rom 10:12; Gal 3:28; cf. Col 3:11). On these texts, see the discussion in William S. Campbell, *The Nations in the Divine Economy: Paul's Covenantal Hermeneutics and Participation in Christ* (Lanham, MD: Lexington Books/Fortress Academic, 2018), 129–52.

27 Given the relative ubiquity of circumcision language in Paul, this is a topic that has been discussed by effectively every interpreter who identifies with this perspective.

ment of these texts, then perhaps they will come to find merit in the larger Paul within Judaism movement. I hope my particular reading—and its varying degrees of agreement and disagreement with other interpreters—demonstrates that this perspective has not pre-determined my conclusions.

1.3 Recent Contributions

Given the role circumcision plays in Paul's epistles, it is a topic that frequently appears in the ever-growing body of literature that addresses the question of Paul's relationship to Judaism and its law. While shorter treatments of Paul's views about circumcision make their way into various books and articles, it has rarely received full-length treatment. As far as I can ascertain, the first full-length treatment of Paul and circumcision is Thomas Schreiner's 1983 PhD dissertation, "Circumcision: An Entrée into 'Newness' in Pauline Thought." Schreiner's argument follows a traditional, anti-legalist reading of Paul in which circumcision has become obsolete due to Paul's break with Judaism and the subsequent obsolescence of the law. He argues that physical circumcision has been replaced with circumcision of the heart (Rom 2:28–29), and this "true circumcision" applies to the Christian church (Phil 3:3).[28] As I will demonstrate throughout this book, this conventional understanding of Paul and circumcision is fundamentally misguided and untenable.

The next full treatment of Paul and circumcision is Andreas Blaschke's, *Beschneidung: Zeugnisse der Bibel und verwandter Texte* (1998). In this comprehensive sourcebook, Blaschke not only gives a full exposition of circumcision in the Pauline epistles, but also offers significant discussions of circumcision texts from the Hebrew Bible, Septuagint, Qumran, New Testament, Early Christianity, Greco-Roman sources, Jewish pseudepigrapha, and Rabbinic literature. The breadth and depth of material covered by Blaschke is unmatched and is indispensable for anyone studying circumcision in antiquity. While the contributions of this volume are legion, his treatment of Pauline texts is fairly traditional.[29] He emphasizes Paul's supposed spiritualization and universalization of circumcision, applying spiritual circumcision of the heart (Rom 2:28–29) to "Christians" as the "true circumcision" (Phil 3:3).[30] Like most anti-legalist interpreters of Paul, Blaschke proposes that Paul's rejection of circumcision for gentiles rests primarily in his rejection

---

[28] Thomas R. Schreiner, "Circumcision: An Entrée into 'Newness' in Pauline Thought" (PhD diss., Fuller Theological Seminary, 1983), 198–204, 245–49, passim.
[29] Andreas Blaschke, *Beschneidung: Zeugnisse der Bibel und verwandter Texte*, TANZ 28 (Tübingen: Francke, 1998), 361–425.
[30] Blaschke, *Beschneidung*, 401–14.

of the law as the grounds for salvation (Gal 5:2–6). He is, however, attuned to Paul's ethnic dichotomy and notes that Paul does not abrogate circumcision for Jews (or "Jewish Christians")—although he does devalue it (1 Cor 7:19; Gal 5:6; 6:15).[31] Additionally, Blaschke is to be lauded for his emphasis on the physicality of circumcision[32] and his fairly consistent usage of *Vorhaut* as a gloss for ἀκροβυστία instead of the more typical *unbeschnitten*.[33]

The next contribution also comes from outside of anglophone scholarship: Simon Claude Mimouni's, *La circoncision dans le monde judéen aux époques grecque et romaine: Histoire d'un conflit interne au judaïsme* (2007). Like Blaschke, Mimouni offers an extensive examination of circumcision in ancient Jewish, early Christian, and Greco-Roman sources.[34] His study is particularly interested in understanding the variety of meanings attributed to and arguments for or against circumcision in ancient Judaism. Regarding the Jesus movement in the first century, Mimouni notes that there generally existed a double attitude toward circumcision; it should not be suppressed for Jews and it should not be imposed on non-Jews.[35] Concerning Paul and circumcision, his conclusions are relatively conventional. He argues that Paul abandoned the necessity of circumcision for "Christians" (Gal 5:1–6).[36] While Paul still allows for Jews in the Jesus movement to practice circumcision, he does not consider it to be a necessity for them or of any particular value (1 Cor 7:19; Gal 5:6; 6:15),[37] and he prohibits non-Jews from being

---

[31] Blashke's (*Beschneidung*, 414) reading of Rom 3:1–2 downplays Paul's positive statements about Jewish circumcision. See also pages 419–21, where Blaschke offers an excursus on Paul and the circumcision of "Jewish Christians."

[32] This is especially noticeable in his introduction (*Beschneidung*, 2–18) and his discussion of ancient medical texts related to circumcision and penile aesthetics (350–56).

[33] On the translation ἀκροβυστία, see the discussion below.

[34] Surprisingly, Mimouni does not cite or mention Blaschke's, *Beschneidung*. While Blaschke's work has been broadly well-received as an encyclopedic sourcebook on ancient circumcision, Mimouni's volume has not received much interaction outside of francophone scholarship. The notable exception to this lack of interaction is Thomas R. Blanton IV, "Circumcision in the Early Jesus Movement: The Contributions of Simon Claude Mimouni, 'Paul within Judaism' and 'Lived Ancient Religion,'" *JJMJS* 8 (2021): 131–57.

[35] Simon Claude Mimouni, *La circoncision dans le monde judéen aux époques grecque et romaine: Histoire d'un conflit interne au judaïsme*, CREJ 42 (Paris-Louvain: Peeters, 2007), 242. Mimouni (10) argues that there were five different positions regarding circumcision in the first two centuries of the Jesus movement: 1) circumcision is necessary (James); 2) circumcision was not necessary (Paul); 3) circumcision was necessary for Judaeans, but not for individuals from other nations (Luke): 4) circumcision is abolished (Eph 2:11–22; Gos. Thom. 53; Barn. 9.1–9; Diogn. 4.1–4); 5) circumcision is positive (Odes Sol. 11.1–5; Gos. Phil. 82:26–30).

[36] Mimouni, *La circoncision*, 214–242.

[37] Mimouni, *La circoncision*, 218.

circumcised. Additionally, Mimouni argues that Paul spiritualizes and universalizes circumcision so that the category of "true circumcision" (Rom 2:28–29; Phil 3:3) can be applied to all Christians irrespective of the state of one's penis.[38]

Nina Livesey's 2010 book, *Circumcision as a Malleable Symbol*, also explores the diversity of meanings ascribed to circumcision in select ancient Jewish and Christian texts.[39] Her work highlights how the meaning of circumcision in any given text is contingent upon its context. She argues that Paul discusses circumcision in a variety of senses: a metonym for circumcised Jews (Rom 3:30; 4:9, 12; 15:8; Gal 2:7, 9, 12; 6:13), a metonym that includes the uncircumcised (Phil 3:3), the physical practice (Rom 2:25, 27; 3:1, 4:10; 1 Cor 7:19; Gal 2:3; 5:2–4, 6, 11; 6:12–13, 15; Phil 3:5), a metaphor (Rom 2:26, 28–29), and as an allegory (Rom 4:11).[40] Though I disagree with some of her readings of these texts, Livesey's overall goal in highlighting the varieties of ways circumcision language is employed by Paul—and other ancient writers—is successful, albeit somewhat unremarkable. More notable are some of her synthetic conclusions that demonstrate how the multivalence of circumcision in ancient Judaism is quickly lost amongst the Christian interpretive tradition, which historically relegated discussions of circumcision to its relationship with salvation. Additionally, Livesey rightly emphasizes Paul's gentile audiences and how this shapes his discourse on circumcision: "Paul primarily concerns himself with the issue of circumcision in so far as it pertains to Gentiles desirous of becoming circumcised. In other words, Paul rarely raises the issue of the value of circumcision for contemporary, historic or even biblical Jews."[41]

In her 2014 dissertation, "A Seal of Faith," Asha Moorthy argues—contrary to the vast majority of Pauline scholarship—that Paul did not oppose the circumcision of gentiles. Based on her reading of Gen 17 and Rom 4, she proposes that Paul viewed physical circumcision as an expression of faith and obedience. While circumcision does not have any power leading toward justification, gentile men should follow the example of Abraham in receiving circumcision as a sign and a seal of the righteousness of faith.[42] Unlike standard treatments of Paul where circumcision of the heart replaces the need for physical circumcision, Moorthy argues that Paul "treats circumcision of the flesh as an outward manifestation

---

[38] Mimouni, *La circoncision*, 224–30.
[39] Livesey's study focuses on 1 Maccabees, 2 Maccabees, 4 Maccabees, *Jubilees*, the writings of Josephus and Philo, Paul, and a selection of ancient, medieval, and modern interpreters.
[40] Livesey, *Malleable Symbol*, 77–122.
[41] Livesey, *Malleable Symbol*, 121.
[42] Asha K. Moorthy, "A Seal of Faith: Rereading Paul on Circumcision, Torah, and the Gentiles" (PhD diss., Columbia University, 2014), 119–85.

of circumcision of the heart."⁴³ The texts where Paul explicitly forbids gentiles from undergoing circumcision (esp. Gal 5:2) are the elephant in the room for Moorthy's overall argument. Moorthy deals with these texts by arguing that Paul opposes the circumcision of gentiles when it is done under compulsion or when it becomes the object of one's trust or sense of identity, instead of Christ. Though original and revisionist, Moorthy's reading of Paul and circumcision fails to convince.

Matthew Thiessen's paradigm-shifting work on circumcision has challenged numerous scholarly consensuses about circumcision in ancient Judaism, early Christianity, and in Paul. In his 2011 monograph, *Contesting Conversion*,⁴⁴ Thiessen pushes back against Shaye Cohen's claim that "[b]y the time of the Maccabees, conversion, ritually defined as circumcision, is securely in place, not to be questioned until the middle ages."⁴⁵ Cohen argues that around the second century BCE Jewish identity morphed from an *ethnos* to an ethno-religion—from being Judaean to being Jewish.⁴⁶ Thiessen notes that while this is true amongst some Jews in the Second Temple period, this is not the case for all Jews. Beginning with Gen 17 and moving throughout the Hebrew Bible, Thiessen demonstrates two main points: 1) In the Hebrew Bible, for a circumcision to be valid it must occur on a descendent of Abraham on the eighth-day after birth, and 2) that nowhere in the Hebrew Bible is circumcision viewed as being efficacious for turning a non-Israelite into one. Next, Thiessen explores the important role eighth-day circumcision and genealogical purity play in some ancient-Jewish constructions of Jewish identity. Following the work of Christine Hayes, Thiessen highlights the existence of Jewish groups in this period that adhered to genealogical definitions of Jewishness.⁴⁷ In this primordialist (or "essentialist") construction of Jewish identity, circumcision is not able to overcome the genealogical gap and ontological difference between Jew and non-

---

43 Moorthy, "Seal of Faith," 160.
44 Matthew Thiessen, *Contesting Conversion: Genealogy, Circumcision, and Identity in Ancient Judaism and Christianity* (New York: Oxford University Press, 2011).
45 Shaye J. D. Cohen, "Conversion to Judaism in Historical Perspective: From Biblical Israel to Post-Biblical Judaism," *CJud* 36 (1983): 31–45, at 42. Cohen is one of Thiessen's main interlocutors, but this perspective is prominent in most secondary literature. See Thiessen, *Contesting Conversion*, 5–10.
46 Shaye J. D. Cohen, *The Beginnings of Jewishness: Boundaries, Varieties, Uncertainties*, HCS 31 (Berkeley: University of California Press, 1999), 69–139.
47 Thiessen, *Contesting Conversion*, 67–110; Christine E. Hayes, *Gentile Impurities and Jewish Identities* (New York: Oxford University Press, 2002), esp. 68–91. Hayes' work explores the "holy seed" ideology of Ezra and Nehemiah, and how this conception of genealogical purity is manifested in Jubilees and 4QMMT. Thiessen (89–96) also uses the *Animal Apocalypse* and 1 Esdras as texts that highlight genealogical purity and essentialist constructions of ethnicity.

Jew.⁴⁸ Lastly, Thiessen argues that this perspective on Jewishness as genealogy and the emphasis on eighth-day circumcision is present in Luke-Acts. While this volume does not offer treatment of the Pauline epistles, Thiessen gestures toward how this understanding of Jewishness as genealogy—with an emphasis on eighth-day circumcision—may be instructive for understanding Paul.

In the follow-up to *Contesting Conversion,* Thiessen's 2016 volume, *Paul and the Gentile Problem,* fills the Pauline lacuna of his previous work.⁴⁹ He proposes that Paul belonged to this stream of Judaism that held to a genealogical definition of Jewishness and only viewed eighth-day circumcision performed on a descendant of Abraham as being valid.⁵⁰ On this reading, Paul's main opposition to gentiles in his assemblies undergoing circumcision is threefold: 1) it is not valid for non-Jews, 2) it would not be performed with the proper timing (eight days after birth), and 3) it is not an effective means for making one into Abraham's seed. While this book does not focus solely on circumcision, Thiessen offers a fairly extensive reading of circumcision in Paul. There are, however, a handful of key texts that either go untreated by Thiessen, or are only mentioned briefly (e.g., Rom 4:9–12; 15:8; Gal 5:6; 6:15; Phil 3:3).⁵¹ I find Thiessen's overall project convincing, and his work serves as one of my main interlocutors.

Like Schreiner, Blaschke, Mimouni, and Livesey, this project seeks to be comprehensive in its treatment of circumcision and Paul's epistles. Unlike these works, however, I avoid their spiritualizing, Christianizing, and universalizing tendencies. By reading Paul within Judaism, highlighting the non-Jewish audiences of his epistles, and reassessing the underlying logic of Paul's discussions of circumcision, I offer a fresh reading of all the (undisputed) Pauline circumcision texts. In addition to circumcision, this work also offers a comprehensive treatment of foreskin in Paul's epistles, which has traditionally been overlooked.

---

48 For a discussion of primordial/essentialist ethnic identity construction and the study of Paul, see R. Barry Matlock, "'Jews By Nature': Paul, Ethnicity, and Galatians," in *Far From Minimal: Celebrating the Work and Influence of Philip R. Davies,* ed. Duncan Burns and John W. Rogerson (London: T&T Clark, 2012), 304–15.
49 Matthew Thiessen, *Paul and the Gentile Problem* (New York: Oxford University Press, 2016).
50 This serves as the backbone of the gentile problem for Paul: if gentiles are ontologically different from Jews, and circumcision is not available to them as a means of conversion, then how can they become Abrahamic seed?
51 Since the publication of *Paul and the Gentile Problem,* Thiessen has written an article that discusses circumcision in Phil 3:3. Matthew Thiessen, "Gentiles as Impure Animals in the Writings of Early Christ Followers," in *Perceiving the Other in Ancient Judaism and Early Christianity,* ed. Michal Bar-Asher Siegal, Wolfgang Grünstäudl, and Matthew Thiessen, WUNT 394 (Tübingen: Mohr Siebeck, 2017), 19–32.

1.4 Circumcision, Foreskin, and Paul's Ethnic Map

Circumcision (περιτομή) has historically received much attention from Pauline interpreters, however, the language of foreskin (ἀκροβυστία) is rarely given much thought. The primary reason for this is how scholars typically translate the word ἀκροβυστία[52] as "uncircumcision" and not "foreskin."[53] The Greek term that indicates uncircumcision—ἀπερίτμητος—does not occur in the Pauline corpus, and only appears in the New Testament in Acts 7:51.[54] By conflating ἀκροβυστία with ἀπερίτμητος, interpreters drastically alter Paul's language. Instead of Paul discussing what individuals possess—a foreskin—they make it about what they lack—a circumcision. Karin Neutel refers to this as "the invisibility of ἀκροβυστία" in Pauline scholarship.[55] As Joel Marcus notes, interpreters tend to over-translate περιτομή and ἀκροβυστία; focusing on derived meanings, rather

---

52 The word ἀκροβυστία does not appear outside of Jewish sources until after the Pauline epistles have been written. In non-Jewish, non-Christian, Greek literature, the terms ποσθία, πόσθη, ἀκροποσθία, and ἀκροπόσθιον are used to refer to the foreskin and the tip of the foreskin. On this terminology, see Frederick M. Hodges, "The Ideal Prepuce in Ancient Greece and Rome: Male Genital Aesthetics and Their Relation to *Lipodermos*, Circumcision, Foreskin Restoration, and the *Kynodesmē*," *Bulletin of the History of Medicine* 75 (2001): 375–405. It is possible that the word ἀκροβυστία is a Jewish invention based on the Greek ἄκρος and the Hebrew בשת, meaning "the tip/extremity of the shame." See the discussion in K. L. Schmidt, "ἀκροβυστία," *TDNT* 1:225–26.

53 There are, however, some welcome exceptions to this general tendency; e.g., Joel Marcus, "The Circumcision and the Uncircumcision in Rome," *NTS* 35 (1989): 67–81; Blaschke, *Beschneidung*; Caroline Johnson Hodge, *If Sons, Then Heirs: A Study of Kinship and Ethnicity in the Letters of Paul* (New York: Oxford University Press, 2007), 60–64; Livesey, *Malleable Symbol*; Jorunn Økland, "Pauline Letters," in *The Oxford Handbook of New Testament, Gender, and Sexuality*, ed. Benjamin H. Dunning (New York: Oxford University Press, 2019), 314–32; Karin B. Neutel, "Restoring Abraham's Foreskin: The Significance of ἀκροβυστία for Paul's Argument about Circumcision in Romans 4:9–12," *JJMJS* 8 (2021): 53–74.

54 Unlike Paul, the translators of the LXX/OG use both ἀκροβυστία and ἀπερίτμητος. When comparing the Hebrew text alongside its Greek translation, an interesting pattern emerges. When the adjectival form ערל ("having foreskin") occurs, the various LXX/OG translators render it as ἀπερίτμητος (e.g., Gen 17:14; Exod 12:48; Lev 26:41; Josh 5:7; Jer 9:25; Ezek 44:7, 9). There are a few exceptions to this rule. Interestingly, the LXX/OG translators do not render all metaphorical uses of ערל as ἀπερίτμητος. Rather, they translate the metaphor in a way that indicates that the foreskinned object is unfit for its purpose (Moses' lips; Exod 6:12, 30) or is unclean (food; Lev 26:41). The metaphors of the foreskinned heart and ears, however, are rendered as ἀπερίτμητος (Lev 26:41; Jer 6:10, 9:25; Ezek 44:7, 9). When the nominal form ערלה ("foreskin") is used, it is rendered as ἀκροβυστία (e.g., Gen 17:11, 14, 23–25; 34:14; Exod 4:25; Lev 12:3; Josh 5:3). In these instances, ערל/ἀκροβυστία is usually the object of the verb מול/περιτέμνω ("to circumcise"), but it always refers to physical foreskin, not metaphorical foreskin.

55 Neutel, "Restoring Abraham's Foreskin," 54.

than their basic referents.⁵⁶ Here, Marcus pushes back against the tendency to interpret περιτομή and ἀκροβυστία as stative abstractions—the state of being circumcised or uncircumcised. He proposes that in many cases, περιτομή and ἀκροβυστία should be translated anatomically and concretely as referring to a circumcised penis or a foreskinned penis. By highlighting the physical, fleshly referents of these terms, he de-familiarizes this aspect of Paul's language, opens up new avenues of inquiry, and is arguably closer to what Paul writes and means when he uses these terms.

Interpreters who are attuned to Paul's use of circumcision and foreskin language have highlighted the unusual nature of Paul's metonymic use of these terms. Paul appears to be the only ancient interpreter to use the anatomical language of circumcision and foreskin metonymically to divide up all of humanity⁵⁷ (e.g., Rom 3:30; 4:9–12; Gal 2:7).⁵⁸ Mishnah Nedarim 3:11 is the only other place in ancient literature that uses the noun "foreskin" (ערלה) as a title for non-Jews: "[F]oreskin is a name only for the *goyim*."⁵⁹ Similarly—and somewhat surprisingly—while circumcision came to be chiefly associated with Jews in the ancient world, no one outside of Paul, Luke (Acts 10:45; 11:2), and their interpreters—Jewish or otherwise—refers to Jews by the noun "circumcision."⁶⁰

Paul's division of humanity into the categories of circumcision and foreskin reflects his ethnic binary of Jews (Ἰουδαῖοι) and an undifferentiated group of

---

56 Marcus, "Circumcision and Uncircumcision," 74–76.
57 Note the androcentric nature of Paul's division of humanity. As Johnson Hodge highlights, "Paul's use of these two terms represents a patriarchal categorization of men and women in terms of the status of male bodies" (*If Sons, Then Heirs*, 63). See also Økland, "Pauline Letters." On the question of circumcision and women, see Shaye J. D. Cohen, *Why Aren't Jewish Women Circumcised? Gender and Covenant in Judaism* (Berkeley: University of California Press, 2005); M Adryael Tong, *Difference and Circumcision: Bodily Discourse and the Parting of the Ways* (Oxford: Oxford University Press, forthcoming).
58 Marcus, "Circumcision and Uncircumcision," 76; Johnson Hodge, *If Sons, Then Heirs*, 60–64; Neutel, "Restoring Abraham's Foreskin," 64.
59 This statement is used in m. Ned. 3:11—in conjunction with Jer 9:25, 1 Sam 17:36, and 2 Sam 1:20—as the logic undergirding claims about how an individual making *konam* vows should relate to the circumcised (מולים) and the foreskinned (ערלים). The argument presented is that the foreskinned of Israel (ערלי ישראל) should be treated as though they are circumcised and that the circumcised of the nations (מולי האומות) should be treated as foreskinned (cf. b. ʿAbod. Zar. 27a). Here, the text indicates that circumcised and foreskinned identity do not necessarily have to align with one's physical reality, rather, genealogy and ethnicity determine these identities. On this, see Tong, *Difference and Circumcision*.
60 In the two instances in Acts, the form is "those from circumcision" (οἱ ἐκ περιτομῆς).

non-Jews, the gentiles/nations (ἔθνη; Rom 3:29; 9:24; 1 Cor 1:23; Gal 2:14–15).[61] As highlighted by Thiessen, Hayes, and Fredriksen, Paul's ethnic construction of the world is genealogical and essentialist; the binaries of Jew/gentile and circumcision/foreskin are natural ones (cf. m. Ned. 3:11).[62] Paul notes that he and Cephas (Peter) are Jews by nature (ἡμεῖς φύσει Ἰουδαῖοι, Gal 2:15) in contrast to being sinners from the nations (οὐκ ἐξ ἐθνῶν ἁμαρτωλοί). Similarly, in Rom 2:27, Paul refers to non-Jews as those who are the foreskin from nature (ἡ ἐκ φύσεως ἀκροβυστία). As I argue in the pages below, this natural distinction is one of the core reasons why Paul argues against the adoption of circumcision by the gentiles in his assemblies; this physical and ethnic binary frames Paul's discourse on circumcision.

1.5 Method

The aim of this project is to provide a reading of how Paul employs the language of circumcision and foreskin in his epistles, paying particular attention to the ethnic context of these discourses. My method in this endeavor is fairly conventional; I apply the standard philological, historical, and literary tools of the historical-critical method that are common in biblical studies and its cognate fields to the writings of Paul. I use "Paul" to refer to the author of the seven (generally) undisputed letters: Romans, 1–2 Corinthians, Galatians, Philippians, 1 Thessalonians, and Philemon.[63] From this corpus, four epistles use the language of circumcision and fore-

---

61 In some instances, Paul does use the pair Jew and Greek—not Jews and gentiles—but this is typically due to his reference to singular persons rather than groups of people (Rom 1:16; 2:9–10; 10:12; Gal 3:28). The Greek term he uses to define all non-Jews is ἔθνη ("nations"), but the singular ἔθνος refers to a singular nation, not an individual person. Thus, Paul substitutes Ἕλλην for ἔθνος to stand in as his singular gentile. Paul does occasionally use the plural Ἕλληνες, but this either builds off of his previous use of the singular (Rom 3:9), or it functions similarly to his usage of ἔθνη (1 Cor 1:22, 24; 10:32; 12:13). On Paul's usage of the term ἔθνη in the context of Jewish discourses about non-Jewish nations, see Ishay Rosen-Zvi and Adi Ophir, "Paul and the Invention of the Gentiles," *JQR* 105 (2015): 1–41; idem, *Goy: Israel's Multiple Others and the Birth of the Gentile* (Oxford: Oxford University Press, 2018).
62 Thiessen, *Paul and the Gentile Problem*; Christine Hayes, *What's Divine about Divine Law? Early Perspectives* (Princeton: Princeton University Press, 2015), 141–51; Matthew Thiessen, "Paul, Essentialism, and the Jewish Law: In Conversation with Christine Hayes," *JSPL* 7 (2018): 80–85; Paula Fredriksen, "God Is Jewish, but Gentiles Don't Have to Be: Ethnicity and Eschatology in Paul's Gospel," in *The Message of Paul the Apostle within Second Temple Judaism*, ed. František Ábel (Lanham, MD: Lexington Books/Fortress Academic, 2020), 5–9.
63 The issue of what counts as "Paul" is indeed much more complicated and nuanced than I have presented. For the recent debates on how scholars construct "Paul," see Benjamin L. White, *Remembering Paul: Ancient and Modern Contests over the Image of the Apostle* (New York: Oxford

skin. I examine each of these epistles on their own and in chronological order: 1 Corinthians, Galatians, Philippians, and Romans.[64]

To successfully examine Paul's use of circumcision and foreskin language, I engage in various acts of re-description and de-familiarization. As Anders Runesson argues, in order to make new discoveries and uncover new understandings through historical inquiry, we must first *"disentangle what we have encountered from the familiar that we know."*[65] In other words, we need to "make Paul weird again."[66] One of the key ways Runesson suggests this can be accomplished is through the terminology one chooses to use. He specifically points to removing the etic language of "Christianity," "Christian," and "church," when studying Paul because the modern connotations of these words obscure historical inquiry.[67] I find this general approach to be correct; anachronistic terminology should be avoided when it muddies the historical water.[68] The ancient world is foreign, and the historian should actively resist attempts to domesticate it. Or as Fredriksen puts it, "To do history requires acknowledging difference between us and the objects of our inquiry. Historical interpretation proceeds by acceding to the priority

---

University Press, 2014); Margaret M. Mitchell, "Paul and Judaism Now, Quo vadimus?" *JJMJS* 5 (2018): 55–78. It is worth noting that six of these seven letters have co-authors, and Romans—which is only attributed to Paul—expressly names the scribe who penned it. These authorial points are rightly highlighted by Laura Salah Nasrallah, *Archaeology and the Letters of Paul* (Oxford: Oxford University Press, 2018), 1–4.

64 Other than ordering the chapters of this book, this chronology does not bear any significant weight on the contents of this volume. If I were to adopt an alternative chronology, my findings would remain unchanged. On the relative sequence of events in Paul's career—including the chronological order of his epistles—see Gregory Tatum, *New Chapters in the Life of Paul: The Relative Chronology of His Career*, CBQMS 41 (Washington, DC: Catholic Biblical Association of America, 2006), 126–30. For a similar Pauline chronology, see E. P. Sanders, *Paul: The Apostle's Life, Letters, and Thought* (Minneapolis: Fortress, 2015), 157–60. For other recent important contributions to the discussion of Pauline chronology, see Douglas A. Campbell, *Framing Paul: An Epistolary Biography* (Grand Rapids: Eerdmans, 2014); Jonathan Bernier, *Rethinking the Dates of the New Testament: The Evidence for Early Composition* (Grand Rapids: Baker Academic, 2022).

65 Runesson, "The Question of Terminology," 56 (emphasis original).

66 I borrow this phrase from Matthew Novenson's review of Paula Fredriksen, *Paul: The Pagans' Apostle* (New Haven: Yale University Press, 2017). See Matthew V. Novenson, "Whither the Paul within Judaism *Schule?*" *JJMJS* 5 (2018): 79–88, at 81.

67 Runesson, "The Question of Terminology," 59–77. See also, Jennifer Eyl, "Semantic Voids, New Testament Translation, and Anachronism: The Case of Paul's Use of Ekklēsia," *MTSR* 26 (2014): 315–39.

68 There are some instances where anachronistic or etic terminology can be used in a re-descriptive sense in order to de-familiarize the past. For example, see the use of "divination" in Matthew T. Sharp, *Divination and Philosophy in the Letters of Paul* (Edinburgh: Edinburgh University Press, 2022).

of the *ancient* context. Our frame of reference is the *past.*"⁶⁹ Throughout this work, I have left various words untranslated or have offered alternative translations of words and texts in attempt to de-familiarize the familiar and well-trodden ground of the Pauline epistles (e.g., πνεῦμα, ἀκροβυστία, ἐκκλησία, δικαιοσύνη, Χριστός). In so doing, I hope to challenge many of the common assumptions made regarding the place and function of circumcision and foreskin in Paul's thought. By examining old questions through a hermeneutic of experimentation⁷⁰ and de-familiarization, we can make advances and tread new ground in the study of Paul's epistles.

1.6 Outline

Chapter one examines 1 Cor 7:17–20 and Paul's apparent negation of the identities of circumcision and foreskin. Based on the rule Paul lays out in 7:17, I push back against the prevailing interpretation that Paul views circumcision and foreskin with indifference. I argue that these identities still have value and meaning for Paul and are determinative for how those in the assembly are to live vis-à-vis the commandments of God.

Chapter two comprises an examination of circumcision in Galatians. Given the central role circumcision plays in Galatians, this chapter covers a range of texts and topics. I argue that Paul's position against gentile men undergoing circumcision rests primarily on three points: 1) circumcision cannot turn a non-Jew into an Abrahamic son—only the reception of divine *pneuma* can; 2) for non-Jews in the Messiah, circumcision returns them to their previous state of slavery; and 3) this return to slavery severs their pneumatic union with the Messiah. Like 1 Cor 7:19, I argue that Gal 5:6 and 6:15 do not constitute Pauline indifference toward circumcision and foreskin, but these evaluations of circumcision and foreskin are used in particular rhetorical contexts to make specific arguments. I also offer a revisionist reading of Gal 5:11 ("If I am still proclaiming circumcision…"), proposing that this proclamation of circumcision does not refer to a prior promotion of pros-

---

69 Paula Fredriksen, "Historical Integrity, Interpretive Freedom: The Philosopher's Paul and the Problem of Anachronism" in *St. Paul Among the Philosophers*, ed. John D. Caputo and Linda Martin Alcoff, ISPR (Bloomington, IN: Indiana University Press, 2009), 61–73, at 61–62 (emphasis original).
70 This is Lloyd Gaston's term (Lloyd Gaston, *Paul and the Torah* [Vancouver: University of British Columbia Press, 1987], 3). He regards this as a radical criticism of the assumptions of the interpreter, that suspends as many assumptions as possible in order to look at data afresh. "What if one were to look at the matter from this perspective? Can all the evidence still be accounted for? Is the resultant picture plausible in itself? It is worth reopening old questions. A hermeneutic of experimentation invites the reader to an initial suspension of disbelief and a serious playfulness."

elyte circumcision by Paul, but that it refers to Paul's prior exclusivist stance against gentile inclusion in the people of God. Additionally, the identity of the agitators is commented on, as well as the place of circumcision in Gal 2.

Chapter three explores Paul's declaration, "We are the circumcision!" in Phil 3:3. Here, I situate Paul's declaration in the context of his rhetoric against the "dogs," "wicked workers," and "mutilation" of 3:2. I argue that "the circumcision" refers not to followers of Jesus or the "church," but specifically to Paul and Timothy—the Jewish authors of the epistle. I also briefly comment on Paul's presentation of his Jewish bona fides in 3:5–6, notably his eighth-day circumcision.

Lastly, chapter four looks at circumcision in Romans. Focusing on the dialogical nature of Romans, I argue Paul continues to uphold the distinction between circumcision and foreskin (3:29–30; 4:9–12)—Jews and gentiles—and still sees circumcision as maintaining its value for Jews (3:1–2). This manifests itself in Paul's ongoing discussion with a fictional dialogue partner whom I identify as a circumcised gentile proselyte to Judaism—someone who calls himself a Jew (2:17). I contend that Paul denies the validity of this individual's non-eighth-day circumcision (2:25–27). Notably, I also make that case that Paul's use of heart-circumcision in Rom 2:29 does not constitute a redefinition or universalization of circumcision available to all. In my discussion of Rom 4:9–12, I highlight the importance of the language of foreskin in Paul's treatment of Abraham's circumcision. Finally, I propose that Rom 15:8 refers to the Messiah as an "agent of the circumcision," in the context of his role in bringing about the promise to Abraham to make him the father of many nations.

Returning to the words of Jesus as presented in the Gospel of Thomas with which this chapter began: "His disciples said to him, 'Is circumcision beneficial or not?' He said to them, 'If it were beneficial, their father would beget them already circumcised from their mother. Rather, the true circumcision in spirit has become completely profitable.'" While some have found commonalities between Thomas' Jesus and Paul on the issue of circumcision, I hope to demonstrate in the ensuing chapters that this view of circumcision would have been foreign to Paul. Despite the history of interpretation of circumcision in Paul, Paul's discourse on circumcision is much more nuanced than a mere rejection of the physical practice and promotion of its spiritual counterpart. It is to this nuanced discussion of circumcision in Paul's epistles that I now turn.

2 Keeping the Commandments of God Circumcision in 1 Corinthians

Nevertheless,[1] as the Lord assigned to each one, as God has called each one, in this way he should walk. And thus I make this rule[2] in all the assemblies. Was anyone circumcised when called? Let him not undergo epispasm. Was anyone called in foreskin? Let him not undergo circumcision. Circumcision is nothing and foreskin is nothing, but keeping the commandments of God.[3] Each in the calling in which he was called, in this remain. (1 Cor 7:17–20)

2.1 Introduction

"Circumcision is nothing and foreskin is nothing, but keeping the commandments of God" (1 Cor 7:19). This statement has proved perplexing for many interpreters who rightly point out the apparent contradiction it contains. Since eighth-day circumcision is a central commandment of God for Jews (Gen 17:10–14; Lev 12:3; cf. Jub. 15:25–26), how can Paul assert that both circumcision and foreskin are nothing while maintaining the importance of the commandments of God? For some, the answer is quite simple: Paul no longer thought that circumcision was included amongst the commandments of God. Andreas Blaschke writes, "It is clear: for Paul, circumcision is not one of the ἐντολαὶ θεοῦ that must be fulfilled post Christ."[4] Similarly, E. P. Sanders remarks, "Here 'the commandments of God' refer to the scriptural law, while excluding the requirement of circumcision—just as is the case in Gal 5:14."[5] In addition to this supposed redefinition of the commandments of God, this text is also used to demonstrate Paul's apparent indifference toward and devaluation of circumcision.

---

[1] Here, Εἰ μή likely refers back to the exception Paul makes in 7:15. See, Gordon D. Fee, *The First Epistle to the Corinthians*, NICNT (Grand Rapids: Eerdmans, 1987), 309; J. Brian Tucker, *Remain in Your Calling: Paul and the Continuation of Social Identities in 1 Corinthians* (Eugene, OR: Pickwick, 2011), 70.

[2] The vast majority of manuscripts contain διατάσσομαι, which is likely the original reading, but a few (D* F G latt) replace it with διδάσκω. This variant can be accounted for by looking to 4:17, where Paul writes, "ἐν πάσῃ ἐκκλησίᾳ διδάσκω." Given the similar language found in 7:17, it is likely that some scribes accidentally replaced διατάσσομαι with διδάσκω due to their familiarity with 4:17 or in order to make the two texts have terminological agreement.

[3] "Is something" or "is everything" is often supplied to the elliptical ending of the Greek text: ἀλλὰ τήρησις ἐντολῶν θεοῦ.

[4] Blaschke, *Beschneidung*, 399 (my translation). "Klar ist: Die Beschneidung ist für Paulus keine der ἐντολαὶ θεοῦ, die es post Christum zu erfüllen gilt."

[5] Sanders, *Paul*, 552.

In this chapter, I argue Paul does not devalue circumcision or remove it from being a necessary commandment for Jews. Rather, I propose that Paul's rule in all of the assemblies illuminates what he says about circumcision, foreskin, and the commandments of God. Here, Paul uses circumcision and foreskin metonymically to refer to Jews and non-Jews respectively. Given that Paul's rule is about how those in the assemblies are to live (περιπατέω), I argue that the commandments of God for Jews and non-Jews are different. Jewish followers of Jesus are to continue to observe Torah and non-Jewish followers of Jesus are to observe the commandments relevant to them (cf. Acts 15). In this context, Paul's rhetorical negation of circumcision and foreskin does not function as an actual devaluation of these identities, but serves to highlight the importance of living according to the relevant commandments of God.

2.2 Paul's Rule in All the Assemblies and the Language of Calling

Paul's rule in all of the assemblies calls for individuals to walk in (περιπατέω, 7:17) and remain in (μένω, 7:20, 24) the life that the Lord has assigned and God has called them.[6] This rule is foundational for Paul's understanding of how one's pre-in-Christ identity functions for those who are now in Christ.[7] As Anders Runesson notes, Paul's rule "provides us a valuable point of entry into the apostle's thought world. The rule is, uniquely, said to be universal; if we study what Paul has to say in this passage we may therefore be able to identify some of his core convictions."[8] While it may seem out of place in the context of 1 Cor 7—which is broadly about Paul's instructions related to celibacy, marriage, and sex for Messiah-followers in Corinth—Paul's rule applies to the discussions in what precedes and what follows this passage.[9]

---

6 The two clauses here are effectively the same in their wording and meaning, with calling replacing assignment, and God replacing Lord (ἑκάστῳ ὡς ἐμέρισεν ὁ κύριος, ἕκαστον ὡς κέκληκεν ὁ θεός). See, e.g., C. K. Barrett, *A Commentary on the First Epistle to the Corinthians*, BNTC (London: Black, 1968), 168.
7 Barrett, *First Corinthians*, 168; William S. Campbell, *Paul and the Creation of Christian Identity*, LNTS 322 (London: T&T Clark, 2006), 91–92; Tucker, *Remain in Your Calling*, 70–75.
8 Anders Runesson, "Paul's Rule in All the *Ekklēsiai*," in *Introduction to Messianic Judaism*, ed. David Rudolph and Joel Willitts (Grand Rapids: Zondervan, 2013), 214–23, at 214–15.
9 Cf. Peter J. Tomson, *Paul and the Jewish Law: Halakha in the Letters of the Apostle to the Gentiles*, CRINT 1 (Assen: Van Gorcum, 1990), 270.

Although the rule explicitly requires everyone to remain in the position in which God has called them, Paul does allow for some exceptions. For example, while it would be ideal for those who are single not to be married, for reasons related to *porneia* (7:2) and desire (7:9, 36–38), Paul permits members of the assemblies to marry. Similarly, Paul possibly makes an exception for slaves who are able to become manumitted, however, there is considerable debate around the meaning of this text (7:21).[10] These exceptions notwithstanding, Paul's ideal for the individuals in his assemblies is that they remain in the position that they were in at the time of their call (7:20, 24).[11]

While the majority of interpreters understand calling (κλῆσις) here to be a reference to one's social location—sociorthnic as in 7:18–20, or socioeconomic as in 7:21–24—this interpretation is not universal.[12] For example, James Dunn argues

---

[10] In 7:21, Paul states, "Were you a slave when called? Do not be concerned about it. But even if you are able to become free, make use of it all the more." The debate revolves around the meaning of the vague phrase μᾶλλον χρῆσαι ("make use of it all the more") which lacks an object. What does this refer to? Are they to make use of their status as slaves or are they to make use of the opportunity to gain their freedom? While most interpreters pick one or the other, Brad Braxton (*The Tyranny of Resolution: 1 Corinthians 7:17–24*, SBLDS 181 [Atlanta: Society of Biblical Literature, 2000], 237) argues that the ambiguity of Paul's language "is an explicit feature of the text." This ambiguity could allow for Paul to be understood as both maintaining civil order, but also as providing an exception to his rule. For a brief outline of the various approaches taken to understand this difficult text, see Joseph A. Fitzmyer, *First Corinthians: A New Translation with Introduction and Commentary*, AB 32 (New Haven: Yale University Press, 2008), 309–10; cf. Tucker, *Remain in Your Calling*, 81–86.

[11] Sanders proposes that Paul's rule is shaped by the fact that "time is short" (*Paul*, 295). With the *parousia* of the Lord on the horizon, Paul employs this rule for a people whom he believes will soon be given pneumatic bodies (σῶμα πνευματικόν) that will inherit the kingdom of God (1 Cor 15:42–53). The section that immediately follows this rule points out the coming distress (7:26), the shortening of the appointed time (7:29), and passing away of the present form of this world (7:31) as reasons for virgins and married individuals to remain in those identities. Adam Gregerman ("Response to Papers Presented at the American Academy of Religion Conference," *SCJR* 5 [2010], 1–10, at 4) argues that the immediacy of Paul's eschatology allows for him to be indifferent toward the distinction between individuals—notably circumcision and foreskin. Gregerman's perspective, however, is undermined by the fact that Paul insists that individuals are not to change these distinctions.

[12] Barrett, *First Corinthians*, 168; Fee, *First Corinthians*, 309; Campbell, *Christian Identity*, 91; Fitzmyer, *First Corinthians*, 307; Mark D. Nanos, "The Myth of the 'Law-Free' Paul Standing Between Christians and Jews," *SCJR* 4 (2009): 1–22, at 5; David J. Rudolph, "Paul's 'Rule in All the Churches' (1 Cor 7:17–24) and Torah-Defined Ecclesiological Variegation," *SCJR* 5 (2010): 1–24, at 3; Tucker, *Remain in Your Calling*, 70; Nasrallah, *Archaeology*, 64.

that "Paul did not regard status (e.g., slavery)[13] as a 'calling'; the 'call' in these verses is the call of conversion."[14] Similarly, Scott Bartchy, Brad Braxton, and David Garland contend that in this passage Paul only has the "call of conversion" in mind.[15] Clarity, however, is brought to Paul's rule and usage of calling language when one reads the passage in context, allowing for multiple senses of calling language to be present in the text: 1) one's social location, and 2) the call of God to follow the Messiah.[16]

The use of calling language in 7:20 is instructive for seeing the two senses of calling that Paul employs in this passage. When Paul writes, "Each in the calling (τῇ κλήσει) in which he was called (ᾗ ἐκλήθη), in this remain," the referent of the noun κλῆσις can easily be determined from the surrounding context; this refers to their status as either circumcised or foreskinned. If κλῆσις only refers to the call to trust the Messiah, then the discussions of circumcision and foreskin, and slavery and freedom, are inserted without cause. The verb καλέω is used in 7:20 to refer to the calling of God to be consecrated in Christ Jesus (1 Cor 1:2). The broader context in which this discussion occurs also illuminates Paul's use of calling language. As noted above, in 1 Cor 7 Paul urges the Corinthians to remain as they are, be it single, married, or widowed—although he does provide some concessions to preempt illicit behavior. The ideal scenario for Paul is that everyone remains in their social location and lives out their calling as a Messiah-follower within that location. Paul's rule (7:17) is further illuminated in 7:20 and 7:24: "Each in the calling in which he was called, in this remain" (7:20). "Each in what he was called,

---

[13] Dunn's apprehension to label slavery as a position apportioned by God is understandable in a modern context where slavery is considered reprehensible, but one should not let modern sensibilities interfere with historical inquiry. In the ancient world, many thought that slavishness was a part of the nature of slaves. For example, Aristotle (*Pol.* 1252a–1255b) famously proposes that slaves were so by nature. Similarly, Philo (*Alleg. Interp.* 3.88–89; cf. *Virtues* 209–20) notes that Esau was a slave by nature (φύσει δοῦλον), though he argues in *Spec. Laws* 3.137 that slaves and their masters share the same nature. For a thorough discussion of "natural slavery," see Benjamin Isaac, *The Invention of Racism in Classical Antiquity* (Princeton: Princeton University Press, 2004), 169–224.
[14] James D. G. Dunn, *Beginning from Jerusalem*, Christianity in the Making 2 (Grand Rapids: Eerdmans, 2009), 801n253.
[15] S. Scott Bartchy, *ΜΑΛΛΟΝ ΧΡΗΣΑΙ: First-Century Slavery and 1 Corinthians 7:21*, SBLDS 11 (Missoula, MN: Scholars Press, 1973), 132–37; Brad Braxton, *The Tyranny of Resolution*, 40–48; David E. Garland, *1 Corinthians*, BECNT (Grand Rapids: Baker Academic, 2003), 303. See also, Anthony C. Thiselton, *The First Epistle to the Corinthians: A Commentary on the Greek Text*, NIGNT (Grand Rapids: Eerdmans, 2000), 548–50.
[16] E.g., Niko Huttunen, *Paul and Epictetus on Law: A Comparison*, LNTS 405 (London: T&T Clark, 2009), 28.

brothers, in this remain before God" (7:24). Reading these parallel verses[17] alongside one another confirms that Paul is speaking of the individual's social location, not their call to trust the Messiah, which he does speak about in 7:18, 21, and 22, and in the second occurrence in 20.

The central point around which Paul's rule revolves is the imperative to walk (περιπατέω) according to their calling in life—that is, they should live their lives in accordance with their social location at the time of their call to follow the Messiah.[18] Paul specifically spells this out in reference to one's status as circumcised or foreskinned, or slave or free. The language of walking used here, combined with Paul's establishment of this as a rule that governs all the assemblies, highlights the halakhic nature of this text and 1 Cor 7 more broadly.[19] Paul employs this rule in all of the assemblies as his basic legal position on how those in the Jesus movement are to live.

2.3 Circumcision and Foreskin as Callings

In 7:18, Paul provides the Corinthians with a practical situation to which his rule applies: "Was anyone circumcised when called? Let him not undergo epispasm.[20]

---

[17] For a further discussion on the structure of this passage see Gregory W. Dawes, "'But if you can gain your freedom' (1 Corinthians 7:17–24)," *CBQ* 52 (1990): 681–97, at 684–85; Runesson, "Paul's Rule," 215–16.

[18] Paul typically uses περιπατέω to refer to the conduct of individuals in his assemblies (1 Thess 2:12; Gal 5:16; 1 Cor 3:3; 2 Cor 10:2–3; 12:18; Rom 6:4; 8:4; 13:13; 14:15; cf. Acts 21:21).

[19] For a full overview of scholarship on halakhah and the New Testament, see Peter J. Tomson, "Halakhah in the New Testament: A Research Overview," in *The New Testament and Rabbinic Literature*, ed. Reimund Bieringer et al., JSJSup 136 (Leiden: Brill, 2010), 135–206. On 1 Corinthians more specifically, Tomson notes, "On the whole, the authoritative, halakhic character of First Corinthians is striking" (*Jewish Law*, 86). Similarly, he notes that 1 Cor 7 "can be considered one of the most 'legal' chapters in Paul" (270). Contra Sanders, *Paul, the Law*, 107.

[20] Epispasm is a medical procedure that attempts to elongate a deficient foreskin or to recreate a foreskin that has been removed via circumcision. The earliest text we have that describes this practice in detail comes from Aulus Cornelius Celsus, who wrote in the first century CE. In outlining how to restore a foreskin, he notes that there are slightly different procedures for those who are simply born with a deficient foreskin and those who lost their foreskin to circumcision. Regarding the restoration of a foreskin that was removed he writes, "But in one who has been circumcised the prepuce is to be raised from the underlying penis around the circumference of the glans by means of a scalpel. This is not so very painful, for once the margin has been freed, it can be stripped up by hand as far back as the pubes, nor in so doing is there any bleeding. The prepuce thus freed is again stretched forwards beyond the glans; next cold water affusions are freely used, and a plaster is applied round to repress severe inflammation" (*On Medicine*, 7.25.1 [Spencer, LCL]).

Was anyone called in foreskin? Let him not undergo circumcision." While this example might seem unusual in light of the surrounding context, for Paul, this example is used as the key model to illustrate his rule. Unlike Galatians—and to some extent Philippians (and Acts)—there does not appear to be any controversy over circumcision within the Corinthian correspondence that would necessitate such prohibitions. Why, then, does Paul forbid the circumcised from undergoing epispasm and those in foreskin from being circumcised?

As many interpreters note, Paul's reference to those who were called circumcised and those who were called in foreskin should be understood metonymically.[21] That is, Paul is using circumcision and foreskin to refer to Jews and non-Jews respectively, which he does throughout his epistles (Rom 3:30; 4:9–12; 15:8; Gal 2:7–9, 12; Phil 3:3).[22] Two of the clearest examples of this are in Rom 3:29–30

Similarly, Soranus writes, "If the infant is male and it looks as though it has no foreskin, she should gently draw (ἐπισπάσθω) the tip of the foreskin forward or even hold it together with a strand of wool to fasten it. For if gradually stretched and continuously drawn forward it easily stretches and assumes its normal length, covers the glans and becomes accustomed to keep the natural good shape (τὴν φυσικὴν εὐμορφίαν)" (*Gynecology* 2.16.34 [Temkin]). For a full discussion of epispasm, see Robert G. Hall, "Epispasm: Circumcision in Reverse," *BRev* 8.4 (1992): 52–57; Blaschke, *Beschneidung*, 139–44.

[21] See, e.g., Albert Schweitzer, *The Mysticism of Paul the Apostle*, trans. William Montgomery (Baltimore: Johns Hopkins University Press, 1998 [1931]), 195–96; Fee, *First Corinthians*, 312; Fitzmyer, *First Corinthians*, 307–8; Tucker, *Remain in Your Calling*, 75–76; Runesson, "Paul's Rule," 216–19; Thiessen, *Gentile Problem*, 9; cf. Barrett, *First Corinthians*, 168–69; Thiselton, *First Corinthians*, 550–51; Johnson Hodge, *If Sons, Then Heirs*, 131–32.

[22] Fredriksen (*Pagans' Apostle*, 107) argues metonymy is not at work in 1 Cor 7:17–19 and that Paul only has two types of gentiles in view: those who previously underwent proselyte circumcision and those who remain naturally in foreskin. Given Paul's apparent devaluation of circumcision in 7:19 and his charge to keep the commandments of God, Fredriksen states, "Paul *cannot* be talking about God's commandments to Israel. Circumcision or foreskin does not matter, he must mean, specifically and only for *not*-Israel, that is, for gentiles" (emphasis original). While Fredriksen is correct in highlighting the ongoing validity and value of Jewish circumcision for Paul—and that, for Paul, proselyte circumcision cannot turn a gentile into a Jew—I think this reading of 1 Cor 7:17–19 is incorrect. As I argue below, Paul's apparent negation of circumcision and foreskin is not an actual devaluation of those statuses or identities, but is part of a larger rhetorical move intent on emphasizing the importance of obedience to God's commandments. As Paul argues elsewhere, circumcision and foreskin *do* matter as it pertains to non-Jews (e.g., Gal 5:2). Further, in 7:17 Paul says the state in which one was called is an assignment from the Lord and calling from God. It is improbable that Paul would conceive of the state of circumcised non-Jews as a divine assignment or calling. On understanding the perfect passive participle of περιτέμνω as referring to Jews (circumcised as infants), see Michele Murray, *Playing a Jewish Game: Gentile Christian Judaizing in the First and Second Centuries CE*, SCJud 13 (Waterloo, ON: Wilfred Laurier University Press, 2004), 35. See also Munck, *Paul and the Salvation*, 89n2; Richardson, *Israel*, 86; Thiessen, *Gentile Problem*, 211n82; cf.

and Gal 2:7–12. In Rom 3:29–30, Paul uses the terms circumcision and foreskin interchangeably with *Ioudaios* and *ethnē*. In Gal 2:7–9, Paul uses foreskin and *ethnē* as binary opposites of circumcision in the context of his mission to non-Jews and Cephas' mission to Jews. While Paul's examples in 1 Cor 7:18 refer directly to the state of an individual's penis—and the prohibition of any surgical modification thereof—for Paul, these states are indicative of one's ethnic identity. Read in this context, Paul is stating that Jews must remain Jews, and non-Jews remain non-Jews.

If Paul has these identities in mind, what is the argument undergirding his prohibition of identity modification? For many, the answer is that Paul prohibits one from altering their identity because he thinks that these categories are "nothing" (1 Cor 7:19) and treats them as indifferent things.[23] As I argue below, this explanation is unsatisfactory. Paul's prohibition against changing one's status as circumcised or foreskinned is not because these categories are merely nothing, but because they have been assigned by the Lord and continue to have significance for precisely how one walks in relation to their calling to trust the Messiah (7:17).[24] In some respects, this is how Augustine read this text:

> "Is any called being circumcised? Let him not become uncircumcised." That is, let him not so live, as though he had become uncircumcised, and covered that which he had laid bare...For he was a Jew, and was called being circumcised; therefore he would not become uncircumcised; that is, would not so live as if he had not been circumcised. (*The Work of Monks* 12 [NPNF¹ 3:509])[25]

It is not simply about circumcision or foreskin, but it is about those physical realities as symbols of Jewish and non-Jewish identity from Paul's Jewish point of view. For Paul, those identities are linked with a specific way of life, with a specific way

---

Justin, *Dial.* 19.3. Richardson, Munck, Murray, and Thiessen, however, make their arguments in the context of περιτετμημένοι as a *varia lectio* of περιτεμνόμενοι in Gal 6:13.
[23] E.g., Schweitzer, *Mysticism*, 194; Fee, *First Corinthians* 312; Friedrich Wilhelm Horn, "Der Verzicht auf die Beschneidung im frühen Christentum," *NTS* 42 (1996): 479–505, at 485; Fitzmyer, *First Corinthians*, 307–8; Livesey, *Malleable Symbol*, 102–3.
[24] In 1 Cor 7:17, Paul uses the third person imperative form (περιπατείτω) as a command for individuals to walk (*read:* live) according to their status when called.
[25] Augustine places this discussion within an exposition of 1 Cor 9:19–22 in which he is reacting against a belief held by some that Paul feigns being Jewish in order to win over Jews. He uses 7:18 as evidence that Paul was not feigning being Jewish when he reached out to Jews, but that he continued to remain Jewish and follow the law throughout his life (cf. Augustine, *Letters* 40.4, 6).

of walking.[26] This is further spelled out in the following verse when Paul makes the seemingly enigmatic claim that circumcision and foreskin are nothing, but keeping the commandments of God.

Albert Schweitzer further illuminates this interpretation of Paul's rule, which he refers to as the theory of the *status quo*.[27]

> Applied to the question of the Law and circumcision the theory of the *status quo* requires that he who believed as a Jew must continue to live as a Jew, and the non-Jew as a non-Jew. Paul would have been no more justified in permitting the Jew to abandon the ordinances of the Law...than in requiring the non-Jew who have been baptized to place himself thereafter under the Law. He himself—we must not allow his protestations that he had become a Greek to the Greeks to introduce any confusion on this point—continued to live as a Jew.[28]

Schweitzer is correct to note that the call to remain in one's identity as a Jew (or non-Jew) involves a pattern of living (7:17). Where he and others go wrong in their understanding of the *status quo* is their insistence that one's status as Jew or gentile, circumcised or foreskinned is of "no importance."[29] In light of Paul's rule, it is apparent that these categories do possess importance for him, which is part of the impetus for him instituting this rule.

---

26 See also, J. B. Lightfoot, *Notes on Epistles of St Paul From Unpublished Commentaries* (London: Macmillan and Co., 1895), 228; Adolf von Harnack, *The Date of the Acts and of the Synoptic Gospels*, trans. J. R. Wilkinson, (London: Williams & Norgate, 1911), 43.
27 Schweitzer, *Mysticism*, 193–96.
28 Schweitzer, *Mysticism*, 195–96. In the following section (196–204), Schweitzer ultimately concludes that the *status quo* theory essentially failed Paul and caused his ministry great trouble by being confusing for both Jews in Christ who observed the law and gentiles in Christ who were outside of the law. Where Schweitzer sees this view going awry is his understanding that Paul urges Torah observance for Jews, although he views it as meaningless and ultimately useless. How could Paul persuade Jews to keep the law (although it was of no importance) while urging gentiles to refrain from the law, which is simultaneously useless, yet damnable? For Schweitzer, this becomes a problem that creates a rift in early Christianity. While I disagree with some of Schweitzer's assessment, it does appear that this rule could inhibit long-term social cohesion in mixed assemblies.
29 Schweitzer, *Mysticism*, 194–95.

2.3.1 Epispasm and Jewish Identity

Paul's prohibition forbidding Jews to undergo epispasm is vital for understanding how he views the significance of Jewish identity for those in the Jesus movement.[30] Looking to other Second Temple Jewish texts that discuss epispasm illuminates the interconnectedness between Jewish identity, circumcision, and praxis for ancient Jews. The most notable reference to foreskin restoration is in 1 Macc 1:11–15. Here, the author describes a group of lawless sons from Israel that sought to assimilate into pagan culture: "And they built a gymnasium in Jerusalem, according to the custom of the gentiles and they made themselves foreskins (ἐποίησαν ἑαυτοῖς ἀκροβυστίας) and withdrew from the holy covenant and they united themselves with the gentiles and sold themselves to do evil."[31] In their quest to live like the nations, these Jews made themselves foreskins—that is, underwent epispasm—to blend in with pagan society.[32] For all intents and purposes—from the perspective of the author of 1 Maccabees—by undergoing epispasm they were denying their identity as Jews and functionally becoming gentiles. In so doing, they "withdrew from the holy covenant" and became apostates.

In a similar vein, in Testament of Moses 8:1–5 the author describes a future event in which Israel is punished on account of the impious, wayward priests that will rule them. Central to this punishment is the crucifixion of those who "confess their circumcisions" (8:1) and the forced epispasm of the sons of Israel: "And their wives will be given to the gods of the nations and their young sons will be cut by physicians to bring forward their foreskins" (T. Mos. 8:3 [Priest, *OTP*]). These

---

[30] As far as I can tell, this is the only place in Paul's epistles where he specifically gives instructions for Jews in the assembly. While these may be hypothetical Jews—or may simply be included as a byproduct of establishing the rule so that it encompasses all of humanity—it nevertheless provides the reader with a powerful statement on the status of Jews in the assembly, in the context of an epistle written for gentiles. There are two key texts that potentially pose a problem to this understanding: Rom 2:17–29 and 14–15. In Rom 2:17–29, I understand that the one who calls himself a Jew (σὺ Ἰουδαῖος ἐπονομάζῃ) to be a judaizing gentile and not a natural-born Jew (from Paul's perspective). For a full discussion of this, see § 5.2 below. In Rom 14–15, the "weak" (ὁ ἀσθενῶν) have also been identified as Jews, but here I understand them to be gentile followers of Jesus who are sympathetic to aspects of Jewish praxis. For a full discussion of this, see A. Andrew Das, *Solving the Romans Debate* (Minneapolis: Fortress, 2007), 106–13.

[31] This account is also recorded by Josephus, *Ant.* 12.240–41.

[32] Sara Parks argues that 2 Macc 4:12 offers a similar perspective on modifying penile aesthetics as a form of Hellenizing. She argues that the "Greek hat" (πέτασος) worn by the young men in this text is a euphemistic reference to foreskin restoration or modification in order to appear more Greek when exercising nude. Sara Parks, "When a Hat Isn't a Hat: Continuing the Tradition of Hebrew Penis Euphemisms in a Hellenistic Anti-Hellenistic Text" (presented at the Sheffield Institute for Interdisciplinary Biblical Studies Research Seminar, Sheffield, February 2021).

forced epispasms are a pivotal step in handing Israel over to the nations because it strips them of the mark of the covenant of Abraham (cf. t. Šabb 16:6; m. Abot 3:11; Gen. Rab. 48:8). The author goes on to note how others will be punished by being compelled to revere idols and blaspheme the law (8:4–5), further separating them from their Jewish identity and praxis. Unlike the willful assimilation of Jews into pagan culture in 1 Macc 1, this programmatic punishment forces them to abandon their identity and assimilate into pagan society. While neither of these texts come from Paul's hand, they are representative of a perspective on epispasm that existed during his life that demonstrates the interconnectedness of Jewish identity, circumcision, and praxis.[33]

Paul's epispasm prohibition raises an important question: was this a real problem that was occurring in the early Jesus movement? Bruce Winter frames 1 Cor 7:17–20 and the issue of epispasm in the context of social mobility and the preoccupation with social status in the ancient world.[34] Given the general disdain for circumcision in the Greco-Roman world, Winter envisages a situation in which "young Christian Jews"[35] would consider epispasm as a way of hiding their distinctiveness and preventing ridicule from gentile naysayers.[36] This would, in turn, allow these individuals the opportunity for upward social mobility. Since public nudity was a part of life in the Greco-Roman world, one's circumcised penis could have been put on display, possibly leading to some Jews trying to hide their circumcisions.[37] Robert Hall argues that Paul's technical, medical usage of

---

[33] For a brief discussion of the rabbinic texts that mention epispasm—either directly or by circumlocution—see Robert G. Hall, "Epispasm and the Dating of Ancient Jewish Writings," *JSP* 2 (1988): 71–86, at 74–75; Magnus Zetterholm, *The Formation of Christianity in Antioch* (London: Routledge, 2003), 72–73.
[34] Bruce W. Winter, *Seek the Welfare of the City: Christians as Benefactors and Citizens* (Grand Rapids: Eerdmans, 1994), 146–52; cf. Dale B. Martin, *Slavery as Salvation: The Metaphor of Slavery in Pauline Christianity* (New Haven: Yale University Press, 1990), 65–66; Thiselton, *First Corinthians*, 551.
[35] Winter, *Seek the Welfare*, 147–48.
[36] Greco-Roman attitudes toward circumcision were broadly shaped by their preferred penile aesthetic and the association of an exposed glans with an erection. On the value placed on penile aesthetics in the Greco-Roman world, see K. J. Dover, *Greek Homosexuality*, rev. ed. (Cambridge: Harvard University Press, 1989), 125–35; Hodges, "The Ideal Prepuce"; Thomas R. Blanton IV, "The Expressive Prepuce: Philo's Defense of Judaic Circumcision in Greek and Roman Contexts," *SPhiloA* 31 (2019): 127–45.
[37] It is probable that Martial's discussion of Menophilus and his fibula refers to a Jew trying to conceal his circumcision in settings of public nudity: "So large a sheath (*fibula*) covers Menophilus' penis that it would be enough by itself for all our comic actors. I had supposed (we often bathe together) that he was anxious to spare his voice, Flaccus. But while he was in a game in the middle of the sportsground with everybody watching, the sheath (*fibula*) slipped off the poor soul; he was

ἐπισπάω—a usage that only occurs here and in Soranus (*Gynecology* 2.16.34)—indicates that epispasm was a legitimate, well-known option in the first century.[38]

While epispasm may have been a live option in the first century, there is no reason to believe that any significant number of Jews in the Jesus movement were seeking out foreskin restoration or that Paul's prohibition reflects any relevant situation in Corinth that led to this prohibition. Rather, read in the context of his universal rule, the prohibition should be understood as being reflective of Paul's stance on the permanence and relevance of Jewish identity for Jews in the Jesus movement. Furthermore, since the Jesus movement was thoroughly situated within Judaism in the first century, the prohibition of epispasm would have been an assumed point of consensus for most—if not all—Jesus-following Jews.[39] Additionally, nowhere in Paul's letters or in the discussion of circumcision in Acts 15 and 21 is circumcision viewed as something that can be or should be abrogated by Jews. In the ancient world, circumcision was the marker par excellence of Jews and it continued to remain so for Paul.[40]

2.3.2 Circumcision and Non-Jews

If a Jew undergoing epispasm was broadly conceived as denying one's identity as a Jew, then conversely, a non-Jew undergoing circumcision constitutes a similar attempt to modify or change their identity.[41] As demonstrated by Josephus, the adop-

---

circumcised (*verpus erat*)" (*Epigrams* 7.82 [Shackleton Bailey, LCL]). *Verpa*, like the Greek ψωλός, indicates a penis with the foreskin drawn back and glans exposed (generally linked with an erection or sexual act), but it can also be used to describe a circumcised penis due to the similarity of their appearance. On this, see James N. Adams, *The Latin Sexual Vocabulary* (London: Duckworth, 1982), 13; contra Cohen, *Beginnings of Jewishness*, 358–59.

38 Hall, "Epispasm and Dating," 73. Hall may be overstating his case, as context would easily illuminate Paul's intended meaning.

39 On circumcision and Jews in the early Jesus movement, see Thiessen, *Contesting Conversion*, 111–23.

40 Tacitus, *Hist.* 4.1–5.2; Petronius, *Satyricon* 102.13; *Poems* 24; Martial, *Epigrams* 7.30; Juvenal, *Satires* 14.96–106. See also, Louis H. Feldman, *Jew and Gentile in the Ancient World: Attitudes and Interactions from Alexander to Justinian* (Princeton: Princeton University Press, 1993). 153–58.

41 Other ancient ethnic groups (e.g. Egyptians, Phoenicians, Ethiopians, Cochlians, etc.) were known to practice circumcision to some degree, however, the closer our sources get to the Second Temple period, the early Christian period, and beyond, the more circumcision becomes almost exclusively associated with Jewish identity. For a brief discussion on the practice of circumcision in the ancient near east, see Frans Jonckheere, "La circonsion [sic] des anciens Egyptiens," *Centaurus* 1 (1951): 212–34; Jack M. Sasson, "Circumcision in the Ancient Near East," *JBL* 5 (1966): 473–476. Ancient historians often link the practice of circumcision to Egypt and note that the nations that prac-

tion of circumcision was understood as a key step that effectively made outsiders into Jews. For example, the conquering and assimilation of the Idumeans (*Ant.* 13.257–58) and the Itureans (*Ant.* 13.318–19) into the Jewish nation is accomplished through the adoption of Jewish customs, chiefly circumcision. Josephus also highlights the central role of circumcision in his documentation of the conversion of Izates of Adiabene (*Ant.* 20.38–40). Similarly, the circumcision of Achior the Ammonite in Jdt 14 is portrayed as bringing him into the house of Israel. This phenomenon is also recorded by non-Jewish authors. For example, Juvenal (*Satires* 14.96–106) writes about some who have fathers that respect the sabbath and eventually get rid of their foreskins to become Jews and turn away from their Roman identity. For many in the Second Temple period, a non-Jew undergoing circumcision was broadly understood as one becoming a Jew or closely aligning oneself with the Jews.[42] A gentile in the Jesus movement submitting to circumcision would broadly be considered in the ancient world as an attempt to fully judaize (OG Esther 8:17; Josephus, *J.W.* 2.454), and thus, would constitute a failure to remain in their state at the time of their calling.[43]

Unlike the epispasm prohibition, Paul's prohibition of gentiles undergoing circumcision is also attested elsewhere in his epistles (Gal 2:3–5; 5:2–4; cf. Phil 3:2–3) and in Acts 15. Given the universal nature of Paul's rule, this text should be instructive for reading Paul elsewhere on the issue of gentiles and circumcision. It is important to note that Paul's rule in regard to circumcision and foreskin is unlike the other examples—slavery and celibacy—in 1 Cor 7, in that Paul allows for no concessions to changing this aspect of one's identity; this is a rule to which no exceptions can be made.[44] This is something that is often overlooked due to the exceptions Paul makes elsewhere.[45] Additionally, the following verse in which Paul states

---

tice circumcision learned it from them; Herodotus, *Hist.* 2.36–37, 104; Diodorus Siculus, *Bib. hist.* 1.28.3; 3.32.4; Strabo, *Geogr.* 17.2.5; cf. Barn. 9.6. See also, Blaschke, *Beschneidung*, 43–45.

42 Cohen (*Beginnings of Jewishness*, 109–74) argues that by the time of the Maccabees, all Jews were in agreement that non-Jews could become Jews via circumcision. Thiessen's *Contesting Conversion* offers a careful critique of this perspective, noting that while some ancient Jews did view conversion via circumcision as a possibility, this was never a universally held perspective.

43 On the meaning of ιουδαΐζω ("to judaize," "to adopt the Jewish way of life") see the discussion at the end of §3.8.1.

44 On the puzzling circumcision of Timothy in Acts 16:1–3, see the discussions in Christopher Bryan, "A Further Look at Acts 16:1–3," *JBL* 107 (1988): 292–94; Thiessen, *Contesting Conversion*, 120–22; David J. Rudolph, *A Jew to the Jews: Jewish Contours of Pauline Flexibility in 1 Corinthians 9:19–23*, 2nd ed. (Eugene, OR: Pickwick, 2016), 23–27. I also offer a brief analysis of Timothy's circumcision in an extended footnote in §4.6.

45 Some commentators have picked up on this, e.g., Richard A. Horsley, *1 Corinthians*, ANTC (Nashville: Abingdon, 1998), 101; Fee, *First Corinthians*, 312.

"circumcision is nothing and foreskin is nothing" has led many to conclude that circumcision and foreskin are matters of indifference for Paul.⁴⁶ The opposite is actually the reality; here Paul uses imperative commands—μὴ ἐπισπάσθω and μὴ περιτεμνέσθω—to prohibit one from changing the state of their penis. That should hardly be understood as a position of indifference.⁴⁷

As Paul's rule indicates, neither circumcision nor foreskin are preconditions for participation in the assembly, but the statuses and ethnic realities that they represent should not be altered. The reason for this is not related to Paul's supposed indifference, but because of Paul's view of ethnic fixity: Jews are Jews and non-Jews are non-Jews, and nothing can effectively make one into another.⁴⁸ As Paul argues in Galatians, the genealogical problem facing gentiles cannot be solved by circumcision—it is unable to make non-Jews into Abraham's seed. From Paul's perspective, while one could never truly change their status as a Jew or gentile—these are fixed ethnic boundaries—he urges those in his assemblies to remain in the state in which they were called because those callings are linked with a specific way of living (1 Cor 7:17). Remaining in one's calling as circumcised or foreskinned is less about a passive adherence to the way things are and more about keeping the commandments of God that accord with one's ethnic identity (1 Cor 7:19).

2.3.3 An Objection: "When you were gentiles…" (1 Cor 12:2)

For Paul, the status and praxis of gentiles in the Jesus movement does seem to change more significantly than it does for Jews. One obvious objection to the view I am proposing above is Paul's statement in 1 Cor 12:2: "You know that when you were gentiles, you were continually led and carried away to mute idols."⁴⁹ If one were to take this verse at face value, the phrase, "when you were gentiles" (ὅτε ἔθνη ἦτε), seems to indicate that those to whom Paul is writing

---

46 See the discussion below.
47 Braxton (*The Tyranny of Resolution*, 123) misses this important point: "Although Paul urges his converts not to alter their ethnic status in order to participate in the ἐκκλησία, *he also does not overtly prohibit such actions in general*" (emphasis added).
48 On Jewishness as genealogy, see Hayes, *Gentile Impurities*, 68–91; Thiessen, *Contesting Conversion*. On ethnic essentialism and Paul, see the discussions in Matlock, "Jews by Nature"; Thiessen, *Gentile Problem*; Fredriksen, *Pagans' Apostle*, 65, 114, 124, 215n37; Thiessen, "Paul, Essentialism."
49 The text of 12:2 is notoriously difficult to translate, particularly the clause ὡς ἂν ἤγεσθε ἀπαγόμενοι. For a discussion of the syntax of this passage, see Fee, *First Corinthians*, 576–78; Fitzmyer, *First Corinthians*, 457–58.

are no longer gentiles but something else (cf. Rom 3:22; 10:12; Gal 3:28). This is an interpretation that has been widely adopted. Here, Richard Hays' thoughts are representative: "This formulation implies that he considers them ἔθνη no longer. Within Paul's symbolic world, they are no longer among the *goyim*, because they have been taken up into the story of Israel."[50] While Paul's language lends plausibility to this interpretation, a more nuanced reading is preferable. If these gentiles are no longer gentiles, what are they? In Paul's understanding of things, there are only two types of people: Jews and the gentiles.[51] Does this mean that since they are no longer gentiles that they have now become some kind of Jews?[52] Paul seems adamant that they do not fully adopt Jewish law and circumcision, and that the gentiles in the Jesus movement remain distinct from Jews (Rom 3:29–30; 11:17–24; Gal 2:14; cf. 1 Cor 7:17–20).[53]

In context, Paul is here discussing his audience's prior commingling with idols, not their ethnic identity per se. In the ancient world it is difficult to separate the concepts of ethnicity and cult, as the two are intertwined.[54] What he does here—focusing on their relationship to idols, as he also does in 1 Thess 1:9 and Gal 4:8—makes it clear that he is highlighting the cultic aspect of their identity as non-Jews,

---

50 Richard B. Hays, *The Conversion of the Imagination: Paul as Interpreter of Israel's Scriptures* (Grand Rapids: Eerdmans, 2005), 9. See also, Wright, *Paul*, 541; Concannon, *When You Were Gentiles: Specters of Ethnicity in Roman Corinth and Paul's Corinthian Correspondence* (New Haven: Yale University Press, 2014), 16, 31, 115.
51 As noted in the introduction, Paul neatly divides all humanity into the categories of Jew and gentile (or circumcision and foreskin): Rom 1:16; 2:9–10; 3:9, 29–30; 4:9–12; 9:24; 10:12; 1 Cor 1:22–24; 10:32; 12:13; Gal 2:7, 14–15; 3:28.
52 Some have interpreted Phil 3:3 ("…we are the circumcision…"), Gal 6:16 ("…the Israel of God."), and Rom 2:28–29 ("…not the Jew on display…but the Jew in secret…") as being instances where gentiles are now credited with some kind of Jewish status. I treat Phil 3:3 and Rom 2:28–29 in subsequent chapters. On the identity of the "Israel of God" or "God's Israel" as referring to historic Israel, see Susan Grove Eastman, "Israel and the Mercy of God: A Re-Reading of Galatians 6.16 and Romans 9–11," *NTS* 56 (2010): 385–90; cf. Richardson, *Israel*, 74–84.
53 Paul does, however, require that non-Jews in his assemblies are to Judaize to a certain degree; they are to exclusively worship the god of Israel. See, e.g., Paula Fredriksen, "Judaizing the Nations: The Ritual Demands of Paul's Gospel," *NTS* 56 (2010): 232–52; Mark D. Nanos, "Paul's Non-Jews Do Not Become 'Jews,' But Do They Become 'Jewish'?: Reading Romans 2:25–29 Within Judaism, Alongside Josephus," *JJMJS* 1 (2014): 26–53.
54 In the ancient world, cult does not exist apart from ethnic groups. See, e.g., Fredriksen, "How Jewish is God?"; cf. Denise Kimber Buell, *Why This New Race: Ethnic Reasoning in Early Christianity* (New York: Columbia University Press, 2005), 35–51. For a broad critique of how modern conceptions of "religion" obscure this aspect of ancient cult, see Brent Nongbri, *Before Religion: A History of a Modern Concept* (New Haven: Yale University Press, 2013), 25–64.

which is, presumably, no longer a part of their current identity.[55] The solution to this problem of nomenclature offered by Paula Fredriksen is instructive for understanding 1 Cor 12:2 and the identity of gentile Christ-followers in Paul's letters. She refers to them as "ex-pagan pagans" or "ex-pagan gentiles."[56] Unlike proselytes who change their ethnicity and worship the god of Israel, or god-fearers who retain their ethnicity and add the god of Israel to their pantheon, these ex-pagan pagans retain their native ethnic identity, while abandoning their native deities for the god of Israel. Thus it is possible to understand that in 1 Cor 12:2 Paul depicts gentiles as retaining their ethnic status while abandoning their native deities.

2.4 Circumcision and Foreskin as Nothing

In light of the foregoing discussion, the claim that circumcision and foreskin are nothing appears to be contradictory. If these are identities that Paul upholds with his universal rule, then how can Paul claim that they are both nothing? Furthermore, the emphasis he places on keeping the commandments of God seems to imply that circumcision is not a commandment of God—something that would be problematic for many ancient Jews.[57] This has been thoroughly recognized by commentators on this text.[58] There are two key questions to ask that are helpful for understanding this: 1) What does Paul mean when he says that circumcision and foreskin are nothing? and 2) What does Paul mean by "keeping the commandments of God"? The vast majority of interpreters—irrespective of background or tradition—have answered these questions similarly: Paul believes that circumci-

---

[55] Many commentators have also noticed this. Barrett (*First Corinthians*, 278–79) highlights the "religious" nature of this text, but also notes that they are no longer gentiles, hinting at future constructions of Christians as a third race: "Paul's readers are *Gentiles* no longer; but neither are they Jews. He does not describe them as 'new' or 'third race (e.g. *Diog.* 1), but the thought is not far away." Ciampa and Rosner (Roy E. Ciampa and Brian S. Rosner, The First Letter to the Corinthians, PilNTC [Grand Rapids: Eerdmans, 2010], 563] see Paul as "stressing their religious background and not simply the fact that they were not ethnic Jews." Fee (*First Corinthians*, 576–77) notes that they traded their pagan past for a Christian one. Fitzmyer (*First Corinthians*, 457) highlights the cultic sense of the term here, and rejects a reading that means they are now members of Israel. Garland (*1 Corinthians*, 566) offers a poignant interpretation, here translating ἔθνος as "pagan": "...in the context of idols, the translation "pagans" is apropos."
[56] Fredriksen, *Pagans' Apostle*, 73–77, 165–67.
[57] Even Philo argues that the true allegorical meaning of circumcision cannot be separated from the act itself. In *Migr.* 89–93, he argues against those who allegorize the law and fail to keep its precepts. For Philo the true meaning of an act and the act itself is not an either/or, but a both/and.
[58] E.g., Barrett, *First Corinthians*, 169; Thiselton, *First Corinthians*, 551; Dunn, *New Perspective on Paul*, 456–57; Ciampa and Rosner, *First Corinthians*, 311.

sion and foreskin should be treated as *adiaphora*,[59] and that he no longer believes that circumcision is a commandment of God because the Messiah's coming has modified or redefined the law. N.T. Wright's view is representative: "Like most exegetes, I have in the past taken verse 19 as a deliberate irony. Paul knew as well as anyone that circumcision was itself one of the 'commandments', and here he was saying that it was irrelevant!"[60] Here, Wright understands Paul as treating circumcision as an *adiaphoron*, which is manifested in a redefinition of what it means to keep the commandments of God. Similarly, Daniel Boyarin comments that Paul views circumcision and foreskin as *adiaphora* and that literal observance of the law has become irrelevant.[61] David Horrell, too, notes that identity markers like circumcision and foreskin have been relativized by Paul, "such that they can be described as 'nothing'."[62] Heikki Räisänen also understands this to be a "negative evaluation of circumcision" that points to irrelevance.[63] Elisabeth Schüssler Fiorenza offers similar thoughts when she states that Paul "insists that the religious/biological sign of initiation to Jewish religion is no longer of any relevance to Christians."[64] Further examples could be supplied, but the point has been sufficiently made.

---

[59] This point is often made in conjunction with readings of 1 Cor 7:19 that are conflated with Gal 5:6 and 6:15, where Paul's "neither circumcision, nor foreskin" texts are treated as a Pauline maxim. For a brief discussion of "neither circumcision, nor foreskin" as a Pauline maxim in the context of ancient rhetoric and *adiaphora*, see Rollin A. Ramsaran, "Paul and Maxims," in *Paul in the Greco-Roman World: A Handbook*, ed. J. Paul Sampley (Harrisburg, PA: Trinity, 2003), 429–56, esp. 437–48. For a tempered approach to Paul and *adiaphora*, see Will Deming, "Paul and Indifferent Things," in Sampley, *Paul in the Greco-Roman World*, 384–403. While some recent applications of *adiaphora* in the study of Paul (e.g., Ramsaran and Deming, noted above) have been careful to note the various types of indifferents present in ancient Stoic thought—namely, preferred and unpreferred indifferents—the broad, generic application of *adiaphora* that is common in scholarship has framed circumcision and foreskin as being irrelevant or insignificant without due consideration for the positive and negative spaces they occupy in Paul's world view. By relegating circumcision and foreskin to the realm of indifferent things, scholars downplay the continuing place they have in Paul's understanding of Jews and non-Jews and how they relate to the god of Israel. Even when one is careful enough to employ the sub-categories of preferred and unpreferred indifferents when discussing circumcision and foreskin, these important distinctions are obscured.
[60] Wright, *Paul*, 1434.
[61] Daniel Boyarin, *A Radical Jew*, 112; 290n10.
[62] David Horrell, *Solidarity and Difference: A Contemporary Reading of Paul's Ethics* (London: T&T Clark, 2005), 141.
[63] Räisänen, *Paul and the Law*, 139n56.
[64] Elisabeth Schüssler Fiorenza, *In Memory of Her: A Feminist Theological Reconstruction of Christian Origins* (London: SCM, 1983), 221.

2.4.1 Rhetorical Negation and Comparison

Does Paul really think of circumcision and foreskin as nothing (or irrelevant) as so many exegetes have claimed? The main problem with taking this text at face value is the surrounding context in which Paul outlines his rule for individuals to walk in and remain in the calling in which they were called. Paul commands that both Jews and gentiles remain in their respective identities, upholding their distinctive natures. Does the language of "nothing" point to relativization, unimportance, or the removal of distinction, or is Paul doing something else here? In upholding these identities in 7:17–18, Paul demonstrates that these statuses have a continuing value and function for those in the assembly. To understand what might be going on in 7:19, it is helpful to look at what Paul says elsewhere about things that are "nothing." 1 Cor 3:5–7 is a text ripe for comparison: "What then is Apollos? What then is Paul? Agents through whom you believed, and each as the Lord gave. I planted, Apollos watered, but God gave growth. So neither the one who plants nor the one who waters is anything (οὔτε...ἐστίν τι οὔτε), but God who gives growth." Does Paul here negate the value of his or Apollos' work? Of course not; he is using the language of comparison and hyperbole to highlight how great God's work is when compared to the work of men. Likewise, in 2 Cor 12:11 Paul states, "...for I am not less than the super-apostles, even though I am nothing (οὐδέν εἰμι)." Once again, is Paul really nothing, or is he using hyperbole to make a rhetorical point about the so called "super-apostles"? Both of these texts demonstrate the possibility that Paul's assertion that circumcision and foreskin are nothing could be a similar rhetorical move in 7:19.[65]

David Rudolph proposes that Paul may be employing a "dialectical negation" to demonstrate that the negation of circumcision and foreskin in comparison with keeping the commandments of God is not a strict either/or dichotomy, but serves to show the importance of keeping the commandments.[66] Commenting on this type of negation and comparison (οὐ...ἀλλά [or οὐδέν...ἀλλά in the current text]), G. B. Winer notes: "Or, as in other passages, an absolute negation is, on rhetorical

---

[65] Additionally, David Rudolph (*Jew to the Jews*, 30) has noted that Hos 6:6 could also serve as a helpful comparison: "For I desire ḥesed and not sacrifice, the knowledge of God rather than burnt offerings." Yahweh's relationship with Israel demands sacrifice, but here the author is using hyperbole to say that ḥesed and knowledge are more important.

[66] Rudolph, *Jew to the Jews*, 30. The term "dialectical negation" comes from Heinz Kruse, "Die 'dialektische Negation' als semitisches Idiom," *VT* 4 (1954): 385–400. On dialectical negation, see also Andrew H. Bartelt, "Dialectical Negation: An Exegetical Both/And," in *"Hear the Word of Yahweh": Essays on Scripture and Archaeology in Honor of Horace D. Hummel*, ed. Dean O. Wenthe, Paul L. Schrieber, and Lee A. Maxwell (St. Louis: Concordia, 2002), 57–66.

grounds, employed instead of a conditional (relative), not for the purpose of really (logically) cancelling the first conception, *but in order to direct the undivided attention to the second, so that the first may almost disappear.*"⁶⁷ The reason for Paul's rhetoric is not to erase the difference between circumcision and foreskin—Jewish and non-Jewish identity—nor is it to state their irrelevance, rather, it is used to highlight the importance of keeping the commandments of God. Since Paul is primarily making a legal argument about the way in which Jews and gentiles in Christ should live (περιπατέω, 7:17), he rhetorically negates their respective identities in order to place his emphasis on necessity of keeping the commandments of God.⁶⁸

While Rudolph and Tucker both grasp that this type of comparison is occurring in 7:19, both state that what is being compared is one's status as a Jew or gentile with being in Christ.⁶⁹ Similarly, William Campbell comments, "The crucial point of the verse is not a comparison of the relative merits of circumcision and uncircumcision, but a comparison of both with the call of God."⁷⁰ These claims are incorrect. Paul compares these statuses with *keeping the commandments of God*: "Circumcision is nothing, and foreskin is nothing, but keeping the commandments of God." This is a crucial distinction. Campbell himself notes that this "is not

---

67 G. B. Winer, *A Grammar of the NT Diction*, trans. Edward Masson (Edinburgh: T&T Clark, 1860), 518–19 (emphasis added).
68 Based on this rhetoric, some have argued that Paul is relativizing this aspect of their previous identities, but the language of reprioritization offered by Tucker (*Remain in Your Calling*, 77–79) seems to capture Paul's ideas more thoughtfully. While relativization and reprioritization may seem to be functionally equivalent language, relativizing implies that circumcision and foreskin lose their significance and "downplays the need for [Paul's] rule" (Tucker, *Remain in Your Calling*, 78). Reprioritization, on the other hand, upholds the particular identities of Jews and gentiles without diminishing them. This distinction is important as it directly impacts what it means to keep the commandments of God. Although he uses the language of relativization, William Campbell (*Creation of Christian Identity*, 93) captures the ongoing significance these various aspects of identity have: "We need to be more careful in Pauline studies in our use of words such as "obsolete" or "abrogated" especially in ethical contexts. This world may be passing away but even if it is, the whole of one's Christian calling has to be lived within it… Thus whilst theologically, ethnic, gender, and sexual issues are *relativized* by the call of Christ, they are neither *obsolete* nor *irrelevant* when it comes to real life situations, as liberation theology and other contextual theologies have long since stressed" (emphasis original). Elsewhere, Campbell (*The Nations*, 261) comments, "Thus, Paul's statements are often made in contexts where a reevaluation of priorities needs to be emphasized by powerful rhetorical statements such as 'circumcision is nothing and uncircumcision is nothing' (1 Cor. 7:19, Gal. 6.15), which I have argued elsewhere cannot make any sense if both circumcision and uncircumcision are literally 'nothing'."
69 Rudolph, *Jew to the Jews*, 28; Tucker, *Remain in Your Calling*, 77–80.
70 William S. Campbell, "'I Rate All Things as Loss': Paul's Puzzling Accounting System: Judaism as Loss or the Re-Evaluation of All Things in Christ?" in *Unity and Diversity in Christ: Interpreting Paul in Context* (Eugene, OR: Cascade, 2013), 205.

a comparison between A and B, but between A and B with C,"[71] but he still overlooks this small but significant detail.

Many who have failed to notice the internal comparison taking place in 1 Cor 7:19 have read it alongside the similar texts in Gal 5:6 and 6:15 ("For in Christ Jesus neither circumcision has any power (ἰσχύει), nor foreskin, but faithfulness working through love"; "For neither circumcision nor foreskin is anything, but a new creation") to confirm the interpretation that Paul devalues circumcision or makes it irrelevant.[72] As Heikki Räisänen notes, however, we should be careful not to harmonize this text with those in Galatians because of their difference in content.[73] While these three texts provide helpful points of contact for understanding what Paul has to say about circumcision, the contexts of each letter and the relevant passages convey different ideas. Gal 5:6, for example, is often harmonized with 6:15 and 1 Cor 7:19 so that each can be read as saying that neither circumcision or foreskin "has any value," "counts for anything" or "has any meaning." This harmonization and interpretation rests on translating ἰσχύει in a manner so that it conveys a sense of value.[74] In context, however, ἰσχύει should be translated with the sense of having power or being able to bring about a result (cf. Phil 4:13). In Gal 5, Paul is making an argument about circumcision (and the law) versus the Messiah as sources for eschatological *dikaiosynē*. In 5:6, he declares that neither circumcision or foreskin has power to bring about this *dikaiosynē*, but *pistis* made effective through love does have this power.[75] The comparison of circumcision and foreskin with *pistis* is not one of ontology, but dynamology.

Similar to 1 Cor 7:19, Gal 6:15 follows the pattern of dialectical negation where circumcision and foreskin are said to be nothing in their comparison with something else—new creation. In this passage, Paul is making a point about boasting in circumcision and boasting in the cross. Here, 6:15 is the crescendo where circumcision and foreskin are said to be nothing (to boast in) and new creation is something (to boast in). Therefore, is it reasonable to conclude that 1 Cor 7:19, Gal 5:6, and 6:15 declare that circumcision is meaningless or irrelevant as so many have said? In

---

71 Campbell, "I Rate All Things," 206.
72 E.g., Horn, "Der Verzicht," 485; Martinus C. de Boer, *Galatians: A Commentary*, NTL (Louisville: Westminster John Knox, 2011), 323; Michael F. Bird, *An Anomalous Jew: Paul among Jews, Greeks, and Romans* (Grand Rapids: Eerdmans, 2016), 6, 161.
73 Räisänen, *Paul and the Law*, 68.
74 While the interpretive tradition has attempted to harmonize 5:6 to 6:15, the textual tradition presents the opposite picture; 6:15 is modified to agree in wording with 5:6. Notably, ἰσχύει is inserted in 6:15 by א² D² K L P Ψ 104. 365. 630. 1505. 1881 𝔐 lat sy^H.
75 For a similar understanding of Gal 5:6, see Hung-Sik Choi, "ΠΙΣΤΙΣ in Galatians 5:5–6: Neglected Evidence for the Faithfulness of Christ," *JBL* 124 (2005): 467–90; 482–9.

a word, no. While it is helpful for some purposes to put these texts in conversation with one another, none of them actually convey the idea that Paul believes circumcision and foreskin are nothing, rather, Paul places them in comparison with various things to make specific points.[76] As Christine Hayes notes, "But if we conclude that circumcision is a matter of complete indifference for Paul, we cannot satisfactorily explain his adamant resistance to Gentile circumcision and Law observance nor his own continued torah observance."[77]

2.5 Circumcision and Keeping the Commandments of God

If Paul is offering a rhetorical negation of circumcision and foreskin in order to highlight the importance of keeping the commandments of God, how does the commandment of circumcision (Gen 17, Lev 12:3) fit into the picture? As noted in the introduction, the most prominent answer is that Paul no longer believes circumcision to be a commandment of God. On this reading, the commandments of God are modified in some way due to the work of Israel's Messiah, abrogating circumcision and making it nugatory. For James Dunn and other "New Perspective" interpreters, circumcision is a Jewish distinctive that no longer has a place in an ethnically mixed assembly and is therefore no longer a part of the commandments of God.[78] "Paul could, without qualification or hesitation, describe such a denationalized understanding of the Torah as 'keeping God's commandments'."[79] Similarly, E. P. Sanders writes, "The degree to which he could change the content of the law, while still saying that it should be kept, is strikingly clear in 1 Cor. 7:19, which I regard as one of the most amazing sentences that he ever wrote."[80] In seeking to make sense of this text, C. K. Barrett, argues that Paul redefines the commandments of God through a christological lens: "That *we keep God's commandments* means an obedience to the will of God as disclosed in his Son far more radical than the observance of any code, whether ceremonial or moral, could be."[81] Sim-

---

76 For full treatments of Gal 5:6 and 6:15, see chapter three on Galatians.
77 Hayes, *Divine Law*, 160–61.
78 Dunn, *New Perspective on Paul*, 317–18, 335–37.
79 Dunn, *New Perspective on Paul*, 337.
80 Sanders, *Paul, the Law*, 103. Sanders does not see a christological modification of the law at play, rather, Paul simply removes circumcision: "The passages which favor fulfilling the law, we have seen, all have in mind the Mosaic law, at least in theory, and when Paul deletes circumcision he does so either without explanation (1 Cor. 7:19) or on the basis of Genesis (Galatians 3, Romans 4), not on the basis of the arrival of the messianic age" (102).
81 Barrett, *First Corinthians*, 169 (emphasis original).

ilarly, Wright notes that "Paul has a larger vision of 'keeping God's commandments', which now transcends the questions of 'Torah-observance' as seen through the eyes of the zealous Pharisee."[82]

For many of these interpreters, Paul views the "commandments of God" as being a christologically modified set of commandments. The text, however, does not require or even suggest such a reading, as Paul does not mention any christological modifications to the commandments, nor are they implicit within the text. Additionally, as Matthew Thiessen has commented on Barrett's reading, "…it is not clear why a radical obedience to the will of God as it is disclosed in Christ necessarily precludes the observance of circumcision. Only a reader who comes to the text with later Christian assumptions about the irrelevance of circumcision could find such a reading compelling."[83] This is a severe—but necessary—critique.

Reading 7:19 with Paul's rule and ethnicity in mind is crucial for untangling the supposedly paradoxical element of Paul's emphasis on keeping the commandments of God in light of what he says about circumcision and foreskin.[84] Paul's rule demonstrates that he upholds Jewish and gentile identity in the assembly. Participation in the assembly is not limited to a particular ethnic group; it does not matter if one is a Jew or a gentile for Paul because both receive the same benefits from a proper orientation toward Israel's Messiah: the reception of divine *pneuma* and a future pneumatic existence. What matters for those in the assembly in the present is keeping the commandments of God. As numerous recent interpreters propose, the pertinent commandments for each of these groups are not identical, rather, there are a set of commandments applicable to Jews and a set for non-Jews.

The first fully formed expression of this solution was made by Peter Tomson.[85] Subsequently, this view has been espoused by Markus Bockmuehl,[86] Pamela Eisenbaum,[87] David Rudolph,[88] J. Brian Tucker,[89] Anders Runesson,[90] Matthew Thiessen,[91] and others. While each of these interpreters have their own nuanced reading of this passage, the core argument they make is broadly the same: Jews in the Jesus

---

[82] Wright, *Paul*, 1434.
[83] Thiessen, *Gentile Problem*, 9; cf. Tomson, *Jewish Law*, 273.
[84] Thiessen, *Gentile Problem*, 9. Cf. Markus Bockmuehl, *Jewish Law in Gentile Churches: Halakhah and the Beginning of Christian Public Ethics* (Grand Rapids: Baker Academic, 2000), 170–71; Rudolph, *A Jew to the Jews*, 83–85; Tucker, *Remain in Your Calling*, 77–80.
[85] Tomson, *Jewish Law*, 88–89, 271–74.
[86] Bockmuehl, *Jewish Law*, 170–2.
[87] Eisenbaum, *Paul Was Not a Christian*, 62–63.
[88] Rudolph, *Jew to the Jews*, 82–5.
[89] Tucker, *Remain in Your Calling*, 77–80.
[90] Runesson, "Paul's Rule," 216–19.
[91] Thiessen, *Gentile Problem*, 8–11.

2.5 Circumcision and Keeping the Commandments of God — 43

movement are still responsible for keeping the traditional law of their ancestors and non-Jews—although not responsible for the Jewish law—must keep the commandments that pertain to them. For most of the interpreters above,[92] these commandments are represented in the apostolic decree of Acts 15:20–29, or are akin to —what are later referred to in rabbinic literature[93] as—the Noachide commandments.[94] This view coheres with Paul's rule, specifically the call to walk in the way each was assigned and called (ἑκάστῳ ὡς ἐμέρισεν ὁ κύριος, ἕκαστον ὡς κέκληκεν ὁ θεός, οὕτως περιπατείτω; 7:17). If their callings are different and they are to remain in their respective callings, it plausibly follows that the commandments applicable to each are also different.[95]

Against the view that interprets the commandments of God through a purely christological lens, this perspective understands that Paul is using the phrase "the commandments of God" like his Jewish contemporaries to actually refer to the Jewish law (e.g., Sir 32:23–24; Matt 19:17–19; Josephus, *Ant.* 8.120).[96] Elsewhere in Paul's writings he typically uses "commandment" (ἐντολή) to refer to Jewish law (Rom 7:8–12; 13:9).[97] The Jewish law already had precedents for differentiated law observance because it did not always require the same things of all peoples. Pamela Eisenbaum notes how the commandment of circumcision in the Hebrew Bible is only required for Jewish males; it is not a universal commandment.[98] Elsewhere in the Hebrew Bible the Levitical priests were given their own set of commandments that were specific to their subgroup and were not imposed on the rest of

---

92 On this point, Runesson deviates ("Paul's Rule," 217). He refers to Rom 13:10 ("love is the fulfilling of the law") and Rom 5:5 ("God's love has been poured into our hearts through the holy *pneuma*") to make the argument that since the condensed form of the law is love, and since Christ-believers have love through the *pneuma*, then all are able to obey "the commandments of God, the essence of which is love" (218). Jews in Christ, however, are still responsible for obeying the whole law. Cf. Fredriksen, *Pagans' Apostle*, 108, 111.
93 The first explicit rabbinic mention of the Noachide Commandments is found in t. ʿAbod. Zar. 8:4.
94 For a brief but thorough discussion of the Noachide commandments, their antecedents in Second Temple texts, and their rabbinic development, see Markus Bockmuehl, *Jewish Law*, 145–73. See also, Mark D. Nanos, *The Mystery of Romans: The Jewish Context of Paul's Letter* (Minneapolis: Fortress, 1996), 50–56; Hayes, *Divine Law*, 350–70. For a discussion of how Paul's instruction for his gentile assemblies intersects with the Noachide commandments, see Matthew P. Van Zile, "The Sons of Noah and the Sons of Abraham: The Origins of Noahide Law," *JSJ* 48 (2017): 386–417.
95 Huttunen, *Paul and Epictetus*, 28–29.
96 Thiessen, *Gentile Problem*, 9; cf. Dunn, *New Perspective on Paul*, 336.
97 In 1 Cor 14:37, however, Paul uses ἐντολή to refer to his own divinely authorized instruction ("… what I am writing is a command of the Lord"). This usage in 1 Cor 14:37 has led Ciampa and Rosner (*First Corinthians*, 313) to improbably conclude that Paul's use in 7:19 is also a reference to his own instruction.
98 Eisenbaum, *Not a Christian*, 62–63.

Israel (Lev 8–10, 21).[99] Additionally, the laws governing the resident aliens (*gerim*) who lived alongside Israel but were distinct from Israel are instructive for understanding how various law codes can exist within the same community.[100]

As noted above, the obvious comparative text from the New Testament that can help make sense of these dual commandments is the apostolic decree in Acts 15. There, a particular group of Messiah-following Pharisees sought to impose circumcision and the Mosaic law on gentiles in the Jesus movement (Acts 15:5). Since the early Jesus movement was thoroughly embedded within Judaism, the status and identity of gentiles in the community was contested. What was required of them? Did they need to observe Torah or was there another option? Were they to be regarded as proselytes or as something else? James concluded that the gentiles did not need to be circumcised and were only required to abstain from things polluted by idols, *porneia*, things strangled, and from blood (Acts 15:19–20, 29).[101] In Acts 15 it is simply assumed that Jews in the Jesus movement continue to be Torah observant; they did not view this as a point that was up for debate, nor did Luke find a need to comment on the state of Jewish Torah-observance. This text implies that Jews remain Jews and non-Jews remain non-Jews, and each are to follow a specific set of commandments. While the historicity of the account in Acts is debated, this text still provides us with an interesting point of contact the helps us make sense of 1 Cor 7:19.[102]

By way of summary, the perspective I am proposing is succinctly captured by Michael Wyschogrod: "The distinction that needs to be made, therefore, is not between the law before Christ and after Christ,[103] but the law for Jews and for Gentiles. I believe that the early church (as reflected in Acts 15) expected Jewish Christians to continue Torah observance and to add to it their faith in Jesus as the Messiah. Gentiles would only need to obey the Noachide laws while sharing their faith in Jesus with Jews who believed in him."[104] This approach is faithful

---

[99] Eisenbaum, *Not a Christian*, 62 (cited by Thiessen, *Gentile Problem*, 10).
[100] E.g., Lev 17–26, where some of the laws are specifically listed as applying to both Israel and the *gerim* living among them, and others only apply to Israel. See my discussion of the law and *gerim* in §3.4.2.
[101] The list is slightly different in 15:29, where "things polluted by idols" (τῶν ἀλισγημάτων τῶν εἰδώλων) is replaced with "things sacrificed to idols" (εἰδωλοθύτων).
[102] While Paul's teaching typically agrees with what is required of non-Jews as outlined in the apostolic decree, he does offer his own halakhah on idol-food in 1 Cor 8:1–13 and 10:14–33. See Tomson, *Jewish Law*, 189–220; Van Zile, "The Sons of Noah," 407–9.
[103] Paul does make this type of distinction elsewhere (Gal 3; Rom 10:4; cf. 1 Cor 9:19–22), but it does not play any part in the present discussion of 1 Cor 7.
[104] Michael Wyschogrod, "A Jewish Postscript," in *Encountering Jesus: A Debate on Christology*, ed. Stephen T. Davis (Atlanta: John Knox, 1988), 187.

to Paul's rule by upholding Jewish and non-Jewish identity, while concurrently keeping the observance of the commandments of God at the forefront of his assemblies. Ultimately, for Paul, one's ethnic identity as a Jew or non-Jew has no bearing on their ability to be recipients of divine *pneuma* and eschatological *dikaiosynē*; they both have an equal standing before God in the Messiah (cf. Rom 3:22–23, 28–30; 10:12). The most important thing is that all individuals—whether Jew or gentile—show fidelity to Jesus as the Messiah, which, partially consists of keeping the relevant commandments of God.

2.6 Conclusion

In this chapter, I have argued that understanding Paul's rule in 1 Cor 7:17 is the key to unlocking what he says in 7:19 about circumcision, foreskin, and the commandments of God. Here, Paul offers a halakhic ruling on how the individuals in his assemblies are supposed to conduct themselves. Those who were called as circumcised are to remain circumcised, and those who were called in foreskin are to remain in foreskin. As he does throughout his epistles, Paul uses the language of circumcision and foreskin in this passage metonymically to refer to one's identity as a Jew or a non-Jew. Contrary to the dominant reading of this text, I proposed that Paul's exhortation for individuals to remain as they are is not because circumcision and foreskin—and the identities they represent—are irrelevant or indifferent things for him, but rather, one's identity as either circumcised or being in foreskin has implications for how one lives.

Next, I argued that Paul's negation of circumcision and foreskin in 7:19 is not a true negation of those identities, but serves to highlight the importance of keeping the commandments of God. Paul employs the rhetoric of negation and comparison (οὐδέν...ἀλλά) to draw his readers attention to what he thinks truly matters. While one's identity as circumcised or foreskinned does not matter as it pertains to membership within the assembly, what does matter is keeping the commandments of God. Given that circumcision is a commandment from God for Jews, this statement has perplexed many interpreters. This has led to the common conclusion that Paul either no longer believed circumcision to be a commandment of God, or that the commandments referenced in 7:19 are something other than the Jewish law. The solution to this conundrum is that God does not require the same things from all people. Like the specific laws only applicable to the Levitical priests, and the differentiated laws for Israel and the *gerim* that lived within her borders, Paul understood that the commandments of God for Jews and non-Jews were different. Jews in the assembly are to continue to keep their ancestral law and non-Jews are to keep the commandments applicable to them. Acts 15 presents this perspective as the consensus view held by the Apostles. There, it is simply assumed that Jews in the Jesus movement continue to follow their ancestral law; what required clarification was the legal requirements of non-Jews. In Acts 15 it is agreed upon that gentiles in the Jesus movement only need to abstain from things polluted by idols, *porneia*, things strangled, and from blood. It is likely that Paul thought that the commandments applicable to non-Jews were those outlined in Acts 15 or were akin to the Noachide laws found in rabbinic literature.

3 Do You Not Hear the Law? Circumcision in Galatians

> Pay Attention! I, Paul, am saying to you that if you let yourselves be circumcised, the Messiah will be of no benefit to you. (Gal 5:2)

3.1 Introduction

There is little doubt that conflict over the circumcision of non-Jews lies at the heart of Paul's epistle to the Galatians. Unlike the brief discussion of circumcision in 1 Corinthians, Paul's discourse on circumcision in Galatians is penned as a direct response to a crisis facing the Galatian assemblies.[1] While many have taken Paul's statements about circumcision in Galatians and universalized them, within the context of the epistle, he is writing specifically to an audience of non-Jews[2] who are considering undergoing proselyte circumcision at the behest of a certain group of "agitators" (Gal 1:7; 5:10) and "unsettlers" (Gal 5:12).[3] Sometime after Paul left Galatia, the agitators came to them proclaiming a different message than the one which Paul proclaimed. This alternative non-gospel (1:6–7) included the necessity of circumcision (5:2–3; 6:12–13) and some level of Torah observance (2:16; 3:2, 5, 11, 18; 4:21) for gentiles in the assembly. Upon hearing that the Galatians are considering undergoing circumcision in light of the agitators' message, Paul sends this urgent, polemical letter in order to dissuade them from undergoing cir-

---

[1] While the message of Galatians has long been universalized and construed as Paul's apology for law-free Christianity—over against legalistic Judaism—this letter is just as contingent and occasional as any other. This interpretation can trace its roots back to Marcion and Tertullian (Tertullian, *Marc.* 5.2).

[2] On the non-Jewish identity of the addressees, see Mark D. Nanos, *The Irony of Galatians: Paul's Letter in First-Century Context* (Minneapolis: Fortress, 2002), 75–85.

[3] Throughout this chapter I refer to these individuals as "the agitators." I do so following Paul's language, though I acknowledge the explicit bias this title conveys. Paul is writing a polemical letter and refers to them with negative language. This language, however, should not distort our perception of these individuals. Like Paul, they likely thought they were accurately serving their god and promoting the truth amongst the Galatian assemblies. While Paul portrays their motives in a negative light (6:12–13), it is possible that this is only due to the distorting nature of polemics. Others have offered more neutral titles for these individuals—e.g., "Teachers" or "Influencers"—but I have consciously chosen to mirror Paul's language. For discussions of these alternatives, see J. Louis Martyn, *Galatians: A New Translation with Introduction and Commentary*, AB 33 A (New York: Doubleday, 1997), 117–18; Nanos, *Irony*, 115–31, 193–99.

cumcision, and to affirm their Abrahamic sonship through the reception of divine *pneuma*.[4]

In this chapter, I seek to explain the logic undergirding Paul's argument against gentile circumcision in Galatians. The chapter begins with a brief discussion of the circumcision of gentiles in Gal 2 and the apparent apostolic consensus on the issue. Next, I offer an overview of some of the common explanations for why Paul opposes the circumcision of gentiles. In contrast to previous solutions, I argue that Paul's allegorical reading of the Sarah and Hagar narrative (Gal 4:21–5:1) offers crucial insights for understanding his opposition to gentile circumcision. Focusing on the themes of slavery, sonship via *pneuma*, and pneumatic union with the Messiah, I argue that gentile proselyte circumcision severs an individual's pneumatic union with the Messiah (5:2–4). Building on the discussion of circumcision and foreskin in the previous chapter, I then offer a reading of the "neither circumcision, nor foreskin" texts in Gal 5:6 and 6:15. Next, I suggest a new interpretation of Paul's previous proclamation of circumcision (5:11), proposing that it refers not to the previous promotion of proselyte circumcision, but to an exclusivist stance toward non-Jews. Though it does not directly mention circumcision or foreskin, I also offer a reading of Gal 5:12 and Paul's call for the agitators to "cut themselves off." The chapter concludes with a discussion of the identity of the agitators, based on my reading of Gal 6:12–13.

3.2 Galatians 2

Paul does not explicitly name the circumcision controversy in Galatians until 5:2, however, he uses his brief discussions of the so-called Apostolic council and the incident in Antioch to prepare his audience for his arguments related to gentile circumcision and the status of non-Jews within the assembly. While Paul presents these accounts as historical events within his apostolic biography, he recounts them to the Galatians within the context of his polemic against the agitators who promoted proselyte circumcision.[5] For Paul, these two incidents were analo-

---

[4] On the various potential pitfalls of interpreting an ancient, polemical letter, see the classic essay by John M. G. Barclay, "Mirror-Reading a Polemical Letter: Galatians as a Test Case," *JSNT* 31 (1987): 73–93. For a tempered critique of mirror-reading Galatians, see Justin K. Hardin, "Galatians 1–2 Without a Mirror: Reflections on Paul's Conflict with the Agitators," *TynBul* 65 (2014): 275–303.
[5] Munck, *Paul and the Salvation*, 123. While the men from James' objections and Cephas' withdrawal were probably not specifically related to circumcision, Paul frames this narrative in a way that supports his rhetorical goals. On this point, Fredriksen (*Pagans' Apostle*, 98) comments: "In other words, the 'Judaizing' in Antioch as reported in Galatians 2 had nothing to do with urging circum-

gous to the crisis in Galatia and further served to prove his point that gentile Messiah-followers should not be circumcised. From Paul's perspective, the apostles were always in agreement on this important point; only pseudo-brothers, rogue men from Jerusalem, and the agitators argued otherwise.

3.2.1 The Apostolic Consensus on Gentile Circumcision

In Gal 2:1–10, Paul gives his account of the Apostolic council (cf. Acts 15). Though the accounts in Acts 15:1–29 and Gal 2 likely recount the same events, they do so from different perspectives and convey slightly different information.[6] What is clear, is that in both accounts the issue at hand is determining the status and position of gentiles within the majority-Jewish Jesus-movement.[7] Though this meeting did not directly impact or influence the situation in the Galatian assemblies, Paul inserts this narrative into the letter as a means of clarifying his mission and the apostolic stance on the adoption of circumcision by gentiles. While gentile inclusion in the assembly is most closely associated with Paul's apostleship and mission to the gentiles, gentiles were admitted into the assembly from the very beginning. As Fredriksen notes, gentile Messiah-followers were initially an accidental consequence of the spread of the gospel message throughout the communities of the Jewish diaspora.[8] The reception of the gospel amongst gentiles caused the budding assembly and its leaders to determine their policy on gentiles; how they relate to Israel's god and what was required of them. This improvised policy, Fredriksen argues, drew on Jewish prophetic traditions that established that at the end of the age, gentiles would worship Israel's god as gentiles, and not as proselytes. That is, these gentiles did not convert and become Jews, but abandoned their native dei-

---

cision on gentile members—despite Paul's deliberate rhetorical framing of the incident—and probably everything to do with avoiding pagan wine by/or avoiding pagan households."

6 Here, I follow the majority of scholars in understanding that Gal 2:1–10 records the same events as Acts 15 and not the famine relief visit recorded in Acts 11:25–30 and 12:25. For an overview of the various position see the discussion in Richard N. Longenecker (*Galatians*, WBC 41 [Waco, TX: Word, 1990], lxxii–lxxxii), though he ultimately determines that Gal 2:1–10 corresponds to Acts 11. For the Acts 15 view, see Craig S. Keener, *Galatians*, NCBC (Cambridge: Cambridge University Press, 2018), 4–7.

7 Magnus Zetterholm rightly comments: "*Both accounts of the apostolic council contain a common denominator; the new situation needs halakhic clarification*" (*Formation of Christianity*, 144 [emphasis original]).

8 Fredriksen, *Pagans' Apostle*, 146–47. See also, Sanders, *Paul*, 465–66.

ties and worshipped the Jewish God as "eschatological gentiles."[9] This policy of non-conversion and the non-necessity of circumcision for gentiles was thus likely the majority opinion of the apostles from the earliest days of the Jesus movement, which is attested by various accounts in Acts.[10] In Acts 10 and 11, the narrative focuses on Peter's dream and revelation that gentiles are to be accepted into the Jesus movement as they are. After Peter receives some pushback for his acceptance of gentiles qua gentiles, he lays his case before some of the circumcised (i.e., Jewish) leaders of the assembly in Jerusalem, and they end up praising God for these repentant gentiles. The controversy ends without any mention of the necessity of circumcision for these gentiles in the assembly; they appear to be in agreement that gentiles do not need to be circumcised.[11]

3.2.2 "Not even Titus was Compelled to be Circumcised"

While this seems to have been the general consensus, not all Jews in the Jesus movement gave assent to this policy. By the time the apostolic council convenes to discuss this issue, there was a small but vocal minority that were demanding circumcision for gentiles in the Jesus movement (Acts 15:1, 5).[12] In Paul's depiction

---

[9] On eschatological gentiles, see Fredriksen, *Pagans' Apostle*, 73–77. Some of the main texts Fredriksen and others cite in favor of the eschatological gentile motif are Isa 56:3–7; Zeph 3:8–13; Zech 8:20–23; Tob 14:6. For a critique of this prophetic tradition as used by Fredriksen and others to demonstrate the eschatological inclusion of the gentiles, see Terrence L. Donaldson, "Paul Within Judaism: A Critical Evaluation from a "New Perspective" Perspective" in Nanos and Zetterholm, *Paul within Judaism*, 284–93; Matthew V. Novenson, "What Eschatological Pilgrimage of the Gentiles?," in *Israel and the Nations: Paul's Gospel in the Context of Jewish Expectation*, ed. František Ábel (Lanham, MD: Lexington Books/Fortress Academic, 2021), 61–73. For discussions of the various Jewish views on the eschatological fate of gentiles, see E. P. Sanders, *Jesus and Judaism* (Philadelphia: Fortress, 1985), 213–18; Zetterholm, *Formation of Christianity*, 136–42.
[10] Sanders, *Paul*, 462–63.
[11] See the discussion in Joshua D. Garroway, "The Pharisee Heresy: Circumcision for Gentiles in the Acts of the Apostles," *NTS* 60 (2013): 20–36, at 23–27.
[12] According to Acts 15, the circumcision of gentiles was the presenting issue that created the necessity for the meeting. Paul's account of the meeting, however, states that it was not the issue of circumcision that necessitated it, but that Paul went up to Jerusalem after receiving a revelation (ἀποκάλυψις) to do so (Gal 2:2). On Paul's revelation, Markus Bockmuehl comments: "The ἀποκάλυψις in Gal 2:2…clearly consists of a concrete instruction pertaining to Paul's visit to Jerusalem" (*Revelation and Mystery in Ancient Judaism and Pauline Christianity*, WUNT 2/36 [Tübingen: Mohr Siebeck, 1990], 144). Contra Keener (*Galatians*, 66), who asserts that the revelation that led Paul to go up to Jerusalem was simply Paul's revelation of the gospel for the gentiles (Gal 1:11, 16).

of the meeting, the issue of circumcision arises somewhat abruptly[13] when he mentions that Titus—a Greek who accompanied him and Barnabas to Jerusalem—was not compelled to be circumcised (οὐδὲ Τίτος...ἠναγκάσθη περιτμηθῆναι, Gal 2:3).[14] Apparently there were some pseudo-brothers (ψευδάδελφος) that snuck into the meeting and sought to have Titus circumcised, but Paul did not submit to their demands and the issue was abandoned (Gal 2:4–5).[15]

Paul states they did not assent to the circumcision of Titus in order that the truth of the gospel would remain with the Galatians. For Paul, the truth of the gospel—particularly his gospel of the foreskin (τὸ εὐαγγέλιον τῆς ἀκροβυστίας, Gal 2:7)—required that gentiles did not submit to proselyte circumcision and that they remained non-Jews, but were equal in status in the Messiah to Jews in the Messiah. Kathy Ehrensperger highlights the fact that Paul's inclusion of Titus in this narrative is not an afterthought: "...Titus is strategically mentioned here as the paradigmatic Christ-Follower from the nations serving as the template for the addresses' identity in Christ. The fact that Paul mentions that there was not pressure by the Jerusalem leaders for Titus to be circumcised serves as a kind

---

[13] The syntax of Gal 2:1–5 is notoriously difficult. F. C. Burkitt somewhat sarcastically comments on this section: "...for who can doubt that it was the knife which really did circumcise Titus that has cut the syntax of Gal. ii 3–5 to pieces?" (*Christian Beginnings: Three Lectures* [London, University of London Press, 1924], 118). On the various syntactical issues, see the discussion in Ernest de Witt Burton, *A Critical and Exegetical Commentary on the Epistle to the Galatians*, ICC (Edinburgh: T&T Clark, 1921). 77–86; cf. William O. Walker Jr. "Why Paul Went to Jerusalem: The Interpretation of Galatians 2:1–5," *CBQ* 54 (1992): 503–10.

[14] A small minority of interpreters have proposed that Titus actually was circumcised, though it was on his own free-will and not under any outside compulsion. For example, Moorthy ("A Seal of Faith," 192–95) argues that Paul only mentions that Titus was not compelled to be circumcised, not that he never was circumcised or never had any intention of becoming circumcised. Based on her reading of circumcision in Rom 4 and the example of Abraham, she argues that Paul did expect gentiles in Christ to be circumcised as a "seal of faith," like Abraham ("A Seal of Faith," 183–85). For her, the main reason why Paul rejects circumcision in Galatians, Philippians, and 1 Corinthians is because it is being forced upon individuals and is not an act of their own volition (cf. Pirqe R. El. 29:9). Similarly, D. W. B. Robinson argues that Titus was circumcised, but he does so based on appeal to "Christian freedom." For his full argument, see D. W. B. Robinson, "The Circumcision of Titus, and Paul's 'Liberty'," *ABR* 12 (1964): 24–42. Against these interpreters, I agree with Munck's (*Paul and the Salvation*, 95) assessment of the supposed circumcision of Titus, "This interpretation is, of course, impossible, because it assumes that Paul consented to the circumcising of a baptized gentile—a thing that is out of the question."

[15] Perhaps these are the Pharisees within the Jesus movement that are mentioned in Acts 15:5 (τῶν Φαρισαίων πεπιστευκότες). Though the reference to them in Acts legitimates their membership within the assembly, Paul does not grant these individuals the same status—assuming that these groups correspond to one another.

of confirmation seal of acceptance of the identity of non-Jews in Christ."[16] In the context of Galatians, the rejection of circumcision for Titus serves to reinforce Paul's message and invalidate the message of the agitators. The solidarity shown to Paul by the "pillars" in Jerusalem (Cephas [Peter], James, and John; Gal 2:9) further substantiates Paul's claim to the legitimacy of his gospel and the invalidity of the agitators' gospel (Gal 1:6–7). With the support of the leaders in Jerusalem, Paul demonstrates that the apostolic position on gentile circumcision is clear: gentiles in the Messiah are not to be circumcised.[17]

3.2.3 The Antioch Incident

After stating the agreement between Paul and the leaders in Jerusalem on the status of gentiles and their respective missions, Paul recounts the incident in Antioch where he had to rebuke Cephas for separating himself from eating with gentiles and leading other Jews and Barnabas into hypocrisy for doing the same (Gal 2:11–13). According to Paul, certain men from James (τινας ἀπὸ Ἰακώβου) came to Antioch and exerted some influence upon Cephas that led to his withdrawal. The precise identity of these men from James is not entirely clear, but it is clear that they are from the circumcision (τοὺς ἐκ περιτομῆς), that is, they are Jews. Some have attempted to read into the phrase "those from the circumcision" as referring to some kind of circumcision party or circumcision faction in Jerusalem,[18] but this identification should be taken in its normal sense to simply refer to a group of Jews.[19] The reference to James is ambiguous, but it may simply indicate that these individuals came from the assembly in Jerusalem and were likely en-

---

[16] Kathy Ehrensperger, "Trouble in Galatia: What should be Cut? (On Gal 5:12)," in Ábel, *The Message of Paul*, 186.
[17] Against this view of agreement between Paul and the leaders in Jerusalem is the influential view of F. C. Baur and the so-called Tübingen School. Baur and those who followed him asserted that there was consistent conflict between Paul (the representative of "Gentile Christianity") and the leaders in Jerusalem (the representatives of "Jewish Christianity"). Here, Baur's thesis relied less on the texts of the New Testament and more on a Hegelian dialectic derived from his reading of the Pseudo-Clementine writings. For the classic refutation of Baur and the Tübingen school, see Munck, *Paul and the Salvation*, 69–86.
[18] E.g., Philip F. Esler, *Galatians* (London: Routledge, 1998), 136–37; Mark D. Nanos, "How Could Paul Accuse Peter of "Living Ethné-ishly" in Antioch (Gal 2:11–21) If Peter Was Eating According to Jewish Dietary Norms?" *JSPL* 6 (2016): 205; Keener, *Galatians*, 87–88.
[19] E.g., Burton, *Galatians*, 107–8; Longenecker, *Galatians*, 73–74; Fredriksen, *Pagans' Apostle*, 96. Cf. Acts 10:45; 11:2; Rom 4:12, Col 4:11.

dowed with some authority from James.[20] What did these individuals say that caused Cephas to withdraw himself and separate from eating with the gentiles in Antioch? What did they find to be wrong with Cephas' commensality with gentiles? Was it simply the fact that they were gentiles (i.e., had foreskin)? Was it the food they ate or the location in which they ate it?

The issue of Jewish and non-Jewish table-fellowship is not unanimously agreed upon by our ancient sources. Did Jews eat with non-Jews? Yes and no. Both non-Jewish and Jewish sources supply us with evidence for a range of positions. Diodorus Siculus notes that Jews do not have table-fellowship with other nations (τὸ μηδενὶ ἄλλῳ ἔθνει τραπέζης κοινωνεῖν; *Bib. hist.* 34.1.2). In Tacitus' famous scathing comments against the Jews, he says that they dine separately (*separati epulis*; *Hist.* 5.5.2).[21] In Jub. 22:16, Isaac implores Jacob to separate from the nations and prohibits eating with them. Joseph and Aseneth 7.1 states that Joseph did not eat with Egyptians, but that he ate separately. There are other sources that focus on not eating gentile food, but they do not seem to be concerned with eating *alongside* gentiles (Tob 1:11, Dan 1:3–17, 2 Macc 7:1–2; Jdt 10:5; 12:17–19). In these instances, when a Jew eats alongside a gentile, they are to eat their own food and drink their own wine, or eat only vegetables and avoid the gentile wine. In the Letter of Aristeas (181–294), the Jewish translators dine alongside the King of Egypt for seven days and it is noted that the food was prepared in a fitting manner for the Jews.

This varied data has caused interpreters to come to different conclusions about how to understand the situation in Antioch. Philip Esler takes this data to mean that the vast majority of Jews did not engage in any meaningful kind of table-fellowship or shared meals with gentiles.[22] Therefore, the issue for the

---

20 Munck, *Paul and the Salvation*, 102. J. B. Lightfoot (*Saint Paul's Epistle to the Galatians* [London: Macmillan & Co., 1896], 112) notes that this likely only indicates that they came from Jerusalem, but it may also indicate that they had some authority given to them by James, which they abused. This is not to say that they came specifically to police Peter and the other Jewish Messiah-followers in Antioch; there is no indication of their motives or the reason for their visit in the text.
21 It is possible that this refers to dining in separate locations, but it could also refer to dining in the same venue but at different tables. See Esler, *Galatians*, 104.
22 Esler, *Galatians*, 93–116. Writing in response to Esler, E. P. Sanders correctly notes that while there were some Jews who refused to eat with gentiles, the majority of the texts Esler uses to support his argument actually state that Jews should not eat gentile food, but may eat alongside gentiles as long as idolatry is avoided. If Sanders is correct, then the issue for separation may have been over consuming gentile food and wine or the possibility of coming in contact with idolatrous practices, not the table-fellowship itself (E. P. Sanders, "Jewish Associations with Gentiles and Galatians 2:11–14," in *The Conversation Continues: Studies in Paul & John in Honor of J. Louis Martyn*, ed. Robert T. Fortna and Beverly R. Gaventa [Nashville: Abingdon, 1990], 170–88). Furthering his point, Sanders highlights the various ways in which Jews and gentiles interacted in the ancient world.

men from James in Antioch was over table-fellowship with non-Jews.²³ Similarly, Mark Nanos contends that the issue was not over food, but over who was eating with whom. The men from James only permitted that mixed meals could take place if the gentile men became circumcised.²⁴ James Dunn argues that the issue was likely over the non-observance of tithing and purity laws pertaining to food.²⁵ E. P. Sanders concludes that the issue was that the men from James perceived that these meals constituted excessive fraternization with gentiles, which could have led Cephas and the other Jews to come into contact with idolatry and would have damaged Cephas' reputation and mission to the circumcision.²⁶ Similarly, Paula Fredriksen asserts that it is likely that the issue was over the location of these meals—pagan households—which could have tainted the status of the food and wine.²⁷ This would have scandalized the men from James—who would have been uncomfortable within a diaspora context—and would have damaging effects on Cephas' mission to the circumcision. Bengt Holmberg and Magnus Zetterholm both put forth the idea that the men from James wanted to separate the community into two commensality groups—one for Jews and one for gentiles—to avoid collapsing the distinction between the two groups.²⁸

While diaspora Jews actively avoided idolatry and forbidden foods, they lived alongside gentiles and regularly interacted with them. On the interaction of Jews in gentile spaces and gentiles in Jewish spaces, see Fredriksen, *Pagans' Apostle*, 38–60. The perspective that many Jews would eat with gentiles on specific terms and that some never would is also reflected in Tannaitic halakhah. On this point, see Tomson, *Jewish Law*, 230–36.
23 Esler, *Galatians*, 136–37.
24 Nanos, "How Could Paul," 205–6. Here, Nanos overemphasizes the reference to τοὺς ἐκ περιτομῆς in 2:12. He writes, "Those whom Paul said Peter fears were identified by Paul as 'from circumcision,' not 'from the (kosher) dietary or menu committee'.... more than likely Paul's phrase was designed to connote that they were *advocating* that...(male) *ethnē* participants be circumcised" (emphasis original).
25 James D. G. Dunn, "The Incident at Antioch (Gal. 2:11–18)," *JSNT* 18 (1983): 31–32. Sanders ("Jewish Association with Gentiles," 171–76) rightly notes how the tithing and purity laws Dunn discusses are either irrelevant in a diaspora context or are overstated as it pertains to Jewish and gentile table-fellowship. For a full treatment of the issue of food, tithing, and purity laws, see E. P. Sanders, *Jewish Law From Jesus to the Mishnah: Five Studies* (London: SCM, 1990), 258–308.
26 Sanders, "Jewish Association with Gentiles," 186–87.
27 Fredriksen, *Pagans' Apostle*, 97–99. Fredriksen argues that Paul's charge that Cephas was living "paganly" refers to his participation in meals at gentile households. By withdrawing and only eating in Jewish households, Cephas was in effect "compelling" the gentile Christ-followers to judaize through the avoidance of pagan wine and/or households by only eating mixed meals in a Jewish settings.
28 Bengt Holmberg, "Jewish *Versus* Christian Identity in the Early Church?" *RB* 105 (1998): 397–425; Zetterholm, *Formation of Christianity*, 161–62.

While all of these proposals have some degree of plausibility in light of the ancient evidence, the brief details of the incident recounted by Paul obscure the exact reasons that motivated the men from James to intervene and cause Cephas and the others to withdraw. What is clear is that before these men came, Cephas and other Jews ate with (συνεσθίω) gentile Christ-followers in Antioch. After the men from James came, Cephas withdrew and separated himself from these meals.²⁹ Paul calls this hypocrisy (ὑπόκρισις), indicating that Cephas, the other Jews, and Barnabas were not walking in accordance with their true beliefs regarding the valid status of gentile Christ-followers. Paul then highlights that these actions were contrary to the truth of the gospel (τὴν ἀλήθειαν τοῦ εὐαγγελίου), which recalls Paul's use of the same phrase in 2:5, where he emphasizes that gentile Christ-followers should not be circumcised and should be treated as equal with Jewish Christ-followers. The incident culminates with Paul rebuking Cephas and accusing him of compelling the gentile Christ-followers to judaize (ἀναγκάζεις ἰουδαΐζειν).³⁰ The result of Cephas' withdrawal was that it placed pressure on the gentile Christ-followers in Antioch to judaize—or in Paul's hyperbolic phraseology—Cephas' withdrawal effectively *compelled* them to judaize if they wanted to be treated as equals.³¹ While one could judaize to various degrees, given the intertextual callbacks to the Titus narrative, Paul appears to be implying that he has full judaization in mind, which would entail undergoing circumcision. And as Paul goes on to discuss in the rest of the letter, this is entirely out of the question.

3.3 The Presenting Issue: Gentile Circumcision

In Gal 5:2, Paul makes the first explicit mention regarding the present controversy in the Galatian congregations. It is here that the reader first learns that the agitators are urging the men in these assemblies to undergo circumcision.³² "Pay Attention! I, Paul, am saying to you that if you let yourselves be circumcised, the Messiah

---

29 Nanos ("How Could Paul," 202) interprets this as withdrawing from eating with certain people, whereas Fredriksen (*Pagans' Apostle*, 98) takes it as withdrawing from eating in certain locations.
30 Elsewhere in Galatians, "compel" (ἀναγκάζω) is used to refer to the compulsion of circumcision (2:3; 6:12).
31 Sanders, *Paul*, 491. Sanders proposes that all three of these situations in Gal 2 "had to do with circumcision and *compulsion*, attempted compulsion, or indirect compulsion."
32 Presumably, the audience would be aware of the agitators' teaching about circumcision and would have known that this is what Paul's letter was about prior to reading (or hearing) 5:2. For example, it seems likely that 1:6 ("I am astonished that you are so quickly deserting the one who called you in the grace of Christ and are turning to a different gospel...") would have indicated to the audience the exigency that led to the creation of Paul's letter.

will be of no benefit to you" (5:2). While the force and gravity of Paul's terse warning are obvious, the logic that undergirds his warning is opaque. Why will the adoption of circumcision sever their connection with the Messiah (5:4)? How does this actually work? What is it about the circumcision of gentiles that takes away the benefits afforded to them by the Messiah (5:2)? Here, I offer an overview of some representative examples of prominent proposals used to explain Paul's logic of exclusion in 5:2–4: anti-legalist (Moo), anti-ethnocentric (Dunn and Watson), and Barclay's anti-conditioned-gift approach.

3.3.1 Why Does Paul Oppose Circumcision in Galatians? Some Prominent Proposals

Given the long history of anti-legalist readings of Paul, the most prominent explanation found in the secondary literature understands that submission to circumcision would obligate the Galatians to fulfill the whole law (5:3), an impossible task based on anti-legalist interpreters' understanding of Judaism. Because they are now responsible for doing the impossible, they are condemned to live under the damning burden of the law apart from Christ. Douglas Moo's exposition of Gal 5 represents a fairly standard anti-legalist reading of Galatians. Understanding that some of the Galatians have already taken the first steps toward law observance by observing the Jewish calendar (4:10), Moo notes that through their adoption of circumcision they would be taking the decisive step toward proselytism and would therefore be cut off from Christ: "One cannot choose circumcision *and* Christ: it is circumcision *or* Christ."[33] He is careful, however, to qualify this statement, noting that the context of the circumcision does matter. The circumcision of gentiles whose purpose is to bring about their membership into the people of God is to be rejected without question, whereas Paul does not have an issue with the circumcision of Jews so long as it is not a requirement for salvation.[34] It is the choice to undergo circumcision and the significance that they attach to it that leads toward their severing from Christ.[35] He furthers this claim by linking it to obliga-

---

[33] Douglas J. Moo, *Galatians*, BECNT (Grand Rapids: Baker Academic, 2013), 322 (emphasis original).
[34] Moo, *Galatians*, 322. Moo cites the circumcision of Timothy in Acts 16:1–3 as evidence for Paul's acceptance of non-salvific, Jewish circumcision. This point is also noted by Martyn who asserts that Paul would have no problem with continued law observance from Jewish Christians as long as their relationship to the law "has become for them a matter of no consequence" (*Galatians*, 471).
[35] Similarly, F.F. Bruce comments: "For the Galatians to submit to circumcision as a legal obligation would be an acknowledgement that law-keeping (in this particular form) was necessary for

tion of law observance in 5:3: "[T]he person who is circumcised will receive no benefit from Christ because circumcision entails obedience to the entire law of God—and as Paul has made clear earlier in the letter (3:11, 21–22) and says again in verse 4, no person can be justified in the law."[36] For him, the key issue at play with the adoption of circumcision—and law observance more generally—is that it is centered on one's own doing in a way that invalidates or denies what the Messiah has done by "bringing [them] into a sphere of a works-oriented approach to justification."[37] While he acknowledges the occasional nature of the letter, he pushes Paul's message beyond a historical circumstance to address the "more fundamental and universal issues of doing versus believing."[38] Despite the fact that he acknowledges the grace that was present in Judaism—a fact that has been highlighted by the various proponents of the New Perspective(s)—Moo ultimately concludes that the logic of exclusion rests on a "traditional but currently unfashionable" faith/works dichotomy (cf. Gal 3:10).[39]

James Dunn and Francis Watson have both offered anti-ethnocentric readings of Gal 5 that, at their core, drive a wedge between Jewish and gentile identity in the assembly. To be sure, Paul too clearly demarcates Jew and gentile in the assembly (e.g., Rom 3:29–30, 1 Cor 7:18; Gal 2:9, 15), but Dunn and Watson do so based on a supposed incompatibility between Jewish identity and distinction, and gentile (i.e., non-Jewish) identity in the context of the assembly. Where Jews and gentiles in Christ are gathered together, Jews must give up their distinction for the sake of their gentile neighbors. Neither Dunn nor Watson offer concrete expositions of Paul's logic of exclusion in 5:2, but their interpretations of Paul's circumcision language in chapter 5 are helpful for understanding how anti-ethnocentric interpreters perceive Paul's argument against circumcision in Gal 5.

---

the achievement of a righteous status in God's sight. Such an acknowledgement would be to nullify the grace of God" (*The Epistle to the Galatians: Commentary on the Greek Text*, NIGTC [Grand Rapids: Eerdmans, 1982] 229). See also Martyn, *Galatians*, 471.

36 Moo, *Galatians*, 322.
37 Moo, *Galatians*, 325. Campbell (*The Nations*, 312) offers a nuanced view on the incompatibility of law observance and Christ that focuses on ethnicity and who the law was given for. Since the law was given to Jews and not to gentiles, any gentiles in Christ who undergo circumcision—and thus submit to full law observance—put themselves in slavery to a law that was not intended for them.
38 Moo, *Galatians*, 325. This type of expansion from historical circumstance to universal theological principle is a critique that John Barclay presents against this type of anti-legalist, works righteousness reading of Gal 5. Barclay's critique, however, emerges out his desire to separate his view from that of Luther's ("Paul, the Gift," 41). For another critique of the doing/believing dichotomy in Galatians, see E.P. Sanders, *Paul, the Law*, 159.
39 Moo, *Galatians*, 27; cf. 324–25.

Beginning with Dunn, he rightly notes that in the ancient world circumcision was the marker par excellence of Jewish males.[40] Not only was this true from a Jewish perspective, but also from a Greek or Roman one. As with most interpreters of Galatians, Dunn understands that the opposing teachers are proclaiming a gospel that includes circumcision as a necessary requirement for inclusion into the covenant community.[41] This emphasis on the necessity of circumcision privileges Jewish ethnicity over against all other people groups. By requiring gentile males to submit to circumcision—and therefore become Jewish proselytes—the opposing teachers were in effect restricting membership in the people of God along national and ethnic lines. There are three key factors that Dunn believes play a role in Paul's rejection of circumcision for gentiles as presented in Gal 5. First, circumcision carried with it the weight of the whole law (5:3).[42] Second, circumcision—as a marker in one's flesh—created physical, fleshly boundaries between Jews and gentiles, and gave grounds for boasting in the flesh.[43] Lastly, Dunn sees in Galatians an antithesis between Christ and the cross and circumcision (5:11; 6:12–14). He comments: "The sharpness of the antitheses (Christ/circumcision, cross/circumcision) can be explained only by recognizing that Christ and cross had become as fundamental and axiomatic for Christian identity as circumcision was for Jewish identity."[44] While Dunn does not explicitly state this, this antithesis is presumably the underlying logic of exclusion that he finds in 5:2. For one to undergo circumcision and identify with Jewish ethnic practices, they are in a sense rejecting the core of Christ-faith and their new mode of being in the *pneuma* (3:3–5, 14; 4:6–7).

Francis Watson's anti-ethnocentric, sociological reading of Gal 5 relies heavily on how he understands Paul's conception of the assembly as a separate entity from the Jewish community: "Christ is incompatible with circumcision not because 'Christ' involves a theological principle (receiving salvation as a sheer gift) which is incompatible with an alleged principle underlying circumcision (earning salvation), but because Paul has already decided that the church is only the church when it is separate from the Jewish community."[45] The incompatibility between the Messiah and gentile circumcision in 5:2 is not because circumcision represents an outmoded form of salvation or a denial of grace, but because Paul says it is.

---

40 Dunn, *New Perspective on Paul*, 315–18.
41 Dunn, *New Perspective on Paul*, 317.
42 Dunn, *New Perspective on Paul*, 318.
43 Dunn, *New Perspective on Paul*, 321–23.
44 Dunn, *New Perspective on Paul*, 323.
45 Francis Watson, *Paul, Judaism and the Gentiles: A Sociological Approach*, SNTSMS 56 (Cambridge, Cambridge University Press, 1986), 69.

3.3 The Presenting Issue: Gentile Circumcision — 59

Here, Watson focuses on Paul's appeal to his own authority at the beginning of 5:2: "Now I, Paul, say to you..." For him, Paul does not explicitly give the rationale for this reality, but simply states that the necessary antithesis of synagogue and assembly is the reality. Here, circumcision in and of itself poses no theologically damning element for the Galatian community, but as "the condition for sharing in salvation is belonging to the Jewish people"[46] it would collapse the distinction necessary for Paul's assembly to remain a separate entity.[47]

In his 2010 *Australian Biblical Review* article, "Paul, The Gift, and The Battle Over Circumcision," John Barclay sets out to explain the very logic undergirding the exclusion created by gentile Christ-followers who undergo circumcision.[48] At the center of his argument is the idea that the "Christ-event was a singular, unconditioned and therefore norm-breaking gift."[49] Unlike other gifts in the ancient world that were distributed according to one's symbolic capital (i.e., worth/value as expressed in non-financial terms), and therefore cementing and affirming this system of value, the Christ-gift pays no attention to an individual's symbolic capital. The Christ-gift is entirely unconditioned and is not distributed on the basis of anything, be it ethnic identity, one's standing in regard to Torah observance, etc. This understanding of the gift (Christ-event) is what drastically changes Paul's value system and his understanding of why he is to conduct his Torah-free, circumcision-free mission.[50] If the Galatians were to submit to circumcision and full law observance (5:3) at the urging of the Teachers, they would thereby be undercutting the Christ-gift and conditioning the gift based on their circumcision and subsequent law observance: "[T]o reinstate the Torah, whose authority as the arbiter of sin and righteousness has been undercut, would efface the fact that they are reconstituted and reoriented by participation in the Christ-gift (co-crucified with Christ, 2:17–19)."[51] For Barclay, this conditioning of the gift based on Jewish standards of value is what separates them from Christ and makes him useless to them. There is utter incompatibility between the Jewish system of value and the

---

[46] Watson, *Paul, Judaism*, 69; citing Bultmann, *Theology of the New Testament*, 1:55.
[47] In his unpacking of this separation, Watson (*Paul, Judaism*, 69–70) goes as far as saying that Paul's opponents see Jesus as the Jewish Messiah, but Paul himself no longer does.
[48] This content of this article is briefly summarized in Barclay, *Paul and the Gift*, 391–94. Here, it appears as a part of broader exploration of the relationship between the Christ-gift and systems of worth in Galatians.
[49] Barclay, "Paul, The Gift," 38. Also: "The death of Christ is not just *an expression of* divine gift/favour: it *is* the χάρις of God" (47).
[50] Barclay ("Paul, The Gift," 52) is careful to note that the gift "does not rule the Torah in principle incorrect," but that it is unable to uphold the Torah as the means by which to attribute moral or social worth.
[51] Barclay, "Paul, The Gift," 52.

system of value inaugurated by the Christ-gift. Since the Christ-gift was given to Jews and gentiles regardless of their circumcised or foreskinned state—or any other human category of differentiation—perverting the gift by conditioning it ultimately amounts to a rejection of the gift on its own terms.

3.3.2 Critiquing Previous Proposals

To my mind, none of these proposals accurately convey Paul's reasoning. First, anti-legalist interpreters rely on an outdated understanding of Judaism that would be foreign to Paul. Their general insistence that law observance was an impossible task is not a sentiment he shares. In fact, Paul declares that he was blameless in his past law observance (Phil 3:5–6) and that he does not overthrow the law in light of the Messiah (Rom 3:31). Additionally, neither Paul nor his opponents would see law observance as a nullification of their fidelity to Christ.[52] Despite the fairly scant evidence we have about the actual message of the agitators, Paul's description of their message in 1:6–7 as "another gospel" and that they "pervert the gospel of Christ" indicates that their gospel included Christ alongside circumcision and law observance, not circumcision and law observance over against Christ. Commenting on the supposed dichotomy between doing and believing, E. P. Sanders correctly notes, "The dispute in Galatians is not about 'doing' as such. Neither of the opposing factions saw the requirement of 'doing' to be a denial of faith. When Paul makes requirements of his converts, he does not think that he has denied faith, and there is no reason to think that Jewish Christians who specified different requirements denied faith. The supposed conflict between 'doing' as such and 'faith' as such is simply not present in Galatians."[53]

Second, the anti-ethnocentric readings offered by Dunn and Watson do not fully explore the logic of exclusion created by circumcision in 5:2, instead they attempt to highlight the core problem they believe Paul had with circumcision in his assemblies: the upholding of Jewish identity as the boundary-marker of covenant membership. On their reading of Paul, the assembly must move away from the traditional boundary-markers of Judaism (circumcision, *kashruth*, sabbath observance) in order to create a more universal community. When Jewish boundary markers are allowed to flourish in the assembly, it creates grounds for boasting for Jews and creates boundaries between Jews and gentiles. This is an argument

---

[52] The depiction of Jewish Christ-followers in Acts 15 assumes that they are to continue in their observance of Torah; an abandonment of Torah is not remotely entertained. The question they are debating is the role of the law in the life of the non-Jew in the assembly.
[53] Sanders, *Paul, The Law*, 159.

that attempts to privilege "Christian universalism" against "Jewish particularism"; the core issue is not one of soteriology, but sociology.[54] As John Barclay notes, this perspective relies heavily on Enlightenment and 20th-century ethical values related to universalism and inclusion that would have been foreign to Paul and his readers.[55] It is not as if the agitators saw themselves as excluding the gentiles by encouraging them to circumcise; the very opposite is actually the case. By encouraging them to adopt circumcision and a Jewish ethnic identity, they were seeking to include them in the community.[56] They saw a connection between Christ-faith and Jewish identity but did not deny the necessity of Christ-faith in their promotion of Jewish identity. Nevertheless, Dunn and Watson do not answer the question of why circumcision invalidates Christ for gentiles, or why it is wrong for gentiles to be included in the community based on Jewish ethnic conversion (and Christ), only that it is wrong for Jewish distinction to flourish in the assembly.[57] In their own way, Dunn and Watson both present their own form of particularism that privileges non-Jewish identity over Jewish identity and excludes Jewish identity in the same way they believe that the agitators exclude non-Jewish identity.

Barclay's anti-conditioned-gift approach falters in a similar way to some anti-legalist readings. While his interpretive schema is formidable and highly nuanced, the logic of exclusion he finds in Gal 5 is strikingly similar to anti-legalist readings.[58] Anti-legalist interpreters generally posit that reverting to Torah observance

---

[54] The creation of a dichotomy between so-called "universalism" and "particularism" is a fundamentally misguided approach to understanding to this problem. See Runesson, "Particularistic Judaism," 55–75.
[55] Barclay, "Paul, the Gift," 45–46.
[56] On the various ways ancient Jews allowed for gentile inclusion, see Terrance L. Donaldson, *Judaism and the Gentiles: Jewish Patterns of Universalism (To 135 CE)* (Waco, TX: Baylor University Press, 2007), 467–513.
[57] The closest Dunn gets to answering why Christ and circumcision are mutually exclusive for gentiles is the unconditional nature of the Gospel. See James D. G. Dunn, *A Commentary on the Epistle to the Galatians*, BNTC (London: Black, 1993), 265: "Consequently, to make circumcision necessary in addition, was so to shift the focus from Christ as to abandon that solid foundation, so to modify the unconditional character of the grace expressed in the gospel, as to nullify the benefit of Christ completely."
[58] Barclay notes the possible confusion that could arise between his approach and a traditionally Lutheran one, and does a commendable job at making those distinctions clear. In regard to this specific text, however, the results of both perspectives are functionally the same, albeit Barclay's is wrapped in apocalyptic language and critical anthropological theory. This is the most pertinent quote from Barclay's article where he distinguishes his view from Luther's: "Against this, it is necessary to insist that the matters under dispute in Galatia—circumcision, and the Torah-observance that it entails—are specific practices within a particular framework of cultural allegiance: what is being discussed here is not a way of understanding practice *per se* (a legalistic attitude to works),

cuts one off from Christ because it conditions grace based on human effort. Barclay's summary of the logic of exclusion is Gal 5:2 is analogous: "Now we can see why for the Gentile Galatians to get circumcised would disengage them from Christ and tip them out of grace (5:4): because the adoption of circumcision, and with it the Torah, would reinstate a standard of value or worth which denied the truth of the Christ-gift as an unconditioned gift."[59] For Barclay, any attempt to condition the gift constitutes a denial of the gift on its own terms. Or to put it in other words, any attempt to condition grace based on a Jewish value system is ultimately a rejection of the grace present in the Christ-event. While I agree that Paul is fundamentally opposed to conditioning the gift based on one's ethnic heritage (or their standing vis-à-vis Torah), I am not convinced that any subsequent conditioning of the gift via circumcision or Torah observance is the mechanism by which Christ becomes of no benefit to them. Additionally, I find that Barclay's use of value language in Gal 5 is flawed. First, it appears that the value of circumcision in Paul's thought is related to one's ethnic heritage. While the circumcision of a gentile makes Christ of no value or benefit (ὠφελέω) to him (Gal 5:2), in Romans, Paul states that circumcision is actually indeed valuable or beneficial (ὠφέλεια) for Jews (Rom 3:1–2), which has implications for his discussion of Jews in Rom 9–11 and Barclay's understanding of regulative systems. Second, Barclay points to Gal 5:6 ("neither circumcision nor foreskin have value [ἰσχύει]") to demonstrate how Paul understands the value of circumcision in the new value system inaugurated by the Christ-gift.[60] The problem with this interpretation is that his translation of ἰσχύω as value language is misguided; rather, ἰσχύω should be translated in a way that conveys having power or the ability to bring about a desired result.[61]

The theme that runs through all of these perspectives is how the Galatians' acceptance of circumcision will demonstrate where their trust is directed. For the anti-legalist, this is in self-reliant law observance; for the anti-ethnocentrist, this is in the adoption of and privileging of Jewish ethnic identity; and for Barclay's

---

but a Jewish regulative framework, issuing in a set of practices oriented by loyalty to the Torah. This would suggest that Christ-faith...is also a regulative schema for life in the world, a reorientation of concrete practices, rather than the relocation of practices-as-such within an abstract soteriological schema...On this reading, neither Christ-faith nor Torah-observance would stand for something else, at a level of abstraction above the world of actual practices, but would describe the regulative structures of existence and practice operative in two contrasting patterns of life. Christ-faith names the total orientation of life consistent with its generative basis in the Christ-gift; Torah-observance is, in Paul's view, incompatible with that foundation" ("Paul, the Gift," 41–42). See also Barclay's discussion of Luther in *Paul and the Gift*, 97–116.

59 Barclay, "Paul, the Gift," 52.
60 Barclay, "Paul, the Gift," 52–53.
61 See the discussion below on the translation of ἰσχύω.

anti-conditioned-gift approach, it is another regulative system of value or worth. To put it another way, these perspectives assert that Christ-faith plus circumcision actually negates a gentile's Christ-faith. It is clear that—for Paul—there is validity to the claim that a gentile in the Messiah is not to undergo circumcision, but none of these interpretations get Paul's logic quite right. In the discussion that follows, I argue Paul's treatment of Abraham in Gal 3 and 4 and his allegorical reading of Sarah, Hagar, and their respective offspring are crucial for understanding the underlying logic of his rejection of circumcision for the men in Galatia.

3.4 Paul and the Allegory of the Enslaved Woman and the Free Woman: Galatians 4:21–5:1

In Gal 3–4, Paul argues that the Galatians are already seed of Abraham through the promise, which occurs through their reception of the *pneuma* of God's son (3:14; 4:6).[62] In so doing, Paul rules out any other means by which the Galatians can become seed of Abraham. While not explicitly stated at this point in the letter, the Galatians would have been well aware that Paul's arguments about the law and Abrahamic descent were directed toward their potential adoption of circumcision.

To support his argument against their adoption of circumcision, Paul appeals to the narrative of Abraham in Gen 16–21. Here, Paul offers his reader a brief summary and interpretation of the Abraham narrative as it pertains to his two sons—Isaac and Ishmael—and their mothers—Sarah and Hagar.[63] The appeal to this text has often been understood as an unusual one for Paul's apparent purposes. Commenting on this text, F. C. Baur remarks: "His whole proof is nothing but a play of allegory, and has no force whatever to prove anything."[64] Given that many interpreters believe that the agitators were using this narrative to support their circumcising mission, some have concluded that Paul only utilizes this text because his hand is forced by the agitators.[65] Why else would Paul appeal to a narrative

---

[62] Gal 4:6 says that God sent the *"pneuma* of his son" (τὸ πνεῦμα τοῦ υἱοῦ αὐτοῦ) into our/your hearts. 𝔓46 does not contain "τοῦ υἱοῦ" and simply reads, "God sent his *pneuma*."
[63] Paul only mentions the first two sons of Abraham and ignores the other six sons that Keturah bore him (Gen 25:1–2).
[64] Baur, *Paul the Apostle*, 2:284. Baur continues: "Not only have the apostle's allegorical demonstrations out of the Old Testament no objective basis in the Old Testament itself,—they actually conflict with it" (2:284).
[65] C. K. Barrett, "The Allegory of Abraham, Sarah, and Hagar," in *Essays on Paul* (Philadelphia: Westminster, 1982) 154–70, esp. 162; Richard B. Hays, *Echoes of Scripture in the Letters of Paul* (New Haven: Yale University Press, 1989), 111–12; de Boer, *Galatians*, 286–87; contra Dunn, *Galatians*, 243; Francis Watson, *Paul and the Hermeneutics of Faith* (London: T&T Clark, 2004), 207n51.

about the necessity of circumcision for Abraham and his seed as part of his argument against circumcision? Terrence Donaldson notes, "The fact that Genesis 17 declares circumcision to be the unconditional prerequisite for membership in Abraham's 'seed' means that the story of Abraham provided much more evident support for the position of the rival teachers than for that of Paul."[66] Hays teases out this interpretive strand: "No sane reader could appeal, without some flicker of irony, to the Law in order to nullify circumcision as the definitive sign of covenant relation with God."[67] Matthew Thiessen has commented on the propensity for this type of interpretation amongst scholars, noting that these interpreters effectively conclude that the Abraham narrative does not—and cannot—support Paul's circumcision-free gospel to the gentiles.[68]

If the supposed "plain meaning of the text" is on the side of the agitators, then Paul has to resort to an allegorical—and in the perception of many, an inferior—interpretation in order to make the text to fit his narrative.[69] As will be discussed below, however, not even a literal interpretation of this text necessarily supports the agitators' circumcising mission. The account in Gen 17 does not mention the

---

[66] Terence L. Donaldson, *Paul and the Gentiles: Remapping the Apostle's Convictional World* (Minneapolis: Fortress, 1997), 120. See also Donaldson's essay, "Paul, Abraham's Gentile 'Offspring,' and the Torah" (in *Torah Ethics and Early Christian Identity*, ed., Susan J. Wendel and David M. Miller [Grand Rapids: Eerdmans: 2016], 135–50), where he writes: "Here [Gen 17] we encounter a significant step beyond the more general use of the term; here 'seed of Abraham' is defined in such a way as to make circumcision a *sine qua non*. Abraham's σπέρμα are circumcised – end of discussion. Read alongside Gen 17, then, Paul's insistence that the uncircumcised ἔθνη belong to Abraham's σπέρμα by virtue of their being in Christ – and, even more, his insistence that this is according to 'scripture' (see Gal. 3:8; Rom. 4:3) – would seem to be a flat-out contradiction in terms, an attempt to square the covenantal circle" (136–37).

[67] Hays, *Echoes*, 111–12. On this point, Hays cites the work of Barrett ("The Allegory," 162); cf. Frank J. Matera, *Galatians*, SP 9 (Collegeville, MN: Liturgical Press, 1992), 175.

[68] Thiessen, *Gentile Problem*, 74–75. For the most recent version of this interpretation see, David A. deSilva *The Letter to the Galatians*, NICNT (Grand Rapids: Eerdmans, 2018), 393.

[69] Paul's usage of ἀλληγορέω has consistently vexed interpreters. On the translation and meaning of ἀλληγορέω, I follow Ben Witherington III, *Grace in Galatia: A Commentary on St. Paul's Letter to the Galatians* (Grand Rapids: Eerdmans, 1998), 330: "The verb is a compound of ἄλλο and ἀγορεύω which literally means to say something else. As we have noticed above in our discussion of rhetoric and allegory, the idea is that the words say and mean one thing but now are used to *refer* to something else. This is not a concept of a deeper meaning but rather a concept of another referent. Allegorizing an historical text is a way of contemporizing it, giving it a secondary referent not a deeper meaning" (emphasis original). The goal of the allegory is not necessarily to offer historical insights about the characters within the story, but rather to reappropriate insights from the story and have them speak into the present context. Cf. Steven Di Mattei, "Paul's Allegory of the Two Covenants (Gal 4.21–31) in Light of First-Century Hellenistic Rhetoric and Jewish Hermeneutics," *NTS* 52 (2006): 102–22.

merit or possibility of proselyte circumcision for a non-Jew seeking to be included as an Abrahamic son.[70] As Ellen Juhl Christiansen has pointed out, "…the idea that circumcision is a boundary rite for *entry* is not present in Genesis 17."[71] If the agitators are using the Abraham narrative in this way, neither they nor Paul are "reading the text literally." Rather, both are interpreting, contextualizing, and utilizing it in the context of their broader mission and theology, however, the majority of modern interpreters have missed this fact in relation to the agitators' hypothetical message.

While it is possible that the agitators used the narrative pertaining to Abraham's sons (Gen 16–21) in their promotion of proselyte circumcision,[72] that does not mean that Paul's use of this text is forced or an act of "hermeneutical jujitsu."[73] Perhaps Paul is actually buying what he is selling. Paul introduces his audience to the discussion of the enslaved and the free woman with an ironic tone: "Tell me, you who desire to be under the law, do you not hear the law?" (4:21).[74] The irony Paul employs here implies that he believes in the viability of his reading and that if his audience were attentive enough, they too would come to the same conclusions as he does.[75] Since the Galatians have been misinformed about the law—or have fundamentally misread it—Paul invites them to hear the law so that their behavior might be corrected and their foreskins preserved.[76] Paul seems convinced that he has been able to present the Abraham narrative in a way that affirms his position.

---

[70] This is noted by Origen, *Comm. Rom.* 2.13.11–12.

[71] Ellen Juhl Christiansen, *The Covenant in Judaism and Paul: A Study of Ritual Boundaries as Identity Markers*, AGJU 27 (Leiden: Brill, 1995), 43 (emphasis original).

[72] Both Martyn (*Galatians*, 302–6) and Thiessen (*Gentile Problem*, 75–77) have created reconstructions of the content that may have been part of the agitators' message. Martyn offers a hypothetical sermon that he believes the agitators may have preached, whereas Thiessen focuses on their potential exegesis of Gen 17. While both are theoretical and rely heavily on mirror-reading, they are heuristically valuable for understanding what Paul *might* have been responding to. I do find, however, Martyn's reconstructed sermon to be an example of excessive mirror-reading in many regards, based on his tendency to offer one-to-one connections between many of Paul's statements in Galatians to proposed counterstatements in the agitators' message.

[73] Hays, *Echoes*, 111–12.

[74] The present participle θέλοντες supports the notion that the Galatians have yet to submit to the law with specific reference to circumcision.

[75] Hans Dieter Betz, *Galatians: A Commentary on Paul's Letter to the Churches in Galatia*, Hermeneia (Philadelphia: Fortress, 1979), 241; Nanos, *Irony*, 80–81.

[76] Cf. Watson, *Hermeneutics of Faith*, 207. See also Peter Oakes, *Galatians*, PCNT (Grand Rapids: Baker Academic, 2015), 155–56.

3.4.1 Competing Mothers, Missions, and Offspring

The entire context of Gal 4:21–31 revolves around birthing and the production of offspring. In Gal 4:19, Paul writes that he is once again in labor pains (ὠδίνω) for his children until Christ is formed in them.[77] Despite having already birthed this community, Paul has once again found himself in the throes of labor, presumably due to the confusion caused by the agitators. This maternal imagery provides the perfect segue for Paul to discuss the various offspring that came from Abraham and that are now being birthed. In his ground-breaking essay, "The Covenants of Hagar and Sarah," J. Louis Martyn highlights the importance of the theme of birthing for Paul's argument, demonstrating that this theme is the hermeneutical key to understanding how and why Paul employs the allegory of the two women.[78] Of primary importance to his interpretation is the observation that Paul departs from the Greek translation of the Ishmael and Isaac narratives in one very important way: his preference for γεννάω ("to beget") instead of τίκτω ("to give birth to"), which is used throughout the Genesis (LXX) account to narrate their respective births. Martyn notes that these verbs are used by the Greek translators in a remarkably consistent way; γεννάω is used to describe the begetting done by men, and τίκτω is used to describe the begetting done by women.[79] One would expect that Paul would follow this convention—using γεννάω to describe Abraham and τίκτω for Hagar and Sarah—but throughout Gal 4:21–31, he consistently uses γεννάω to describe begetting by all parties involved, save for his quotation of OG Isa 54:1 in 4:27 where he preserves the use of τίκτω. How can this terminological substitution be accounted for?

Elsewhere in Paul's letters, he employs the verb γεννάω to speak of the individuals and assemblies he begat as part of his mission. In Phlm 10, he describes Onesimus as a child (τέκνον) whom he begat (γεννάω). Similarly, in 1 Cor 4:14–15, Paul speaks of the saints in Corinth as his children (τέκνον) whom he begat (γεννάω). For Martyn, these comparative uses are instructive for explaining

---

77 For the pioneering treatment of the maternal imagery in Gal 4:19, see Beverly R. Gaventa, "The Maternity of Paul: An Exegetical Study of Galatians 4:19," in *The Conversation Continues: Studies in Paul and John In Honor of J. Louis Martyn*, ed. Robert T. Fortna and Beverly R. Gaventa (Nashville: Abingdon, 1990), 189–201. For full treatments of Paul's usage of maternal imagery, see Beverly R. Gaventa, *Our Mother Saint Paul* (Louisville: Westminster John Knox, 2007); Grace Emmett, "Becoming a Man: Un/Manly Self-Presentation in the Pauline Epistles" (PhD diss., Kings College London, 2020); eadem, "The Apostle Paul's Maternal Masculinity," *JECH* (2021): 1–23.
78 J. Louis Martyn, "The Covenants of Hagar and Sarah," in *Faith and History: Essays in Honor of Paul W. Meyer*, ed. John T. Carroll, Charles H. Cosgrove, and E. Elizabeth Johnson (Atlanta: Scholars Press, 1990), 160–92.
79 Martyn, "The Covenants," 174–75.

what Paul is doing in Gal 4, particularly his substitution of τίκτω with γεννάω; he is using it to compare his mission and the agitators' mission, and the two types of offspring they beget.[80] This is also highlighted by the tense shift that occurs in 4:24.[81] In 4:22–23, when Paul is introducing Abraham, the women, and their offspring, he does so by using the aorist and perfect tenses. Once he declares that these things should be understood allegorically in 4:24, he switches to the present tense, which serves to join his allegorical reading with the present crisis.[82] The agitators are aligned with Hagar and are bearing children according to the flesh into slavery, whereas Paul is aligned with Sarah and is bearing children of the promise according to *pneuma*.[83]

In both the historical example and the present allegory, the two sons, their modes of birth, and the identities of the mothers are the central points of focus for Paul. "For it is written that Abraham had two sons, one from the enslaved woman and one from the free woman. The one from the enslaved woman was begat according to the flesh, and the one from the free woman, through promise" (Gal 4:22–23). "Now, brothers, you are children of promise, like Isaac. But just as it was then—the child begat according to the flesh persecuted the child according to the *pneuma*—thus it is also now" (Gal 4:28–29).[84] According to the argument Paul

---

80 See also Susan Eastman, *Recovering Paul's Mother Tongue: Language and Theology in Galatians* (Grand Rapids: Eerdmans, 2007), 131; Thiessen, *Gentile Problem*, 89–90.
81 Martyn, "The Covenants," 177.
82 This temporal shift is also illustrated in 4:29: "But just as at that time the one who was born according to the flesh persecuted the one who was born according to the Spirit, so it is now also." Paul describes the historical event in the past and then brings it into the present to further demonstrate how his allegorical interpretation is functioning.
83 Paul also identifies himself as a child of Sarah in 4:26, 31: "But the free woman is the Jerusalem above; she is our mother...Therefore, brothers, we are not children of the enslaved woman, but the free woman." While he is now bearing children through the *pneuma*, he himself has also received the *pneuma* and is able to identify himself with the Galatians in this regard.
84 The claim that Ishmael persecuted Isaac is not entirely clear from the Genesis account. Some appeals are made to Gen 21:9, where Sarah witnesses Ishmael playing (or "laughing") with her son Isaac, which leads her to make a request (or demand) to Abraham to cast out the enslaved woman and her son (21:10). In the MT, the phrase "with her son Isaac" is absent, but it is preserved in the LXX ("μετὰ Ισαακ τοῦ υἱοῦ αὐτῆς"). In the account given in Jub. 17:4, Sarah is not so much concerned by Ishmael's playing, but by the response it elicits from Abraham: "And Sarah saw Ishmael playing and dancing, and Abraham rejoicing with great joy, and she became jealous of Ishmael and said to Abraham, 'Cast out this bondwoman and her son; for the son of this bondwoman will not be heir with my son, Isaac.'" In rabbinic discussions, various appeals to some type of persecution or dispute are made. In Gen. Rab. 53:11, Rabbi Azariah claims that Ishmael would shoot arrows in the direction of Isaac and pretend that he was just playing. In Gen. Rab. 55:4, Ishmael and Isaac have a dispute over the merits of their respective circumcisions and the timing at which they took place.

has made thus far, the Galatians have already received *pneuma* because of their trust (Gal 3:2, 5). Since they already have *pneuma*, it is foolish for them to attempt to complete in the flesh (i.e., undergo circumcision) what was begun with *pneuma* (Gal 3:3).[85] If they undergo circumcision, they follow the fleshly birth pattern of Ishmael and become slaves. In the Genesis account, once Sarah had come to terms with her fruitless womb, she proposed the idea to Abraham that he should bear her children through her slave, Hagar (Gen 16:1–4). The account given in Gen 16 focuses on the human activity involved in Ishmael's birth; Sarah speaks to Abraham and he listens, Sarah gives Hagar to Abraham, he went into Hagar, and she conceives.[86] On the other hand, the birth of Isaac is depicted as being brought about through divine means; the Lord visits Sarah, he does as he said he would, and she conceives (Gen 21:1–2). Unlike the account of Ishmael's birth, Abraham does not play a physical role in the narrative of Isaac's conception; he does not go into Sarah.[87] Isaac is born through the promise.

Just like Hagar and Sarah, the agitators and Paul are both trying to bring forth descendants of Abraham; one through the flesh and one through the promise. The focus here is on the correct mode of inclusion into Abraham's lineage—the mode of birth that produces the proper type of son. For Paul, gentiles can only become the right kind of descendants of Abraham through the promise and the *pneuma* (3:7–9, 14, 18, 29; 4:6, 26–31), whereas the agitators are advocating that they be in included through proselyte circumcision and law observance (Gal 3:3–5; 5:2–4, 12).[88] For Paul, circumcision and law observance cannot turn gentiles into the

---

Targum Pseudo-Jonathan (Gen 21:10) mentions that part of Sarah's rejection of Ishmael is due to him making war with Isaac.

[85] Thiessen (*Gentile Problem*, 77) makes an interesting connection between "completion in the flesh" in Gal 3:3 with Abraham's being "whole/complete" (תמים) in Gen 17:1. There are some lexical incongruities between LXX Gen 17:1 (ἄμεμπτος) and Paul's vocabulary in 3:3 (ἐπιτελέω), however, Thiessen notes that there are some witnesses to the LXX that use τέλειος instead of ἄμεμπτος. Additionally, Thiessen points out that Targum Pseudo-Johnathan's paraphrase of Gen 17:1 contains the Aramaic equivalent (הוי שלים בבישרך) of σαρκὶ ἐπιτελεῖσθε, found in Gal 3:3.

[86] On the human activity involved in Ishmael's conception and divine activity involved in Isaac's conception, see Thiessen, *Gentile Problem*, 88–91.

[87] On divine agency in the conception of Israel's patriarchs, see Philo, *Cherubim* 40–47; *QG* 3.18. Cf. Gen 4:1, where Adam "knew" Eve to conceive and birth Cain, yet Eve attributes his birth as being "with the help of the Lord" (NRSV) or, literally, "I have procreated a man with Yahweh." On the connections between the divine role in the birth of Cain and its relation to Isaac's birth, see David E. Bokovoy, "Did Eve Acquire, Create, or Procreate with Yahweh? A Grammatical and Contextual Reassessment of קנה in Genesis 4:1," *VT* 63 (2013): 19–35, esp. 34–35.

[88] In various treatments of Gal 4:21–31, many have incorrectly and anachronistically concluded that Paul is comparing Christianity (Paul) with Judaism (the agitators). For the development of this view, which goes back to Marcion (Tertullian, *Marc.* 5.4.8), see Martyn, "The Covenants,"

right type of Abrahamic son (Isaac); it puts them in line with the fleshly descendants of Ishmael and forces them back into a state of slavery from which they have already been set free (Gal 4:8; 5:1).

3.4.2 Where is Circumcision?

Surprisingly, however, direct references to circumcision are missing from Paul's discussion of Abraham, Sarah, Hagar, and their respective sons. Considering the role circumcision plays in the Genesis account of God's covenant with Abraham and his offspring—and the circumcision crisis present in the Galatian assemblies—it is notable that Paul makes no specific reference to circumcision in 4:21–31.[89] Given this—and that Paul explicitly links this passage with circumcision in the ensuing section (i.e., Gal 5:2 onward)—exploring circumcision in the Genesis narrative adds another interpretive layer to Paul's allegorical reading and his opposition toward Galatian adoption of circumcision.

In Genesis, we are first introduced to circumcision in 17:10–14, where Yahweh institutes circumcision as the sign of the covenant (אות ברית) between Abraham and himself. In 17:12, the command is stated to apply to all of the males in Abraham's household and is temporally limited to occur on the eighth day (cf. Lev 12:3). In 17:14, the seriousness of the institution and implementation of circumcision is made known by Yahweh: "Any uncircumcised male who is not circumcised in the flesh of his foreskin shall be cut off from his people; he has broken my covenant" (NRSV). Following these instructions, Yahweh states that he will give Abraham a son through his wife Sarai (who will now be called Sarah), his name will be Isaac, and that he will make his covenant with Isaac, not Ishmael (17:15–21). Immediately—on the same day—Abraham did as Yahweh commanded, and he circumcised himself, his son Ishmael, and all of the men in his house (17:23–27). Interestingly, here the author includes the ages of Abraham (ninety-nine years old) and Ishmael (thirteen years old), which clearly differ from the temporal stipulation of 17:12.[90] In 21:1–7, we are told of the birth of Isaac, who is the first son of Abraham to be circumcised on the eighth day as Yahweh had commanded. The author of Ju-

---

164–69. He traces it from Marcion to Luther to Lightfoot to Schlier and Betz. While this history is not exhaustive, it is representative.

89 Troy Martin, "Apostasy to Paganism: The Rhetorical Stasis of the Galatian Controversy," *JBL* 114 (1995): 437–61, at 456; Martyn "The Covenants," 173.

90 On the delayed circumcision of Abraham at the age of ninety-nine, Gen. Rab. 46:2 says that this was so Isaac would come from a holy source. The text contrasts this with the birth of Ishmael who was born when Abraham was eighty-six, and therefore in a foreskinned state.

bilees here says, "And Abraham circumcised his son [Isaac] on the eighth day. He was the first one circumcised according to the covenant which was ordained forever" (Jub. 16:14, [Wintermute, *OTP*]).

Matthew Thiessen's work on the temporal stipulations of circumcision further illuminates how important the timing of circumcision was in certain streams of Jewish thought.[91] Particularly relevant for our current purposes are his observations regarding Gen 17:14. Notably, the Greek version of this text, which Paul would have been familiar with, includes the eighth-day temporal stipulation alongside the punishment for not being circumcised. "And an uncircumcised male who is not circumcised in the flesh of his foreskin on the eighth day (τῇ ἡμέρᾳ τῇ ὀγδόῃ), that soul will be eliminated from his descendants because he has disbanded my covenant" (cf. Lev 12:3). It is not only that one needs to be circumcised to be included in the covenant, *but they must also be circumcised properly*.[92] This reading is preserved across ancient Greek translations of Genesis and is also attested to by the Samaritan Pentateuch and the book of Jubilees (15:14, 25–26).[93] R. H. Charles highlighted this in his pioneering work on Jubilees in the early twentieth century: "Again the strict halacha in [Jubilees] xv. 14 regarding circumcision on the eighth day was a current, probably the current, view in the second cent. B.C. and earlier, *since it has the support of the Samaritan text and the LXX.*"[94] In Jub. 15:25–26, we find the harshest articulation of this stipulation:

> This law is for all the eternal generations and there is no circumcising of days and there is no passing a single day beyond eight days because it is an eternal ordinance ordained and written in the heavenly tablets. And anyone who is born whose own flesh is not circumcised on the eighth day is not from the sons of the covenant which the LORD made for Abraham since (he is) from the children of destruction. And there is therefore no sign upon him so that he might belong to the LORD because (he is destined) to be destroyed and annihilated from the

---

91 Thiessen, *Contesting Conversion*, 17–42; *Gentile Problem*, 80–82. Here, Thiessen builds on some of the insights made by David A. Bernat, *Sign of the Covenant: Circumcision in the Priestly Tradition*, AIL 3 (Atlanta: SBL Press, 2009).
92 Paul mentions that his own circumcision was carried out with the proper timing on the eighth day in Phil 3:5 (περιτομῇ ὀκταήμερος).
93 Matthew Thiessen, "The Text of Genesis 17:14," *JBL* 128 (2009): 625–42; idem, *Contesting Conversion*, 18–30. Based on careful text-critical analysis, Thiessen concludes that the reading of Gen 17:14 found in the MT—which does not include the eighth-day (ביום השמיני) stipulation—is not the original reading of this text. Rather, he argues that the reading which includes the eighth-day stipulation found in the Greek versions, Samaritan Pentateuch, and Jubilees is likely the original form. Thiessen also offers a convincing reconstruction of 8QGen that preserves this reading. For other ancient witnesses to this reading of 17:14, see Philo, *QG* 3.52; Justin, *Dial.* 10; 23.
94 R. H. Charles, *The Book of Jubilees or The Little Genesis* (London: Black, 1902), lxv (emphasis added).

earth and to be uprooted from the earth because he has broken the covenant of the LORD our God (trans. Wintermute, *OTP*).

While the legitimacy of the non-eighth-day circumcision of Abraham does not seem to be questioned by the text of Genesis—or Jubilees—neither Ishmael's circumcision nor the circumcision of the men in Abraham's house are afforded the same leniency.⁹⁵ This is a crucial point that can be—and has been—easily overlooked: Abraham's son Ishmael was circumcised, yet he did not gain entry into the covenant by it.⁹⁶ It is only Isaac's eighth-day circumcision that is viewed as being covenantally legitimate (Gen 21:1–7; cf. Jub. 15:14; 16:14). Gen 17 demonstrates that even at the earliest institution of the covenant of circumcision, not all circumcisions have equal value. While circumcision is a necessary requirement for participation in the covenant with Abraham, circumcision alone does not offer one inclusion in the covenant.⁹⁷ Ellen Juhl Christiansen rightly highlights this important distinction: "Even if [circumcision] functions as a boundary rite, it does not qualify as a symbol of entry. Rather it becomes the sign that *affirms* the covenantal relationship without it being a condition or a means of entry."⁹⁸

---

95 While all the men of Abraham's house are also circumcised, this does not make them Abrahamic sons or give them any discernible privileges. Their circumcisions serve as a means of demonstrating their ownership by Abraham, which is made clear by the repeated use of the second person possessive pronoun in Gen 17:13. Notably, Yahweh says, "And so my covenant will be in your flesh (בבשרכם/ἐπὶ τῆς σαρκὸς ὑμῶν) as an eternal covenant." Even though Yahweh is addressing Abraham alone here, the second person plural is used to demonstrate the bodily ownership he has over these men (see David Kimchi [Radak] on Gen 17:13). On the relationship of the body of the circumcised slave to his master, see Saul M. Olyan, *Rites and Rank: Hierarchy in Biblical Representations of Cult* (Princeton: Princeton University Press, 2000), 94–97; Bernat, *Sign of the Covenant*, 45–46; Cf. Catherine Hezser, *Jewish Slavery in Antiquity* (Oxford: Oxford University Press, 2005), 30–31.
96 For example, Richard Hays (*Echoes*, 111) notes that Isaac was circumcised properly and was Abraham's only legitimate heir. He, however, follows this up by noting that in light of this the agitators would have taught that circumcision was necessary for inclusion in the covenant, because "after all, even Ishmael was circumcised when he was thirteen years old." While he acknowledges the importance of Isaac's proper circumcision, he still appears to promote the idea that all circumcisions have some value vis-à-vis the Abrahamic covenant. Philip Esler (*Galatians*, 209–10) highlights the importance of circumcision for Abrahamic sonship, but fails to note that Ishmael was also circumcised. He does this while emphasizing the benefits of circumcision for inclusion as a son of Abraham through Sarah and highlighting the exclusion of Hagar and Ishmael.
97 Contra Jakob Wöhrle, "The Integrative Function of the Law of Circumcision," in *The Foreigner and the Law: Perspectives from the Hebrew Bible and the Ancient Near East*, ed. Reinhard Achenbach, Rainer Alberts, and Jakob Wöhrle, BZABR 16 (Wiesbaden: Harrassowitz, 2011), 71–87.
98 Christiansen, *Covenant in Judaism and Paul*, 41 (emphasis original). Similarly, John Barclay ("Paul And Philo on Circumcision: Romans 2.25–9 in Social and Cultural Context," *NTS* 44

God establishes his covenant specifically with Isaac and not with Ishmael, despite both being circumcised sons of Abraham (Gen 17:19–21). As noted, however, the modes of their births—according to the flesh and according to the promise/*pneuma*—and the timing of their circumcisions—at the age of thirteen and on the eighth day—distinguish them from one another.

The idea of non-covenantal circumcision is further attested by Exod 12:43–49 and Jer 9:25–26 where non-Israelites are circumcised, yet the value and efficacy of their circumcisions are differentiated from that of Israel.[99] In Exod 12:43–49, Yahweh lays out the ordinances for the Passover and who can partake in the meal. It is stated that a slave (עבד) can partake in the meal if he is circumcised. Similarly, a *ger* (גר, "resident alien") can partake in the Passover provided that he and all of the males in his house are circumcised.[100] After stating that the circumcised *ger* can partake in the Passover, it is noted that "he shall be as a native of the land" (והיה כאזרח הארץ). This clause has led some to believe that circumcision makes the *ger* an Israelite, but this is incorrect.[101] The *ger* is to be regarded as a native of the land as it pertains to partaking in the Passover, not as it pertains to his ethnic status. This is clarified by 12:49: "There will be one law for the native and for the *ger* dwelling in your midst"; even after being circumcised, they remain a *ger*. As it is written elsewhere in the Torah, there are some statutes that govern both Israel and the *ger* in the same manner (e.g., Exod 12:19; Lev 18:8–16; 24:16, 22; Num 15:14–16), and some that treat them differently (e.g., Lev 23:42; 25:45–46).[102] The requirement of circumcision for participation in the Passover applies to both Isra-

---

[1998]: 536–56, at 545) writes, "[I]t was the physical sign of belonging to the covenant of Abraham, the fleshly inscription of genealogical identity marking the ancestral heritage of every male Jew (cf. Phil 3.5)."

99 In his discussion of texts that indicate non-covenantal, non-Israelite circumcisions, Thiessen (*Contesting Conversion*, 56–57) also includes Ezek 32:17–32 (cf. Blaschke, *Beschneidung*, 64–70). He argues that since we have sources that attest to the circumcision of the Egyptians, Phoenicians, and Edomites (e.g., Herodotus, *Hist.* 2:36–37, 104; Jer 9:25–26), the fact that Ezekiel's oracle indicates that they die the death of the foreskinned demonstrates that Ezekiel viewed their circumcision as affording them no benefit.

100 It should be noted that the *ger* is not required to partake in the Passover or become circumcised; these are both voluntary actions. Thus rightly Origen, *Comm. Rom.* 2.13.16.

101 E.g., James G. Murphy, *A Critical and Exegetical Commentary on the Book of Exodus*, ICC (New York: I.K. Funk & Co., 1881), 85; Christiana van Houten, *The Alien in Israelite Law*, JSOTSup 107 (Sheffield: JSOT Press, 1991), 131–38; cf. Keener, *Galatians*, 231.

102 For a concise treatment of how the *ger* and Israelite function as distinct entities in the Hebrew Bible, see Olyan, *Rites and Rank*, 68–81. See also Bernat, *Sign of the Covenant*, 43–48; Rainer Albertz, "From Aliens to Proselytes: Non-Priestly and Priestly Legislation Concerning Strangers," in Achenbach, Alberts, and Wöhrle, *The Foreigner and the Law*, 53–69, esp. 56–63; Ophir and Rosen-Zvi, *Goy*, 28–33. Cf. Origen, *Comm. Rom.* 2.13.11–17.

elites and *gerim*, but as distinct entities. While circumcision does appear to afford some communal benefits to these two non-Israelite groups—slaves and *gerim*—they still remain separate and distinct from Israel.[103]

In Jer 9:25–26, the reader is introduced to various circumcised nations, but here they are regarded as being in foreskin:

> Behold, the days are coming, says Yahweh, when I will attend to all who are circumcised in the foreskin: Egypt, Judah, Edom, the sons of Ammon, Moab, and all those with shaven temples who live in the desert. For all the nations are foreskinned, and all the house of Israel has a foreskinned heart.

Jeremiah's oracle rightly indicates that there were other nations in the ancient near east that practiced circumcision. Here, however, the circumcision practiced by the non-Israelite nations is not viewed as legitimate but is deemed as being foreskin.[104] While various proposals have been made as to how or why this could be from a physical standpoint,[105] what is important for our present purposes is that Jeremiah's oracle indicates that not all circumcisions are deemed as being legitimate. In some way their circumcisions are not equivalent to the circumcision of Israel and are effectively still foreskin.[106]

In addition to these texts that indicate that not all circumcisions have the same value *vis-à-vis* Israelite covenantal identity, it can also be stated that nowhere in the Hebrew Bible do its authors or editors envision circumcision as a sufficient means by which non-Israelites *become* Israelites.[107] Or to put it in language rele-

---

[103] Significantly, those who are only residing within Israel temporarily (שכיר/תושב) or are foreign sons (בן נכר) with no relation to Israel are not permitted to undergo circumcision and partake in the Passover meal (Exod 12:43–45).
[104] See the discussions in Blaschke, *Beschneidung*, 57–60; Thiessen, *Contesting Conversion*, 52–56.
[105] E.g., Richard C. Steiner, "Incomplete Circumcision in Egypt and Edom: Jeremiah (9:24–25) in the Light of Josephus and Jonckheere," *JBL* 118 (1999): 497–505.
[106] M Adryael Tong (*Difference and Circumcision*) argues that Jer 9:25–26 is a textbook case of "identitarian circumcision." She offers the heuristic category of identitarian circumcision to discuss discourse on circumcision and foreskin that is used to convey ethnic difference, regardless of physical morphology. Thus, while these nations are physically circumcised, Jeremiah still considers them to be foreskinned due to the fact that they are not Israel.
[107] Thiessen, *Contesting Conversion*, 43. See also, Bernat, *Sign of the Covenant*, 43–38, 125. While Gen 34 appears to present circumcision as the stipulation that allows for intermarriage and union between Israel and a foreign, foreskinned nation, the entire proposition is presented by the sons of Jacob on deceptive grounds. As the narrative makes clear, they had no intention in actually joining the two nations, rather, they used the covenant sign of circumcision as a means to debilitate the Hivites in order to enact revenge upon them. The disingenuous terms presented by the sons of Jacob should not be understood as legitimating the idea that circumcision can

vant for this current discussion, nowhere in the Hebrew Bible does circumcision itself make one a proper son of Abraham. In Gen 15 and 17 when Yahweh establishes his covenant with Abraham and gives the sign of circumcision, it is explicitly noted that this covenant is for Abraham and his seed (זרע/σπέρμα) and their subsequent generations (דור/γενεά). This is genealogical language that delineates those who are included in the covenant and who eighth-day circumcision applies to. If an individual is not part of Abraham's offspring through the line of Isaac, then they are excluded from the covenant and its stipulation for eighth-day circumcision by default. This emphasis on genealogy persisted as one of the primary markers of Jewish identity until the second century BCE when Jewish identity became more fluid in some circles.[108] There are, however, some groups that maintained strict genealogical boundaries for Jews and non-Jews in the second-temple period.[109]

Taking this understanding of circumcision, timing, and genealogy into account, it seems possible that this could be undergirding Paul's rejection of circumcision for the Galatians. They are non-Jews who would be undergoing non-covenantal circumcision with the goal of becoming Abrahamic sons through this act. This is why Paul highlights the two sons of Abraham in his introduction of this story: "You who want to be under the law, do you not hear the law? For it is written that Abraham had *two* sons..." (Gal 4:21–22). If the Galatians are seeking to become sons of Abraham, they have to answer this question: Which kind of son do you want to become? If they seek to be Abrahamic sons through the flesh (i.e., circumcision) as the agitators are proposing, then they will become sons that follow after Ishmael. If they seek to be Abrahamic sons through the promise and *pneuma*, then they will become sons that follow after Isaac. Based on what Paul has argued thus far in

---

allow one to become a part of Israel through intermarriage (contra Blaschke, *Beschneidung*, 30–34). Notably, in the account of this story in Jub. 30, the author fails to disclose that the Hivites were circumcised because the author understood that circumcision practiced outside of Israel is not valid (Christiansen, *Covenant in Judaism and Paul*, 100). On Gen 34 and Ezek 44:6–9, see also Thiessen, *Contesting Conversion*, 45–51.

108 Shaye Cohen (*Beginnings of Jewishness*, 69–106) argues that a shift occurs in Jewish identity around the second century BCE where it moves from an *ethnos* to an ethno-religion. This is most clearly demonstrated by the mass circumcisions of non-Israelite nations in Josephus, and the account of the circumcision of Izates of Adiabene (*Ant.* 13.257–58, 318–19; 20.38–40).

109 As previously noted, see Hayes, *Gentile Impurities*, 8–9, 58–67; Thiessen, *Contesting Conversion*. For a discussion of genealogical boundaries in Qumran, see Daniel R. Schwartz, "Ends Meet: Qumran and Paul on Circumcision" in *The Dead Sea Scrolls and Pauline Literature*, ed., Jean-Sébastien Rey, STDJ 102 (Leiden: Brill, 2013), 295–307; Carmen Palmer, *Converts in the Dead Sea Scrolls: The Gēr and Mutable Ethnicity*, STDJ 126 (Leiden: Brill, 2018), esp. 129–57.

Gal 3 and 4, he believes that the Galatians have already become sons of Abraham, like Isaac, through the promise and *pneuma*.

> Just as Abraham trusted in God and it was reckoned to him as *dikaiosynē*, then you know that those who come from faithfulness (οἱ ἐκ πίστεως), these are Abraham's sons (Gal 3:6–7)
>
> So that the blessing of Abraham might come to the gentiles in Christ Jesus, so that we might receive the promise of the *pneuma* through faithfulness (Gal 3:14)
>
> And if you are of Christ, then you are Abraham's seed, heirs according to the promise (Gal 3:29).
>
> And because you are sons, God has sent the *pneuma* of his son into our hearts, crying, "Abba, Father!" So you are no longer slaves but sons, and if sons, also heirs through God (Gal 4:6–7).

By virtue of being born from faithfulness, being of Christ, and having Christ's *pneuma*, Paul asserts that Galatians are in fact the seed of Abraham (Gal 3:29), which fulfills God's promise to Abraham to make him the father of many nations (LXX Gen 17:4; πατὴρ πλήθους ἐθνῶν). If the Galatians undergo improper circumcision, they will remain sons of Abraham, albeit enslaved sons like Ishmael who have no inheritance. Paul is not arguing that circumcision is inherently bad, but that it is incapable of making a non-Jew the right kind of Abrahamic son, and can only make them a slave. And since circumcision is incapable of making a gentile into Abrahamic seed, Paul forges a genealogy through the Messiah that connects them to Abraham.[110] While Paul has often been interpreted as promoting a universal, non-ethnic "Christianity," his emphasis on the necessity of being Abraham's offspring indicates otherwise.[111] For Paul, this genealogical link is not a metaphor but a concrete reality.

---

[110] Elsewhere in ancient Jewish literature, other groups have attempted to forge a genealogical link to Israel through a shared kinship with Abraham. Notably, there is an account preserved in 1 Macc 12:21 and Josephus' *Antiquities* (12.226) in which the Spartans argue that they share a common ancestry with *Ioudaioi* through Abraham. For a thorough examination of this peculiar genealogical link, see Jan M. Bremmer, "Spartans and Jews: Abrahamic Cousins?" in *Abraham, the Nations, and the Hagarites: Jewish, Christian, and Islamic Perspectives on Kinship with Abraham*, ed. Martin Goodman, George H. van Kooten, and Jacques T. A. G. M. van Ruiten, TBN 13 (Leiden: Brill, 2010), 47–59.

[111] Johnson Hodge, *If Sons, Then Heirs*, 3–6; Stephen L. Young, "Paul's Ethnic Discourse on 'Faith': Christ's Faithfulness and Gentile Access to the Judean God in Romans 3:21–5:1," *HTR* 108 (2015): 30–51; Thiessen, *Gentile Problem*, 115. For readings that discuss a third-race model of ethnic Christianity, see Kimber Buell, *Why This New Race*; Love L. Sechrest, *A Former Jew: Paul and the Dialectics of Race*, LNTS 410 (London: T&T Clark, 2009), esp. her critique of Johnson Hodge on 217–24.

3.5 Sonship via *Pneuma*, Not Circumcision

Caroline Johnson Hodge, Stanley Stowers, and Matthew Thiessen have all argued that Paul uses the reception of Christ's *pneuma* as a means to form a genealogical link between Abraham and the Galatians.[112] Since Jesus is the seed of Abraham (Gal 3:16) and because the Galatians have Jesus' *pneuma* (Gal 4:6; cf. 3:2–3, 5, 14, 27; 4:29) they are genealogically linked to Abraham and are his sons. Now many assume that—for Paul—this genealogical connection is *spiritual*[113] (i.e., not physical) and fictive or metaphorical, but this is not necessarily what the language suggests.[114] Pauline scholars are increasingly discussing—and defending—the possibility that Paul's conception of *pneuma* is not immaterial and abstract in one, common modern sense of the term *spirit*;[115] rather, Paul's understanding of *pneuma* is physical like many of his contemporaries.[116] In Paul's ancient context, nota-

---

[112] Caroline Johnson Hodge, *If Sons, Then Heirs*, 72–76; Stanley K. Stowers, "What Is 'Pauline Participation in Christ'?" in *Redefining First-Century Jewish and Christian Identities: Essays in Honor of Ed Parish Sanders*, ed. Fabian E. Udoh et al., CJAn 16 (Notre Dame: University of Notre Dame Press, 2008), 352–71; Thiessen, *Gentile Problem*, 105–28. Against this interpretive trend, see J. Thomas Hewitt, "Πνεῦμα, Genealogical Descent and Things That Do Not Exist According to Paul," *NTS* 68 (2022): 239–52.
[113] The standard translation of πνεῦμα as "spirit" has tended to give readers the impression that things that are pneumatic are not physical but are immaterial or metaphorical. On the anachronistic application of this dichotomy to the ancient world, see Dale B. Martin, *The Corinthian Body* (New Haven: Yale University Press, 1999), 3–6, 127.
[114] Caroline Johnson Hodge (*If Sons, Then Heirs*, 15–16) suggests that since the language of fictive kinship implies "that it is less real, less true, less 'natural' than other kinds of kinship," it should be avoided when describing the genealogical lineage that Paul makes when connecting the Galatians to Abraham. While fictive kinship can accurately be used in second-order discourse to indicate the socially constructed nature of kinship as conceived by individuals, in Paul's first-order discourse this lineage is physical and real in the material sense. David Rhoads ("Children of Abraham, Children of God: Metaphorical Kinship in Paul's Letter to the Galatians," *CurTM* 31 [2004]: 282–97, at 284–85.) rejects fictive kinship language for the same reason but opts to use the language of metaphorical kinship. He believes that "Paul would say that [these relationships] are more real than blood relations" (284) but operate within the sphere of immateriality. This reading fails to ascertain the physicality of this relationship as Paul describes it in Galatians.
[115] For a summary on the importance of distinguishing between spirit and *pneuma* in the study of Paul, see Paul Robertson, "De-Spiritualizing *Pneuma*: Modernity, Religion, and Anachronism in the Study of Paul," *MTSR* 26 (2014): 365–83.
[116] Using 1 Cor 15:35–58 as a test case, both Dale Martin (*Corinthian Body*, 104–36) and Troels Engberg-Pedersen (*Cosmology and Self in the Apostle Paul: The Material Spirit* [Oxford: Oxford University Press, 2010], 8–38) demonstrate the physicality and materiality of *pneuma* in Paul's thought. Both highlight the fact that—for Paul—the resurrected body is still a physical body but is composed solely of incorruptible *pneuma* (1 Cor 15:44). Here, Paul is not concerned with a physical/spiritual or material/immaterial dichotomy, rather, he is focusing on a hierarchy of physical substances. Some

bly in medical texts and Stoic philosophy and physics, *pneuma* is understood to be the highest order of physical substances.[117] *Pneuma* is the stuff that animates the body, gives rationality to the brain or heart (depending on where an author believed the seat of the mind to be), allows the body to experience sight, smell, sound, and touch, gives life to the body, makes up the soul, and regulates the general health of an individual.[118] *Pneuma* is one of the basic elements that makes up

---

translations—notably the NRSV—have obscured Paul's thought by translating σῶμα ψυχικόν as "physical body" and σῶμα πνευματικόν as "spiritual body," which has led readers toward a dualistic understanding of the present and future body in this text. For Paul, however, both are physical, material realities. Whereas the current body is composed of flesh, blood, *psychē*, and *pneuma*, the resurrected body sheds the corruptible aspects of human corporeality and is raised composed solely of *pneuma*. Paul quotes Gen 2:7 (1 Cor 15:45) to illustrate that just as Adam became a living *psychē* (ψυχὴν ζῶσαν), the last Adam (i.e., Jesus) became a life-giving *pneuma* (πνεῦμα ζῳοποιοῦν). Just as humans currently bear the earthy *psychic* form of the man from the earth, at the resurrection they will bear the heavenly pneumatic form of the man from heaven (1 Cor 15:47–49, cf. Schweitzer, *Mysticism*, 219). The reason for the necessity of this transformation is because flesh and blood are unable to inherit the kingdom of God; the corruptible cannot inherit the incorruptible (1 Cor 15:50). Just as humans, land animals, birds, and fish have different types of bodies made up of different types of flesh suited for their environments, so too celestial bodies have their own distinct type of body in contrast to the earthly (1 Cor 15:38–41). If those in Christ are going to inherit the incorruptible kingdom of God, they need pneumatic bodies suited for such an environment. See Thiessen, *Gentile Problem*, 151–53; David A. Burnett, "A Neglected Deuteronomic Scriptural Matrix for the Nature of the Resurrection Body in 1 Corinthians 15:39–42," in *Scripture, Texts, and Tracings in 1 Corinthians*, ed. Linda L. Belleville and B. J. Oropeza (Lanham, MD: Lexington Books/Fortress Academic, 2019), 187–211; cf. Matthias Klinghardt, "Himmlische Körper. Hintergrund und arguemtative Funktion von 1Kor 15,40f," *ZNW* 106 (2015): 216–44. In Phil 3:20–21, Paul says that for those whose citizenship is in heaven, Christ will transform (μετασχηματίζω) their lowly bodies into glorious bodies like his. For a recent critique of this line of interpretation and the material *pneuma* in Paul, see Wright, *Paul*, 1398–1402. While Wright affirms the necessity of physical, bodily resurrection, he understands it to be a body that is animated by *pneuma*, not composed of it. Here Wright leans on philological and exegetical traditions while failing to take into account the entire content of Paul's argument (e.g., Paul's comparison between the earthy body and the heavenly body, and his claim that "flesh and blood cannot inherit the kingdom of God"). For another argument against the relevance of the material *pneuma* in Paul, see Volker Rabens, *The Holy Spirit and Ethics in Paul*, WUNT 2/283 (Tübingen: Mohr Siebeck, 2010).

117 On *pneuma* and Pauline physics, see Stanley Stowers, "The Dilemma of Paul's Physics: Features Stoic-Platonist or Platonist-Stoic?" in *From Stoicism to Platonism: The Development of Philosophy, 100 BCE–100 CE*, ed. Troels Engberg-Pedersen (Cambridge: Cambridge University Press, 2017), 231–53.

118 For a concise overview of *pneuma* in ancient medical texts as *comparanda* for Pauline studies, see Troy W. Martin, "Paul's Pneumatological Statements and Ancient Medical Texts," in *The New Testament and Early Christian Literature in Greco-Roman Context: Studies in Honor of David E. Aune*, ed. Paul Fotopoulos, NovTSup 122 (Leiden: Brill, 2006), 105–26; and for Galatians specifically, see Jeremy W. Barrier, "Jesus' Breath: a Physiological Analysis of πνεῦμα Within Paul's Letter to the

the universe; it is like a rarified form of air—or a mixture of fire and air—that pervades the universe, holds the cosmos together, and comprises celestial bodies.[119] To translate this understanding of *pneuma* for modern readers, Dale Martin describes it this way: "Pneuma is, to Paul, something like what a combination of oxygen and electricity might be for us. Pneuma is the electricity-oxygen stuff-force of the body and the cosmos. It is a cosmic stuff of life, energy, movement, and thought. It can be experienced individually and shared, both with the persons of God and Jesus but also among ourselves with one another."[120]

While *pneuma* can generally be understood as a physical substance in the ancient world and in Paul's epistles, that does not mean all instances of *pneuma* have the same intended referent. In the New Testament, *pneuma* is used to refer to a variety of things: the *pneuma* of human beings—that is—the substance that animates the body and allows humans to move and think (e.g., Luke 8:55; Acts 7:59; 1 Cor 14:14; Jas 2:26); the *pneuma* of the universe that makes up the cosmos, both clean and unclean, good and bad (e.g., Luke 6:18; 1 Cor 2:12); the *pneuma* of God (e.g., 1 Cor 2:11; Phil 3:3); the *pneuma* of Jesus/Christ (e.g., Gal 4:6; Phil 1:19); and the holy *pneuma* (e.g., Luke 3:22; Acts 2:4).[121] *Pneuma* is also employed with similar diversity in ancient Jewish texts.[122] For example, OG Isa 11:2–3 speaks about the *pneuma* of God (πνεῦμα τοῦ θεοῦ), the *pneuma* of wisdom and understanding (πνεῦμα σοφίας καὶ συνέσεως), the *pneuma* of resolution and power (πνεῦμα βουλῆς καὶ ἰσχύος), the *pneuma* of knowledge and piety (πνεῦμα γνώσεως καὶ εὐσεβείας), and the *pneuma* of the fear of God (πνεῦμα φόβου θεοῦ). We also see references to the

---

Galatians," *JSNT* 2 (2014): 115–38. For a more general presentations of *pneuma* in ancient medical contexts, see Owsei Temkin, *The Double Face of Janus and Other Essays in the History of Medicine* (Baltimore: Johns Hopkins University Press, 1977), 154–61; Martin, *Corinthian Body*, 21–25.

119 Terence Paige, "Who Believes in 'Spirit'? πνεῦμα in Pagan Usage and Implications for the Gentile Christian Mission," *HTR* 95 (2002): 425; David E. Hahm, *The Origins of Stoic Cosmology* (Columbus: Ohio State University Press, 1977), 70–71, 142, 157–65; Thiessen, *Gentile Problem*, 143–47.

120 Dale B. Martin, *Biblical Truths: The Meaning of Scripture in the Twenty-First Century* (New Haven: Yale University Press, 2017), 233.

121 On the various referents of *pneuma* in Paul, see Engberg-Pedersen, *Cosmology and Self*, 66–80. See also Friedrich Wilhelm Horn (*Das Angeld des Geistes: Studien zur paulinischen Pneumatologie*, FRLANT 154 [Göttingen: Vandenhoeck & Ruprecht, 1992]. 60), who argues for six different conceptual uses of *pneuma* in Paul: functional (*funktionalen*), substantive (*substanzhaften*), material (*stofflichen*), hypostasis (*hypostatischen*), normative (*normativen*), and anthropological (*anthropologischen*).

122 On the wide range of meaning and usage of spirit/*pneuma* in the varieties of Jewish thought of Paul's day, see John R. Levison, *The Spirit in First-Century Judaism*, AGJU 29 (Leiden: Brill, 1997). Levison concludes that the diversity of thought surrounding the spirit in this period is so broad that it is impossible to pin down any systematic usage of the idea, even for singular authors (notably Philo).

pneuma of individuals (e. g., Gen 45:27; Num 14:23; 1 Kgdms 30:12), divine *pneuma* (e. g., Exod 31:3; 35:31), and a *pneuma* of various character traits (e. g., Num 5:14; Deut 34:9; 3 Kgdms 22:22–23).

Since the use of *pneuma* is diverse and its references and functions are not monolithic, one has to work from context to determine what is going on in any particular passage.[123] In our present exploration of Galatians, Paul uses the *pneuma* of Christ as the means by which gentiles become sons of Abraham.[124] Since Christ is the promised seed of Abraham (Gal 3:16), and because the Galatians have received his *pneuma* (Gal 4:6; cf. 3:2–3, 5, 14, 27, 29; 4:29), they have the physical stuff of Abraham's seed within them that makes them true genealogical seed of Abraham, or—to put it modern medical parlance—they undergo a kind of gene therapy and share his DNA.[125] Thiessen—building on the work of Johnson Hodge and Stowers—notes that the Stoic theory of *krasis* (blending) offers a helpful model for understanding how Christ's *pneuma* enters and interpenetrates the body of an individual.[126] In regards to this type of blending, when *pneuma* penetrates another substance or body, it is evenly diluted throughout the entirety of the other body. It creates a perfect, even, homogeneous mixture so that the every bit of the body equally shares the *pneuma*, but in a way that preserves the qualities of each substance.[127] On the importance of each substance retaining its own qualities,

---

[123] Many interpreters do not engage in discussing what this *pneuma* actually is, but given the general proclivity to capitalize "spirit" in these contexts, it seems that they equate this with the Holy Spirit, the third person of the trinity. E. g., Bruce, *Galatians*, 198–9; Martyn, *Galatians*, 391; Barclay, *Paul and the Gift*, 389–90.

[124] It is worth noting that the relationship between faith, sonship, baptism, and reception of the *pneuma* is not easily placed in a tidy chronology in Galatians. In Gal 4:6, Paul writes, "And *because* you are sons, God has sent the *pneuma* of his son into our hearts..." Here, the *pneuma* of his son is given to those who are already sons. Previously, in Gal 3:2–7 Paul had said that they received the *pneuma* from the hearing of faith/faithfulness (ἐξ ἀκοῆς πίστεως) and those who are out of faith/faithfulness (οἱ ἐκ πίστεως) are the sons of Abraham. Similarly, in Gal 3:27–29 the idea of baptism and being clothed with Christ (i.e., receiving his *pneuma*, see Thiessen, *Gentile Problem*, 112–13) is linked to being Abrahamic sons. On this, Martyn (*Galatians*, 391n11) comments: "For Paul there is no chronological order between adoption into God's family and receipt of the Spirit." See also the discussion in Engberg-Pedersen, *Cosmology and Self*, 67–70.

[125] On this imperfect but apt analogy, see Thiessen, *Gentile Problem*, 117–18.

[126] Thiessen, *Gentile Problem*, 112–22; Johnson Hodge, *If Sons, Then Heirs*, 75–76; Stowers, "Pauline Participation," 358–60.

[127] This conception of *krasis* is generally attributed to Chrysippus and is preserved in a number of extant texts. See Alexander, *On Mixture* 216.14–218.6 (=SVF 2.473); Stobaeus 1.155.5–11 (=SVF 2.471); Plutarch, *Against the Stoics on Common Conceptions* 1078B-E (=SVF 2.465; 2.480). For a fuller exploration of how *krasis* functions in Stoic physics, see Samuel Sambursky, *Physics of the Stoics* (London: Routledge & Kegan Paul, 1959), 10–16.

Thiessen writes: "Since *krasis* permits the perfect mixture of two substances, while allowing those two substances to retain their own distinctive aspects, Paul's gentiles-in-Christ both remain gentiles, and yet are distinguished from gentiles who are not in Christ. That is to say, gentile believers are both fully flesh-and-blood gentile bodies, and fully infused with the *pneuma* of Christ."[128] While they remain in fleshy bodies, in some way that flesh has been modified or upgraded by its fusion with divine *pneuma*.[129]

Paul's body imagery in 1 Corinthians further elucidates the interconnectedness that exists between Christ and those who are in him, of him, and clothed with him. "For in one *pneuma* we were all baptized into one body" (1 Cor 12:13a). Paul notes that God has blended together this body (συνεκέρασεν τὸ σῶμα, 1 Cor 12:24) from many members into a single unified body (1 Cor 12:27) and that all who are united to Christ are one *pneuma* with him (1 Cor 6:17). Just as Christ's *pneuma* exists in the body of the believer, so too do they exist within the body of Christ. "The important conclusion is that 'being in Christ'—and indeed, 'being one in Christ'—as a result of 'having been clothed in Christ' should be understood as having a quite concrete ontological underpinning, which is that of having received the material pneuma."[130] It is this real, functional, physical union with Christ that makes them sons of Abraham: "And if you are of Christ (ὑμεῖς Χριστοῦ) then you are the seed of Abraham, heirs according to the promise" (Gal 3:29).

3.6 Pruning Circumcised Gentiles in Christ: Galatians 5:2–4

What does all of this have to do with Paul's argument against gentile circumcision? Why does he highlight that the Galatians are in and of Christ through the *pneuma* —a feat that is impossible to perform through circumcision—and are therefore sons of Abraham? And how does circumcision nullify this sonship? Many interpreters fail to see the connection between 4:21–5:1 and 5:2 onward, instead opting to

---

128 Thiessen, *Gentile Problem*, 114.
129 They were formerly enslaved to the *stoicheia* of the cosmos—the elements that compose their flesh, which brings forth weakness, corruptibility, sin, and mortality—but since their earthy (1 Cor 15:47), fleshy bodies have been infused with this divine material, they are no longer susceptible to corruption in the same way. As Paul notes in 1 Cor 15, he knows of a future in which the flesh and its associated weakness, limitations, and mortality will be finally done away with, but as it stands in the present, pneumatically-infused mortal earth-flesh is a solid down payment (2 Cor 1:22; 5:5) until they receive their final upgrade to pneumatic, immortal, celestial bodies.
130 Engberg-Pedersen, *Cosmology and Self*, 69.

see 5:2 as beginning a new, somewhat unrelated section.[131] If, however, we read these passages organically—without imposing modern versification—the logic of exclusion that Paul is attempting to elucidate becomes clearer.

3.6.1 Schweitzer, *Pneuma*, and *die Todsünden*

In 5:2 Paul states: "Pay Attention! I, Paul, am saying to you that if you let yourselves be circumcised, Christ will be of no benefit to you." What Paul has been arguing up until this point is that through the Galatians' reception of Christ's *pneuma* they have become free sons of Abraham. This is the benefit (ὠφελέω) they receive by being in Christ. If they undergo circumcision, they lose this benefit. As Paul has been arguing in the preceding chapters (Gal 3–4), Christ and his *pneuma* are the means by which the Galatians become Abrahamic sons. If freedom, inheritance, and sonship are the benefits received through their reception of Christ's *pneuma*, then losing these benefits must also mean they lose the *pneuma*. If they seek to rightwise[132] themselves by the law (i.e., undergo circumcision) then they are cut off from Christ and have lost the gift (Gal 5:4).[133] How, then, does undergoing circumcision cause one to lose Christ's *pneuma* and their status as an Abrahamic son?

In his classic work, *The Mysticism of Paul the Apostle*, Albert Schweitzer explores what he calls the mystical idea of being-in-Christ. While he does not explicitly conceive of the being-in-Christ is terms of the reception of Christ's material *pneuma*, he does note that the connection between those who participate in Christ and Christ is of a physical character (*naturhaften Charakter*).[134] Due to the physical

---

131 E.g., Moo, *Galatians*, 319; cf. deSilva, *Galatians*, 407–8.
132 Δικαιόω and δικαιοσύνη are notoriously difficult to translate into English, both literally and conceptually. See, e.g., E. P. Sanders, *Paul and Palestinian Judaism: A Comparison of Patterns of Religion* (Philadelphia: Fortress, 1977), 470–72. Looking at Gal 3:6–9, the *dikaiosynē* the Galatians have is directly dependent on their Abrahamic sonship; it is relational. If Abrahamic sonship—and therefore *dikaiosynē*—are through reception of Christ's *pneuma*, then *dikaiosynē* cannot be accomplished through circumcision. For a helpful exploration of Gal 3:6–9 and the connection between Abraham and *dikaiosynē*, see Richard B. Hays, *The Faith of Jesus Christ: The Narrative Substructure of Galatians 3:1–4:11*, 2nd ed. (Grand Rapids: Eerdmans, 2002), 173–76.
133 On circumcision in Gal 5 as a "ritual failure," see Peter-Ben Smit, "In Search of Real Circumcision: Ritual Failure and Circumcision in Paul," *JSNT* 40 (2017): 79–82. Though Smit and I disagree on why the ritual of circumcision fails the Galatian men, it is constructive to think about circumcision in these terms. I.e., what does the ritual of circumcision accomplish and signify, and why does circumcision not do this for the Galatians?
134 Schweitzer, *Mysticism*, 110 (original German: *Die Mystik des Apostels Paulus*, 2nd ed. [Tübingen: Mohr Siebeck, 1954], 111). Throughout the translated volume of *Mysticism*, Montgomery inter-

union that the elect—to use Schweitzer's idiom—share with Christ, there is the possibility that they can invalidate this union by committing acts that are contrary to this union and existentially threaten the body of Christ. Schweitzer finds three deadly sins (*Todsünden*) that Paul describes as being incompatible with one's physical union with Christ: union with a prostitute (πόρνη, 1 Cor 6:15–19), participating in pagan sacrifices and therefore being connected to *daimonia* (1 Cor 10:14–22), and a non-Jew undergoing circumcision after having been baptized (Gal 5:2–4).[135] These actions would theoretically create unions between Christ and something with which his body is completely incompatible. Since Paul cannot conceive of such things damaging the body of Christ, the one who participates in such acts is severed from the body like a gangrenous limb. They lose Christ's *pneuma* and are separated from his body and the benefits afforded to his members.

To understand how union with a prostitute is physically damning for a brother, we must briefly look at how Paul understands the union between spouses. In Paul's mind, the corporeal union between a husband and a wife is the same sort of corporeal union that exists between Christ and those who are in him; they become a one-flesh entity.[136] Even if a fellow believer has an unbelieving (ἄπιστος) spouse, the unbelieving spouse—by virtue of their one-flesh relationship with a believer—is sanctified through that union (1 Cor 7:12–14; cf. Rom 11:16). The unbelieving spouse shares in the flesh of their spouse and is connected to Christ and receive his *pneuma* through the *pneuma* that their spouse has received. Paul also presents the idea that the union of a believer and unbeliever—and presumably two believers—produces holy children (1 Cor 7:14).[137] The *pneuma* of

---

prets *naturhaft* in various ways, and here he translates it as "quasi-physical" whereas in other instances it is simply "physical" (127; orig. 128) or "realistic" (34; orig. 35). Throughout *Mysticism*, however, Schweitzer consistently uses the word *naturhaft* to describe a physical reality (e.g., 10–11, 127–29, 285; orig. 10–11, 127–29, 277–78). Despite the physicality that Schweitzer ascribes to this union, Engberg-Pedersen offers this critique of Schweitzer's use of the term *mysticism* to refer to the physical union with Christ: "There is nothing mystical about this, as Albert Schweitzer would have it. It is all a question of elemental pneumatic cosmology" (*Cosmology and Self*, 69). Mark A. Seifrid, however, argues the exact opposite of Engberg-Pedersen, and states that Schweitzer's usage of *naturhaft/naturlich* to describe one's union with or being in Christ is completely groundless (*Justification by Faith: The Origin and Development of a Central Pauline Theme*, NovTSup 68 [Leiden: Brill, 1992], 17–19).

135 Schweitzer, *Mysticism*, 128–30.
136 Schweitzer refers to the physical union of spouses as corporeally belonging to one another ("die Ehegatten einander körperlich angehören"; *Mysticism*, 127–28; orig., 128).
137 In some ancient texts, semen is thought to contain *pneuma* (e.g., Galen, *On Semen* 1.5.18). It is conceivable that Paul believes that Christ's *pneuma* could be transmitted seminally between spouses to produce holy offspring. On the connection between semen, *pneuma*, and procreation, see Alicia D. Myers, *Blessed Among Women? Mothers and Motherhood in the New Testament* (New York:

Christ that one receives is communicable between themself and those with whom they share corporeality. If a believer—by virtue of being united to Christ—sleeps with a prostitute, they unite Christ to a prostitute in the same way that spouses are united; they make Christ a member of a prostitute (1 Cor 6:15–19). Since this union is completely impossible for Paul, he does not fully tease out the implications for this individual, but it can be inferred that since this union is so antithetical to the nature of the body of Christ that Paul would prefer that the man be severed from the body rather than risk joining Christ to a prostitute. On this union Dale Martin comments, "The Christian man penetrating a prostitute constitutes coitus between two beings of such different ontological status that Paul can hardly contemplate the consequences."[138] This is akin to what Paul says about the man who is sleeping with his stepmother in 1 Cor 5:1–11. Paul calls for the Corinthians to expel this man from the assembly for the sake of the *pneuma*. While many translations add the possessive pronoun "his" before *pneuma* to help identify which *pneuma* is to be preserved (τὸ πνεῦμα σωθῇ), it is also possible that this refers to the *pneuma* that unites believers and exists within the assembly (i.e., Christ's *pneuma*).[139] If the Corinthians allow this man to remain within their community, then they will be allowing this man to pollute their shared *pneuma*, because "a little leaven leavens the whole batch of dough" (1 Cor 5:6); he has to be removed for the sake of the *pneuma*.

Similarly, in 1 Cor 10:14–22, Paul argues that those who are members of the body of Christ cannot partake in sacrifices and cultic meals to idols because it will cause them to be partners with *daimonia*.[140] Paul likens partaking in sacrifices to idols to partaking in the eucharist. In the same way that partaking in the body

---

Oxford University Press, 2017), 44–51. On the transmission of a parent's covenantal status via *pneuma* to their children, see Daniel H. Weiss, "Born Into Covenantal Salvation? Baptism and Birth in Early Christianity and Classical Rabbinic Judaism," *JSQ* 24 (2017): 318–38, at 332–35; cf. Taylor G. Petrey, "Semen Stains: Seminal Procreation and the Patrilineal Genealogy of Salvation in Tertullian," *JECS* 22 (2014): 343–72, at 368–369. On intermarriage in Paul, see Hayes, *Gentile Impurities*, 92–98.

138 Martin, *Corinthian Body*, 177.

139 Tertullian, *Pud.* 13; Karl P. Donfried, "Justification and Last Judgment in Paul," *Int* 30 (1976): 140–52, at 150–52; Engberg-Pedersen, *Cosmology and Self*, 206–7; Contra David Raymond Smith, 'Hand This Man Over to Satan': Curse, Exclusion and Salvation in 1 Corinthians 5, LNTS 386 (London: T&T Clark, 2008), 175–78. For an extensive list of translations and interpreters and the readings they espouse—either "his *pneuma*" or "the *pneuma*"—see Michael K. W. Suh, "τὸ πνεῦμα in 1 Corinthians 5:5: A Reconsideration of Patristic Exegesis," *VC* 72 (2018): 121–41, at 122–23.

140 For a detailed discussion of this passage, see Martin Sanfridson, "Paul and Sacrifice in Corinth: Rethinking Paul's Views on Gentile Cults in 1 Corinthians 8 and 10" (McMaster University, PhD diss., 2022), 248–81.

and blood of the eucharistic meal joins the individual to the body of Christ, so too does partaking in cultic activity to idols join the individual to *daimonia*. These two unions are mutually exclusive for Paul, and therefore participation in one of these unions makes the opposing union an impossibility. "You are not able to drink the cup of the Lord and of *daimonia*; you are not able to participate in the table of the Lord and of *daimonia*" (1 Cor 10:21).[141] If one participates in these sacrifices and meals, they lose Christ's *pneuma* and their union with him.

When looking at Gal 5:2 in light of these comparative examples, it is not immediately clear how circumcision invalidates one's union with Christ and strips them of his *pneuma*. As previously discussed, the majority of interpreters believe that undergoing circumcision is damnable because it demonstrates a reliance on works righteousness and the law in opposition to Christ-faith. Or to look at it from a more sociological perspective, others focus on the ethnic-boundary-bending that gentile adoption of circumcision leads to, which presumably reinstates ethnic boundaries that Christ has abolished. Or to put it in Barclay's system, it places the Christ-gift within an incompatible system of value and therefore denies it on its own terms. Schweitzer's view on the logic of exclusion brought about by undergoing circumcision seems to affirm the underlying assumptions of these other perspectives, but strays from the corporeal and union-centric logic he gives for the exclusion of individuals in the case of sleeping with a prostitute or communing with demons. Schweitzer argues that circumcision separates one from Christ because the act of circumcision affirms the significance of one's being-in-the-flesh—and therefore the importance of law observance and Jewish ethnicity—which is incompatible with being in Christ.[142] "But a man can only be either in Christ or in the flesh, not both at once."[143]

---

[141] The phrase "you are not able" (οὐ δύνασθε) should be understood as conveying the idea of impossibility. Thiselton (*First Corinthians*, 776) notes that this dual union is impossible for three reasons: logically (these two possibilities logically exclude each other), empirically (something will be destroyed if you try and do both), and institutionally (those in Christ cannot do both and remain in Christ).

[142] Schweitzer, *Mysticism*, 129. Cf. Karin B. Neutel, "Circumcision Gone Wrong: Paul's Message as a Case of Ritual Disruption," *Neot* 50 (2016): 373–96, at 383. Neutel rightly emphasizes genealogical concerns in her interpretation, but wrongly assumes that—for Paul—gentiles could become Jews and Abrahamic sons through circumcision. She writes: "Therein appears to lie the problem for Paul: in becoming Jews through circumcision, gentiles would be alienated from Christ. Since Paul argued earlier in the letter that if gentiles are in Christ, they are Abraham's seed and heirs to God's promise to him (Gal 3:27–29), it seems likely that becoming associated with Abraham through circumcision would for Paul entail a rejection of the Abrahamic lineage that already exists through Christ" (383).

[143] Schweitzer, *Mysticism*, 129.

If, however, we take Paul seriously on what he says the agitators' non-covenantal, non-eighth-day circumcision does to an individual's relationship to the Messiah, the logic of exclusion becomes more straightforward. Throughout Gal 4, Paul has been making it clear that the Galatians have been set free from their slavery to the *stoicheia* of the cosmos (Gal 4:8–9) and are now free sons of Abraham (4:5–7, 31). "For freedom Christ has set us free, therefore do not subject yourselves again to a yoke of slavery" (Gal 5:1). In undergoing circumcision, those who are already sons of the promise like Isaac through their reception of Christ's *pneuma* become sons that follow in the fleshly pattern of Ishmael, which returns them to their enslavement under the *stoicheia* of the cosmos.[144] How can one have the *pneuma* of Christ, yet be enslaved to the cosmic elements that Paul says are by nature not God (Gal 4:8–9)? The answer—for Paul—is that this is an ontological impossibility. In the same way that sleeping with a prostitute and communing with *daimonia* cuts one off from Christ's body for the sake of preserving it, so too does subjecting the body of Christ to this particular form of slavery cause one to be cut off. Paul cannot conceive of Christ becoming a slave (Phil 2:7 notwithstanding!); he is the seed of Abraham to whom the promises were made (Gal 3:16–19). It is precisely this impossible subjugation of Christ to enslavement to the *stoicheia* of the cosmos that causes one to lose his *pneuma* and to be cut off from him.[145]

This interpretation also offers a possible explanation of the physics related to how one can lose Christ's *pneuma* and their status in him. Given the general tendency to overlook the materiality of *pneuma*, interpreters have not sought to explain the mechanics of how one actually loses his *pneuma*. For the vast majority of interpreters, it seems to be that one's exclusion through circumcision happens due to a shift in their trust that is represented by the act itself—that is—they now trust in works of the law, Jewish ethnicity, etc. This does not explain how this actually works; how do they actually, physically lose Christ's *pneuma*? If we understand the reception of this *pneuma* through the Stoic concept of *krasis*, there is a possible explanation for how this can occur. Some Stoics believed that *krasis*—though a perfect interpenetrative blend—can be undone through physical inter-

---

[144] On the *stoicheia* in Gal 4, see Johnson Hodge, *If Sons, Then Heirs*, 71, 183n21; Martinus C. de Boer, "The Meaning of the Phrase τὰ στοιχεῖα τοῦ κόσμου in Galatians," *NTS* 53 (2007): 204–24; cf. Emma Wasserman, *Apocalypse as Holy War: Divine Politics and Polemics in the Letters of Paul*, AYBRL (New Haven: Yale University Press, 2018), 151–54.

[145] This subjugation of Christ upends a proper divine hierarchy. On Paul's divine hierarchy see, Wasserman, *Apocalypse as Holy War*, esp. 124–28, 134–37. See also, Matthew T. Sharp, "Courting Daimons in Corinth: Daimonic Partnerships, Cosmic Hierarchies and Divine Jealousy in Paul," in *Demons in Judaism and Christianity: Characters, Characteristics, and Demonic Exegesis*, ed. Hector M. Patmore and Josef Lössl, AGJU 113 (Leiden: Brill, 2022), 112–29.

vention. The example often cited by the ancient sources is attributed to Chryssipus and recounts how one can undo the mixture of water and wine. Chryssipus believed that this mixture was a *krasis* and therefore it could be undone by dipping an oiled sponge into it, which would separate out the water (Stobaeus 1.155.5–11; Philo, *Confusion* 184–86; Alexander, *On Mixture* 252.1). In the case of circumcision, it is possible that the incision itself causes the *pneuma* to flow out of the individual in the same way that *pneuma* flows out of the wounds of an animal (Galen, *On the Doctrines of Hippocrates and Plato* 7.3.30).[146] While this explanation is speculative, it is important to note that in ancient physics *krasis* is able to be undone through physical intervention—e.g., circumcision.

3.6.2 Circumcision and the Whole Law

To rebut this interpretation of why non-covenantal circumcision is incompatible with being in Christ, one might look to the next verse where Paul declares that anyone who is having himself circumcised is obligated to do the whole law (ὅλον τὸν νόμον, Gal 5:3). Since the traditional anti-legalist line of interpretation generally presumes that perfect law observance is an impossible task, this would indicate that Paul believes circumcision condemns them because it forces them to rely on law observance for *dikaiosynē*.[147] Paul, however, does not think that blameless law observance is an impossibility—he himself did so (Phil 3:6)—nor does this text explicitly state the idea that law observance is an impossibility, only that it is required of the circumcised.[148] What Paul does say to his Galatian audience is that

---

[146] The interconnection of *pneuma* and blood was a prevalent idea in ancient medical theory, including the work of Herophilus and Galen. See Heinrich von Staden, *Herophilus: The Art of Medicine in Early Alexandria* (Cambridge: Cambridge University Press, 1989), 264–67; Michael Boylan, "Galen: On Blood, the Pulse, and the Arteries," *Journal of the History of Biology* 40 (2007): 207–30. Similarly, Philo (*QG* 2.59) speaks of the intermingled nature of *pneuma* and blood.

[147] E.g., Bruce, *Galatians*, 229–31; Thomas R. Schreiner, "Paul and Perfect Obedience to the Law: An Evaluation of the View of E. P. Sanders," *WTJ* 47 (1985): 246–78; Blaschke, *Beschneidung*, 384–85; cf. Barclay, *Paul and the Gift*, 334.

[148] Fredriksen (*Pagans' Apostle*, 67) succinctly points out important interpretive questions that are overlooked in the vast majority of scholarship on Paul and the law— especially commentaries on Galatians—that interact with Gal 5:3. "Still: what did "keeping the whole Law" mean? According to whose interpretation? The evidence of vigorous Jewish variety of practice in the late Second Temple period should give us pause." See also, Karin H. Zetterholm, "The Question of Assumptions: Torah Observance in the First Century," in Nanos and Zetterholm, *Paul within Judaism*, 79–103, at 80–81; Anders Runesson, "Entering a Synagogue with Paul: First-Century Torah Observance," in Wendel and Miller, *Torah Ethics*, 11–26. Presumably Paul would have appealed to his own hala-

dikaiosynē is not from the law (Gal 3:21) and therefore any attempt to bring about *dikaiosynē* through the law is futile (Gal 5:4). So even if Paul's exhortation here to the Galatians is that undergoing circumcision carries with it the obligation to keep the whole law, this does not necessarily consign them to fulfill the unfulfillable.[149]

Some have also suggested that the agitators only encouraged the Galatians to adopt circumcision and certain aspects of the Law, and here Paul is making sure they know that *full* Torah observance is required of the circumcised.[150] This implies that the agitators may have promoted circumcision under false pretenses and did not actually preach observance of all of the law, but only emphasized the necessity of circumcision.[151] While this does somewhat accord with Paul's polemic in Gal 6:12–13, one cannot be certain that Paul's characterization of the agitators' motives there is entirely fair and accurate.[152] In light of the various accounts we have from the ancient world regarding gentile adoption of Jewish ways of life, the general rule of thumb is the circumcision was one of the final steps in judaizing—not the first—so it seems unlikely that this would have been their strategy.[153] If, however, this view is accepted as correct, it is possible that

---

khah, but that remains broadly concealed in his epistles, which were written to non-Jewish audiences.

149 Michael Cranford, "The Possibility of Perfect Obedience: Paul and an Implied Premise in Galatians 3:10 and 5:3." *NovT* 36 (1994): 242–58; cf. R. Barry Matlock, "Helping Paul's Argument Work? The Curse of Galatians 3.10–14" in *The Torah in the New Testament*, ed. Peter Oakes and Michael Tait, LNTS 401 (London: T&T Clark, 2009), 154–79.

150 E.g., Franz Mußner, *Der Galaterbrief*, 5th ed., HThKNT 9 (Freiburg: Herder, 1988), 347–48; Sanders, *Paul, The Law*, 29; Cranford, "Perfect Obedience," 255; Longenecker, *Galatians*, 226–27; deSilva, *Galatians*, 417–18.

151 A potential stumbling block for this interpretation is Gal 4:10, where Paul indicates that some of the Galatians have begun to adopt aspects of the Jewish law as it pertains to calendrical observances. On this point, I disagree with Troy Martin ("Pagan and Judeo-Christian Time-Keeping Schemes in Gal 4.10 and Col 2.16," *NTS* 42 [1996]: 105–19) who argues that the days, months, seasons, and years mentioned in Gal 4:10 refer to the Roman imperial cult, not the Jewish one. While Martin acknowledges the relative ambiguity of these references and appeals to context for guidance (112), I'm not convinced that his appeals to the pagan past of the Galatians supports his argument. In 4:3 Paul links the law with the *stoicheia*, so it seems that—for Paul—the Galatians' observance of the Jewish calendar would constitute a return to the way things were when their bodies were enslaved to the *stoicheia*. Here, I understand that to be "enslaved under the cosmic elements" (Gal 4:3) refers to the normal situation of mortal humans that have not have their flesh "upgraded" with divine *pneuma*, and therefore need to be regulated by the law (Gal 3:23–4:5). See note 129 above.

152 Barclay, *Mirror-Reading*, 75.

153 Josephus, *J.W.* 2.454; *Ant.* 20.17–47; Juvenal, *Satires* 14.96–106. Sanders (*Paul, the Law*, 29, 56n58) argues that adopting circumcision, sabbath, and *kashruth* is a kind of a gradual introduction into a Jewish way of life since it is a selection of commandments and not the entirety of the law. Circum-

Paul's thought reflects the sentiment of Sifra Kedoshim 8:3, where it explicitly states that a proselyte must take on all the words of Torah and an omission of any part of Torah leads to their rejection as a proselyte.[154]

Given the strict legislation surrounding circumcision, Thiessen argues that the "whole law" in Gal 5:3 could be referencing all of the laws that pertain to circumcision—that covenant circumcision only applies to Abraham's descendants from Isaac and is only valid if performed on the eighth day after birth.[155] If any Galatian man were to undergo circumcision, then he fails to keep the law of circumcision from a temporal and genealogical standpoint. A similar understanding of the laws pertaining to circumcision is represented in Jub. 15:33, where the author speaks about the sons of Israel not being circumcised according to "all of this law," which leads to their condemnation.[156] Thiessen also points to LXX Deut 24:8–9 to demonstrate the plausibility that "the whole law" can be a reference to the entirety of a law that pertains to a particular concept. Here, the author refers to the law regarding *lepra*, and tells the Israelites to be extremely careful to keep all of the law (πάντα τὸν νόμον) that the priests instruct them in. Lastly, Thiessen finds support in John Chrysostom's exposition of Gal 5:3 (*Hom. Gal.* 5:3), where Chrysostom notes that the commandment of circumcision contains various sub-commandments that must be observed in order for a circumcision to be properly carried out.[157]

While Thiessen rightly highlights the importance of carrying out a circumcision in the proper manner—and Paul presumably would have agreed with this, he even highlights his own proper eighth-day circumcision (Phil 3:5)—I am not convinced that this is Paul's concern in this particular text. If Paul holds a strict halakhah regarding circumcision, then why would he make this statement in 5:3? It seems doubtful that Paul would attempt to regulate the illegitimate circumcisions of grown, non-Jewish men by insisting that they observe the whole law of circumcision, which they will have already broken by simply undergoing the procedure.

---

cision, however, was likely the most daunting part of judaizing for a gentile male due to cultural and physical reasons, so it seems inaccurate to call this a type of gradualism.
154 See also, b. Sanh. 81a; b. Mak. 24a.
155 Thiessen, *Gentile Problem*, 91–95.
156 In the context of this passage in Jubilees, the failure pertains to the amount of foreskin that is removed, not the timing or ethnicity of the individuals undergoing the rite. Cf. m. Šabb. 19:6.
157 While Chrysostom does highlight the various elements required for a proper circumcision to take place, he does so within the wider context of keeping all of Torah. In the same way that all of the laws pertaining to circumcision need to be followed in order for a circumcision to be valid, so too does all of the Torah need to be followed in order for one's law observance to be valid. Consequently, he states that Paul is a debtor to the whole law—implying all of Torah—not just the various laws pertaining to circumcision.

On the other hand, it is possible that Paul is simply pointing out to these individuals that in their attempt to keep the law of circumcision, they are actually doomed to break it by undergoing belated circumcision.

The key for interpreting Paul's statement in 5:3, is understanding his use of the adverb πάλιν ("again") at the beginning of the verse: "And I insist again (πάλιν), that any man who is having himself circumcised is obligated to do the whole law." Has Paul already insisted that whole Torah observance is required of the circumcised? The general scholarly consensus is that Paul has not said this explicitly, but he does say other things about the law that can be understood as being the referent of this phrase. Due to this ambiguity, some scribes even went as far as removing πάλιν from their manuscripts.[158] There are presently four main views represented in scholarship on what Paul could be referencing here. The most prominent interpretation is that 5:3 is referring back to what Paul had immediately said in 5:2.[159] Proponents of this view contend that since circumcision requires perfect law observance, then circumcision makes Christ of no benefit to them (5:2) and cuts them off from Christ (5:4) due to the incompatibility between Christ and circumcision and the law. Other interpreters say that 5:3 recalls back to 3:10 where Paul declares that all who are from works of the law (ἐξ ἔργων νόμου) are under a curse because they are required to observe the whole law.[160] Here, Paul quotes Deut 27:26: "Cursed are all who do not observe and do all that is written in the book of the law." Given that these two interpretations are broadly in agreement regarding the impossibility and incompatibility of law observance and Christ-faith, some propose that Paul could have both 5:2 and 3:10 in mind when he makes his statement in 5:3.[161] Lastly, there are some interpreters who acknowledge the lack of an explicit direct referent elsewhere in the letter and argue that Paul must have said this in some prior communication with the Galatians.[162]

Another interpretive possibility is that Paul's previous usage of the word *law* can be instructive for understanding his usage here. Prior to this text, Paul's most recent appeal to the law occurs in Gal 4:21: "Tell me, you who desire to be under the

---

[158] πάλιν is omitted in D* F G 1739. 1881 it; Ambst.
[159] Lightfoot, *Galatians*, 203; Bruce, *Galatians*, 229; de Boer, *Galatians*, 312–13; A. Andrew Das, *Galatians*, ConC (St. Louis: Concordia, 2014), 523–24; Moo, *Galatians*, 322.
[160] E.g., Watson, *Paul, Judaism*, 71; Thomas R. Schreiner, *Galatians*, ZECNT (Grand Rapids: Zondervan, 2010), 314.
[161] Keener (*Galatians*, 232) and deSilva (*Galatians*, 314) both think that 5:2 is likely what Paul was immediately referring to, but that 3:10 also supports Paul's overall polemic against the law and should be kept in mind when interpreting 5:3.
[162] Betz (*Galatians*, 295n58) leaves this previous communication unidentified, but Mußner (*Galaterbrief*, 347) speculates that Paul could possibly have in mind some of his previous conflicts related to circumcision in Jerusalem (Acts 15:5; Gal 2:5) and Antioch (Acts 15:1).

law, do you not hear the law?" Since the instructions and warnings in the first part of Gal 5 directly build off of his explanation of the law in Gal 4:21–5:1, it is worth exploring how this may impact our reading of this present verse. In regard to doing all of the law from Gen 16–21 as portrayed in Paul's allegorical reading, there is one command that stands out—and is actually a quote from the law. As some interpreters have highlighted, a potential point of climax in Paul's allegorical unpacking of Genesis is his quotation of Gen 21:10 in Gal 4:30, "Cast out (ἔκβαλε) the enslaved woman and her son."[163] Here, Paul quotes the command of Sarah as a call to action for his Galatian community. They are to cast out the enslaved woman and her children, that is, they are to rid themselves of the agitators and those who follow them in promoting—and adopting—circumcision for gentile men in the assembly.[164] Commenting on Gal 4:30 in light of 4:21, G. Walter Hansen writes, "The way to be under the law is to follow the commands of the law."[165] If the Galatian men want to be under the law and get circumcised, then they are obligated do the whole of the law which Paul just expounded for them and remove themselves from the assembly. Here, the call to do the whole law is a call for them to remove themselves from assembly. The imperative (ἔκβαλε) in 4:30 serves to remind the Galatians that if they are to adopt circumcision, then they must realize that they are choosing to identify with the son that has no inheritance and is cast out.

Susan Eastman argues that Gal 4:30 should not be interpreted as a command to the Galatians, but rather should be understood as serving as a warning for what is in store (i.e., exclusion) for any of the men in the assembly who undergo the procedure.[166] Her reading focuses on the second-person singular imperative in the quotation of Sarah from Gen 21:10: ἔκβαλε. She argues that since Sarah's command is in the singular and directed at Abraham, Paul uses this quote to serve as a warning for the Galatians. When the Galatians "overhear"[167] Sarah's words to Abraham, they would not identify it as a command, but would understand it as a warning for their potential fate if they align themselves with the agitators. The crux of her argument is that when Paul quotes commands from scripture and intends for them to apply to his audience, he modifies the quote by pluralizing singular commands.[168]

---

163 Hays, *Echoes*, 116; Longenecker, *Galatians*, 217; Keener, *Galatians*, 227.
164 Thiessen (*Gentile Problem*, 94–95) also proposes this view alongside the one noted above, but he does not indicate which one he ultimately finds to be correct.
165 G. Walter Hansen, *Abraham in Galatians: Epistolary and Rhetorical Contexts*, JSNTSup 29 (Sheffield: JSOT Press, 1989), 146.
166 Susan G. Eastman, "'Cast Out the Slave Woman and Her Son': The Dynamics of Exclusion and Inclusion in Galatians 4.30," *JSNT* 28 (2006): 309–36, esp. 313–14, 326–27.
167 Eastman, "Cast Out," 314, 321, 324, 326, 333.
168 Eastman, "Cast Out," 321–24.

For example, in 1 Cor 5:13 when Paul quotes the Deuteronomic command (17:7; 19:19; 21:21; 22:21, 24; 24:7) to "drive out the evil person from you," he pluralizes the verb from ἐξαρεῖς to ἐξάρατε.[169] While it is true that Paul leaves the call to cast out the enslaved woman and her offspring in the singular, he does modify the quote in another way—which goes unnoticed by Eastman—when he changes "my son Isaac" (τοῦ υἱοῦ μου Ισαακ/עם בני עם יצחק) to "the son of the free woman" (τοῦ υἱοῦ τῆς ἐλευθέρας).[170] This modification indicates that Paul does not simply want the Galatians to "overhear" Sarah's words to Abraham, but rather by distancing the words from Sarah's lips and obscuring Sarah from view, Paul injects the Galatians into the narrative because he wants them to see themselves within it.[171] While this surely does function as a warning to the Galatians—as Eastman asserts—it also functions a command to the Galatians to remove the agitators and their offspring from the community.[172] Hansen even goes as far as saying that "the focal point in the Hagar-Sarah allegory *is* the imperative to expel the bondwoman and her son."[173]

The call to cast out the agitators—and those who are their offspring—functions within a broader discourse of exclusion that further bolsters this interpretation. There is an interesting progression that occurs in Gal 5:2–4.[174] In 5:2, Paul speaks to those who are still contemplating circumcision and says that if they undergo the procedure, Christ will not benefit them (οὐδὲν ὠφελήσει).[175] In 5:3, Paul speaks to those who are committed to undergoing the procedure (περιτεμνομένῳ) and reminds them that they must do the whole law. Lastly, in 5:4, Paul appears to speak to those who have already been circumcised, with the result that they have separated themselves from Christ (κατηργήθητε ἀπὸ Χριστοῦ). While these may be hypothetical categories referring to hypothetical individuals, the progression of 5:2–4 points to the reality of exclusion that comes about through the adoption of circumcision and serves as a warning to anyone who is considering having himself circumcised.[176] In each of these verses Paul references the exclusion that is brought about through gentiles in Christ improperly adopting circumcision.

---

[169] Notably, he also changes it from a future indicative to an aorist imperative.
[170] Seeing that Paul modified the quote from Gen 21:10, a handful of manuscripts preserve the LXX reading of τοῦ υἱοῦ μου Ισαακ in Gal 4:30: D* F G it vg^ms.
[171] Cf. Hays, *Echoes of Scripture*, 116. On the function of the singular command in the context of other Pauline letters, see John Anthony Dunne, *Persecution and Participation in Galatians*, WUNT 2/454 (Tübingen: Mohr Siebeck, 2017), 63–64.
[172] Dunne, *Persecution and Participation*, 64.
[173] Hansen, *Abraham in Galatians*, 146 (emphasis added).
[174] This is noted by Das, *Galatians*, 525.
[175] The third class conditional (ἐὰν περιτέμνησθε) plus the future result (οὐδὲν ὠφελήσει) further confirms that this is a still a pending fact for some of Paul's addressees.
[176] These three potential groups are also noted by Eastman, "Cast Out," 329.

As Paul goes on to say, "A little leaven leavens the whole batch of dough" (Gal 5:9). The leaven—that is the agitators and those they persuade to undergo circumcision—must be removed from the community before their leaven permeates throughout. Similarly, in 1 Cor 5:5–6, Paul urges the Corinthian assembly to expel the man who is sleeping with his father's wife from their community in order that the *pneuma* may be preserved (τὸ πνεῦμα σωθῇ). Paul says they must expel the man because "a little leaven leavens the whole batch of dough" (1 Cor 5:6). Any influence that damages the assembly and its *pneuma* needs to be expelled before its leaven infects the rest of assembly. If the Galatian men submit themselves to be circumcised, they must obey the whole law which Paul has expounded for them, and they must remove themselves from the assembly. While it has generally been interpreted as referring to castration, Paul's exclamation in Gal 5:12 can also be understood as furthering this discourse of exclusion: "I wish that the ones unsettling you would cut themselves off!"[177]

3.7 Are Circumcision and Foreskin Actually Nothing? Galatians 5:6 and 6:15

As briefly discussed in the previous chapter, Gal 5:6 and 6:15 are used alongside 1 Cor 7:19 as evidence that Paul came to believe that circumcision and foreskin are "nothing." The tendency of interpreters to flatten these three verses into a singular Pauline maxim that views circumcision and foreskin as nothing has obscured Paul's thought in these texts.[178] By overlooking these verses' epistolary contexts and the comparisons that Paul is making, the majority of interpreters have misunderstood what Paul is trying to accomplish by employing these terms. I argue that in Gal 5:6 Paul is not discussing the value of circumcision or foreskin, but their relative power to bring about eschatological *dikaiosynē*. Similarly, I argue that in Gal 6:15 Paul is not discussing the value of circumcision or foreskin, but their individual merit as things to boast in.

---

[177] See full discussion of this text below in §3.9.
[178] Similarly, some scholars who focus solely on the text of Galatians attempt to argue that Gal 5:6 and 6:15 are functionally equivalent. E.g., Simon Butticaz, *La crise galate ou l'anthropologie en question*, BZNW 229 (Berlin: de Gruyter, 2018), 227, 247.

3.7.1 Galatians 5:6

After stating the damning nature of circumcision for gentiles in 5:2–4, Paul says, "For[179] we, by *pneuma* from faithfulness, eagerly await the hope of righteousness. For in Christ Jesus, neither circumcision has any power (τι ἰσχύει), nor foreskin, but faithfulness working through love" (Gal 5:5–6). The critical thing to note for our current investigation is Paul's usage of ἰσχύω in 5:6 instead of the simple negations (a negative + ἐστιν) found in 1 Cor 7:19 and Gal 6:15. While some interpreters translate ἰσχύω as being related to power,[180] the majority translate it in a way the conveys value (i.e., neither circumcision nor foreskin has value/means anything/ counts for anything).[181] If one turns to most modern English Bible translations, a variant of this reading is what they will find.[182]

In the context of his work on ancient gift-giving, John Barclay argues that ἰσχύω should here be translated in a financial sense related to value.[183] Since— for Barclay—Paul has put aside the old Jewish system of value, he can now say that circumcision and foreskin no longer have any value in the divine economy; the only thing that now has worth is faith.[184] Barclay argues that ἰσχύω must be translated as conveying value based on syntactical and lexical grounds. He contends that ἰσχύω plus an accusative—here, τι ἰσχύει—should be translated in financial terms, and that translations conveying power are not applicable.[185] This,

---

179 The γάρ ("for") in verse 5 serves to establish a contrast between those who seek *dikaiosynē* in the law (Gal 5:4) and those who wait for *dikaiosynē* by *pneuma* from faithfulness; de Boer, *Galatians*, 315; cf. Martyn, *Galatians*, 472.
180 Notably, Martyn, *Galatians*, 472–3.
181 E.g., Dunn, *Galatians*, 270; Sanders, *Paul*, 551–2; Keener, *Galatians*, 235.
182 E.g., NRSV, NASB, ESV, NIV, CEB. The notable exception to this rule is the KJV. Similarly, most German, French, and Spanish translations also follow this interpretive trend.
183 Barclay, "Paul, the Gift," 37, 52–53.
184 For Barclay's reading of Galatians in relationship to ancient gift-giving and systems of value, see Barclay, *Paul and the Gift*, 351–446.
185 Barclay, "Paul, The Gift," 52n51; Barclay, *Paul and the Gift*, 392–93. Here, Barclay cites Josephus (*Ant.* 14.106) to demonstrate his point about value and financial terminology. The account in Josephus, however, does not necessarily discuss value, rather, it discusses equivalence. There Josephus mentions what a mina is equal to: 2.5 pounds (ἰσχύει λίτρας δύο ἥμισυ). If one were to insert a negation into Josephus' discussion of what a mina is equivalent to—as Paul does in Gal 5:6—it would not make the mina worthless or valueless, but would indicate that it is not equal to 2.5 pounds. If we adopt this understanding of ἰσχύω in terms of equivalence and apply it to Gal 5:6, the reading is similar to the one I propose below. If Paul argues that circumcision and foreskin are not equal to something (τι ἰσχύει, which should be understood as referring to *dikaiosynē*), that does not mean that they are worthless or meaningless, but that those things or statuses in

however, is incorrect. The only other instance in the Pauline Corpus[186] where ἰσχύω is employed is in Phil 4:13, when Paul says πάντα ἰσχύω ἐν τῷ ἐνδυναμοῦντί με, "I am able to do/have power to do all things in the one who strengthens me." Here, Paul employs ἰσχύω plus an accusative to convey power or the ability to accomplish something.[187] In a few cases, some scholars translate ἰσχύω in Gal 5:6 as conveying power, but their interpretation of the text falls back onto a reading that conveys value. For example, Wright correctly translates τι ἰσχύει as "has any power," but in his explanation of this text he immediately reverts to language that conveys value or worth without any explanation.[188] Similarly, Hans Dieter Betz states that τι ἰσχύει conveys the idea that circumcision does not have power to achieve righteousness, but when explaining the second half of the verse (ἀλλὰ πίστις δι' ἀγάπης ἐνεργουμένη), he reverts to value language.[189]

Further confirming a translation related to power is the context of this passage. The emphasis in 5:4–6 is on what has the ability to bring about eschatological *dikaiosynē* for those who are in Christ.[190] Paul denies that circumcision and the law have the ability to bring about *dikaiosynē* for the Galatians, rather, *dikaiosynē* comes to them through *pistis*.[191] Thus, when we read "neither circumcision has power, nor foreskin," we should understand this statement in the context of bringing about *dikaiosynē*. That is, neither circumcision nor foreskin have the power or

---

and of themselves are not equal to eschatological *dikaiosynē*. I am indebted to Isaac Soon for showing me this reading of ἰσχύω in *Ant*. 4.106.

186 Outside of the Pauline corpus, Matt 5:13 and Jas 5:16 also attest to the translation of 'power' when ἰσχύω is paired with an accusative.

187 John Reumann, *Philippians: A New Translation with Introduction and Commentary*, AB 33B (New Haven: Yale University Press, 2008), 703; Paul A. Holloway, *Philippians*, Hermeneia (Minneapolis: Fortress, 2017), 187.

188 Wright, *Paul*, 1140.

189 Betz, *Galatians*, 263–64. Betz comments, "The symbol of circumcision (or its absence) no longer has any power," and "It does not have the power to achieve (ἰσχύει τι [sic]) salvation and righteousness before God..." He follows this up by saying, "...what *matters* to those 'in Christ Jesus' is instead ἀλλὰ πίστις δι' ἀγάπης ἐνεργουμένη ('but faith working through love')" (emphasis added).

190 Choi, "ΠΙΣΤΙΣ in Galatians 5:5–6," 487–89; cf. Dunn, *Galatians*, 271.

191 Throughout Galatians—most notably in Gal 3:2–14—the concepts of *dikaiosynē*, *pistis*, and *pneuma* are all interrelated and linked to Abrahamic sonship; see Johnson Hodge, *If Sons, Then Heirs*, 93–107; Thiessen, *Gentile Problem*, 106–28. In the passage preceding our current text (Gal 4:21–31), Paul argues that the Galatians are sons of Abraham through their reception of *pneuma* and not through the acceptance of circumcision. When we arrive at 5:4–6, we find *dikaiosynē*, *pistis*, and *pneuma* once again. It is likely that Abrahamic sonship is also in view here as it pertains to those, who, by the *pneuma* and out of *pistis* wait for *dikaiosynē*, which is brought about by *pistis* and not circumcision or foreskin.

ability to confer eschatological *dikaiosynē*, but *pistis* does.¹⁹² Circumcision, however, does have the power to cut someone off from Christ and sever them from the benefits of being in Christ (Gal 5:2–4). The comparison of circumcision and foreskin with *pistis* is not one of ontology, but dynamology. This picture of circumcision and *pistis* agrees with what Paul says throughout Galatians about *dikaiosynē*; it is not from works of the law (ἐξ ἔργων νόμου, Gal 2:16; 3:2, 5, 10–11), but it is from faithfulness (ἐκ πίστεως, Gal 2:16; 3:8–9, 11–12, 22, 24). "[A]nd we have trusted in Christ Jesus, so that we may be rightwised from faithfulness (ἐκ πίστεως) and not from works of the law (ἐξ ἔργων νόμου)" (Gal 2:16).

The inclusion of foreskin in this text appears to be superfluous. While it could simply be the counterpart to circumcision, Paul could also be using it emphasize to the Galatians that their continuation in a state of foreskin in and of itself does not have power to bring about *dikaiosynē*. That is, though Paul thinks it is imperative that the Galatian males do not modify their foreskins, this preservation does not have any power.

Like 1 Cor 7:19 and Gal 6:15 (see below), Paul compares circumcision and foreskin to something else to make a specific rhetorical point. Here, when commenting on what has power to bring about *dikaiosynē*, Paul rejects the idea that circumcision and foreskin can bring about this desired result. Rather, the only thing that can bring about *dikaiosynē* is *pistis*. This text does not claim that circumcision and foreskin are irrelevant or indifferent things for Paul; rather, Paul only states that they do not have a specific type of power.

3.7.2 Galatians 6:15

In Gal 6:15, Paul makes the assertion that "neither circumcision is anything, nor foreskin, but new creation." Like the similar phrase in 1 Cor 7:19, many interpreters have concluded from this text that circumcision and foreskin are now nothing for Paul, and all that matters is "new creation."¹⁹³ In this section of Galatians, Paul continues his argument against the agitators' imposition of circumcision on the Galatian men. He states that those who are compelling the Galatians to be circumcised do so to make a good showing in the flesh and to avoid persecution (Gal 6:12–13). Furthermore, the reason they want to have the Galatians circumcised

---

192 Betz (*Galatians*, 263) notes that *pistis* functioning as a power is surprising. See also, Choi, "ΠΙΣΤΙΣ in Galatians 5:5–6," 482–89.
193 E.g., Martyn, *Galatians*, 565.

is so that they can boast in their flesh.[194] In contrast to the agitators, Paul notes that he himself will only boast in the cross of the Lord Jesus Christ, through which the cosmos has been crucified to him and he to the cosmos. Paul then makes the familiar declaration in 6:15: "For neither circumcision is anything, nor foreskin, but new creation."

When approaching Gal 6:15, it is important to note the context in which it occurs, specifically how 6:15 is connected to what precedes it in 6:14.[195] The first thing we must do when reading 6:15 is to establish the connection Paul makes between 6:14 and 6:15 through the conjunction γάρ. It seems most likely that Paul here uses γάρ in 6:15 in its basic sense to explain the cause or reason for his statement in 6:14.[196] If Paul is using the conjunction γάρ in this manner, we must then determine what Paul is using 6:15 to explain in 6:14. Is he using it to explain the main clause or the subordinate clause?[197] Does Paul use his negation of circumcision and foreskin, and his emphasis on new creation to explain his reason for boasting in the cross, or to explain the mutual crucifixion between the cosmos and himself? The subordinate clause, "through which the cosmos has been crucified to me and I to the cosmos," serves to lay out one of the results that is effected by the cross of Christ, so it does not seem plausible that Paul is using 6:15 to explain this sub-clause.[198] If 6:15 served to build on Paul and the cosmos' mutual crucifixion, one would expect to find οὖν rather than γάρ in 6:15, which would read thusly: "…through which the cosmos has been crucified to me and I to the cosmos. *Therefore*, neither circumcision is anything, nor foreskin…" Rather, in 6:15 we have γάρ, which serves to explain the main clause of 6:14, that is, why Paul only boasts in the cross of Christ. The reason that Paul only boasts in the cross of Christ is because circumcision and foreskin are both nothing, but new creation—full stop. While we have established the syntactic relationship between the two verses, the meaning of 6:15 is still slightly opaque.

---

194 Dunn (*Galatians*, 340) describes the fleshly boast of the agitators as a "(typically Jewish) attitude" that Paul was no longer able to share. This is unhelpful for a number of reasons, notably because the boast that Paul attributes to the agitators in not related to the agitators' flesh (i.e., their circumcised penises or ethnic origin), but the flesh of the Galatians ("boast in *your* flesh"; ἐν τῇ ὑμετέρᾳ σαρκὶ καυχήσωνται, Gal 6:13) As far as I am aware, there no evidence that points to Jews boasting in the flesh of circumcised converts. Here, Dunn incorrectly reads his ethnocentric depiction of Judaism into this text.
195 Jeff Hubing, *Crucifixion and New Creation: The Strategic Purpose of Galatians 6:11–17*, LNTS 508 (London: T&T Clark, 2015), 229–45.
196 BDF §452.
197 Hubing, *Crucifixion and New Creation*, 237.
198 Contra Martyn, *Galatians*, 565.

3.7 Are Circumcision and Foreskin Actually Nothing? Galatians 5:6 and 6:15

In Galatians, it is especially clear that circumcision and foreskin are not simply nothing for Paul. It seems unlikely that Paul would now conclude this letter—with his own pen (6:11)—stating that circumcision and foreskin are now nothing, as this could potentially be interpreted as undoing much of what he previously wrote. Since 6:15 serves to explain Paul's reason for boasting in the cross of Christ— and not in the flesh, like the agitators (6:13)—Paul's declaration that circumcision and foreskin are nothing should be interpreted as relating to their relevant merits as things to boast in.[199] That is, circumcision is nothing to boast in and neither is foreskin.[200] As was the case with 5:6, the inclusion of foreskin here may seem a bit unusual; who would boast in foreskin? Paul may simply have included it as the counterpart to circumcision, but there are two other possible explanations: 1) like the agitators who desired to boast in the circumcised flesh of the Galatians, Paul too could have been tempted to boast in the preservation of their foreskins as an accomplishment of his mission; or 2) in the Greco-Roman world, foreskin was valorized and an important aspect of the ideal penis and male body. It is possible that foreskinned Galatian males could have had cultural reasons for boasting in their foreskin over against circumcised Jews or judaized gentiles.[201]

Situating this verse within the context of boasting also helps us make sense of Paul's abrupt utterance, ἀλλὰ καινὴ κτίσις, "but new creation" (6:15). Like 1 Cor 7:19, Paul is here using the rhetoric of comparison[202] to demonstrate that—while circumcision and foreskin are not things to boast in—new creation *is* something to boast in.[203] This new creation corresponds to the cross of Christ and being in

---

[199] So Campbell, "'I Rate All things," 210–11. While Campbell rightly highlights the context of boasting in which this statement is made, his overall reading of this text focuses on the relative value of circumcision and foreskin in relationship to the cross and new creation.

[200] Alternatively, one could read circumcision and foreskin as metonymically referring to Jewish and non-Jewish identity, but given the context of this passage, it seems more probable that Paul is referring specifically to the practice of circumcision.

[201] On the value placed on penile aesthetics in the Greco-Roman world, see Hodges, "The Ideal Prepuce"; Blanton IV, "The Expressive Prepuce."

[202] Contra Martyn (*Galatians*, 565), who explicitly denies the possibility that Paul is speaking in comparative terms.

[203] It is possible to understand Paul's reference to new creation as representing the product of his mission. The agitators' desire was to boast in the circumcised flesh of their Galatian proselytes, which was the product of their fleshly mission. Paul's mission, however, resulted in new sons of Abraham being born through *pneuma*, which could be understood as being a new creation; at one point they were not sons of Abraham, but through their reception of Christ's *pneuma* they have become sons of Abraham (Gal 3:3, 29; 4:6, 21–31). On this interpretation, Paul is saying that the agitators wrongfully boast in what their mission produces, whereas Paul correctly boasts in what his mission produces. Though he comes to more traditional conclusions about the interpretation of Gal 6:15, John W. Yates (*The Spirit and Creation in Paul*, WUNT 2/251 [Tübingen: Mohr Sie-

Christ. As Paul writes in 2 Cor 5:17, "So if anyone is in Christ—new creation!"[204] Throughout his epistles Paul describes proper and improper boasting. In Romans, Galatians, 1 Corinthians, and Philippians—all of the Pauline epistles that deal with circumcision and foreskin in some manner—boasting in the flesh, in appearances, or in status is always excluded (Rom 2:17, 23; 4:2; 11:8; 1 Cor 1:29; 3:21; 4:7; 5:6; 13:3; Gal 6:13). In these epistles, boasting is confined to being in Christ, in God, in the Lord, in hope, in suffering, or in the faithfulness of the assembly (Rom 5:2–3, 11; 15:17; 1 Cor 1:31; 9:15–16; 15:31; Gal 6:14; Phil 1:26, 2:16; 3:3; cf. 1 Thess 2:19).[205] Of these boasting passages, Phil 3:3–8 offers a close parallel to 6:15. Here, Paul notes that his boast is in Christ and not in his fleshly pedigree despite it being pristine in every respect: "an eighth-day circumcision, from the race of Israel, of the tribe of Benjamin, a Hebrew born from Hebrews; as to the law, a Pharisee; as to zeal, a persecutor of the assembly; as to *dikaiosynē* in the law, blameless" (Phil 3:5–6). Although he has confidence in his flesh (Phil 3:4),[206] Paul only boasts in Christ and has come to consider *all* things as a loss in order to know and gain Christ (Phil 3:7–8). Paul's assessment of his own pedigree and of all things is that in comparison with Christ, they are to be regarded as loss. That is not to say that they are actually worthless, but within the rhetoric of comparison, Christ is exceedingly more profitable and something to boast in.[207]

Like 1 Cor 7:19 and Gal 5:6, Gal 6:15 should not be read as a standalone declaration that circumcision and foreskin are nothing, rather, read in its rhetorical and

---

beck, 2008], esp. 120–21) succinctly demonstrates the important connection between the *pneuma* and new creation.

204 This verse also appears in a wider context related to boasting in appearances (2 Cor 5:12) and knowing individuals "according to the flesh" (κατὰ σάρκα, 2 Cor 5:16).

205 The issue of boasting in 2 Corinthians is complex and outside the scope of this project. While boasting there does seem to follow the general schema Paul lays out in his other epistles, there are many perplexing texts as well. Notably, in a letter like 2 Corinthians where circumcision, foreskin, and the law are not issues, positive boasting is much more prevalent than his other epistles. I have also excluded Gal 6:4 from the aforementioned boasting texts. This is because positive boasting is presented here as being directed inward toward oneself and not outwardly toward others (καὶ τότε εἰς ἑαυτὸν μόνον τὸ καύχημα ἕξει καὶ οὐκ εἰς τὸν ἕτερον). This seems to be a different type of boasting altogether.

206 In Phil 3:4, Paul is almost universally translated as saying he has "*reason for* confidence in the flesh," but the text actually says he *does* have confidence in the flesh (καίπερ ἐγὼ ἔχων πεποίθησιν καὶ ἐν σαρκί). The interpretive tendency to include "reason for" seems to be a way to ensure that Paul does not contradict what he said in the previous verse: "...and have no confidence in the flesh" (καὶ οὐκ ἐν σαρκὶ πεποιθότες).

207 For a judicious study of Phil 3 and its relationship to these "neither...nor" statements, see Campbell, "'I Rate All Things'." See also, Rudolph, *Jew to the Jews*, 45; Novenson, "Did Paul Abandon," 247.

syntactical context, it serves to demonstrate why Paul only boasts in the cross of Christ. This is because circumcision and foreskin are not things to boast in, but new creation as effected by the cross of Christ is something to boast in. Paul uses this to set himself in contradistinction to the agitators based on what each party respectively boasts in. For the agitators, it is the flesh of the Galatian males, which seems to euphemistically refer to their foreskinned penises becoming circumcised.[208] Paul, however, states he only boast in the cross of Christ, because circumcision and foreskin are not things to be boasted in. This type of boasting is important for Paul, and he urges the Galatians to follow his model of boasting in the following verse: "And for anyone who follows this standard (τῷ κανόνι τούτῳ; i.e., boasting not in circumcision or foreskin, but in the cross and new creation), peace be upon them" (Gal 6:16a).[209]

3.8 Paul: Proclaimer of Circumcision? Galatians 5:11

Paul's claim in Gal 5:11 that he used to proclaim circumcision is a *crux interpretum* for scholars exploring Paul's relationship to circumcision: "But brothers, if I am still (ἔτι)[210] proclaiming circumcision, why am I still (ἔτι) being persecuted? If that is the case, the offense of the cross has been removed."[211] At what point in

---

208 Thus, Keener (*Galatians*, 285) writes, "Paul's depiction of the rivals' desire to show off in the flesh (Gal 6:12) now takes a grotesque turn: they want to boast in your flesh, i.e., the flesh of your sliced foreskins."
209 The majority of scholars rightly interpret τῷ κανόνι τούτῳ (6:16) as referring back to the content of 6:15; e.g., Dunn, *Galatians*, 343; Martyn, *Galatians*, 566–67.
210 For all of the interpretations below, an important crux is determining the use and function of the double ἔτι in 5:11. The presence of the ἔτι in the first clause is particularly difficult because it implies that Paul at one point proclaimed circumcision, something that we do not necessarily have straightforward evidence for. Due to the ambiguity surrounding Paul's previous proclamation of circumcision, some scribes and copyists decided to remove the first ἔτι from their manuscripts (D* F G 0278.6.1739. 1881 ar b vg^mss; Ambrosiaster). It is probable that the omission of ἔτι can be attributed to the difficulty it posed to interpreters when they attempted to determine when—or if—Paul previously proclaimed circumcision. It is preferable to take both occurrences of ἔτι as being original. For an in-depth discussion of this adverb in this text, see Donaldson, *Paul and the Gentiles*, 278–82.
211 While most interpreters agree that Paul is responding to specific claims made by the agitators about his prior or current proclamation of circumcision based on a mirror-reading of the passage, this does not have to be the case. On this point see, Justin K. Hardin, "'If I Still Proclaim Circumcision' (Galatians 5:11a): Paul, the Law, and Gentile Circumcision," *JSPL* 3 (2013): 145–63, at 153–54. Hardin argues that instead of Paul responding defensively to claims made by the agitators, he could be on the attack by constructing a "biographical foil to the agitators" (154).

Paul's life did he proclaim circumcision and to whom? Was this prior to his call to be the apostle to the gentiles or after? What constitutes proclaiming circumcision? There are generally five ways that interpreters have understood what Paul means by his previous proclamation of circumcision: 1) Paul proclaimed circumcision to Jews for a period of time after his call;[212] 2) The agitators understood that Paul was proclaiming a form of ethical circumcision, which inevitably encouraged the practice of physical circumcision;[213] 3) Paul is responding to a false charge the he occasionally proclaimed circumcision to gentiles when it was beneficial;[214] 4) Paul proclaimed circumcision to gentiles for a period of time after his call;[215] and 5) Paul proclaimed circumcision to gentiles before his call.[216]

3.8.1 Prevailing Perspectives

The first position—that Paul proclaimed circumcision to Jews at some point after his call—has been proposed by Francis Watson and James Dunn, albeit for different reasons. Watson argues that at the earliest stage of his gospel proclamation Paul only preached to Jews, which he argues is equivalent to proclaiming τὸ εὐαγγέλιον τῆς περιτομῆς (Gal 2:7)—i.e. proclaiming circumcision.[217] When Paul speaks about his halakhic principle of accommodation in 1 Cor 9:20–21, Watson argues that these do not represent concurrent realities, but a linear change in mission;

---

212 Dunn, *Galatians*, 279–80; Watson, *Paul, Judaism*, 28–31.
213 Peder Borgen, "Paul Preaches Circumcision and Pleases Men" in *Paul and Paulinism: Essays in Honour of C. K. Barrett*, ed. Morna D. Hooker and Stephen G. Wilson (London: SPCK, 1982), 37–46; idem, *Philo, John and Paul: New Perspectives on Judaism and Christianity*, BJS 131 (Atlanta: Scholars Press, 1987), 233–54.
214 Martyn, *Galatians*, 475–7.
215 Douglas Campbell, "Galatians 5.11: Evidence of an Early Law-Observant Mission by Paul?" *NTS* 57 (2011): 325–47; Joshua D. Garroway, *The Beginning of the Gospel: Paul, Philippi, and the Origins of Christianity* (Cham: Palgrave Macmillan, 2018), 9, 48–52.
216 Burton, *Galatians*, 286; Bruce, *Galatians*, 236; Longenecker, *Galatians*, 233; Donaldson, *Paul and the Gentiles*, 277–83; Blaschke, *Beschneidung*, 388; Thiessen, *Gentile Problem*, 37–41.
217 Here, Watson looks to 2 Cor 11:24 for support that Paul used to preach to Jews and therefore was subject to the authority of the synagogue. The fact that Paul was subject to synagogue punishment is not necessarily an indication that he was preaching exclusively to Jews, but that he still identified as a Jew and was considered by his coreligionists to still be a Jew. On synagogue punishment and the identity of Paul as a Jew, see Sanders, *Paul, the Law*, 192; Sven Gallas, "»Fünfmal vierzig weniger einen...«. Die an Paulus vollzogenen Synagogalstrafen nach 2Kor 11,24," *ZNW* 81 (1990): 178–91. Sanders comments, *"Punishment implies inclusion.* If Paul had considered that he had withdrawn from Judaism, he would not have attended synagogue. If the members of the synagogue had considered him an outsider, they would not have punished him" (*Paul, the Law*, 192).

Paul used to live as a Jew to win Jews, but once he broke with the Jewish way of life and Torah observance, he only saw himself as the apostle to the gentiles.[218] So while Paul used to proclaim circumcision to Jews when proclaiming the Messiah to them, he no longer does and only proclaims the Messiah to gentiles without circumcision. Dunn, however, focuses on 1 Cor 9:20–21 and the issue of consistency. If the agitators in Galatia knew that Paul proclaimed Jesus to Jews and allowed or encouraged them to continue to practice circumcision, then Paul's inconsistency could have led the agitators to accuse him of proclaiming circumcision.[219] Both of these perspectives are improbable. We do not have any evidence that Paul ever discouraged Jews from circumcising their sons. On the contrary—as demonstrated by 1 Cor 7:17–20—Paul encouraged circumcision and law observance amongst Jewish followers of Jesus. There does not seem to be a point at which he ever stopped promoting circumcision for Jews.[220] Since Paul seems emphatic that he no longer does the activity of proclaiming circumcision, this must refer to something other than affirming the necessity of circumcision amongst Jews. If he is being charged with inconsistency by the agitators, that is not what Paul is responding to here.

The second interpretive option belongs to Peder Borgen. Borgen argues that Paul's preaching against pagan immorality—as typified by his various references to the flesh (σάρξ; Gal 5:13, 16, 17, 19, 24)—was interpreted by the agitators as encouraging ethical—and therefore physical—circumcision.[221] Borgen primarily draws on Philo's interpretation of what circumcision signifies and accomplishes for an individual. Throughout his writings on circumcision, Philo consistently argues that circumcision physically accomplishes the excision of excessive desire and sexual impulses from men, and also metaphorically portrays this excision (*Migration* 92; *Spec. Laws* 1.9–11; 1.305; *QG* 3.46–52; cf. Origen, *Hom. Gen.* 3.6).[222] Philo

---

[218] Watson, *Paul, Judaism*, 29.
[219] Dunn (*Galatians*, 279–80) also notes that if the agitators were aware of Acts 16:3 and the circumcision of Timothy, they could have also used this as evidence that Paul proclaimed circumcision.
[220] Watson's argument that Paul originally only proclaimed Jesus to Jews is also dubious; see Campbell, "Galatians 5.11," 338–9.
[221] Borgen, "Paul Preaches Circumcision," 38. Borgen's view has also been adopted by Timo Laato, *Paul and Judaism: An Anthropological Approach*, SFSHJ 115 (Atlanta: Scholars Press, 1995), 172–76.
[222] This interpretation of circumcision did not gain much traction in the ancient world, however, it was proposed a millennium later in the teaching of Maimonides (*The Guide of the Perplexed* 3.49). On Philo, Maimonides, and the ethical effect of circumcision, see Shaye J. D. Cohen, *Jewish Women*, 61–64, 144–54. On Maimonides and circumcision specifically, see Josef Stern, "Maimonides on the Covenant of Circumcision and the Unity of God," in *The Midrashic Imagination: Jewish Exegesis*,

understood that circumcision must be applied to both the foreskin of the penis and also the mind and heart. He was also critical of Jews who rightly perceived the ethical (i.e., true) meaning of circumcision, but abandoned the physical practice (*Migration* 89–93); one cannot divorce the ethical meaning of the act from the act itself. Borgen argues that the agitators are Philonic Jews who believed that Paul was preaching ethical circumcision and therefore physical circumcision as well. They did not necessarily see themselves as being Paul's opponents, rather they understood themselves as completing the work that Paul started; solidifying the Galatian's ethical circumcision by means of physical circumcision.[223] For Borgen, this could explain why in Gal 3:3 Paul says, "Having started with *pneuma* are you now completing it in the flesh?"[224]

While Borgen's interpretation rightly highlights the existence of non-literal interpretations of circumcision amongst some ancient Jews, his argument is ultimately unpersuasive for a few reasons.[225] Based on his mirror-reading of the passage, Borgen argues that the agitators' claim that Paul ever proclaimed circumcision is false, however, the use of the double ἔτι ("still") in 5:11 indicates otherwise.[226] Here, Paul concedes that at one time he proclaimed circumcision. If he simply wanted to deny that he ever proclaimed circumcision and that this accusation is a misunderstanding, he would not have employed the first ἔτι. Borgen's presentation that Paul denied preaching ethical circumcision seems unlikely based on what Paul says elsewhere in Galatians about circumcision. From the wider context of Galatians, Paul only discusses circumcision in the physical sense and as it pertains to Jewish identity; it would be unusual for him to switch to an assumed ethical meaning of the phrase without indicating otherwise.[227] Given that the entire insertion of ethical circumcision into Borgen's discussion is based on a mirror-reading that identifies the agitators as Philonic Jews who misconstrued Paul's message about overcoming aspects of the flesh via the *pneuma* as referring to preach-

---

Thought, and History, ed. Michael Fishbane (Albany: State University of New York Press, 1993), 131–54.

223 Borgen, "Paul Preaches Circumcision," 39–40.

224 In the wider context of Gal, 3:3 seems to be a reference to how one receives Abrahamic sonship (3:14, 29; 4:28–29), not how one excises the desires of the flesh (see Thiessen, *Gentile Problem*, 129–36).

225 In addition to Philo, he also highlights this view in 1QpHab 11:13 and 1QS 5:5–6; cf. Jub. 1:22–24.

226 Borgen, *Paul Preaches Circumcision*, 41, 44.

227 Notably, the concept of ethical circumcision does not feature elsewhere in Paul's epistles. While he does make a reference to pneumatic heart circumcision in Rom 2:29, the argument there is about Jewish identity and receiving praise from God, not the ethical meaning of circumcision.

ing ethical circumcision, this argument seems implausible.²²⁸ This mirror-reading is excessive and relies more on reconstructing what the agitators' may have said and believed about a misinterpretation of Paul's message, rather than focusing on what Paul himself says in the text.

The third view has been most prominently proposed by J. Louis Martyn.²²⁹ His reading of Gal 5:11 hinges on how he translates the adverb ἔτι in 5:11a. Here, he does not translate it temporally ("still"), but additively ("additionally"), so that the idea Paul is arguing against is that he occasionally adds circumcision to his gospel message when preaching to gentiles when it suits him.²³⁰ Martyn paraphrases 5:11a thusly: "If, on occasion, I am preaching, as part of the gospel message, that one should be circumcised..." and "If I were on occasion advocating circumcision of Gentile converts..."²³¹ The logic of Paul's argument is that if he occasionally proclaims circumcision, then he should not be being persecuted and he has removed the offense of the cross, but he has never proclaimed circumcision on occasion to gentiles and therefore he is being persecuted and affirms the offense of the cross. While this interpretation solves a key problem with this text, it also creates another. Importantly, this reading removes the ambiguity around when Paul might have proclaimed circumcision and the possibility that he ever did. By denying the fact that he ever occasionally proclaimed circumcision, the interpretation removes the burden from readers to try to determine the elusive point in Paul's career when he did proclaim circumcision. The crucial problem with this reading that renders it unlikely is its grammatical improbability. If one renders the first ἔτι additively, then one would expect the second ἔτι in the following clause to be rendered similarly, but this translation does not make sense.²³² It does not seem likely that Paul would have used ἔτι with two starkly different meanings in the same sentence.

---

228 To be sure, in Gal 5:13–26 Paul links possession of divine *pneuma* with the ability to overcome the desires of the flesh, but in that context he makes no reference to ethical or pneumatic circumcision. See Campbell, "Galatians 5.11," 334n31.
229 Similarly, Mußner, *Galaterbrief*, 358–59.
230 Robinson ("The Circumcision of Titus," 37–38) argues that while Paul may have allowed for gentiles to be circumcised in some instances, it was not a part of his gospel proclamation, and therefore he could deny the charge that he proclaimed circumcision.
231 Martyn, *Galatians*, 575–77.
232 This would be translated as: "If I am on occasion proclaiming circumcision, why am I on occasion/additionally being persecuted?" Martyn (*Galatians*, 476) concedes that this poses a problem for his translation and interpretation, but he concludes that his translation solves more problems than it creates.

The fourth position has been recently espoused by Douglas Campbell and Joshua Garroway.[233] They argue that there was a period after Paul's call to be the apostle to the gentiles in which he included circumcision and Torah observance for gentiles.[234] Douglas Campbell highlights the possibility of theological and missiological development in Paul's thought; arguing that at an earlier stage in Paul's ministry he proclaimed circumcision—and Torah observance—but after he realized this was ineffective with a gentile constituency, Paul removed the necessity of circumcision. Campbell argues that like many modern missionaries, Paul learned to contextualize his message for a gentile audience and eventually removed the need for circumcision from his gospel. His argument rests less on positive evidence from exegetical data and more on the example of various missionaries whose ministries and beliefs evolved over time based on their experiences. This supposedly renders his reading as a viable possibility.[235] Joshua Garroway argues that a similar development occurred in Paul's thought and that some of the earliest Jewish followers of Jesus saw the invitation for gentiles to follow Jesus as an invitation to be circumcised and join Judaism.[236] Based on Gal 5:11 and Phil 4:15 ("...the beginning of the gospel..."), Garroway claims that while after Paul's initial call he proclaimed Christ (Gal 1:16) and proclaimed faith (Gal 1:23), he did not actually proclaim the (circumcision-free) gospel until his second revelation, which he recounts in Gal 1:11–12.[237] After this second revelation, Paul came to understand that gentiles who were baptized into Christ did not need to be circumcised; up until that point, Paul proclaimed circumcision alongside Christ (cf. Acts 15:1–5).[238]

A key problem with this view is that Paul does not seem to indicate that his understanding of his calling to be the apostle to the gentiles ever changed over

---

[233] This position is briefly suggested by Alan F. Segal, *Paul the Convert: The Apostolate and Apostasy of Saul the Pharisee* (New Haven: Yale University Press, 1990), 332n1.

[234] This view was advocated in some late nineteenth-century and early twentieth-century scholarship, but never gained much mainstream traction. For a brief list of older expositions of this view, see Campbell, "Galatians 5.11," 340n40. See also, Mimouni (*La circoncision*, 218), who proposes this view alongside the view that Paul was possibly a Pharisaic missionary prior to his call.

[235] A core assertion that Campbell makes is that one of the key reasons people are averse to this reading rests on the fact that it would mean Paul was inconsistent and interpreters—particularly Lutheran ones—have found this embarrassing ("Galatians 5.11," 341–47). Campbell comments: "But I suggest that this very embarrassment within the tradition attests to the probably truth *of* this reading" ("Galatians 5.11," 344; emphasis original). For the most complete argument against Campbell's post-call reading of Gal 5:11, see Hardin, "'If I Still Proclaim.'"

[236] Garroway, *Beginning of the Gospel*, 6.

[237] On Garroway's reading, the first place where Paul actually proclaimed the gospel is Philippi; prior to that, Paul was just proclaiming Christ—which is somehow different than the gospel (*Beginning of the Gospel*, 45–52).

[238] Garroway, *Beginning of the Gospel*, 11, 45–58.

time—though it is possible that he might not have admitted this if it were the case. To be sure, Paul's thought likely developed—as is expected with any individual—but that he drastically altered his core message to gentiles seems unlikely. Garroway offers a more substantial argument than Campbell, focusing on how Paul employs the verb εὐαγγελίζομαι and its cognate noun εὐαγγέλιον throughout his epistles. He notes that in all but four occurrences of Paul's use of εὐαγγελίζομαι, the verb has no object, or the implied object is "the gospel."[239] Of the four instances where εὐαγγελίζομαι has an object, only two of them actually refer to the act of proclaiming: Gal 1:16 and 1:23. Garroway posits that since the object or implied object in these instances is not the gospel, this indicates that Paul was proclaiming something other than the gospel, namely Christ and faith. While Garroway's reading interprets the data in creative ways, it is not fully compelling. Notably, Garroway fails to mention how "the gospel of Christ" (τὸ εὐαγγέλιον τοῦ Χριστοῦ, Gal 1:7) fits into his framework. If Paul is proclaiming Christ (1:16), what would be he proclaiming other than the good news of Christ (i.e., τὸ εὐαγγέλιον)?[240] Garroway's underdevelopment of what proclaiming Christ and proclaiming faith entail raises the question of how they are substantially different from "proclaiming the gospel." Despite Garroway's meticulous parsing of how Paul uses εὐαγγελίζομαι, Gal 1:11–2:10 does not seem to indicate that Paul ever changed the content of his message. While he does admit to a change of heart based on his previous ways in *Ioudaismos*, he does not indicate that his message to gentiles ever changed.[241]

---

239 Garroway, *Beginning of the Gospel*, 54. There are 17 instances of εὐαγγελίζομαι in the uncontested letters of Paul: Rom 1:15; 15:20; 1 Cor 1:17; 9:16, 18; 15:1, 2; 2 Cor 10:16; 11:7; Gal 1:8, 9, 11; 4:13.
240 If Paul argues that proclaiming circumcision implies that the offense of the cross has been removed, then if Paul was proclaiming Christ alongside circumcision, would this mean that Paul proclaimed Christ without the cross? Garroway does not tease out this implication of his argument.
241 Both Campbell ("Galatians 5.11," 344–45) and Garroway (*Beginning of the Gospel*, 50) place a great deal of importance on the idea that if Paul is responding to a claim from the agitators, his response that he no longer proclaims circumcision only has rhetorical weight if it refers to a period of time after his call. "For their accusation to have held esteem among the Galatians, so much so that Paul felt obligated to refute it, the opponents *must* have alleged that Paul advocated circumcision for Gentiles at some point after his turn to Christ" (Garroway, *Beginning of the Gospel*, 50; emphasis added). This, however, does not have to be the case. Any prior proclamation of circumcision by Paul could have been sufficient ammunition for the agitators to charge Paul as preaching circumcision. If one removes the mirror from their reading, it is possible that Paul simply denies the charge that he is still proclaiming circumcision because he is acknowledging his former ways and demonstrating that they are incompatible with the offense of the cross. Or as Justin Hardin has noted ("If I Still Proclaim," 153), it is also possible that Paul is on the attack and by separating himself from the act of proclaiming circumcision he is arguing against the folly of the agitators' message.

The final and most prominent view is that at one point prior to his call to be the apostle to the gentiles—in his "pre-Christian past"[242]—Paul proclaimed the necessity of circumcision to gentiles who wanted to become Jews.[243] While it is highly unlikely that Paul was acting in any official missionary capacity where he was actively converting gentile pagans to Judaism, recent supporters of this perspective highlight the possibility that Paul was open to gentile converts to Judaism.[244] Arguing for this interpretation of Gal 5:11, Terence Donaldson highlights presence of openness toward gentile proselytes in Jewish thought.[245] Donaldson gives the example of Eleazar from Josephus' account of the conversion of Izates of Adiabene (*Ant.* 20.34–48) as a possible model for what Paul's former proclamation of circumcision may have looked like.[246] Eleazar strictly held the traditions of his ancestors and urged Izates to undergo circumcision if he wanted to become a proselyte (*Ant.* 20.43). It is not simply that Eleazar was open to proselytes, but he urged those who were contemplating converting to undergo circumcision. Paul, too, strictly held the traditions of his ancestors (Gal 1:13–14) and seemed to be involved in some kind of circumcising activity (Gal 5:11), so—for Donaldson—it is possible that Eleazar's and Paul's prior actions were analogous.

Justin Hardin and Matthew Thiessen rightly note that Paul leaves us a helpful piece of biographical data in Gal 1:13–14 that can help us understand Paul's former proclamation of circumcision.[247] Here, Paul refers to his previous involvement in *Ioudaismos*: "For you have heard of my former conduct in Ἰουδαϊσμῷ, that I was

---

242 Blaschke, *Beschneidung*, 388.
243 E.g., Burton, *Galatians*, 286; Longenecker, *Galatians*, 233; Witherington, *Grace in Galatia*, 372–74; Sanders, *Paul*, 553; Fredriksen, *Pagans' Apostle*, 126, 164.
244 There is no evidence that attests to the idea that ancient Judaism was a missionary religion, especially in any modern sense of the idea of a missionary. For the—now classic—arguments against ancient Judaism as a missionary religion, see Scot McKnight, *A Light Among the Gentiles: Jewish Missionary Activity in the Second Temple Period* (Minneapolis: Fortress, 1991); Martin Goodman, *Mission and Conversion: Proselytizing in the Religious History of the Roman Empire* (Oxford: Clarendon, 1996). See also Munck, *Paul and the Salvation*, 264–71; Paula Fredriksen, "Judaism, the Circumcision of Gentiles, and Apocalyptic Hope: Another Look at Galatians 1 and 2," *JTS* 42 (1991): 532–64, at 537–40; eadem, *Pagans' Apostle*, 211n18. Against this, Hans Hübner argues that Paul's proclamation of circumcision combined with his former activity in Gal 1:13–14 points in the direction that Paul was a Jewish missionary that promoted the circumcision of gentiles ("Gal 3,10 und die Herkunft des Paulus," *KD* 19 [1973]: 215–31, at 222).
245 Donaldson (*Paul and the Gentiles*, 275) notes the presence of this motif in Tannaitic material (t. Sanh. 13:2; b. 'Abod. Zar. 3b; b. Yeb. 24b; Pesiq. Rab. 161a) which could suggest that this idea was present among the Pharisees. For Donaldson's fullest treatment of the various ways that gentiles were able to relate to ancient Judaism, see Donaldson, *Judaism and the Gentiles*, 467–513.
246 Donaldson, *Paul and the Gentiles*, 276–77.
247 Hardin, "If I Still Proclaim," 150; Thiessen, *Gentile Problem*, 38–41.

exceedingly pursuing the assembly of God and destroying it. And I was advancing in *Ioudaismos* beyond many of the contemporaries in my nation, being exceedingly zealous for the traditions of my ancestors" (Gal 1:13–14). While translators have almost been unanimous in their translation of Ἰουδαϊσμός as "Judaism" (i.e., the ancestral religion of Jews), the ground-breaking work of Steve Mason has challenged this standard translation.²⁴⁸ Mason argues that *Ioudaismos* does not refer to Judaism, but that "[t]he Greek –ισμός noun represents in nominal form the ongoing action of the cognate verb in –ίζω."²⁴⁹ Therefore, the meaning of Ἰουδαϊσμός is dependent on the meaning of ἰουδαΐζω ("to judaize," "to adopt the Jewish way of life") and conveys the idea of judaization (i.e., the promotion of the Jewish way of life among non-Jews).²⁵⁰ So from this understanding of *Ioudaismos*, in Gal 1:13–14 Paul does not recount his former ways in a religion called Judaism, but his former occupation as one who promoted the Jewish way of life—notably circumcision—amongst non-Jews.²⁵¹ Both Hardin and Thiessen identify Paul's former occupation in *Ioudaismos* with his proclamation of circumcision in Gal 5:11, indicating that he previously promoted circumcision—and therefore conversion—amongst non-Jews.²⁵²

---

248 Steve Mason, "Jews, Judaeans, Judaizing, Judaism: Problems of Categorization in Ancient History," *JSJ* 38 (2007): 457–512. On the standard translation of Ἰουδαϊσμός as "Judaism," see the classic article by Yehoshua Amir, "The Term Ἰουδαϊσμός (*IOUDAISMOS*), A Study in Jewish-Hellenistic Self-Identification," *Imm* 14 (1982): 34–41.
249 Mason, "Jews, Judaeans, Judaizing, Judaism," 461.
250 On the meaning of –ίζω verbs, see Cohen, *Beginnings of Jewishness*, 175–80. Here, Cohen demonstrates that –ίζω verbs with an ethnic root indicate the adoption of ethnic practices by a foreigner. It does not refer to the activity of those within the particular ethnic group, but to those outside of it who are adopting a particular set of ethnic practices. So in the case of ἰουδαΐζω ("to judaize"), only a non-Jew can do this, in the same way that a Greek cannot hellenize, but only a non-Greek can. See also, Murray, *Playing a Jewish Game*, 3–4; Mason, "Jews, Judaeans, Judaizing, Judaism," 460–70.
251 This promotion is not to be confused with missionary activity amongst non-Jews. Rather, as noted above by Donaldson, this refers to the acceptance of gentile proselytes and affirming the necessity of circumcision for them.
252 While both Hardin and Thiessen come to similar conclusions about the meaning of Paul's former proclamation of circumcision—that he previously promoted the adoption of circumcision and the Jewish way of life amongst non-Jews—they disagree about precisely what *Ioudaismos* means. Thiessen closely follows the definition of *Ioudaismos* espoused by Mason, which leads him to conclude that "Galatians 1:13–14 and 5:11, therefore, suggest that Paul at one point in his past preached circumcision and the necessity of conversion to gentiles" (*Gentile Problem*, 41). Hardin, however, follows the meaning of *Ioudaismos* proposed by Matthew Novenson (see discussion below), and situates Paul's promotion of circumcision within the context of protecting the purity of Judaism. For Hardin, when Paul speaks of proclaiming circumcision, then, he is referring to his former way in defending Judaism through guarding the law by promoting the circumcision of would-be

3.8.2 A New Proposal

The assumption that undergirds the majority of interpretations of Paul's former activity in Gal 5:11 is that "proclaiming circumcision" (κηρύσσω περιτομήν) means that at some point Paul encouraged or condoned the circumcision of non-Jews. Donaldson's interpretation of this phrase is representative: "For in the context of Galatians, 'preaching circumcision' *means* insisting that Gentiles be circumcised if they want to be members of Abraham's family."[253] This interpretation makes two crucial assumptions: 1) that at one point, Paul thought non-Jews could become Jews in order to be included in Abraham's family, and 2) that circumcision was an effective means for bringing about this change.[254] To proclaim the necessity or importance of circumcision, however, is not necessarily an open invitation for foreskinned non-Jews to adopt circumcision.[255] Rather, it could be understood as

---

gentile proselytes ("If I Still Proclaim," 149–51). On this point, Hardin cites his previous work on what it means to guard the law (Justin K. Hardin, *Galatians and the Imperial Cult*, WUNT 2/237 [Tübingen: Mohr Siebeck, 2008], 88–89). There, Hardin understands that guarding the law (νόμον φυλάσσουσιν; Gal 6:13) refers to preserving the law from being disregarded by gentiles. It does not refer to the agitators' law observance, but to "zeal for preserving Torah by having gentiles circumcised" (89). Others who have tried to read Paul as remaining within Judaism, yet still translate Ἰουδαϊσμός as "Judaism," have come up with various solutions to the problem this creates. For example, David Rudolph (*A Jew to the Jews*, 44–45) attempts to read *Ioudaismos* as a particular type of Judaism. Paul's former occupation in *Ioudaismos* refers to his right-wing Pharisaic past, which has now be replaced by his present occupation in "the Way" or "the Nazarenes" sect of Judaism (Acts 9:2; 19:23; 24:5, 14, 22; 28:22).

253 Donaldson, *Paul and the Gentiles*, 270 (emphasis original).

254 One of the main disadvantages of Thiessen's interpretation of Gal 5:11 is that—within the context of his broader arguments about Paul and circumcision—he implies that Paul's halakhah on circumcision actually became more stringent after his *apocalypsis* of Jesus (Gal 1:12, 16). Thiessen (*Gentile Problem*, 40–41) proposes that prior to this *apocalypsis*, Paul thought that proselyte circumcision was effective for conversion and could remedy the gentile problem. After it, however, Paul recognized that circumcision could not bring about the required genealogical change for gentiles and came to believe only eighth-day circumcision was valid. Though not impossible, this shift in thinking seems unlikely. While religious experiences can lead someone to be more stringent in their understanding of religious praxis/law, as I argue below, the way Paul presents his former life in *Ioudaismos* seems to be quite legally rigorous and would also exclude the possibility of gentile inclusion (via circumcision or otherwise). It is possible that the individuals in Acts 15:1 who state that one must be circumcised in accordance with the custom of Moses (τῷ ἔθει τῷ Μωϋσέως) in order to be saved can be understood as promoting something similar. If one views eight-day circumcision as necessary, then there is no reason to even bother with non-Jews.

255 Paul's proclamation of circumcision does not necessarily mean that he encouraged the adoption of the practice by non-Jews. Proclaiming (κηρύσσω) is not always indicative of announcing a message that the proclaimer wants their audience to adopt, but is simply the public declaration or heralding of something (e.g. Xenophon, *Cyr.* 8.4.4; OG Jonah 1:2; Matt 10:27; Mark 5:20; Luke 12:3; Rev

excluding the foreskinned. Contrary to Donaldson, proclaiming circumcision could mean proclaiming that *only* the circumcised (i.e., Jews) are members of Abraham's family or the people of God.[256] In the context of Paul's larger argument in Galatians and his emphasis on Abrahamic sonship, this reading is worth exploring.

Throughout Paul's letters, circumcision does not always refer to the practice itself, but rather, it can refer to a class of people (i.e., Jews/Israel; Rom 3:30; 4:9; 15:8; 1 Cor 7:17–19; Phil 3:3; cf. Eph 2:11; Col 3:11) and in Galatians, Paul has already referred to circumcision as a metonymy for Jews (2:7–9, 12).[257] It is possible, then, that Paul's proclamation of circumcision does not refer to the promotion of circumcision amongst non-Jews, but the promotion of Jewish identity or the Jewish people as typified by circumcision.[258] If Paul had been proclaiming that non-Jews should be circumcised, one would expect him to use a verbal form like περιτέμνεσθαι or περιτέμνεσθε, not the noun περιτομή (cf. Acts 15:24 *varia lectio*: λέγοντες περιτέμνεσθαι). As is discussed above, if we situate Paul within the stream of Judaism which affirms that eighth-day circumcision is the only kind of valid circumcision, then proselyte circumcision is excluded. Further, this perspective also highlights the impossibility that circumcision is able to effect the genealogical change to make a non-Jew into a Jew; that is, circumcision is not a rite of initiation or conversion, but a confirmatory marker of Abrahamic lineage.[259]

5:2). Alternatively, if one interprets κηρύσσω as implying the adoption of the message proclaimed, it could be argued that Paul was proclaiming a message stating that circumcision was the only means of inclusion amongst the people of God. This does not necessarily imply that Paul was going around encouraging non-Jewish men to excise their foreskins but can be interpreted as Paul proclaiming a strict halakhah on circumcision and Jewish identity to less stringent Jews who welcomed in gentiles with open arms. Both Watson (*Paul, Judaism*, 30) and Campbell ("Galatians 5.11," 337n34) assert that κηρύσσω is a technical term that implies proclamation in an apostolic capacity, but this is an overstatement.

256 Thiessen (*Gentile Problem*, 23–24) notes that the impossibility of gentile inclusion in the people of God was a live option for some Second Temple Jews.

257 While Paul typically employs the article when using circumcision to refer to a class of people, in 5:11 it is anarthrous. Paul also uses circumcision anarthrously in Rom 3:30 and Rom 15:8 to refer to a class of people. On using anarthrous nouns to refer to classes or groups of people, see Smyth §1129, BDF §262, Heinrich von Siebenthal, *Ancient Greek Grammar for the Study of the New Testament* (Oxford: Peter Lang, 2019), §134c.

258 Hardin's interpretation of proclaiming circumcision shares elements of this view, but still includes and highlights proselyte circumcision within its meaning. For him, proclaiming circumcision means "that circumcision was not optional for Jews or for would-be proselytes" ("If I Still Proclaim," 152n22). Hardin also links the proclamation of circumcision with the fulfillment of Torah; i.e., that Torah can be summed up by the requirement of circumcision (151–52).

259 Christiansen, *Covenant in Judaism and Paul*, 41.

Notably, Paul juxtaposes his previous proclamation of circumcision and the offense of the cross (τὸ σκάνδαλον τοῦ σταυροῦ). If he was still proclaiming circumcision, then this would be tantamount to removing the offense of the cross. But what is this offense? Various proposals have been made,[260] but given the context of this passage and the broader discussion of gentile inclusion in Galatians as a whole, the offense of the cross likely has something to do with the acceptance and incorporation of gentiles into the people of God as gentiles.[261] When Paul was proclaiming that only the circumcision (i.e., natural born Jews) could be seed of Abraham, he rejected the offense of the cross. Now that he embraces the cross and boasts in it (Gal 6:14), he rejects his former proclamation that Abrahamic sonship was only available to the circumcision and now believes that Abrahamic sonship is also available to gentiles through the work of the Messiah. Paul also links circumcision and the cross with persecution. Whereas he currently receives persecution because of his embrace of the cross and abandonment of his proclamation of circumcision, the agitators are compelling the Galatians to be circumcised—which is different from, but adjacent to Paul's prior activity—in order to avoid the persecution associated with embracing the cross (Gal 6:12).

If this proposal is correct—that Paul's prior proclamation of circumcision refers to an exclusionary stance on gentile participation in the people of God—is there any evidence of this kind of proclaiming activity? If Paul proclaimed circumcision in this manner, what would this have entailed? Here, like Hardin and Thiessen have proposed, the answer is found in Gal 1:13–14 and Paul's former occupation in *Ioudaismos*. While Hardin and Thiessen conclude that the circumcision of non-Jews was a component of Paul's former occupation in *Ioudaismos*, this is un-

---

[260] The most common proposal is that the offense of the cross has something to do with crucifixion itself (Keener, *Galatians*, 240; deSilva, *Galatians*, 439). On this point it is commonly assumed that the notion of a crucified Messiah was offensive to Jews because it would demonstrate that he was cursed by God (Gal 3:13; cf. Deut 21:21; 1 Cor 1:23). This view, however, falls short for a number of reasons. First, it fails to take into account the contrast that Paul sets up between proclaiming circumcision and the offense of the cross. How would proclaiming circumcision invalidate the scandal of an accursed Messiah? Second, Fredriksen (*Pagans' Apostle*, 83–84) has demonstrated how baseless this claim actually is in ancient Jewish thought. Outside of Paul's reference in Gal 3:13 —which functions within the rhetorical chiasm of blessing and curse in Gal 3:10–14—we have no evidence of the existence of the connection between crucifixion and being accursed in ancient Judaism. Other common proposals focus on the cross in contrast to Judaism. On these readings, the cross has done away with Torah and works righteousness (de Boer, *Galatians*, 323–24) or has made the Jewish religion obsolete (Martyn, *Galatians*, 477) and is therefore offensive to Jews. These views, however, rely on outmoded and faulty conceptions of ancient Judaism and should be rejected.
[261] Though they do not phrase it this way, Dunn (*Galatians*, 281) and Oakes (*Galatians*, 165) both highlight the fact that while the offense may have something to do with a crucified Messiah, the main referent of the offense relates to the status of gentiles in the divine economy.

likely to be the case.²⁶² Contrary to the important proposal made by Mason, Matthew Novenson has argued that *Ioudaismos* does not refer to the practice of promoting the judaization of non-Jews, but that it refers to "the defense and promotion of Jewish customs by Jewish people" or "a cause, a political movement, a program of activism. It is not the ancestral religion itself, it is one's party program for defending the ancestral religion."²⁶³ As typified by its origin and use in 2 Maccabees (2:21; 8:1; 14:38; cf. 4 Macc 4:26), *Ioudaismos* refers to the defense and practice of Jewish ancestral traditions by *some* Jews—not all Jews—because it is not the name of the Jewish religion, but an activist movement.²⁶⁴

---

262 The way Paul speaks about gentile judaization and circumcision in Galatians does not support this interpretation of *Ioudaismos*. In Gal 2:3, 2:14, and 6:12, Paul refers to compelling or forcing circumcision and judaization upon non-Jews, but in none of these instances does Paul refer to those imposing circumcision and judaization as operating within *Ioudaismos* as he formerly did. If—as Thiessen proposes—Paul's past activity in *Ioudaismos* was equivalent to what Paul charges Cephas with (2:14) or what the agitators were actively doing amongst the Galatians (6:12), then why does Paul not use the language of *Ioudaismos* to describe their behavior? Outside of describing his own previous activity in Gal 1:13–14, *Ioudaismos* does not appear elsewhere in his writings or the New Testament. If Paul is seeking to draw a contrast between himself and those encouraging circumcision and full-on gentile judaization, then comparing his past activity in *Ioudaismos* and their present activity in *Ioudaismos* would be rhetorically beneficial. For Paul, however, this type of activity is not a component of *Ioudaismos*. Whenever Paul speaks in Galatians of the compelled adoption of Jewish practices by non-Jews he never speaks of *Ioudaismos*, instead he uses a form of ἀναγκάζω plus an accompanying verb (περιτέμνω or ἰουδαΐζω) to convey the activity that was being encouraged. Like Paul, when referring to forced or coerced circumcision, Ptolemy also used ἀναγκάζω plus περιτέμνω (*GLAJJ*, 1:356). Additionally, based on his reading of 1 Macc 2:46 in light of the use of *Ioudaismos* in 2 and 4 Maccabees, Thiessen (*Gentile Problem*, 40) proposes that *Ioudaismos* included encouraging or forcing circumcision upon non-Jews. This understanding of the circumcising activity in 1 Macc 2:46, however, has been convincingly refuted by Isaac T. Soon, "'In Strength' Not 'by Force': Re-Reading the Circumcision of the Uncircumcised ἐν ἰσχύι in 1 Macc 2:46," *JSP* 29 (2020): 149–67.

263 Matthew V. Novenson, "Paul's Former Occupation in *Ioudaismos*," in *Galatians and Christian Theology: Justification, the Gospel, and Ethics in Paul's Letters*, ed. Mark W. Elliot et al. (Grand Rapids: Baker Academic, 2014), 33, 34–35. See also Elias J. Bickerman, *The God of the Maccabees: Studies on the Meaning and Origin of the Maccabean Revolt*, trans. Horst R. Moehring, SJLA 32 (Leiden: Brill, 1979), cited by Novenson; Lionel J. Windsor, *Paul and the Vocation of Israel: How Paul's Jewish Identity Informs his Apostolic Ministry, with Special Reference to Romans*, BZNW 205 (Berlin: de Gruyter, 2014), 89–90; Daniel Boyarin, "*Ioudaismos* within Paul: A Modified Reading of Gal 1:13–14," in Ábel, *Message of Paul*, 167–78.

264 Novenson notes that according to 2 Maccabees, Ἰουδαϊσμός is "what Jews who reject Hellenization do," "what zealous Jews do," or " what manly Jews do" ("Paul's Former Occupation," 34). In the ancient world there was no one term that is equivalent to what we would refer to as "Judaism." He (35) rightly highlights that when speaking about Jewish religion, culture, and praxis, ancient authors would do so by using the standard vocabulary of laws (νόμοι), customs (ἔθη), traditions

Paul's advancement in *Ioudaismos* as a zealous defender and protector of Jewish identity and praxis (cf. Phil 3:5–6)—which was typified by eighth-day circumcision—caused him to oppose the Christ-assembly for its open acceptance of gentile members.[265] Here, Paul describes himself as acting within a Maccabean-like partisan program that grew out of his zeal for his ancestral traditions (cf. 1 Macc 2:27).[266] In Paul's mind, the practice of full gentile inclusion in the assembly was a rejection of his conviction that only the circumcision were members of the people of God. Thus, Paul's proclamation of circumcision was made manifest in his opposition to the assembly when he was advancing in his career in *Ioudaismos*. Notably, after Paul recounts his former occupation in *Ioudaismos*, he contrasts his past persecution of the assembly with his calling to proclaim the good news of the Messiah to gentiles (Gal 1:15–16). He went from a proclaimer of circumcision and enactor of persecution based on his exclusionary policy toward gentiles, to a proclaimer of the good news to gentiles.[267]

3.9 "Cutting Off" The Agitators: Galatians 5:12

While there is no explicit reference to circumcision in Gal 5:12, the echo of circumcision from the preceding passages reverberates up through this text. Here, Paul's polemic against the agitators and their imposition of circumcision reaches its crescendo: "I wish that the ones unsettling you would cut themselves off."

(παραδόσεις), ancestral ways (πάτρια), etc., but they never do so by using Ἰουδαϊσμός. On this point, see also Fredriksen, *Pagans' Apostle*, 35–36. For examples of this in ancient works, see Plato, *Leg.* 959b; Josephus, *Ant.* 4.139; 20.100; Philo, *Spec. Laws*, 2.13; 2 Macc 6:1; 7:2, 37; 4 Macc 4:23; 5:33; Acts 6:14; 15:1; 28:17; Gal 1:14.

265 Cf. James D. G. Dunn, *The Parting of the Ways: Between Christianity and Judaism and Their Significance for the Character of Christianity*, rev. ed. (London: SCM, 2006), 158–60.

266 Esther Kobel—building off of the work of Novenson—comments that Paul's activity in Ἰουδαϊσμός should be understood as his adherence to a partisan program within Pharisaism that focused on the preservation of his paternal traditions (Esther Kobel, *Paulus als interkultureller Vermittler: Eine Studie zur kulturellen Positionierung des Apostels der Völker*, SCCB 1 [Paderborn: Schöningh, 2019], 163; cf. 100–1). It is possible that Paul's strict/precise interpretation of the law of circumcision was the result of his Pharisaism, since the Pharisees were known for their precise interpretation of the law (Josephus, *Ant.* 17.41; *J.W.* 1.110; *Life* 191; Acts 26:5; cf. Acts 22:3). Not all Pharisees, however, would have necessarily held this view (e.g., Acts 15:5). On the Pharisees and their precision in interpretation, see Albert I. Baumgarten, "The Name of the Pharisees," *JBL* 102 (1983): 411–28, at 413–17.

267 Like most interpreters, I agree that Paul likely brought up his past proclamation in Gal 5:11 due to a false claim by the agitators.

3.9.1 Galatians 5:12 and Castration

The overwhelming consensus is that in this text Paul is sarcastically attacking the agitators by calling for them to castrate themselves.[268] Paul takes their circumcising mission, turns it back upon them, and amplifies it in an absurd manner. This is attested by the standard translations of ἀποκόπτω as "castrate," "mutilate," and "emasculate" found in most English Bibles.[269] In his colorful rendering of this verse, Craig Keener captures this general interpretive tendency: "I wish their knives would slip and they'd sever their own dicks."[270]

This standard reading of Gal 5:12 has been amplified by interpreters' conflation of it with Phil 3:2.[271] Based on this conflation, many have concluded that Paul's wish for the agitators to cut themselves off (ἀποκόψονται) is functionally equivalent to Paul's biting reference to mutilation (κατατομή) in Philippians.[272] For example, James Carleton Paget writes that in Gal 5:12 Paul compares circumcision to a form of mutilation and then he cites Phil 3:2.[273] Similarly, Betz comments: "The term ἀποκόπτω is used here in a specific sense ("castrate") as a caricature of the Jewish ritual of circumcision."[274] There is, however, no direct comparison be-

---

[268] E.g., Mußner, *Galaterbrief*, 363; Dunn, *Galatians*, 282; Longenecker, *Galatians*, 234; Blaschke, *Beschneidung*, 389; James R. Edwards, "Galatians 5:12: Circumcision, the Mother Goddess, and the Scandal of the Cross." *NovT* 53 (2011): 319–37; Keener, *Galatians*, 241–43.

[269] Castration and mutilation language are also found in German (*abschneiden* and *kastrieren*, see Blaschke, *Beschneidung*, 389) and French (*mutiler* and *castrer*) translations.

[270] Keener, *Galatians*, 242. Keener notes that while this crude translation is what Paul meant by his invective, Paul likely used insinuation to make his statement a bit less crude for his intended audience. Cf. Epictetus, *Diatr.* 3.1.31 for a similar use of insinuation to imply castration or emasculation. Edwards ("Galatians 5:12") argues that Paul is not simply being sarcastic or crude in this verse, but that this is a serious condemnation of the agitators' message as being no better than promoting the pagan cult of Cybele. Similarly, Albrecht Oepke, *Der Brief des Paulus an die Galater*, THKNT 9 (Berlin: Evangelische Verlagsanstalt, 1960) 126; Martyn, *Galatians*, 478.

[271] E.g., Longenecker, *Galatians*, 234; Dunn, *Galatians*, 284; Horn, "Der Verzicht," 501; Blaschke, *Beschneidung*, 403; Matthew Kuefler, *The Manly Eunuch: Masculinity, Gender Ambiguity, and Christian Ideology in Late Antiquity* (Chicago: University of Chicago Press, 2001), 257; Jeremy F. Hultin, *The Ethics of Obscene Speech in Early Christianity and Its Environment*, NovTSup 128 (Leiden, Brill, 2008), 148; Karin B. Neutel, *A Cosmopolitan Ideal: Paul's Declaration "Neither Jew Nor Greek, Neither Slave Nor Free, Nor Male and Female" in the Context of First Century Thought*, LNTS 513 (London: T&T Clark, 2015), 99; Keener, *Galatians*, 243.

[272] On mutilation in Phil 3:2, see §4.4.

[273] James Carleton Paget, "Barnabas 9:4: a Peculiar Verse on Circumcision," *VC* 45 (1991): 242–54, at 244, 252n14. Similarly, Edwards ("Galatians 5:12," 335) remarks: "Other lexicons affirm [that ἀποκόπτω can refer to castration], as does Paul in Phil 3:3, where he describes the effort of the Judaizers as κατατομή, the physical mutilation of circumcision."

[274] Betz, *Galatians*, 270.

tween circumcision and mutilation in Gal 5:12, nor does Paul characterize Jewish circumcision as castration.²⁷⁵ After all, Paul does not think of himself and his fellow Jews as mutilated. While it is true that castration can be interpreted—from both ancient Jewish and non-Jewish perspectives—as a form of mutilation, Paul is not making an explicit comparison between the two practices in this text—or any text for that matter. Some have also appealed to the idea that circumcision was understood as being on par with castration in the Roman world, but the connection between circumcision and castration is grossly overstated.²⁷⁶ While a circumcised penis would undoubtedly be seen as a defective—or even mutilated—penis from the perspective of the Greco-Roman conception of an ideal male body,²⁷⁷ any connection between circumcision and castration is never explicitly mentioned until much later after Paul's death.²⁷⁸

---

275 Blaschke (*Beschneidung*, 389–90) rightly notes that Paul does not equate circumcision with castration, neither in regard to the Galatians nor the agitators. Rather, he argues that Paul is participating in the general Greco-Roman distain for circumcision to make the demands of the agitators seem absurd (Cf. Horn, "Der Verzicht," 501; Neutel, *Cosmopolitan Ideal*, 99–100). This point, however, wrongly assumes that Paul is showing distain for circumcision itself, and not the agitators or their misapplication of circumcision to gentiles. On this point, see also Ehrensperger, "Trouble in Galatia," 182.

276 E.g., Witherington, *Grace in Galatia*, 374; Blaschke, *Beschneidung*, 389–90. Hultin (*Ethics of Obscene Speech*, 148n209) states that Dio Cassius (*Hist. rom.* 80.11) understands that ἀποκόπτω is the completion of περιτέμνω, but this is incorrect. There, Dio notes that "fully cutting oneself off" (i.e., emasculation/castration; παντάπασιν αὐτὸ ἀποκόψαι) can occur after circumcision, but not that it is the logical result of or completion of circumcision.

277 On the ideal penis in the ancient Greco-Roman world, see Hodges, "The Ideal Prepuce"; Blanton IV, "The Expressive Prepuce." See also, Strabo, *Geogr.* 16.4.17; Celsus, *On Medicine* 7.25.1; Soranus, *Gynecology* 2.9.14; 2.16.34; Galen, *Method of Medicine* 14.16.

278 Mimouni, *La circoncision*, 218. Some have pointed to Hadrian's supposed ban on circumcision to substantiate the claim that circumcision and castration were equal in the eyes of the Roman law. While the historicity and impetus of Hadrian's ban on circumcision is debated, the lone reference we have to this particular ban does not mention castration, but refers to banning Jews from mutilating their genitals (*mutilare genitalia*; Hist. Aug., Hadr. 14.2), which undoubtedly refers to circumcision. For two different minimalist approaches to understanding the historicity of the ban, its timing, and the reliability of this source, see E. Mary Smallwood, *The Jews Under Roman Rule*, SJLA 20 (Leiden: Brill, 1976), 429–32; Ra'anan Abusch, "Negotiating Difference: Genital Mutilation in Roman Slave Law and the History of the Bar Kokhba Revolt," in *The Bar Kokhba War Reconsidered: New Perspectives on the Second Jewish Revolt against Rome*, ed. Peter Schäfer, TSAJ 100 (Tübingen: Mohr Siebeck, 2003), 71–91. Hadrian did ban castration (Dig. 48.8.4.2), but this was likely separate from his supposed ban on circumcision. Alfredo Mordechai Rabello ("The Ban on Circumcision as a Cause of Bar Kokhba's Rebellion," *IsLR* 29 [1995]: 176–214) takes a maximalist approach and argues that Hadrian's ban on castration included circumcision based on his interpretation of *circumcidere* as being included under the umbrella of *excidere* in Dig. 48.8.4.2. On this point, Rabello argues that *excidere* essentially refers to all types of genital cutting (189–92). While circumcision is never ex-

The Anatolian context of Galatians has also led some interpreters to read Gal 5:12 in light of the self-castration performed by the *galli* associated with the cult of Cybele.[279] On this reading, Paul is associating or equating the circumcision promoted by the agitators with pagan ritual castration. For example, Susan Elliott comments: "…Paul opposed circumcision for pastoral reasons given the Galatians' context. Circumcision was too similar to the ritual castration of the *galli*.... He saw circumcision as a particular threat that would return them to their previous condition."[280] James Edwards offers a similar approach, but positions the ritual castration of the cult of Cybele alongside Jewish circumcision as "works of flesh" that are in opposition to Paul's gospel.[281] Joseph Marchal has also added to this conversation by situating Paul's comments about castration—and the potential link to the *galli*—in the wider context of ancient discourses about eunuchs and masculinity.[282] While the presence of the *galli* and the cult of Cybele may have caused some of Paul's readers to make an association between his statement and their cultural knowledge of cultic castration associated with the cult of Cybele, given the relative opaqueness and ambiguity of this reference, this connection should not be understood as an intentional move by Paul in this text.[283]

---

plicitly described as a form of castration in any of these ancient sources, after it was reinstated for Jews by Antoninus Pius and remained outlawed for non-Jews, the punishment for both an illicit circumcision and castration were the same: death (Dig. 48.8.11). On this text, see Rabello, "The Ban," 211–14; Abusch, "Negotiating Difference," 85–89.

279 The most comprehensive study that situates Paul's letter to the Galatians within this cultic context is Susan Elliott, *Cutting Too Close for Comfort: Paul's Letter to the Galatians in its Anatolian Cultic Context*, JSNTSup 248 (London: T&T Clark, 2003). For a representative list of scholars who read Gal 5:12 as a reference to the castrated *galli*, see Elliott, *Cutting Too Close*, 235n10.

280 Elliott, *Cutting too Close*, 14.

281 Edwards, "Galatians 5:12," 336–37. Edwards incorrectly notes that Elliot's approach is more sociological, whereas his approach is more theological. On his reading of Elliott, Paul opposes circumcision in Galatians because of the cultural significance it has, where Edwards sees Paul opposing it because of his understanding of works of the law and their supposed opposition to grace. Elliott does, however, agree with Edwards' overall theological point that Paul pits both Jewish circumcision and Anatolian pagan ritual castration against his gospel: "By equating the Anatolian pagan context with the Jewish context, Paul also begins to articulate his gospel as something distinct from both" (*Cutting too Close*, 254).

282 Joseph A. Marchal, *Appalling Bodies: Queer Figures Before and After Paul's Letters* (New York: Oxford University Press, 2020), 79–112. For Marchal's critiques of Elliott, see *Appalling Bodies*, 91–92. On eunuchs, ancient masculinity, and early Christianity, see Kuefler, *The Manly Eunuch*, 245–82.

283 Even if Paul is subtextually gesturing toward the castrated *galli* in Gal 5:12, these recent treatments that place the Mother Goddess and the *galli* at the interpretive center of this verse are overstated. Cf. Smit, "Real Circumcision," 81–82.

Critical for interpreting this text and what Paul is doing in it is understanding the verb ἀποκόπτω.²⁸⁴ In the LXX/OG, ἀποκόπτω is primarily used to refer to the physical removal of body parts.²⁸⁵ Deuteronomy 23:2 refers to those who have had their penises cut off (ἀποκεκομμένος)²⁸⁶ and are no longer allowed to enter into the assembly of the Lord. In Deut 25:12 it refers to the cutting off of a hand. Similar references to the physical removal of digits on the hands and feet are found in Judg 1:6 – 7. 2 Kingdoms 10:4 refers to the cutting off of garments and in OG Isa 18:5 κατακόπτω is used to refer to the cutting off of tree limbs. Psalm 76:9 differs slightly from these texts and uses ἀποκόπτω to refer to God cutting off or ceasing his mercy. In the NT, ἀποκόπτω is used to refer to cutting off of hands and feet (Mark 9:43, 45), ears (John 18:10, 26), and the severing of ropes (Acts 27:28). Elsewhere in Greek Jewish literature, Philo uses ἀποκόπτω figuratively to refer to cutting off of emotions from one's self (*Alleg. Interp.* 3.129, 134, 140), separating falsehood from truth (*Alleg. Interp.* 3.127), the cutting away or separation of Jews from their way of life (*Flaccus* 53), and the removal of positive mental characteristics (*Drunkenness* 23).²⁸⁷ Similar to Philo, Josephus' usage of ἀποκόπτω also focuses on the separation of entities, both physically and metaphorically (e.g., *J.W.* 2.160, 403; 5.512).

The circumcision controversy present in Galatians has led interpreters to read castration into the meaning of ἀποκόπτω, but the lexical range of the word is much broader than mere castration. While it is possible that castration is a component of Paul's wish, a broader understanding of how Paul may be employing ἀποκόπτω in this text is worth exploring.

3.9.2 Galatians 5:12 and Exclusion

Based on this textual evidence, Kathy Ehrensperger has argued that the claim of many interpreters that Paul uses ἀποκόπτω to clearly refer to castration is overstated.²⁸⁸ Given the various uses of ἀποκόπτω in Jewish literature—all of which in-

---

284 For a classic treatment of ἀποκόπτω as castration in Gal 5:12, see Pierre Debouxhtay, "Le sens se ἀποκόπτομαι (Gal, V, 12)," *REG* 39 (1926): 323 – 26.
285 This is also widely attested in classical Greek literature, but can also refer to metaphorical cutting off, i.e., exclusion (LSJ, s.v. ἀποκόπτω). For example, Epictetus (*Diatr.* 2.20.19) uses it in the same sentence to refer to both castration and the metaphorical cutting off of desire (και οι ἀποκοπτόμενοι τάς γε προθυμίας τας των ανδρών ἀποκόψασθαι ου δύνανται).
286 This is a euphemistic translation of the MT (וכרות שפכה), but the context of the indicates that the translators are trying to portray an individual who has removed his penile shaft.
287 Philo also uses συγκόπτω in *Drunkenness* 23 to refer to the metaphorical "chopping up" of souls for destruction (cf. *Alleg. Interp.* 3.8).
288 Kathy Ehrensperger, "Trouble in Galatia," 187.

dicate some form of separation—Ehrensperger explores the possibility that Paul is wishing for the agitators to separate themselves from the Galatian assemblies, rather than sarcastically wishing for them to castrate themselves and become eunuchs.[289] On this point, Ehrensperger explores the idea that Paul may be using this type of separation language within the context of a broader discourse of separation present in Galatians.[290] Given the dire nature of the Galatian situation and the threat that the agitators pose to the Galatian assemblies, Paul wishes that they would cut themselves off and remove themselves from their midst. While Ehrensperger rightly grasps the gravity of the situation and highlights the presence of separation language in Galatians, she unfortunately rules out any possibility that Paul could be employing a play on words or any kind of sarcasm. On her reading of the situation, Paul could not be doing anything other than calling for the separation of agitators because—for her—that is the only interpretation in which Paul seriously tries to cut off the problem at its source. On this point, Ehrensperger seems to overstate her case.[291]

One cannot simply reject the idea that a double-meaning or play on words is present based on the idea that too much is at stake for Paul to do so.[292] Interpreters should not limit themselves to a strict "either-or" reading of exclusion or castration when a double-entendre accomplishes similar ends, while being contextually and lexically plausible. A double entendre invoked by Paul's use of ἀποκόπτω could accomplish the necessary emphasis on the exclusion of the agitators while sardonically attacking them by calling for their self-castration. Paul even inserts cutting language in 5:7 as a wordplay to set up his wish in 5:12: the ones who "cut in on you" (ὑμᾶς ἐνέκοψεν) should now "cut themselves off" (ἀποκόψονται). Given the overwhelming evidence that places circumcision at the center of the Galatian crisis, it seems probable that Paul did have some form of phallus-cutting in mind when he wishes for the agitators to "cut themselves off." The texts in Galatians that point to the exclusion of those who improperly adopt and promote gentile proselyte circumcision (Gal 4:30, 5:2–4; cf. 6:13) also allow the interpreter to see

---

289 Here, Ehrensperger interpretation agrees with the Vulgate's rendering of Gal 5:12: *utinam et abscindantur, qui vos conturban.* Similarly, there is also a cadre of ancient interpreters who read Gal 5:12 metaphorically or allegorically, and downplay any overt reference to castration. For examples of this line of interpretation, see Martin Meiser, *Galater,* NTP 9 (Gottingen: Vandenhoeck & Ruprecht, 2007) 252–54.
290 Ehrensperger, "Trouble in Galatia," 187–89. Here, she cites Gal 1:6–9; 2:1–15; 3:28; 5:4, 7, but does not highlight the exclusion discourse presented in 4:30.
291 Ehrensperger ("Trouble in Galatia", 186, 189) does not see a valuable rhetorical purpose for Paul calling for the agitators to castrate themselves. While it would be humiliating, she does not see that a sufficient explanation for Paul's language in light of the situation.
292 Ehrensperger, "Trouble in Galatia," 189.

Paul's language as functioning in an exclusionary manner. Unlike the command in Gal 4:30 for the Galatians to remove the agitators and their offspring from their midst (cf. 1 Cor 5:5–6), in 5:12 Paul wishes that the agitators would remove themselves from the community.[293] Perhaps Paul wishes for the agitators to remove themselves from the Galatian assemblies in order to relieve the Galatians of this pressure and to prevent further conflict between the two groups.[294] However this exclusion occurs—either through expulsion or self-exclusion—they must be cut off before their leaven metastasizes throughout the body of the Galatian assemblies (Gal 5:9).

An important text that is often put into conversation with Gal 5:12 is LXX Deut 23:2. Here, the Deuteronomist notes that a man whose testicles are crushed or who is "a cut off one" (ἀποκεκομμένος)—euphemistically referring to a eunuch—is not able to enter into the assembly of the Lord (ἐκκλησίαν κυρίου).[295] It may be the case that Paul is drawing on this tradition and weaponizing it for his own use against the agitators. As I argue below, the agitators are not natural-born Jews, but are judaizing gentiles who have undergone non-covenantal circumcision.[296] On this reading, it is not merely that Paul wishes for them to separate from the assembly, but that they are excluded from it based on their invalid circumcisions (Gal 4:30; 5:2–4; 6:13). In Paul's mind they may as well be like the eunuchs in Deut 23:2 that are de jure excluded from participation in the assembly. If they carry out his wish for self-castration, they would be acknowledging and confirming their position as those who are excluded from the assembly.

---

[293] As noted above, my reading of 5:3 blends the command for expulsion and self-removal by calling for those Galatians who follow the agitators in undergoing circumcision to heed the command of 4:30 and remove themselves from the assembly.
[294] The identity of the upsetters (οἱ ἀναστατοῦντες) may extend beyond the agitators and may also include any Galatian males who have adopted circumcision and are encouraging others to follow in their footsteps.
[295] E.g., Dunn, *Galatians*, 282–83; de Boer, *Galatians* 326–27; Keener, *Galatians*, 242. Surprisingly, Ehrensperger does not cite Deut 23:2 in this regard. It should be noted that the assembly of the Lord (קהל יהוה) refers to the sanctuary/temple, not the nation of Israel (cf. Lam 1:10; Ezek 44:7, 9), and is primarily concerned with preventing defective bodies from polluting sacred space. On this point, see Olyan, *Rites and Rank*, 79, 111–14.
[296] Paul's wish for the agitators to castrate themselves is arguably more effective if they are judaizing gentiles and not natural-born Jews. Richardson, *Israel*, 89; Murray, *Playing a Jewish Game*, 36.

3.10 Identifying the Agitators: Galatians 6:12–13

While the traditional understanding of the identity and ethnicity of those who Paul is writing against in Galatians has been generally assumed to be Jews of some sort, the exact identity of these individuals is a point of scholarly contention.[297] Are these individuals Jews, Jewish Christ-followers, gentile proselytes to Judaism, or something else? Complicating matters is how different interpreters understand Jewish identity in the ancient world and how Paul himself would have thought of these individuals in relationship to Jewish identity. For some, these individuals are clearly Jews by birth that have since become followers of Jesus.[298] For others these may be gentile Christ-following proselytes who have fully judaized and have—for all intents and purposes—become Jews.[299] The question that has generally been overlooked in this conversation is not if they thought themselves to be Jews or if they presented as Jews, but what or who did Paul think they were? Did they fit Paul's understanding of what a Jew is? In other words, did Paul consider them to be Jews and identify them as such?

The most illuminating text we have in Galatians on the identity of the agitators is 6:12–13: "It is those who want to make a good showing in the flesh that try to compel you to be circumcised—only that they may not be persecuted for the cross of Christ. Even the circumcised (οἱ περιτεμνόμενοι) do not themselves obey the law, but they want you to be circumcised so that they may boast about your flesh" (NRSV). Here, the present participle περιτεμνόμενοι is the crucial data point that can inform our understanding of the identity of the opponents.[300]

---

[297] On this point, F. C. Baur writes, "In one word, they were Jews or Jewish Christians of the genuine old stamp, who could so little find a place in the more liberal atmosphere of Pauline Christianity that they thought the very ground of their existence would be cut from under them, if Judaism was no longer to have its absolute power and importance" (*Paul the Apostle*, 1:263). For a comprehensive list and discussion of the various permutations of the identity of the agitators in Galatians, see Nanos, *Irony*, 115–99. See also Robert Jewett, "The Agitators and the Galatian Congregation," NTS 17 (1971): 198–212; Jerry L. Sumney, '*Servants of Satan*', '*False Brothers*' *and Other Opponents of Paul*, JSNTSup 188 (Sheffield: Sheffield Academic, 1999), 134–59.
[298] E.g., Jewett, "The Agitators," 205; Betz, *Galatians*, 7; Longenecker, *Galatians*, 95; Oakes, *Galatians*, 9.
[299] See discussion in Nanos, *Irony*, 234–42.
[300] Complicating this is the textual variant found in a handful of manuscripts that replaces περιτεμνόμενοι with περιτετμημενοι ($\mathfrak{P}^{46}$, B, L, Ψ, 6, 365, 614, 630, 1175, Ambrosiaster). This variant in the perfect form—"those who have been circumcised"—likely refers to Jews who were circumcised as infants (Richardson, *Israel*, 86; Murray, *Playing a Jewish Game*, 35). It is likely that the variant emerged as a scribal modification that sought to clarify that the opponents were Jews and had received circumcision at birth, not those who had received it as adult proselytes (Thiessen, *Gentile Problem*, 211n82). The present form found in the majority of manuscripts is to be preferred as

While translations tend to ignore the passive (or middle/reflexive) nature of the participle in 6:13, they tend to highlight it in their translations of 5:3: "who lets himself be circumcised" (NRSV).[301] A similar translation should also be adopted in 6:13, which is also confirmed by the presence of αὐτοί after οἱ περιτεμνόμενοι. While most interpreters apply αὐτοί to φυλάσσουσιν ("those undergoing circumcision do not *themselves guard* the law"), Thiessen notes that it is also grammatically possible that αὐτοί could apply to περιτεμνόμενοι ("those who *circumcise themselves* do not guard the law").[302] On this reading, περιτεμνόμενοι should be understood to be a reflexive middle and not just a simple middle/passive. Therefore, the preferable translation of οἱ περιτεμνόμενοι αὐτοί in 6:13 is "those who circumcise themselves" or "those who have themselves circumcised."[303] Thus in 6:13, the individuals that Paul is writing against are not natural-born Jews, but are judaizing gentiles who have adopted circumcision; they were not infants when they passively underwent eighth-day circumcision, but are those who have had themselves circumcised.[304]

---

the original reading, as it is the *lectio difficilior* that can better explain how the other variant emerged. On this variant, see Burton, *Galatians*, 352–53; Murray, *Playing a Jewish Game*, 35–36.
301 Additionally, both of the participles are also in the present tense.
302 Thiessen, *Gentile Problem*, 96. Since interpreters of Galatians have typically assumed that these individuals were Jews and that the inability of perfect law observance was at the heart of the letter, this has impacted how they understand the function of αὐτοί. This general presupposition has led many interpreters to conclude that αὐτοί is functioning as an intensifier for φυλάσσουσιν, and that Paul is thus critiquing these individuals for their own insincere or insufficient law observance; e.g., Lightfoot, *Galatians*, 222; Longenecker, *Galatians*, 293; Blaschke, *Beschneidung*, 393; de Boer, *Galatians*, 400; Keener, *Galatians*, 284–85.
303 For a full discussion of the various interpretive options for περιτεμνόμενοι, see Mark Nanos *Irony*, 234–42. Notably, Nanos notes that regardless if one takes the present participle as a middle or a passive the resulting picture painted by the word would indicate that the agitators are gentile proselytes (278).
304 While this view has most famously been proposed by Johannes Munck (*Paul and the Salvation*, 87–89), it can be traced back to August Neander (*Geschichte der Pflanzung und Leitung der christlichen Kirche durch die Apostel*, 2 vols, 4th ed. [Hamburg: Perthes, 1847], 1:366–67). For others who have also come to similar conclusions about the identity of the Agitators, see Emanuel Hirsch, "Zwei Fragen zu Galater 6," *ZNW* 29 (1930): 192–97; Richardson, *Israel*, 84–97; Murray, *Playing a Jewish Game*, 34–36; eadem, "Romans 2 Within the Broader Context of Gentile Judaizing in Early Christianity," in *The So-Called Jew in Paul's Letter to the Romans*, ed. Rafael Rodríguez and Matthew Thiessen (Minneapolis: Fortress, 2016), 163–82, at 166–69; cf. Martin Goodman, "The Politics of Judaea in the 50s CE: The Use of the New Testament," *JJS* 70 (2019): 225–36, at 229–31. Goodman argues that the agitators in Galatians are Jews, but that those named in 6:13 as οἱ περιτεμνόμενοι are a different group of gentile Christ-followers within the Galatian community who are urging circumcision upon fellow gentiles.

Furthermore, Thiessen has also made sense of the present tense of περιτε-μνόμενοι, which has either been ignored by or confused interpreters.³⁰⁵ Thiessen argues that the use of the present participle does not necessarily demonstrate that the action of circumcising has taken place around the same time as Paul's writing, but that the act of circumcising is taking place concurrently with the main verb: φυλάσσουσιν.³⁰⁶ That is, the act of circumcising is taking place at the same time as their failure to guard the law. Their apparent act of guarding the law through circumcision is itself a failure to guard the law that necessitates that circumcision be performed on eight-day-old boys, not adult men.

Looking elsewhere in Galatians, Paul never identifies the agitators as Jews. He only directly refers to them as οἱ περιτεμνόμενοι in 6:13 and as "agitators," "confusers," or "upsetters" (ταράσσοντες, 1:7; ταράσσων, 5:10; ἀναστατοῦντες, 5:12). Throughout the epistle, Paul refers to Jews either by using Ἰουδαῖος ("Jews"; Gal 2:13–15; 3:28) or περιτομή ("the circumcision"; Gal 2:7–9, 12; cf. 5:6; 6:15), but never as "those who have themselves circumcised." As noted above, the present passive/reflexive participle is used in both 5:3 (περιτεμνομένῳ) and in 6:13 (περιτε-μνόμενοι). In 5:3 it refers to gentiles who are considering undergoing the procedure, and there is no reason to believe that Paul now applies it to a group of Jews in 6:13.³⁰⁷ Similarly, in his other epistles, Paul uses "the circumcision" to refer to Jews (Rom 3:30; 4:12; 15:8; Phil 3:3; cf. Eph 2:11; Col 3:11; 4:11; Titus 1:10), but they are always "the circumcision," and never "those who have themselves circumcised" or "those who receive circumcision."³⁰⁸ Furthermore, the *only* place where Paul specifically identifies his epistolary opponents as Jews is in 2 Cor

---

305 E.g., Longenecker, *Galatians*, 292–93; Dunn, *Galatians*, 338; de Boer, *Galatians*, 399–400.

306 Thiessen, *Gentile Problem*, 96; cf. Robert W. Funk, *A Beginning-Intermediate Grammar of Hellenistic Greek*, 2nd ed. (Missoula, MT: Scholars Press, 1973), §849.

307 Michele Murray comments, "The existence of the present tense of the same verb in Galatians 5:2, 3, and 6:12, further strengthens the argument the present participle is the original form in verse 13 as its sense is "to get circumcised," or "to receive circumcision"—that is, it refers to someone undergoing circumcision, rather than a circumcised person" (*Playing a Jewish Game*, 35). In Gal 5:2 the present passive subjunctive participle (περιτέμνησθε) refers to those in Galatia who are contemplating circumcision. The "all men who have themselves circumcised" (παντὶ ἀνθρώπῳ περιτε-μνομένῳ) in 5:3 should not be understood as referring to all circumcised men, but specifically to the men in Galatia.

308 The lone exception is 1 Cor 7:18 where Paul uses περιτετμημένος to refer to Jews circumcised from birth. Here, the perfect tense distinguishes this instance from Paul's usage in Gal 5:3 and 6:13. See my comments on this in §2.3.

11:22, where he makes this point abundantly clear: "Are they Hebrews? So am I. Are they Israelites? So am I. Are they seed of Abraham? So am I" (NRSV).[309]

In light of all of this data, it becomes apparent that the ones who are having themselves circumcised are not natural-born Jews, but are gentiles who have judaized to the point of undergoing proselyte circumcision. While they may think of themselves as Jews, Paul does not grant them that honored status. From his perspective they are not his Jewish kin (τῶν συγγενῶν μου κατὰ σάρκα; Rom 9:3) but are simply those who have had themselves circumcised. While they may have been urging the Galatians to undergo circumcision as an act of law observance (cf. Gal 4:21), Paul does not attribute such pious motives to their imposition of circumcision.[310] From his perspective, they desire to "secure a good status"[311] in the flesh and have the Galatians circumcised only in order to (μόνον ἵνα) avoid persecution for the cross of Christ (6:12). In 6:13,[312] Paul highlights that their circumcising mission was never actually rooted in a desire to guard the law—after all, their circumcisions themselves are an affront to the law—but they wanted to have the Galatians circumcised in order to boast in the missing flesh of their foreskins. Here, Paul characterizes their desire to avoid persecution as actually resulting in boasting in the Galatians' flesh. Whereas Paul only boasts in the cross (6:14) and not the flesh, the agitators avoid the persecution associated with the cross and boast in the flesh.[313]

---

[309] Notably, in 2 Corinthians there is no discussion of circumcision, nor any indication from Paul that this group of Jews in 2 Cor 11 advocated for the circumcision of non-Jews.

[310] As noted by Barclay ("Mirror-Reading," 75–76), we should take Paul's depiction of the agitators' motives *cum grano salis* due to the distorting nature of polemics. Contra Horn (*Das Angeld des Geistes*, 348–49), who takes Paul's statement in 6:12 at face value. He understands that the agitators are preaching circumcision solely in order to avoid persecution and not because they believe it is necessary for Abrahamic sonship.

[311] On this translation of εὐπροσωπέω, see Hardin, *Imperial Cult*, 91.

[312] Verse 13 serves as an explanatory clause (γάρ) for verse 12. This is missed by most interpreters.

[313] The kind of persecution they are avoiding is not entirely clear. This may simply be a Pauline invention or mischaracterization, but it may also be evidence that their judaization and adoption and promotion of circumcision were done in order to avoid persecution from the state and/or from non-Christ-following Jews. It is possible that since the Jesus movement encouraged gentile pagans to abandon their native cult and instead worship the one God and one Lord (1 Cor 8:6) of the assembly that they received persecution for either joining an unfamiliar superstition or for upsetting the cosmic order by failing to participate in the cult of their native deities. If they judaize and adopt circumcision then they would disambiguate their ex-pagan gentile status and would effectively become Jews in the eyes of those concerned. They would no longer look like deviant pagans and would have joined an acceptable alternative cult. On the various possibilities of why they might have faced persecution and from whom, see Hardin, *Imperial Cult*, 101–15; Fredriksen, *Pagans' Apostle*, 87–93; Goodman, "Politics of Judaea," 227–32.

3.11 Conclusion

In this chapter, I sought to expose the underlying logic of Paul's rejection of circumcision for gentiles in Galatians and why it alienates them from the Messiah. While interpreters often explain this logic in light of Paul's supposed anti-legalism, anti-ethnocentrism, or his understanding of the Christ-gift, I proposed that Paul uses his allegorical interpretation of the Hagar and Sarah narrative to provide this logic. Paul uses this allegory to represent two competing missions and two modes of Abrahamic sonship. Hagar is linked to the agitators in Galatia who sought to create Abrahamic sons though human agency and circumcision, whereas Sarah is linked with Paul and his mission that produces Abrahamic sons through the promise and divine *pneuma*. Their circumcising mission produces slaves and Paul's circumcision-free mission produces heirs. Although the language of circumcision is absent from Paul's allegorical treatment, I argued that an understanding of how circumcision functions in the Genesis accounts of Abraham, Ishmael, and Isaac sheds further light on Paul's logic. Following the work of Matthew Thiessen, I noted that not all circumcisions are created equal. According to Gen 17, for a circumcision to have covenantal value it must be performed on a descendent of Abraham on the eighth-day after birth. Unlike Ishmael's circumcision, which was performed when he was thirteen years of age, Isaac's circumcision is the first to be performed properly on the eighth-day. Since the Galatians who are contemplating circumcision are not descendants from Abraham (and grown men), circumcision has no positive covenantal value for them. Paul argues that since they have received Christ's *pneuma*, they are already Abraham's sons who follow after the pattern of Isaac (Gal 3:6–7, 14, 29; 4:6–7). If they submit themselves to circumcision, they will remain Abrahamic sons, albeit slaves like Ishmael that have no inheritance. Here, Paul does not argue that circumcision is bad or flawed, only that it cannot make a gentile into the right kind of Abrahamic son.

Since those who share Christ's *pneuma* are united to him and become one body (1 Cor 12:13, 27) with him, their actions can affect this union because of their shared, pneumatic corporeality. Schweitzer proposed that there were three deadly sins that could sever this union: sleeping with a prostitute (1 Cor 6:15–19), communing with *daimonia* (1 Cor 10:14–22), and undergoing proselyte circumcision (Gal 5:2–4). While Schweitzer argued that sleeping with a prostitute and communing with *daimonia* created incompatible unions that would pollute Christ's body—and thus led to the severing of this union—his explanation for how circumcision cuts one off from Christ strayed from this union-centric logic. Building upon Schweitzer's work, I proposed that Paul's argument that circumcision returned an individual to a state of slavery (like Ishmael) created an incompatible union that severed one from Christ. By undergoing circumcision the men were submitting once again to a yoke of slavery under the *stoicheia*. Because one cannot be enslaved to the *stoicheia* and at the same time be pneumatically united to Christ, this return to slavery severs them from Christ and the benefits gained by that union. This logic of exclusion also offers insights into Paul's statement in 5:12 about his desire for the agitators to cut themselves off. Since I identify the agitators as judaizing gentiles who have undergone circumcision (Gal 6:13), Paul's wish for the agitators to cut themselves can be understood as having a double meaning. Not only does this indicate a sarcastic wish for their self-castration, it also indicates Paul's desire for the agitators to remove themselves from the Galatian assemblies because of their negative influence and disqualifying circumcisions.

In addition to exploring Paul's rejection of proselyte circumcision and the underlying logic of exclusion, this chapter also offered readings of the rest of Paul's statements about circumcision in Galatians. Like my reading of 1 Cor 7:19, I made the case that Gal 5:6 and 6:15 should not be interpreted as declarations that circumcision and foreskin are actually nothing. Rather, when read in their epistolary and rhetorical contexts, Paul is using these negations to make specific points and specific comparisons. Next, I offered a new reading of Paul's past proclamation of circumcision in 5:11. While the majority of interpreters have understood this passage as indicating that at one point in his life, Paul was a proponent of proselyte circumcision, I argued that this refers to Paul's previous exclusionary stance on gentile participation in the people of God. Here, I linked Paul's former occupation in *Ioudaismos* (Gal 1:13–14) with his past proclamation of circumcision.

As I have attempted to demonstrate, the discussion of circumcision in Galatians is complex. Prominent readings of Galatians tend to argue that Paul rejects circumcision for non-Jews and diminishes it for Jews based his supposed anti-legalism or anti-ethnocentrism. I have proposed, however, that Paul's rejection of circumcision for non-Jews is rooted in his understanding of circumcision in Gen 17, God's promises to Abraham concerning his offspring, and pneumatic union with the Messiah. As is the case with his other epistles, Paul has very little to say about the circumcision of Jews in Galatians, and much to say about making sure non-Jews do not have themselves circumcised.

4 We Are the Circumcision
Circumcision in Philippians

> Beware the dogs! Beware the wicked workers! Beware the mutilation! For we are the circumcision; the ones who serve by the *pneuma* of God and boast in Christ Jesus and put no confidence in the flesh. (Phil 3:2–3)

4.1 Introduction

Paul's claim that "we are the circumcision" (Phil 3:3) has longed served interpreters as one of the key texts that supposedly illustrates Paul's redefinition of what it means to be a member of "the circumcision." On this supposed redefinition, N. T. Wright declares, "The covenant God has not given up on the category of 'circumcision', on the idea of there being an elect people; he has merely *redefined it*, as in Philippians 3:3."[1] Similarly, Peter Richardson notes that in Phil 3:3, "Christians are the circumcision."[2] Here, it is often claimed that Paul reappropriates the language of circumcision and transfers it from ethnic Israel to the so-called "new Israel"—the Christian church. Thus goes the reading offered by John Reumann: "All this makes 'we' Christians and 'the Circumcision' synonymous and raises ecclesiological questions. 'The Circumcision' fits use by Paul of 'Israel terms' for the church."[3] From this interpretation, many scholars jump to the conclusion that Paul must be talking about the circumcision of the heart mentioned in Deuteronomy and Jeremiah (Deut 10:16; 30:6; Jer 4:4; 9:25–26; cf. Ezek 44:7), not physical circumcision or Jewish identity, which leads to a conflation of this text with their readings of Rom 2:28–29.[4] Through his supposed spiritualization and redefinition of circumcision, many argue Paul points to the "true" circumcision that physical circumcision

---

[1] Wright, *Paul*, 921 (emphasis added).
[2] Richardson, *Israel*, 115.
[3] Reumann, *Philippians*, 474–75. See also, Blaschke, *Beschneidung*, 403–4; Ralph P. Martin and Gerald F. Hawthorne, *Philippians*, WBC 43, rev. ed. (Nashville: Nelson, 2004), 175; Michael Wolter, *Paulus: Ein Grundriss seiner Theologie* (Neukirchen-Vluyn: Neukirchener Verlag, 2011), 363, 443.
[4] Origen, *Hom. Gen.* 3.4; Jean-François Collange, *The Epistle of Saint Paul to the Philippians*, trans. A. W. Heathcote (London: Epworth, 1979), 125; Gordon D. Fee, *Paul's Letter to the Philippians*, NICNT (Grand Rapids: Eerdmans, 1995), 298–99; Markus Bockmuehl, *The Epistle to the Philippians*, BNTC (London: Black, 1997), 191; Blaschke, *Beschneidung*, 408; Martin and Hawthorne, *Philippians*, 175; Dunn, *New Perspective on Paul*, 472; Mimouni, *La circoncision*, 229; Wright, *Paul*, 921; 1076; 1146; 1432–33; Bird, *Anomalous Jew*, 81; cf. Justin, *Dial.* 18.2–19.3; Joshua D. Garroway, "The Circumcision of Christ: Romans 15.7–13," *JSNT* 34 (2012): 303–22, at 318.

pointed to all along. The idea of true circumcision, however, is a theological invention that appears nowhere in the Hebrew Bible or New Testament.

Like the discussion of circumcision in Galatians, Paul introduces the topic of circumcision due to the threat of a group of rival teachers who seek to promote circumcision amongst the Philippians (3:2). Unlike Galatians, however, these individuals do not appear be an active force in Philippi. Instead of the immediate and present danger Paul believes his opponents pose in Galatians, Paul only offers a harsh tripartite warning to alert the Philippians of the potential threat this group poses: "Beware the dogs! Beware the wicked workers! Beware the mutilation!" (3:2). Given that many interpreters conclude that Paul is using the title "circumcision" for all Messiah-followers in 3:3, the majority argue that Paul's rivals in 3:2 must be a group of Jews, who are themselves claiming to be the "circumcision."[5] Additionally, many contend that the components of Paul's invective single out Jews as the object of his warning: "dogs" constitutes an ironic inversion of a supposed Jewish slur about non-Jews; "wicked workers" may indicate Jewish missionary activity or be a play on "works of the law"; and lastly, "mutilation" constitutes Paul's harshest critique of physical circumcision.

In this chapter, I argue that Paul does not redefine circumcision in Phil 3:3 as a title for Messiah-followers, but he uses it in his conventional way to refer to Jews. Here, circumcision refers specifically to himself and Timothy, the Jewish authors of the epistle (Phil 1:1). Based on Paul's philippic in 3:2, his further description of his rivals in 3:18–19, and the juxtaposition he sets up between this group of rivals and the circumcision, I propose that his rivals in Philippians are not a group of Jews, but rather—like the agitators in Galatians—are a group of judaizing gentiles who have undergone proselyte circumcision. Their false claim to the title "circumcision" is further highlighted by Paul when he appeals to the superlative nature of his Jewish bona fides (3:5–6) to further distinguish himself from his opponents. Here, Paul draws attention to the fact that his circumcision conforms to the requirements of the law and was performed on the eighth-day (περιτομῇ ὀκταήμερος).

---

[5] Despite the fact that he believed Philippians to be inauthentically Pauline, Baur concluded that these individuals were Jews simply because the author recognized that is who Paul's opponents always were. "There is certainly polemic against Jewish opponents, yet one can hardly avoid the impression that this is there simply because it seemed to belong to the character of Pauline Epistles" (*Paul the Apostle*, 2:53). For an overview of the proposals on the identity of these individuals, see John J. Gunther, *St. Paul's Opponents and Their Background: A Study of Apocalyptic and Jewish Sectarian Teachings*, NovTSup 35 (Leiden: Brill, 1973). See also, Mark D. Nanos, "Paul's Polemic in Philippians 3 as Jewish-Subgroup Vilification of Local Non-Jewish Cultic and Philosophical Alternatives," *JSPL* 3 (2013): 47–91, at 48n4.; Murray, "Romans 2," 171–75.

4.2 The Dogs[6]

The scholarly trope that ancient Jews commonly referred to non-Jews as dogs has colored interpretations of Phil 3 for centuries.[7] With this trope in mind, many then assume that Paul must here be inverting the epithet dogs ironically as a way of diminishing the validity of the claims of supposedly Jewish opponents.[8] Regarding this reading, Mark Nanos notes, "It is universal enough to generalize that every interpreter of Philippians believes [Jews commonly referred to Gentiles contemptuously as dogs]."[9] The earliest instance we have of this understanding comes from John Chrysostom:

> But whom does he style "dogs"? There were at this place some of those, whom he hints at in all his Epistles, base and contemptible Jews, greedy of vile lucre and fond of power, who, desiring to draw aside many of the faithful, preached both Christianity and Judaism at the same time, corrupting the Gospel. As then they were not easily discernible, therefore he says, "beware of the dogs": the Jews are no longer children; *once the Gentiles were called dogs, but now the Jews.* (Hom. Phil. 11 [NPNF¹ 13:230; emphasis added])[10]

Since Chrysostom, this claim has made its way into countless treatments of Phil 3. Only recently have scholars begun to question this often cited assumption by returning to the sources and investigating the data behind this claim.[11] Recent studies on the place of dogs in the ancient Near East, Hebrew Bible, Second-Temple Judaism, Greco-Roman world, and the New Testament challenge this prevailing

---

6 For an expanded version of this section, see Ryan D. Collman, "Beware the Dogs! The Phallic Epithet in Phil 3.2," *NTS* 67 (2021): 105–20.
7 E.g., Otto Michel, "κύων," TDNT 3:1101–4; Pierre Bonnard, *L'épître de saint Paul aux Philippiens*, CNT 10 (Neuchatel: Delachaux & Niestle, 1973), 60; A. F. J. Klijn, "Paul's Opponents in Philippians III," *NovT* 7 (1965): 282; Watson, *Paul, Judaism*, 75; Horn, "Der Verzicht," 501; Herbert W. Batement IV, "Were the Opponents at Philippi Necessarily Jewish?" *BSac* 155 (1998): 39–61, at 55; Fee, *Philippians*, 295; Demetrius K. Williams, *Enemies of the Cross of Christ: There Terminology of the Cross and Conflict in Philippians*, JSNTSup 223 (London: Sheffield Academic, 2002), 156–57; Martin and Hawthorn, *Philippians*, 174; Dunn, *New Perspective on Paul*, 470–71; Peter-Ben Smit, "Real Circumcision," 85.
8 Kenneth Grayston ("The Opponents in Philippians 3," *ExpTim* 97 [1986]: 170–72, at 171) argues the opposite. He proposes that if ancient Jews commonly referred to gentiles as "dogs," then it is likely that Paul is using this slur in its normative sense to refer to non-Jews.
9 Mark D. Nanos, "Paul's Reversal of Jews Calling Gentiles 'Dogs' (Philippians 3:2): 1600 Years of an Ideological Tale Wagging an Exegetical Dog?" *BibInt* 17 (2009): 448–82, at 452n7.
10 See also Chrysostom, *Adv. Jud.* 1.2.1–2.
11 Reumann notes how scholars often cite that Jews referred to gentile as "dogs," but remarks that "there is less documentation than might be supposed" (*Philippians*, 461). See also, Holloway, *Philippians*, 153.

interpretation by demonstrating the lack of evidence for such claims and push back on the perceived consensus of New Testament scholars on the status of dogs in the ancient world.[12]

4.2.1 The Deconstruction of an Ideological Tale: Dogs in Ancient Jewish Sources and the Gospels

Mark Nanos' *Biblical Interpretation* article, "Paul's Reversal of Jews Calling Gentiles 'Dogs' (Philippians 3:2): 1600 Years of an Ideological Tale Wagging an Exegetical Dog?" is the first and only major work to undertake the task of fully evaluating the claim the ancient Jews were in the habit of calling gentiles dogs. In this article, Nanos concludes that no ancient Jewish sources can offer support for this common claim that would impact Paul's usage of the word. Examining pre-rabbinic sources, one finds that dogs are used to refer to a variety of things: actual dogs (Deut 23:19;[13] Judg 7:5; 1 Sam 17:43; 24:14; 1 Kgs 14:11; 16:4; 21:19–24; Job 30:1; Tob 6:2; 11:4; Jdt 11:19), and enemies (Ps 22:16; 59:6), and it is used as a metaphor for a place of lowliness (2 Sam 3:8; 9:8, 2 Kgs 8:13) and as a general insult (2 Sam 16:9; Prov 26:11).[14] Surprising for some, dog can also be used negatively to refer to Israelites (2 Sam 16:9; Isa 56:10–11).[15]

---

[12] For an overview of dogs in the ancient world, see Kenneth F. Kitchell Jr., *Animals in the Ancient World from A to Z* (New York: Routledge, 2014), 47–53. For specialist treatments, see Joshua Schwartz, "Dogs in Jewish Society in the Second Temple Period and in the Time of the Mishnah and Talmud," *JJS* 55 (2004): 246–77; Geoffrey David Miller, "Attitudes Toward Dogs in Ancient Israel: A Reassessment," *JSOT* 32 (2008): 487–500; Christiana Franco, *Shameless: The Canine and the Feminine in Ancient Greece*, trans. Matthew Fox (Oakland: University of California Press, 2014); Fabio Tutrone, "Barking at the Threshold: Cicero, Lucretius, and the Ambiguous Status of Dogs in Roman Culture" in *Impious Dogs, Haughty Foxes and Exquisite Fish: Evaluative Perception and Interpretation of Animals in Ancient and Medieval Mediterranean Thought*, ed. Tristan Schmidt and Johannes Pahlitzsch (Berlin: de Gruyter, 2019), 73–102.
[13] A common translation of מחיר כלב/ἄλλαγμα κυνὸς in Deut 23:19 is "male prostitute" (e.g., NRSV). This interpretation is unlikely and "dog's price" is to be preferred (Miller, "Attitudes toward Dogs," 497). This interpretation is also attested by Josephus, *Ant.* 4.206.
[14] These references are not exhaustive, but merely illustrative of the range of meaning in pre-rabbinic, Jewish sources.
[15] On the positive function of dogs in ancient Jewish texts, see Miller, "Attitudes Toward Dogs." Miller highlights the use of dogs as working animals (Job 30:1; Josephus, *Ant.* 4.206) and as companions (Tob 6:2; 11:4).

These generic uses of "dog" are also echoed by Josephus and Philo, with no clear instance of dog being used to signify non-Jews *qua* non-Jews.[16] In addition to these texts, some scholars also cite rabbinic literature to substantiate this trope.[17] Nanos' exploration of the rabbinic literature yields similar results. While there are some texts that mention dogs and non-Jews in the same breath (e.g., m. Ned 4:3; m. Bek 5:6; Midr. Tanḥ., *Terumah* 3), none of them demonstrate that Jews were in the habit of calling non-Jews "dogs."[18] In light of this data, it appears that interpreters of Paul have been broadly uncritical in their repetition of this trope.

In addition to these texts, some interpreters of Phil 3:2 have also looked to the texts in Mark and Matthew where Jesus refers to a gentile woman as a dog as being evidence that Jews were in the habit of calling gentiles "dogs."[19] Mark 7:24–30 recounts an interaction between Jesus and a Syrophoenician women who asks for healing for her daughter who is plagued by an unclean *pneuma*. After hearing her request, Jesus replies, "Allow the children to be fed first, for it is not good to take the children's bread and throw it to the dogs" (7:27). While the meaning of the illustration is not fully elucidated, because Mark has doubly identified the gentile otherness of the woman—she is a Greek, from the people of Syrophoenicia (7:26)—it is likely that in the metaphor the children are Israel and the dogs are gentiles.[20] In Matthew's account of this story (Matt 15:21–28), the woman is portrayed as a Canaanite and the ethnic reasoning behind Jesus' words is spelled out in more detail: "I was sent only to the lost sheep of the house of Israel" (15:24). He goes on to say, "It is not good to take the children's bread and throw it to the dogs" (15:26).

---

16 Philo uses dogs to describe treacherous and hypocritical enemies who have occupied Palestine and Syria (*Good Person* 89–91). In *Spec. Laws* 4.91, gluttonous banquet behavior is described as being dog-like. Josephus and Philo both comment on Egyptians false worship of dogs (*Embassy* 139; *Ag. Ap.* 2.85). Many of the references to dogs in Josephus' *Antiquities* mirror those found in the Hebrew Bible.
17 E.g., David E. Garland, "The Composition and Unity of Philippians: Some Neglected Literary Factors." *NovT* 27 (1985): 141–73, at 167n92; Fee, *Philippians*, 295n44; Bockmuehl, *Philippians*, 186; Martin and Hawthorne, *Philippians*, 174; cf. Horn, "Der Verzicht," 501n72.
18 Nanos, "Paul's Reversal," 464–69. See also, Collman, "'Beware the Dogs!'," 108–9. Nanos, however, does note one occurrence in *Pirke de Rabbi Eliezer* 29 that does link gentiles with dogs due to both being uncircumcised, but this is not a smoking gun. This text is problematic due to its late date (~8th century) and the fact that it is not present in all manuscripts. It should have no bearing on how one understands Paul's language in Phil 3. For a general overview of dogs in the Mishnah and Talmud, see Schwartz, "Dogs in Jewish Society."
19 E.g., Garland, "Composition and Unity," 167; Bockmuehl, *Philippians*, 186; Martin and Hawthorne, *Philippians*, 174; Moisés Silva, *Philippians*, 2nd ed., BECNT (Grand Rapids: Baker Academic, 2005), 147; Dunn, *New Perspective on Paul*, 471.
20 Adela Yarbro Collins, *Mark: A Commentary*, Hermeneia (Minneapolis: Fortress, 2007), 366.

Matthew is more explicit than Mark, but the result is similar. Matthew portrays Jesus' mission as being to Israel (sheep) and not to gentiles (dogs). While these texts in Mark and Matthew do rely on ethnic reasoning to demonstrate that there is an essential ethnic difference that divides Jew from non-Jew, the term dog is not necessarily used here as a slur to belittle gentiles as unclean or to comment on their unscrupulous behavior. While Jesus uses the term to distinguish non-Jews from Jews, he does so in the context of a household illustration[21] to explain his present mission to Israel, not to belittle the woman for her ethnic or moral status. It is an image used in a narrative to separate insider from outsider—not a common racial slur—and does not constitute positive evidence for the motif under discussion.

Matthew Thiessen—highlighting the underlying ethnic essentialism in these passages in Mark and Matthew—proposes that Paul uses the term dog as an ethnic identifier in Phil 3:2 in the same way.[22] For Thiessen, Paul's usage of dog indicates that his rivals are a group of (judaizing) gentiles. While I agree that the opponents are judaizing gentiles, I am not confident that the information from the Gospels should be used as an exact correlate for what is going on in Philippians. It appears that the Gospels are using the term somewhat differently than how Paul is using it in Phil 3; Mark and Matthew use it ethnically—but not as a slur—whereas Paul's usage is unabashedly abusive. Unlike the account in the Gospels, it is not immediately clear if Paul is using dog as an ethnic identifier or something else. The core problem with this interpretation is that in light of the lack of evidence for the "Jews called gentiles dogs" trope, it is likely that an ethnic employment of dog would not have been grasped by the Philippian audience. If Paul is using dog as an ethnic identifier, who would have picked up on this? Additionally, since the recipients of the letter themselves are non-Jews, how would Paul's use of dog as an ethnic identifier not apply to them? Or, if they were to perceive such ethnically charged language, would they take offense at it?[23] While it is possible that Paul is employing dog ethnically in Phil 3:2, it is important to note that if he is using it in this manner, it is much more subtle than in the Gospels and would seemingly only apply to a specific subset of gentiles—judaizing gentiles who also encourage

---

21 Sharon R. Ringe, "A Gentile Woman's Story" in *Feminist Interpretation of the Bible*, ed. Letty M. Russell (Oxford: Blackwell, 1985), 65–72, at 68.
22 Thiessen, "Gentiles as Impure Animals," 25–26.
23 Elsewhere in Philippians, Paul refers to the Philippians as his brothers (ἀδελφοί, 1:12; 3:1, 13, 17; 4:1, 8, 21) and as his beloved (ἀγαπητοί, 2:12; 4:1). This distinguishes them from the opponents and could have further prevented them from identifying with ethnic dog-language if any of them did have the capacity to perceive it.

other gentiles to judaize. In light of these points, it seems unlikely that ethnic identification is what Paul has in mind by his reference to dogs.

4.2.2 A New Proposal: An Overlooked Meaning of κύων

In light of this data, any further meaning attributed to the usage of dog in Phil 3:2 is still opaque; as it stands now, it is merely functioning as a biting insult of reproach.[24] But is there more going on here? Since the "gentiles were commonly referred to as dogs" hypothesis has been proven false in light of the textual evidence, this allows for the interpreter to look for new and refreshing ways to approach the data. Cristiana Franco notes the flexibility with which dog can be employed as an insult in the ancient world; no one meaning can account for the variety of uses of dog as an insult, rather, it takes on meaning from its broader textual and social contexts.[25] Why, then, does Paul call them dogs when he already uses two other insults in his warning? Does dog add anything to these other invectives? One obvious answer is that κύων (dog) also begins with a kappa, as do the following invectives—κακοὺς ἐργάτας ("wicked workers") and κατατομή ("mutilation")—which creates assonance and possibly added rhetorical force to Paul's warning.[26] There is, however, one more element in play here that has gone unnoticed by scholars. Due to the fact that this insult occurs in a polemic about circumcision, it is surprising that no interpreter of Philippians has commented on the fact that κύων was also used in the ancient world as a slang term for penis.[27] This oversight can be attributed to the history of scholarship on this

---

[24] This broadly fits within the usage in the Hebrew Bible and Greco-Roman literature. Koester (Helmut Koester, "The Purpose of the Polemic of a Pauline Fragment," *NTS* 8 [1962]: 317–32), Batement ("Opponents at Philippi," 55), and Nanos ("Paul's Reversal," 117–20) note that dog was a common insult in the ancient world, not a particular one of Jewish origin against gentiles. See also the description of dogs in Philo, *Moses* 1.130–31.

[25] Franco, *Shameless*, 7–16. Her research primarily highlights the way that *dog* is used as an insult when an author is highlighting ethological concerns. See also Tutrone ("Barking at the Threshold"), who highlights the liminality of dogs in the ancient world. While dogs were often utilized for work or noted as being companions, they are generally not something you want to be called or compared to.

[26] Fee, *Philippians*, 296n49.

[27] Nanos briefly mentions a possible interpretation related to male prostitution (cf. Deut 23:19, see note above) in which dog could imply "the penis that has been dogged, that is, suffered a flesh wound from sexual activity," but he does not expound upon this interpretation ("Paul's Polemic," 71). On the usage of κύων as a slang term for penis, see Françoise Skoda, *Médecine ancienne et métaphore: Le vocabulaire de l'anatomie et de la pathologie en grec ancien* (Paris: Peeters/Selaf, 1988), 307n17; Jeffrey Henderson, *The Maculate Muse* (Oxford: Oxford University Press, 1991), 127; Konstan-

passage, which was preoccupied with identifying Jewish opponents based on a supposed slur about gentiles.

In Greek comedy, the penis is referred to as a dog in various colorful ways. In Aristophanes' *Lysistrata*, the phrase "skin a skinned dog" (κύνα δέρειν δεδαρμένην) is used by Lysistrata to refer to the manual stimulation of a penis.[28] Similarly, Suetonius defines the term κύνειρα as "the one who pulls the dog" (τὴν τὸν κύνα εἰρύουσαν), referring to a prostitute who manually stimulates her clients.[29] In Plato Comicus, the penis and testes are referred to as "the dog and dog-leaders" (κυνί τε καὶ κυνηγέταιν).[30] The fifth-century CE lexicographer Hesychius of Alexandria provides ἐξέδειραν as a gloss for κυνέπασαν, meaning "to pull back the skin" (i.e., to get an erection).[31] Since κυνέπασαν is a compound of κύων and σπάω, the basic meaning of term is "to draw the dog" (i.e., like drawing a sword), referring to the foreskin retracting and revealing the glans when erect.

Another key place where κύων is used to refer to the penis is the κυνοδέσμη, the "dog leash," which was used in athletic competitions as a primitive way to bind up the penis and ensure that the glans was not exposed. Paul's use of athletic imagery elsewhere in his writings (1 Cor 9:24–26; cf. Gal 2:2; 5:7; Phil 2:16; 3:13–14) could demonstrate a potential awareness of the κυνοδέσμη and the phallic connotations of κύων. Depictions of the κυνοδέσμη are common in athletic vase paintings and statues—dating from the fifth century BCE to the first century CE—where it is typically portrayed as a thin piece of leather tied around the tip of the foreskin and secured to the waist.[32] The κυνοδέσμη was also used for aesthetic

---

tinos K. Kapparis, "The Terminology of Prostitution in the Ancient Greek World," in *Greek Prostitutes in the Ancient Mediterranean 800 BCE–200 CE*, ed. Allison Glazebrook and Madeleine M. Henry (Madison: University of Wisconsin Press, 2011), 222–55, at 236–37.

28 Henderson (*The Maculate Muse*, 133), citing Aristophanes (*Lys.* 158), also comments that κύων could refer to female genitalia, but this is incorrect. From the broader context of the passage, "skinning a skinned dog" refers to women getting their husbands' attention by teasing and arousing them through manual stimulation.

29 This is cited by Eustathius in *Comm. Od.* 2.147. The original quote from Suetonius is from one of his lost works, *Concerning Profanity*, but the fragmentary text containing this reference can be found in Jean Taillardat, *Suétone: ΠΕΡΙ ΒΛΑΣΦΗΜΙΩΝ. ΠΕΡΙ ΠΑΙΔΙΩΝ (Extraits Byzantins)* (Paris: Les Belles Lettres, 1967), 51. On κύνειρα, see Kapparis, "Terminology of Prostitution," 203, 236–37. Henderson (*The Maculate Muse*, 133) incorrectly identifies κύνειρα as a vulgarity referring to female genitalia.

30 Pl. Com. 174.16.

31 Hsch. κ 4573; also, Com. Adesp. 1057.

32 For a brief overview of artwork that depicts the κυνοδέσμη, see Hodges, "The Ideal Prepuce," 381n22; 382n23. Marina Haworth ("The Wolfish Lover: The Dog as a Comic Metaphor in Homoerotic Symposium Pottery," *Archimède* 5 [2018]: 3–23) has noted that the use of dogs in homoerotic Attic black-figure vases also comedically links dogs with penises.

purposes as a means to stretch or elongate the foreskin via traction.³³ Regarding the κυνοδέσμη, the second-century CE grammarian Julius Pollux states: "The cord with which they tie up the foreskin, they call the dog leash."³⁴ Also writing in the second-century CE is the grammarian Phrynichus Arabius, who further spells out the etymological reasoning for calling this cord a dog leash. "The thing with which the people of Attica who have their glans exposed bind their penis. They call the penis 'dog' (κύων)."³⁵ Hesychius also notes that the word can refer to the penis: "…the male member, and the barking animal, and the shameless one, and the star, and the sea animal."³⁶ Elsewhere in medical and etymological texts, the frenulum, which is the elastic piece of tissue on the underside of the penis that connects the foreskin to the vernal mucosa, is also referred to as κύων.³⁷

Given that the context of Paul's polemic is about the opponents' claim to a circumcised identity (Phil 3:3), it is possible that Paul could here be invoking a phallic definition as a kind of vulgar title that he is conferring on these potential agitators.³⁸ Such vulgarity is not out of character for Paul.³⁹ Just a few verses later in Phil 3:8, Paul describes all things as σκύβαλον ("crap" or "shit")⁴⁰ in comparison to gaining the Messiah. Further on, in Phil 3:19, Paul states that his opponents' "god is the belly (κοιλία) and the glory in their shame (ἡ δόξα ἐν τῇ

---

33 Hodges, "The Ideal Prepuce," 381–83.
34 Pollux, *Onomastikon* 2.4.171; translated by Waldo E. Sweet, *Sport and Recreation in Ancient Greece: A Sourcebook with Translations* (Oxford: Oxford University Press, 1987) 130.
35 Phrynichus, *Sophistae Praeparatio Sophistica*, ed. J. de Borries (Leipzig, 1911), 85, cited by Eric John Dingwall, *Male Infibulation* (London: John Bale, Sons & Danielsson, 1925), 70.
36 Hsch. κ 4762. Hesychius (κ 4594) gives δεσμός ἀκροποσθίας ("tip of the foreskin cord") as the gloss for κυνοδέσμη. Nanos also cites Hesychius on the meaning of κύων, instead focusing on the "shameless one" to provide evidence for his reading that the opponents Paul is warning about may have been Cynics ("Paul's Polemic," 77).
37 Oribasius, *Collectionum Medicarum Reliquiae*, 50.3.1; EM 549.27. See also Henderson, *The Maculate Muse*, 127.
38 Given that κύων can reference both the penis and—more specifically—the foreskin in some of these examples, Isaac Soon has pointed out to me the possibility that Paul not only uses it as a phallic reference, but also as a reference to the opponents' true identity as naturally foreskinned gentiles (cf. Rom 2:27). Thus, κύων could also be functioning as a kind of circumlocution for ἀκροβυστία, which would enhance Paul's contrast with περιτομή in Phil 3:3 and is supported by Paul's contrast between ἀκροβυστία and περιτομή elsewhere in his epistles (Rom 2:25–27; 3:30; 4:9; 1 Cor 7:18–19; Gal 5:6; 6:15; cf. Eph 2:11; Col 3:11).
39 On the use of obscenity in the ancient world and early Christian texts, see Hultin, *Ethics of Obscene Speech*; cf. Jakob Jónsson, *Humour and Irony in the New Testament*, BZRGG 28 (Leiden: Brill, 1985).
40 Hays, *Echoes*, 122; John David Punch, "Σκύβαλα Happens: Edification from a Four-Letter Word in the Word of God?" *BT* 65 (2014): 369–84; Contra Hultin, *Ethics of Obscene Speech*, 150–54.

αἰσχύνη αὐτῶν)." Here, I understand Paul to be using κοιλία and αἰσχύνη euphemistically to refer to his opponents' circumcised genitals.[41] In effect, he is accusing them of phallus-worship. Additionally, in Gal 5:12 Paul states his desire for the ones imposing circumcision on the Galatians to cut their penises off. In short, Paul is no stranger to harsh and obscene language. In the Philippian opponents' quest to be recognized as "the circumcision," Paul confers on them another phallic title, "the dogs." Here, Paul uses this canine language as a "four-letter word" in the same way that modern vulgarities also use animal-language as crude references to genitals. Not only it is a word of reproach, but it also demonstrates where these opponents focus their attention and what the Philippians should be on the lookout for.

4.3 The Wicked Workers

Of Paul's tripartite warning, his identification of his rivals as wicked workers has been understood as the most ambiguous and generic.[42] The prevailing interpretation of this title is that it indicates some form of missionary activity.[43] Many who argue for this reading look to Paul's usage in 2 Cor 11:13 (cf. Matt 10:10; Luke 10:7) where he refers to another group of rival teachers as "deceitful workers" (ἐργάται δόλιοι). Throughout Paul's epistles, he also refers to those whom he works with in his capacity as an apostle as his "co-laborers" or "co-workers" (συνεργός; Rom 16:3, 9, 21; 1 Cor 3:9; 2 Cor 8:23; Phil 2:25; 4:3; 1 Thess 3:2, Phlm 1, 24), so interpreting his use of ἐργάτης in 3:2 as indicating some form of missionary or proclaiming activity seem plausible. Paul's pairing of ἐργάτης with the negative adjective κακός creates a clear contrast between these individuals and Paul and the co-workers he mentions in Phil 2:25 and 4:3. The identity of this group as rival missionaries or teachers, however, does not hinge on Paul's use of the term ἐργάτης. Rather, this fact seems to be implied by the warning of 3:2 itself. So while Paul may be using ἐργάτης in this manner, it is possible that he may be signaling something in addition to this aspect of their identity and praxis.

---

41 See the discussion in §4.5.
42 Schreiner, "Circumcision," 243; Nanos, "Paul's Polemic," 58–59. Nanos comments, "For the most part, the identity signified by this phrase is filled out on the basis of decisions made about Paul's use of dogs and mutilation..." (59).
43 Koester, "Purpose of the Polemic," 320; Klijn, "Paul's Opponents," 282; Schreiner, "Circumcision," 243; Watson, *Paul, Judaism*, 74; Martin and Hawthorne, *Philippians*, 174; Mimouni, *La circoncision*, 229; Reumann, *Philippians*, 472; Holloway, *Philippians*, 153; cf. Bockmuehl, *Philippians*, 188; Fee, *Philippians*, 294–95.

Other interpreters have proposed that Paul may be employing some kind of deliberate wordplay on the "works of the law" (ἔργων νόμου; Rom 3:20, 28; Gal 2:16; 3:2, 5, 10).[44] Based on the circumcision-focused language in Phil 3:2–5, it may be the case that Paul is speaking against their promotion of—and/or reliance on—the so-called works of the law, namely circumcision. In Galatians, Paul's discussion of works of the law is directly connected to his to rejection of the circumcision of gentiles. There, he contrasts those who seek *dikaiosynē* "from works of the law" (Gal 2:16; 3:2, 5, 10–11) with those who do so "from *pistis*" (Gal 2:16; 3:8–9, 11–12, 22, 24). According to Paul, Jews know that one is not rightwised from works of the law but from *pistis*, which is why he and Cephas trust in the Messiah (Gal 2:16). Gentile sinners on the other hand, do not know this and are in need of proper instruction about how one is rightwised. Paul has no patience for those who lead gentiles astray through the promotion of the works of the law as the means of obtaining eschatological *dikaiosynē*.[45] Just as he rebuked Cephas for effectively compelling non-Jews to judaize (Gal 2:11–14),[46] Paul rebukes these rival teachers for their insistence on the necessity of circumcision for non-Jews in the assembly. Those who come promoting the works of the law are not good workers but are wicked workers. As Paul notes in Gal 5:2–4, the adoption of circumcision by a non-Jew severs them from the Messiah and returns them to a state of slavery.[47] While these teachers may think they are including non-Jews through circumcision, they may actually be damning them. For this, Paul deems them to be wicked workers. Further, if these individuals are judaizing gentiles—which I think is most clearly indicated by the title "mutilation" and Paul's contrasting presentation of his Jewish bona fides—then, like the agitators in Galatians,

---

[44] Garland, "Composition and Unity," 168–69; Bockmuehl, *Philippians*, 188; Martin and Hawthorne, *Philippians*, 175; Thiessen, "Impure Animals," 27–28; cf. Fee, *Philippians*, 296.

[45] Paul speaks about this type of *dikaiosynē* in Phil 3:9: "[T]he *dikaiosynē* through the faithfulness of Christ, the *dikaiosynē* from God based on faithfulness." On the ineffectual nature of circumcision and works of the law as a means of obtaining *dikaiosynē*, Smit comments, "Paul understand the 'dogs' and 'evil workers' to be performing a ritual act (circumcision) as *pars pro toto* for achieving righteousness; they seek to belong to the people of God throughout the 'performance' of the law, and yet it does not produce the desired effect, that is, righteousness" ("Real Circumcision," 86). Here, Smit argues from the perspective of ritual studies and the concept of ritual failure.

[46] This is why Paul rebukes Cephas for confusing some gentiles on this point through his hypocrisy that inadvertently compelled some non-Jews to judaize. As noted in §3.2.3, "compel" (ἀναγκάζω) is used elsewhere in Galatians to refer to the compulsion of circumcision (2:3; 6:12). It may be that Paul has full judaizaiton in mind in Gal 2:14, indicating the adoption of circumcision. Cf. Josephus, *J.W.* 2.454, where Metilius commits "to judaize as far as circumcision" (μέχρι περιτομῆς Ἰουδαΐσειν ὑποσχόμενον).

[47] See the discussion in §3.6.1.

Paul would consider their own circumcisions a transgression of the law (Gal 6:13). It may be the case that Paul also has this in mind when conferring the title "wicked workers" upon them.

4.4 The Mutilation

The final component of Paul's tripartite warning has been regarded as his harshest: "Beware the mutilation!" Here, Paul employs paronomasia, contrasting mutilation (κατατομή) with circumcision (περιτομή) for powerful rhetorical effect.[48] While κατατομή and περιτομή are aurally similar and share a common root, their intended meanings in Paul's Jewish milieu could not be further from one another; one signifies pagan ritualistic cuttings and the other the mark of the covenant with Abraham and the Jewish people. To equate Jewish circumcision with mutilation is to look at God's covenant with Abraham with disdain. Consequently, this line has been construed as the sharp knife with which Paul himself mutilates the image of Judaism.[49]

In the LXX/OG, the verbal form of κατατομή (κατατέμνω) is used four times to signify the self-mutilation that was practiced in the context of non-Israelite cults (Lev 21:5; 3 Kgdms 18:28; Hos 7:14; Isa 15:2; cf. Lev 19:28).[50] This practice is specifically banned in Lev 21:5 for the priests of Israel: "...and in their flesh they shall not cut gashes." In 1 Kgs 18:28, when the prophets of Baal are pleading for fire to fall upon a sacrificial bull, they cry out and cut themselves as a means of invoking Baal, but their blood is met with silence. To demonstrate how far Ephraim has fallen, Hos 7:14 notes that they have resorted to these types of ritualistic cutting practices in order to receive grain and wine. These texts portray this type of cutting as harmful, powerless, and forbidden. For Paul to say that Jewish circumcision is equivalent to this type of cultic self-mutilation would be a denial of the value of God's covenant with Abraham—something he speaks about positively elsewhere (e.g., Rom 4; Gal 3–4). Commenting on Phil 3:2, Hyam Maccoby remarks, "The great mystery about Paul is, how did a person of his allegedly Pharisaic background and upbringing arrive at views so incompatible with Judaism and hold such a contempt for Judaism's

---

48 Paronomasia is also present in the German translation of these terms: *Zerschneidung* and *Beschneidung*.

49 See, e.g., Räisänen, *Paul and the Law,* 258; Horn, "Der Verzicht," 501; John Paul Heil, *Philippians: Let Us Rejoice in Being Conformed to Christ* (Atlanta: Society of Biblical Literature, 2010), 118–19.

50 Nanos ("Paul's Polemic," 82–85) and Ehrensperger ("Trouble in Galatia," 182) both argue that—like these comparative examples in the LXX/OG—Paul's mention of mutilation points in the direction of pagan practices, not Jewish circumcision or its misapplication on gentile bodies (see below).

holiest rite?"⁵¹ Here, Maccoby raises an incisive question: how could Paul—a circumcised on the eighth-day, Hebrew from Hebrews, Pharisaic Jew—come to the point in his life where he believed that circumcision is tantamount to pagan ritualistic mutilation?⁵²

One prevailing answer to this question has been that after Paul's call to be the Apostle to the nations, he forsook his former life in Judaism and spiritualized the meaning of circumcision.⁵³ Combine this with a mirror-reading of Phil 3 that produces Jewish opponents, and you create a Paul who is able to renounce Jewish circumcision as being on par with mutilation. Martin and Hawthorne propose that Paul transfers the title of circumcision from Israel to the "church" because "Israel lost sight of the spiritual significance of circumcision" and "has forfeited its right to the title 'The Circumcision.'"⁵⁴ On this basis, they propose that Paul uses the term mutilation to describe all of ancient Israel (!). This reading extrapolates Paul's invective—directed at a particular group of rivals—to an absurd degree, ignoring that Paul speaks positively about the circumcision of Jews elsewhere (Rom 3:1–2).

Other interpreters who are perceptive to the fact that Paul "never derogates circumcision as such, and especially not that of Jews,"⁵⁵ have found ways to soften the blow of this invective. Instead of equating circumcision with mutilation, Bockmuehl proposes Paul's point is that "circumcision that is not of the heart is *no better than* ritual pagan laceration."⁵⁶ Rather than completely devalue and diminish the fleshly symbol, Bockmuehl thinks Paul is actually driving at the point that in order for circumcision to be valuable, it must be accompanied by a circumcised heart—otherwise it is just as ineffective and meaningless as cul-

---

51 Hyam Maccoby, "Paul and Circumcision: A Rejoinder," *JQR* 82 (1991): 177–80, at 180.
52 The only other place in ancient literature that directly links circumcision with mutilation is Hist. Aug., Hadr. 14.2: "...the Jews began war because they were forbidden from mutilating their genitals (*mutilare genitalia*)." On this, see my previous discussion in §3.9.1. Cf. Strabo, *Geogr.* 16.4.17: "They are not only mutilated (κολοβοί), but some have also been circumcised (περιτετμημένοι)." While κολοβός could be a reference to the size of an individual or an individual's penis, based on Strabo's usage in the surrounding context it indicates being maimed or mutilated. Elsewhere Strabo references those with a "mutilated glans" (κολοβοὶ τὰς βαλάνους)" (*Geogr.* 16.4.5; 16.4.9).
53 E.g., Boyarin, *A Radical Jew*, 81–82; James D. G. Dunn, *The Theology of Paul the Apostle* (Grand Rapids: Eerdmans, 1998), 422, 424; Martin and Hawthorne, *Philippians*, 174–75.
54 Martin and Hawthorne, *Philippians*, 175.
55 Fee, *Philippians*, 296n48.
56 Bockmuehl, *Philippians*, 189; emphasis added; cf. Marvin R. Vincent, *A Critical and Exegetical Commentary on the Epistles to the Philippians and to Philemon*, ICC (Edinburgh: T&T Clark, 1897), 92.

tic mutilation.⁵⁷ Fee takes a different approach and proposes that κατατομή is not a reference to Jewish circumcision, but is Paul's way of speaking about the circumcision of gentiles that the dogs are advocating for. Thus, the invective does not apply to the dogs themselves, but is a reference to their activity.⁵⁸ While Fee rightly perceives that if Paul was describing Jewish circumcision as mutilation it would be out of character for him, his interpretation creates an awkward reading of Paul's tripartite warning. On Fee's understanding, dogs and wicked workers are descriptors of the rivals, but mutilation describes what they promote and do. In solving one problem, Fee creates another. In the wider context of Paul's warning and his juxtaposition between the circumcision and these rivals, it makes most sense to take all of the epithets as titles Paul is conferring upon this group. If Paul were focusing on what they do as mutilators, one would expect him to employ a participial form of κατατέμνω—e.g., "the mutilators" or "the ones who mutilate."⁵⁹ This, however, is not what Paul is driving at with this epithet. Rather, Paul is identifying what they are (mutilation) in contrast to what "we" are (circumcised).

The question is, for whom does Paul deem circumcision to be a mutilation? Despite the prevalent interpretation that Paul's opponents here are Jews, it makes little sense for Paul to refer to other circumcised, Jewish bodies as being mutilated. If this were the case, how would Paul's circumcision not be included under this title? While the possible invocation of heart-circumcision as validating or superseding Paul's physical circumcision in 3:3—and thus ensuring he is a member of the so-called "true" circumcision and not the mutilation—is appealing, it is unlikely for two reasons: 1) Paul makes no direct reference to heart-circumcision here, and 2) Paul goes on to appeal to the confidence he has in his flesh (3:4)—notably his eighth-day circumcision and genealogy—which he portrays as being superior to those of his rivals. Given that Paul elsewhere uses the title circumcision to refer to Jews, and that highlights the validity of his own eighth-day circumcision and Jewish bona fides in 3:5, it is most prob-

---

57 Here, Bockmuehl (*Philippians*, 189) proposes Paul is making a critique of flesh-only circumcision comparable to the critique in Jer 9:25–26.
58 Fee, *Philippians*, 296.
59 The (N)RSV translates κατατομή as if it were a participle: "those who mutilate the flesh." Employing a participle instead of a noun would preserve the play on words between κατατομή and περιτομή—although not the full aural similarity—and would emphasize their actions rather than Paul's characterization of them as mutilated. Cf. Nanos, "Paul's Polemic," 60–61.

able that judaizing gentiles are the object of Paul's warning.⁶⁰ While they may claim to be the circumcision, Paul rejects the validity of their proselyte circumcisions. The marks on their bodies are not actually circumcisions from Paul's perspective, but rather, are mere slashes or incisions that are no more beneficial than the ritualistic cuttings of pagan cults.⁶¹

According to Paul's bifurcated conception of humanity—Jews and gentiles, circumcisions and foreskins—these categories are determined by nature. In Gal 2:15, Paul states that he and Peter are Jews by nature (ἡμεῖς φύσει Ἰουδαῖοι), and not sinners from the nations (οὐκ ἐξ ἐθνῶν ἁμαρτωλοί). Conversely, in Rom 2:27, Paul speaks of those who are the foreskin from nature (ἡ ἐκ φύσεως ἀκροβυστία), which is an unusual thing to say. To modern readers, saying that someone is "the foreskin from nature" or "was born foreskinned" is simply an empirical truth that applies to all male infants—barring some kind of physical anomaly or divine intrauterine circumcision. For Paul, however, this natural state of being foreskinned only applies to gentiles; Jews are Jews by nature and are thus naturally circumcised (cf. m. Ned. 3.11; b. ʿAbod. Zar. 27a).⁶² This brings us back to "the mutilation" of Phil 3:2. If the categories of circumcision and foreskin are ones determined by nature, then the adoption of circumcision by a naturally foreskinned gentile would constitute a mutilation of their natural state. Although their incisions may look like circumcisions, the cut alone does not a circumcision make.⁶³

Paul's equation of his rivals' circumcised status with that of mutilation is therefore not a wholesale rejection of the Jewish rite and its concomitant identity, but a harsh rejection of the validity of circumcision for gentiles. By identifying Paul's opponents as judaizing gentiles who have adopted circumcision, this text should be understood in a way that does not reject circumcision but upholds its application in its proper context. In Phil 3:2, Paul makes no statement about the circumcisions of Jews, only the mutilation of gentiles.

---

60 For other interpreters who identity these opponents as a group of judaizing gentiles, see Grayston, "Opponents"; Batement, "Were the Opponents"; Murray, "Romans 2," 171–75; Thiessen, "Gentiles as Impure Animals," 26–30.
61 Thiessen, "Gentiles as Impure Animals," 28.
62 Fredriksen (*Pagans' Apostle*, 124) notes that in Gal 2:15 Paul's statement implies that gentiles are sinful by nature. In the same way, Rom 2:27 implies that Jews are from nature circumcised. Thus rightly James D. G. Dunn, *Romans 1–8*, WBC 38A (Waco, TX: Word, 1988), 122; Pamela Eisenbaum, "Is Paul the Father of Misogyny and Antisemitism?" *CrossCur* 50 (2000): 506–524, at 517. Cf. Philo, *Spec. Laws* 2.109, "They are under the sway of a very ancient custom, which through long familiarity has won its way to the standing of nature" (γενόμενον εἰς φύσιν ἐκνενίκηκεν).
63 Cf. Smit, "Real Circumcision," 86.

4.5 Further Identifying the Opponents: Philippians 3:18–19

As I have proposed thus far, each element of Paul's warning can be interpreted as relating to his opponents' identity as circumcised, judaizing gentiles: "dogs" as a phallic epithet, "wicked workers" as an indictment of their imposition of judaizing circumcision, and "mutilation" as a harsh critique of their pseudo-circumcisions. In addition to his warning in Phil 3:2, I argue Paul further describes his rivals with phallic imagery in 3:18–19.[64]

> For many live—about whom I have often spoken to you, and now I say with tears—as enemies of the cross of Christ;[65] whose end is destruction, whose god is the belly and the glory in their shame,[66] whose minds are set on earthly things (Phil 3:18–19).

Here, I focus on Paul's claim that their "god is the belly and the glory in their shame." In light of the numerous ways this has been understood, I will offer a brief overview of the various interpretations before offering my own. Belly (κοιλία) has often been interpreted in a way that reflects eating habits and dietary concerns.[67] For most interpreters who see the opponents as being strict adherents and promoters of Torah, κοιλία thus becomes a cypher for Jewish dietary laws.[68] Others see the reference to κοιλία here as a reference to the opponents licentious and unscrupulous desires, ranging from gluttony to unbridled sexual appetites.[69] Looking

---

[64] When identifying the opponents of Phil 3:2, some interpreters are split on whether the group targeted in 3:2 is the same as the group in 3:18–19. I understand Paul's language in 3:18–19 to refer to the same group as in 3:2. Some of the earliest interpreters and copyists of this text also saw this connection, which is attested to by the insertion of βλέπετε before τοὺς ἐχθροὺς τοῦ σταυροῦ τοῦ Χριστοῦ in 𝔓⁴⁶. Some modern interpreters who also follow this interpretation are: Klijn, "Paul's Opponents," 279–83; Koester, "Purpose of the Polemic," 331; Chris Mearns, "The Identity of Paul's Opponents at Philippi," NTS 33 (1987): 194–204, at 202; Watson, Paul, Judaism, 75; Nanos, "Paul's Polemic"; Holloway, Philippians, 148–49, 179.

[65] Like the judaizing gentile agitators in Galatians, Paul portrays these individuals as being in opposition to the cross. On the connection between the cross and circumcision in Galatians, see §3.7.2 and 3.8.2.

[66] Grammatically, κοιλία and δόξα are functioning as a single subject joined by καί with θεός functioning as the predicate (Martin and Hawthorne, Philippians, 225). This is attested by the punctuation in most Greek editions, however, the majority of translations overlook this (e.g., "[T]heir god is the belly; and their glory is in their shame." NRSV).

[67] E.g., "god is their stomach" (NIV); "god is their appetite" (NASB).

[68] Koester, "Purpose of the Polemic," 326; Bonnard, Philippiens, 71; Gunther, St. Paul's Opponents, 98; Martin and Hawthorne, Philippians, 166.

[69] Robert Jewett, "Conflicting Movements in the Early Church as Reflected in Philippians," NovT 12 (1970): 362–90, at 380; Fee, Philippians, 372; Bockmuehl, Philippians, 232; Karl Olav Sandnes, Belly

4.5 Further Identifying the Opponents: Philippians 3:18–19 — 141

at the usage of κοιλία in Rom 16:18, some see this as designating some kind of self-worship or too high self-regard.[70] Given the prior discussion of circumcision in 3:2–3, Watson and Mearns both read κοιλία as a euphemism for penises.[71] Shame (αἰσχύνη) also receives a wide range of treatments from interpreters. Nanos sees αἰσχύνη functioning in a very broad sense: "When Paul writes of those 'who glory in their shame,' this language can naturally refer to any behavior that is contrary to what Paul believes honorable behavior should be."[72] Other interpreters find a contrast between δόξα and αἰσχύνη, which leads them to an understanding that shame is used here to represent the judgement of God.[73] Shame, like κοιλία, is also understood by some scholars as a euphemism for penises.[74]

Given that the core issue of 3:2–3 is the false claim to the title "circumcision" made by judaizing gentile opponents, it is likely that Paul continues that attack here. The use of κοιλία as a reference to male genitalia is well attested in the LXX/OG (2 Kgdms 7:12; 16:11; 1 Chr 17:11; Ps 131:11).[75] In these instances, κοιλία is used as the locus of where one's progeny spring from, i.e., the testes and penis. Similarly, shame (ἀσχημοσύνη) is also used in the LXX to refer euphemistically to nudity and genitalia (Exod 20:26; Lev 18:6ff; cf. Rev 16:15).[76] If both κοιλία and αἰσχύνη can be understood as references to genitals, then Paul is once again crit-

---

and Body in the Pauline Epistles, SNTSMS 120 (Cambridge: Cambridge University Press, 2002), 136–64; Nanos, "Paul's Polemic," 75–77.
70 Klijn, "Paul's Opponents," 283; Batement, "Were the Opponents," 59. Collange sees κοιλία here as a reference to their navels (ὀμφαλός), i.e., they are self-absorbed navel-gazers (Philippians, 138).
71 Watson, Paul, Judaism, 76; Mearns, "Identity," 198–200; Smit, "Real Circumcision," 84.
72 Nanos, "Paul's Polemic," 77. He specifically thinks this points to a group of Cynics who publicly engage in animal-like behavior such as farting, defecating, masturbating, showing off their erections in public, etc. For similar readings that understand αἰσχύνη to reference to lewd behavior, see Jewett, "Conflicting Movements," 381; Bockmuehl, Philippians, 231–32; Fee, Philippians, 373.
73 Koester, "Purpose of the Polemic," 327; Silva, Philippians, 181.
74 Watson, Paul, Judaism, 76; Martin and Hawthorne, Philippians, 224–25; Mearns, "Identity," 198; Smit, "Real Circumcision," 84.
75 While the references in 2 Kingdoms, 1 Chronicles, and Psalms are clearly referencing the κοιλία of a man (David), the instances in Deuteronomy (28:4, 11, 18, 53; 30:9) could be references to either men or women, but they are generally taken as references to a womb and not a penis in most English translations. The Hebrew word used in Deuteronomy is בטן, which is also used as a reference to David's loins in Ps 131:11. Mearns ("Identity," 199) also sees a reference to genitalia in Sir 23:6 (κοιλίας ὄρεξις, desire of the belly), but that text is widely understood as speaking about gluttony. In context, both readings are possible, however, the previous verse's reference to desire (ἐπιθυμία) and the reference to "sexual intercourse" and "a shameless soul," in the rest of 23:6 could give weight to Mearns' reading.
76 This is how Paul is uses the cognate ἀσχήμων in in 1 Cor 12:23; Martin, Corinthian Body, 94–96; Thiselton, First Corinthians, 1008–9.

iquing these rival teachers for their obsession with their circumcised penises. Reumann notes an objection to the understanding that circumcised penises are in view here, stating, "Paul never speaks so disparagingly of circumcision"[77] in regard to Jews, which is correct. However, as I have argued, Jews are not the object of the language here—gentiles who have adopted circumcision are. Fee also rejects this reading, but he does so based on a rigid reading of the use of these terms in the LXX/OG, which fails to take into account the subtlety of euphemism.[78] The reason these texts do not directly say "penis," "testes," or "genitals" is precisely because they are employing euphemism; context indicates that genitals are in view. It is the same in Phil 3:19—Paul uses both κοιλία and αἰσχύνη euphemistically to refer to the circumcised members of his opponents.

Therefore, when Paul says, "whose god is the belly and the glory in their shame," he is characterizing his opponents as a priapic cult.[79] Based on their obsession with circumcision, Paul styles them as elevating their circumcised penises to the status of a deity. They do not direct their worship toward God as they should, but rather, they worship their penises. In an ironic turn of events, according to Paul, their circumcisions are not actually counted as circumcisions but are merely mutilations. The confidence they have in the flesh is groundless and their god has failed them. In fact, their fidelity to this god ultimately leads to their eschatological destruction. Like the portrayal of the damning consequences of proselyte circumcision in Gal 5, Paul points out in 3:19 that their misunderstandings about and misapplication of circumcision lead to their ultimate destruction.[80]

4.6 "We are the Circumcision!"

Having argued that Paul's opponents are a group of circumcised, judaizing gentiles —not Jews—I will now turn to Phil 3:3 where many have interpreted Paul as redefining who the circumcision are. Here Paul proclaims, "For we are the circumci-

---

77 Reumann, *Philippians*, 573.
78 Fee, *Philippians*, 371n36.
79 Watson, *Paul, Judaism*, 76. As Watson mentions, the connection Paul creates between their circumcisions and cultic mutilation may also gesture in this direction. There is archaeological and inscriptional evidence that lends plausibility to the idea that the Philippians would have understood Paul's words as a reference to phallus worship or a priapic cult. In Philippi there was a temple for Egyptian deities, including Harpocrates, who is often depicted like Priapus with an oversized, erect phallus. Cf. Diodorus Siculus, *Bib. hist.* 4.6.1–4. For a list of inscriptions in Philippi that reference Harpocrates see, Peter Pilhofer, *Philippi: Band 2, Katalog der Inschriften von Philippi*, 2nd ed., WUNT 119 (Tübingen: Mohr Siebeck, 2009), 242–43.
80 Cf. Smit, "Real Circumcision," 86.

sion, the ones who serve by Spirit of God and boast in Christ Jesus and put no confidence in the flesh." Interpreters are almost unanimous in understanding that "we" is a reference to the writers of the letter (Paul and Timothy, 1:1) and the assemblies in Philippi.[81] Additionally, the majority of interpreters extend this to include all Christ-followers.[82] Thus for the vast majority of scholars, this text serves as the place where Paul confers the title of circumcision upon all who are in the Messiah, irrespective of the state of one's penis.[83] For example, on this supposed transfer of the title circumcision, Michael Wolter comments: "The concept of circumcision is provided with an expanded meaning, so that a piece of the semantic concept (the function of circumcision as a sign of the election of God's people) is transferred to Christians."[84] Many have also included the adjective "true" to describe the circumcision Paul speaks of in 3:3—indicating that it is different from and superior to the physical circumcision of Jews.[85]

As I have argued throughout this book, Paul frequently uses circumcision metonymically to refer to Jews, in contrast to the foreskin. If Paul is now redefining whom he identifies as the circumcision, this would be a marked deviation from how he uses the term in the rest of his extant writings.[86] Furthermore, nowhere else in Paul's writings are the titles "Israel" or "Jews" applied to all Christ-followers as a redefinition of those categories.[87] Given the rhetorical context of Paul's language, what is more plausible is that "we" (ἡμεῖς) simply refers to Paul and Timothy[88]—the Jewish

---

[81] E.g., Garroway, "Circumcision of Christ," 317–18. Livesey (*Malleable Symbol*, 99) identifies the "we" as Paul and the Philippians, omitting Timothy.
[82] Blaschke, *Beschneidung*, 403–4; Bockmuehl, *Philippians*, 191; Williams, *Enemies*, 162; Martin and Hawthorne, *Philippians*, 175; Silva, *Philippians*, 148; Fee, *Philippians*, 298; Reumann, *Philippians*, 473; Wright, *Paul*, 960.
[83] On this point, many interpreters cite Rom 2:28–29 as further evidence of this hypothesis. For examples, see the note in the introduction above (§4.1).
[84] Wolter, *Paulus*, 443n25 (my translation); cf. 363. "Der Beschneidungsbegriff wird mit einer Bedeutungserweiterung versehen, indem ein Ausschnitt aus semantischen Konzept (die der Beschneidung als Zeichen des erwählten Gottesvolks) auf die Christen übertragen wird."
[85] E.g., Jewett, "Conflicting Movements," 383; Sanders, *Paul and Palestinian Judaism*, 505; Räisänen, *Paul and the Law*, 128; 176n75; Williams, *Enemies*, 162; Silva; *Philippians*, 148; Martin and Hawthorne, *Philippians*, 175.
[86] The peculiarity of Paul's supposed usage of circumcision to include non-Jews in contrast to his consistent usage elsewhere is highlighted by some, e.g., Grayston, "Opponents in Philippians," 170; Dunn, *New Perspective on Paul*, 471–72. Notably, even the deutero-Pauline and Pastoral epistles use περιτομή to refer only to Jews (Eph 2:11; Col 4:11; Titus 1:10).
[87] See my discussion of Rom 2:28–29 in §5.4.2. On the Israel of God in Gal 6:16 referring to historic Israel, see Eastman, "Israel," 385–90; cf. Richardson, *Israel*, 74–84.
[88] There are numerous issues surrounding the ethnicity and circumcision of Timothy. First, all of the direct information we have regarding Timothy's ethnicity and circumcision comes from Acts—not

Paul. Second, the information given in Acts 16:1–3 does not clearly indicate Timothy's ethnicity; his mother was Jewish, but his father was Greek. Third, Acts positions Timothy's circumcision immediately after the recounting of the apostolic council where it was agreed upon that gentiles should not be circumcised. Lastly, the reason given for Paul circumcising Timothy appears to be related to pressure or expectations from other Jews that knew Timothy was of mixed heritage. While I think Phil 3:3 indicates that Paul understood Timothy to be a Jew (at least for his own rhetorical purposes), the presentation in Acts 16:1–3 is problematic and worth a brief discussion.

As Shaye Cohen demonstrates, the matrilineal principle of descent was not firmly established as Jewish law until sometime after the first century (Shaye J. D. Cohen, "Was Timothy Jewish (Acts 16:1–3)? Patristic Exegesis, Rabbinic Law, and Matrilineal Descent," *JBL* 105 [1986]: 251–68). Based on this, the fact that Timothy's father was a Greek, and the history of interpretation regarding Timothy's ethnic identity, Cohen concludes that in all likelihood Luke did not think he was recounting the circumcision of a Jew. While the codification of the matrilineal principle may be later than the events recounted in Acts, this does not rule out the possibility that the ethnicity of one's mother was a determinative factor for some ancient Jews—Luke included. For example, Thiessen (*Contesting Conversion*, 121) notes how the holy seed anthropology of Ezra-Nehemiah placed emphasis on the ethnicity of both parents, not just the father (cf. Jub. 30:11–14). Similarly, in Luke 1:5, Luke highlights that Elizabeth—the mother of John the Baptizer—was a descendent of Aaron. So it may be the case for Luke that the identity of one's mother has some role in the ethnicity of her children. If Luke did not think this was relevant information, he simply could have indicated that Timothy was a gentile. Given that this passage follows immediately after the Apostolic Council and deals with circumcision, the inclusion of this information does not appear to be accidental or superfluous (see Bryan, "A Further Look," 292–94). While one cannot be certain, it is possible that this could be an early attestation of the matrilineal principle of descent (Rudolph, *Jew to the Jews*, 26). Or as Thiessen (*Contesting Conversion*, 121) proposes, it could be Luke's way of acknowledging that some of his readers would understand Timothy's ethnicity in different ways, and Luke is portraying how carefully Paul acts in the face of ethnic ambiguity. Since Luke goes on to portray Paul as being falsely accused of leading Jews to abandon Torah and abstain from circumcising their sons (Acts 21:21), perhaps Luke uses this instance as a way to convince his reader that these claims are false (Bryan, "Acts 16:3," 293; Rudolph, *Jew to the Jews*, 27). If Luke's account is historically accurate, it seems that Paul would have deemed Timothy to be a Jew—or at least Jew-ish. In light of Paul's self-presentation in his epistles, it is highly unlikely that he would have knowingly performed a circumcision upon a non-Jew based on external pressure.

This, however, does not solve the issue of Timothy's circumcision occurring outwith the eight-day stipulation. One can only speculate as to why Paul would perform a non-covenantal circumcision. Assuming Paul believed Timothy was a Jew, perhaps he thinks it is better for him to be circumcised improperly rather than remain in foreskin. Given the interconnectedness of Jewish identity and circumcision in Paul's thought, it may be that Paul could not conceive of the contradiction of a foreskinned Jew. In any case, this is the only discussion of the circumcision of a man with mixed heritage in the New Testament, and the account in Acts 16 presents Paul's ad hoc halakhah on an unusual situation. As far as Paul and the New Testament are concerned, the circumcision of Timothy constitutes a very unique exception, not the rule. Perhaps this is why Paul switches from "we" to "I" when he discusses the basis for his confidence in the flesh and his ethnic bona fides in Phil 3:4–6. Since Timothy could not appeal to such a pristine pedigree, Paul focuses on his own.

authors of the letter.[89] The next occurrence of the first-person plural pronoun in 3:17 ("the example you have in *us*") further supports this interpretation. There, "us" refers to authors of the letter exclusive of the Philippian assemblies.[90]

The contrast Paul is setting up in 3:2–3 is not between the mutilated, wicked-working dogs and Christ-followers or Jews more generally, but between these rival preachers and himself and Timothy—a specific subset of the circumcision. While these individuals *claim* to be the circumcision and are characterized by their obsession with circumcision, Paul and Timothy actually *are* the circumcision and are characterized by serving by the *pneuma* of God, boasting in Christ Jesus, and not placing confidence in the flesh (3:3). This is not to say Paul is claiming that all of the circumcision do these things or that doing these things constitutes membership within the circumcision,[91] but that the circumcised individuals in question do these things in contradistinction to those who claim to be the circumcision but are merely mutilated. Paul's statement about the circumcision in 3:3 has a very specific rhetorical context and—despite the practice of the majority of interpreters—should not be treated as a universal claim about who the circumcision are. Rather, it is simply a description of "us" over against "them."

4.6.1 Paul's Pristine Pedigree

Paul follows up his self-identification as the circumcision with an appeal to his own Jewish bona fides. Not only does the recitation of his ethnic qualifications establish his authority, as Jennifer Eyl notes, but this list demonstrates the rightful claim he has to the title circumcision and the confidence he is able to have in

---

[89] Windsor, *Paul and the Vocation*, 53–55; Thiessen, "Gentiles as Impure Animals," 28. This option is discussed in Bonnard, *Philippiens*, 60; Reumann, *Philippians*, 474. D. W. B. Robinson ("We Are the Circumcision," *ABR* 15 [1967]: 28–35) expands this to include all Jewish Christ-followers. Here, Robinson uses the category of "true circumcision" to describe Jews who trust in the Messiah, over against those who do not recognize Jesus as the Messiah. Within the rhetorical context of 3:2–3, however, it should be understood as simply referring to Paul and Timothy. Given the positive role Epaphroditus plays in Phil 2:25–30 and 4:18, he may also be included among the circumcision in 3:3. While we know little about Epaphroditus and his ethnicity, this would indicate that he was a Jew—though I acknowledge the circularity of this point.

[90] Fee, *Philippians*, 365n14; Bockmuehl, *Philippians*, 229; Martin and Hawthorne, *Philippians*, 218–19; Thiessen, "Gentiles as Impure Animals," 28–29; cf. Robinson, "We are the Circumcision," 34–35.

[91] Contra Smit, "Real Circumcision," 87.

his flesh.[92] The opponents who wrongfully boast in and have confidence in their circumcisions have no grounds for doing so, but Paul on the other hand, has a pristine pedigree that gives him confidence in his flesh.[93]

> For we are the circumcision; the ones who serve by the *pneuma* of God and boast in Christ Jesus and have no confidence in the flesh—even though I also have confidence in the flesh. If anyone thinks he has confidence in the flesh, I more so: an eighth-day circumcision, from the race of Israel, of the tribe of Benjamin, a Hebrew from Hebrews; as to the law, a Pharisee; as to zeal, a persecutor of the assembly; as to *dikaiosynē* in the law, blameless (Phil 3:3–6).

Notably, Paul presents his own circumcision as being carried out on the eighth-day after birth in accordance with the requirements of the law (LXX Gen 17:14; Lev 12:3; Jub. 15:14, 25; cf. Ep. Apos. 31:1). Paul stresses his pedigree here because—from his perspective—this is what determines one's membership in the circumcision, and further demonstrates that the mutilation are not who they say they are. For circumcised gentiles to now claim that they are a part of the circumcision is manifestly false in Paul's mind. They are merely mutilated dogs.

4.7 Conclusion

This chapter argued that Paul does not redefine the title of circumcision in Phil 3:3 as the majority of interpreters have claimed. Instead of redefining or reappropriating circumcision as an identity marker for the assembly, I have proposed that Paul uses it in his standard way as a reference to Jews—specifically himself and Timothy, the Jewish authors of the epistle.

I made this argument based on a fresh reading of Paul's warning in Phil 3:2, "Beware the dogs! Beware the wicked workers! Beware the mutilation!" I suggested that each element of this warning can be understood in a way that draws attention to this group's emphasis on circumcision; both their own penises and the pros-

---

[92] Jennifer Eyl, "'I Myself Am an Israelite': Paul, Authenticity and Authority," *JSNT* 40 (2017): 148–68, at 151.. Thiessen ("Gentiles as Impure Animals," 30) notes some early Christian interpreters of Phil 3:5 highlight the rhetorical value of Paul's appeal to his eight-day circumcision as emphasizing the fact that he was not a proselyte (Ambrosiaster, *Comm. Phil.* 3:5; Chrysostom, *Hom. Phil.* 10; Theodoret, *Comm. Phil.* 3:5).

[93] Todd D. Still ("(Im)Perfection: Reading Philippians 3.5–6 in Light of the Number Seven," *NTS* 60 [2014]: 139–48) proposes that it is significant that Paul's "confidence catalogue" in 3:5–6 contains seven elements. He argues that the numerical symbolism of the number seven in the ancient world points to completion or perfection, indicating that Paul presents his Jewish pedigree as complete. Still notes the comparable list of seven privileges belonging to Israel in Rom 9:4–5: the adoption, the *doxa*, the covenants, the giving of the law, the cultic service, the promises, and the patriarchs.

elyte circumcision they promote. First, I offered a new interpretation of Paul's invective "dogs" as a phallic epithet in light of its ancient usage as a slang term for penises and foreskin. Second, I proposed that "wicked workers" constitutes a negative assessment of their promotion of proselyte circumcision. Lastly, I argued that the invective "mutilation" is not a harsh critique of Jewish circumcision but represents Paul's evaluation of the mark of circumcision on gentile bodies. Based on Paul's understanding that gentiles are naturally foreskinned (Rom 2:27), a circumcised gentile constitutes a mutilation. This invective is where I think the identity of Paul's rivals as judaizing gentiles comes sharply into focus. Lastly, in 3:18–19 Paul say's that this group's "god is the belly and the glory in their shame." Based on the usage of belly and shame in the LXX as euphemisms for nudity and genitalia, I argued that Paul continues to highlight these teachers as being obsessed with their circumcised penises—so much so that he styles them as a priapic cult.

In contrast to the phallus-worshipping, mutilated, wicked-working dogs, Paul claims the identity of circumcision for an unidentified "we." Having identified the opponents as a group of judaizing gentiles, I argued that the "we" in Phil 3:3 refers to Paul and Timothy, the Jewish authors of the epistle. This follows Paul's standard usage of the term and is confirmed by his appeal to his own pristine pedigree in 3:5–6. While his opponents may come to the Philippians claiming to be the circumcision, Paul and Timothy actually are the circumcision. In contradistinction to those who can be identified by their phallic fixations, Paul and Timothy "serve by the *pneuma* of God and boast in Christ Jesus and put no confidence in the flesh."

5 The God of the Circumcision and the Foreskin Circumcision in Romans

> For it is not the Jew on display, nor the circumcision on display in the flesh, but the Jew in secret, and the circumcision of the heart in *pneuma*, not letter, whose praise is not from humans, but from God. What then is the advantage of the Jew? Or what is the benefit of circumcision? Much in every way! First, that they were entrusted with the oracles of God... (Rom 2:28–3:2)

5.1 Introduction

Like Paul's epistle to the assemblies in Galatians, circumcision features prominently in Romans.[1] Unlike, Galatians, however, Paul's discussion of circumcision does not appear to be in response to the immediate threat of the imposition of circumcision on non-Jews. Rather, all but one (15:8) of the occurrences of circumcision in Romans occur within the context of Paul's imagined dialogue with a hypothetical interlocutor.[2] Here, Paul weaves a discussion of circumcision (and foreskin) into this dialogue to cover a variety of topics: circumcision and law-keeping, heart-circumcision, Jewish identity, the benefit of circumcision, God's oneness, *dikaiosynē*, *pistis*, and Abraham's paternity of Jews and non-Jews.

This chapter begins with a discussion of the identity of Paul's imagined interlocutor throughout Romans. After identifying the interlocutor as a gentile-proselyte to Judaism—one who calls himself a Jew (Rom 2:17)—I offer a discussion of circumcision and foreskin in 2:25–29. Here, I make two main points: 1) Paul delegitimizes the interlocutor's circumcision by pointing out that it was not performed in accordance with the law, and 2) Paul's brief discussion of circumcision of the heart does not constitute a redefinition of who is a Jew and what counts for circumcision. Like the prophets before him, I propose that Paul emphasizes the necessity of heart circumcision for circumcised Jews in order to be approved by God. Next, I offer a brief discussion of Rom 3:1–2 and the benefit of circumcision for Jews. Turning to the end of Rom 3, I argue that Paul's metonymic usage of circumcision and foreskin there indicates that he upholds the distinction between the

---

[1] Of all of Paul's extant epistles, Romans contains the most occurrences of the nouns περιτομή and ἀκροβυστία. Περιτομή occurs fifteen times (2:25 [2x], 26, 27, 28, 29; 3:1, 30; 4:9, 10 [2x], 11, 12 [2x]; 15:8) and ἀκροβυστία appears eleven times (2:25, 26 [2x]. 27; 3:30; 4:9, 10 [2x], 11 [2x], 12). The verb περιτέμνω, which appears in Galatians (2:3; 5:2, 3; 6:12, 13) and 1 Corinthians (7:18), does not appear in Romans.
[2] See discussion below.

two groups based on the oneness of God. In the following section I focus on Rom 4:9–12 and Paul's discussion of Abraham's *dikaiosynē*, foreskin, and circumcision, and how it relates to his paternity of Jews and non-Jews. Lastly, this chapter closes with an examination of Paul's identification of Jesus as a διάκονον περιτομῆς in Rom 15:8.

5.1.1 Reading Romans

Before I offer my reading of circumcision in Romans, I will briefly comment on two important points that impact how I read Romans in general. Unlike Paul's other letters, Romans is unique in the fact that Paul did not found the assemblies in Rome, nor had he ever visited Rome in his capacity as the apostle to the gentiles (Rom 1:10–13). Paul's lack of direct relationship to the assemblies in Rome has led scholars to put forward countless numbers of proposals as to why Paul wrote this letter.[3] While fully exploring the so-called "Romans Debate" is beyond the scope of this current work, one component of that debate that is worth commenting on is the intended audience of the letter. In addition to this, I will also briefly comment on the dialogical style of Romans.

While Johannes Munck proposed a solely gentile audience of Romans in the 1950s,[4] this perspective has most notably been associated with Stanley Stowers and his 1994 monograph, *A Rereading of Romans*. In this pioneering work, Stowers forcefully pushes back against the standard view that Paul's audience in Romans is a mixed group consisting of a gentile majority and a Jewish minority.[5] Looking to the explicit statements made by Paul in the text of Romans itself, Stowers argues that the audience Paul encodes therein is solely made up of gentiles.[6] The question

---

[3] See the discussions in, Karl P. Donfried, ed., *The Romans Debate*, rev. and exp. ed. (Edinburgh: T&T Clark, 1991); Das, *Solving*; Jerry L. Sumney, ed., *Reading Paul's Letter to the Romans*, RBS 73 (Atlanta: Society of Biblical Literature, 2012).
[4] Munck, *Paul and the Salvation*, 200–2.
[5] See the representative arguments made by C. E. B. Cranfield, *A Critical and Exegetical Commentary on the Epistle to the Romans*, 2 vols., ICC (Edinburgh: T&T Clark, 1975–1979), 1:18; Dunn, *Romans 1–8*, xlv; Ben Witherington III and Darlene Hyatt, *Paul's Letter to the Romans: A Socio-Rhetorical Commentary* (Grand Rapids: Eerdmans, 2004), 7–8; Robert Jewett, *Romans*, Hermeneia (Minneapolis: Fortress, 2007), 70–71; Richard N. Longenecker, *The Epistle to the Romans*, NIGTC (Grand Rapids: Eerdmans, 2016), 8–9. For an exhaustive list of proponents of this perspective, see Runar M. Thorsteinsson, *Paul's Interlocutor in Romans 2: Function and Identity in the Context of Ancient Epistolography*, ConBNT 40 (Stockholm: Almqvist & Wiksell, 2003), 88n5.
[6] Stanley K. Stowers, *A Rereading of Romans: Justice, Jews, and Gentiles* (New Haven: Yale University Press, 1994), 21–22. For other scholars who also identify a solely gentile audience in Romans,

of the intended or encoded audience is not concerned with who *may* have read the text, but who Paul explicitly states that he is writing to.[7] The problem that Stowers points out is that the vast majority of scholars approach the audience of Romans through reconstructions of the hypothetical makeup of the Roman assemblies, rather than looking at who Paul directs his letter to.[8] Paul writes as an apostle who has been charged to "bring about the obedience of faithfulness among all the gentiles...among whom you also are" (1:5–6).[9] He desires to come to Rome and to "reap a harvest among you" as he did "among the rest of the gentiles, Greeks as well as barbarians, wise as well as foolish" because he is "obligated to proclaim the gospel...to you who are in Rome" (1:13–15).[10] "But I am speaking to you genti-

---

see Nanos, *Mystery of Romans*, 79–83; Thorsteinsson, *Paul's Interlocutor*, 87–122; Livesey, *Malleable Symbol*, 105; Joshua D. Garroway, *Paul's Gentile-Jews: Neither Jew nor Gentile, but Both* (New York: Palgrave Macmillan, 2012), 78–80; A. Andrew Das, "The Gentile-Encoded Audience of Romans: The Church outside the Synagogue," in Sumney, *Reading Paul's Letter*, 29–46; Rafael Rodríguez, *If You Call Yourself a Jew: Reappraising Paul's Letter to the Romans* (Eugene, OR: Cascade, 2014), 7–10; Thiessen *Gentile Problem*, 44–46; Fredriksen, *Pagans' Apostle*, 155–57; J. Brian Tucker, *Reading Romans After Supersessionism: The Continuation of Jewish Covenantal Identity*, NTAS 6 (Eugene, OR: Cascade, 2018), 107.

7 Stowers, *Rereading*, 21–22. Stowers distinguishes between three types of readers: empirical, encoded explicit, and encoded implicit. An empirical reader is anyone who reads a particular text. The encoded explicit reader is the audience manifest in the text. The encoded implicit reader is the ideal reader of a text, which goes a step beyond the encoded explicit reader and gets to an ideal subgroup within it. Contra Philip F. Esler, who dismisses the relevance of identifying the encoded/intended audience of the letter in contrast to the empirical audience (*Conflict and Identity in Romans: The Social Setting of Paul's Letter* [Minneapolis: Fortress, 2003], 110–11). For Esler, if the encoded audience and empirical audience do not match, then the letter would be a "catastrophic failure" and would indicate "communicative incompetence." Since Esler assumes a mixed audience of the letter, he rejects Stowers' taxonomy as a non-starter.

8 Stowers, *Rereading*, 22–33. Here, Stowers notes the general tendency of commentaries to discuss the state of "Roman Christianity" at the time of Paul's writing. From their reconstructions of the hypothetical makeup of the assemblies in Rome, they then conclude that Paul *must* have been writing to a mixed audience. On this point, see also Thorsteinsson, *Paul's Interlocutor*, 91–100; Das, *Solving*, 83–113. Interestingly, Munck argues that because Paul only addresses gentiles in Romans and his other letters, his assemblies must have *only* consisted of gentiles (*Paul and the Salvation*, 200–1). On this point, Munck commits a similar error to those who believe that Paul's intended audience must have been mixed. The makeup of Paul's intended audience and the actual makeup of the assemblies are two different questions that require different modes of historical investigation.

9 For a discussion of the debates surrounding the difficult syntax of Rom 1:6, see Das, *Solving*, 54–60.

10 Here, I follow the punctuation proposed by Harry Parkin, "Romans i. 13–15," *ExpTim* 79 (1967): 95; Runar M. Thorsteinsson, "Paul's Missionary Duty Towards Gentiles in Rome: A Note on the Punctuation and Syntax of Rom 1.13–15," *NTS* 48 (2002): 531–47. On this reading, Ἕλλησίν τε καὶ

les....as I myself am an apostle to the gentiles" (11:13).[11] "I have written boldly to you...because of the grace that was given to me by God to be a priestly servant of Christ Jesus to the gentiles...so that the offering of the gentiles may be acceptable" (15:15–16).[12] Like the rest of his epistles, Paul presents the audience of Romans as being composes solely of gentiles.

5.1.2 Romans and the Diatribe

The dialogical style of Romans is distinctive amongst Paul's epistles[13] and all but one (15:8) of the references to circumcision (and foreskin) in Romans are found within the context of Paul's diatribe with an imagined interlocutor.[14] Like the general use of the diatribe in the ancient world, Paul abruptly addresses an interloc-

---

βαρβάροις and σοφοῖς τε καὶ ἀνοήτοις are in apposition to τοῖς λοιποῖς ἔθνεσιν, and a new sentence begins with ὀφειλέτης εἰμί. This reading highlights that Paul's obligation is to the whole of the gentile world, and thus his eagerness to come to Rome to fulfill his obligation. See also Rodríguez (*If You Call Yourself*, 21–22) on this point, though he follows the traditional punctuation of these verses.

11 Interpreters have made various attempts to argue that this address is to a subset of Paul's mixed audience (e.g., Cranfield, *Romans*, 2:558–59; James D. G. Dunn, *Romans 9–16*, WBC 38B [Waco, TX: Word, 1988], 655; Joseph A. Fitzmyer, *Romans: A New Translation with Introduction and Commentary*, AB 33 (New York: Doubleday, 1993), 612). It should be noted, however, that these interpretations rely on the assumption that the audience is mixed. If we read the passage in its context, it is clear that Paul is shifting from talking about his Jewish kinsmen (third person), to directly talking to his gentile audience (second person); he is explaining their situation as it pertains to the stumbling of Israel. On this, see Thorsteinsson, *Paul's Interlocutor*, 109–11.

12 On the parallels between Rom 1:5–6, 13–15 and 15:15–16 see Das, *Solving*, 64–66. Das rightly argues that both of these sections ground Paul's letter within his apostolic mission to the gentiles, and therefore indicates that his audience is composed of gentiles. Contra Esler (*Conflict and Identity*, 109–16), who notes the parallels between the passages, but concludes that the audience is mixed.

13 While Paul does use a dialogical style elsewhere in his epistles (e.g., 1 Cor 6:15; 10:16–22; Gal 2:17; 3:19–21), it features much more heavily in Romans.

14 The comparison between Romans and the Greco-Roman diatribe has long been noted in Pauline studies and can be traced back to Rudolf Bultmann, *Der Stil der paulinischen Predigt und die kynisch-stoische Diatribe*, FRLANT 13 (Göttingen: Vandenhoeck & Ruprecht, 1910). The first major reassessment of Bultmann's work and advancement of the study of Paul and the diatribe was done by Stanley K. Stowers, *The Diatribe and Paul's Letter to the Romans*, SBLDS 57 (Chico, CA: Scholars Press, 1981). After Stowers, Thorsteinsson's *Paul's Interlocutor* was the next important work on Romans and the diatribe. The latest monograph to advance the study of the diatribe and Romans is Justin King, *Speech-in-Character, Diatribe, and Romans 3:1–9: Who's Speaking When and Why It Matters*, BibInt 163 (Leiden: Brill, 2018). See King (*Speech-in-Character*, 103–28) for an overview of the history of research on the diatribe and Paul.

utor throughout this letter to respond to his potential objections and false conclusions.[15] This generally occurs through a shift from the third-person to the second-person (2:1, 17), vocative addresses like ἄνθρωπε (2:1, 3; 9:20), the introduction of questions and objections with τί οὖν or οὖν (3:1, 9; 4:1; 6:1, 15; 7:7; 8:31; 9:14, 19, 30; 11:1, 11), and negative responses such as μὴ γένοιτο (3:4, 6, 31; 6:2, 15; 7:7, 13; 9:14; 11:1, 11).[16] Throughout this dialogue, Paul employs speech-in-character (προσωποποιία) and places words in the mouth of his interlocutor to which he responds.[17] While older studies generally argued that the diatribe was overtly polemical in nature, Stowers has shown the importance of understanding the pedagogical function of the diatribe.[18] Paul utilizes this dialogue to advance his argument and to correct and educate the misconceptions held by the imagined interlocutor, who represents members of the letter's audience.[19] For my present purposes, identifying who Paul envisages his interlocutor to be is crucial, as it will color how I interpret key elements of the imagined dialogue Paul has with him.[20]

---

15 Here, I follow Rodriguez (*If You Call*, 37n39) in using masculine pronouns to refer to the interlocutor (contra King, *Speech-in-Character*, 240, 267, 271). Given the discussion of the interlocutor's circumcision in Rom 2:17–29, Paul's imagined interlocutor is male.
16 Thorsteinsson, *Paul's Interlocutor*, 125–26.
17 For an overview of speech-in-character of Paul, see King, *Speech-in-Character*, 58–97. See also, Jacob P. B. Mortensen, *Paul Among the Gentiles: A "Radical" Reading of Romans*, NET 28 (Tübingen: Narr, 2018), 79–91.
18 Stowers, *Diatribe*, 76–77. See also the minor critique by King (*Speech-in-Character*, 125–27) who argues that Stowers pushed the pendulum too far from overtly polemical to only pedagogical. He notes that the pedagogical function of a diatribe does not necessarily indicate that it is not polemical.
19 Thorsteinsson (*Paul's Interlocutor*, 140–44) notes that epistolary interlocutors generally function as representatives for the letter's recipient(s). While I am inclined to agree with this general principle based on the evidence Thorsteinsson presents, in the case of Romans it seems that the interlocutor may represent a subset of the audience (gentiles who call themselves Jews; 2:17), and not the entire audience (gentiles more generally). Depending on the origins of the Roman assemblies, their relationship to the synagogue, and the members who would have identified as "God-fearers," this subset may have made up a large portion of Paul's audience (e.g., the reading proposed by Nanos, *Mystery of Romans*, 41–84).
20 On the characterization and identification of imagined dialogue partners, see the discussion Mortensen, *Paul Among the Gentiles*, 81–90. Here, Mortensen primarily explores the rhetorical device of προσωποποιία in Theon, *Progymnasmata* § 8 and Quintilian, *Inst. Or.* 9.2.29–37.

5.2 Paul and An Interlocutor: Romans 2:17

The first discussion of circumcision in Romans occurs in Rom 2:25–29, where Paul names his interlocutor as one who calls himself a Jew or one who is called a Jew (σὺ Ἰουδαῖος ἐπονομάζῃ, 2:17). This identification of the interlocutor has almost always been taken to indicate that Paul is addressing an ethnic Jew. The way that Paul presents this individual, however, should give cause for pause. Paul does not address this individual as *a Jew*, but as one who *calls himself a Jew* (or *is called a Jew*)—a "self-styled Jew" so to speak.[21] On this, Origen comments, "First of all it must be observed that he has not said of him, 'But if you are a Jew,' but rather, 'if you call yourself a Jew.' This is because to be a Jew and to be called a Jew are not the same thing" (*Comm. Rom.* 2.11.4 [Scheck]).[22] Comparably, the twelfth-century monk Euthymius Zigabenus notes that this identification does not square with the way Paul sees it: "'You are called a Jew,' indeed, but you are not..." (*Comm. Rom.* 2.17 ["Ἐπονομάζῃ" μέν, οὐκ εἶ δέ]).[23] Following the groundbreaking work of Runar Thorsteinsson—and subsequent studies by Rafael Rodríguez, Matthew Thiessen, Christine Hayes, Joshua Garroway, Matthew Novenson, Michele Murray, and others—I will argue that this individual is actually a gentile who has judaized and undergone proselyte circumcision.[24] As I argued in chapter three, Paul did not

---

21 See Matthew V. Novenson, "The Self-Styled Jew of Romans 2 and the Actual Jews of Romans 9–11," in Rodríguez and Thiessen, *The So-Called Jew*, 133–62.
22 Similarly, John Chrysostom notes the difference between being something and being called something: "For he does not say, Behold, thou art a Jew, but 'art called' so" (*Hom. Rom.* 6 [NPNF¹ 11:368]). Both Origen and Chrysostom, however, identify this individual as a Jew, but note that his contested identity in 2:17 is based on what Paul says about Jewish identity in 2:28–29. Many modern interpreters argue similarly, e.g., Barclay, *Paul and the Gift*, 469n51.
23 Like Origen and Chrysostom, Euthymius (*Comm. Rom.* 2.17, 28, 29) understands that Paul denies this individual the title of Jew because he does not fulfill the law (μὴ πληρῶν τὸν νόμον) and because Paul does not think Jewishness is based on descent (γένος) or flesh (σάρξ), but that the Jew in the proper sense (Ἰουδαῖος κυρίως) is a noetic Jew (ὁ νοητὸς Ἰουδαῖος).
24 Thorsteinsson, *Paul's Interlocutor*. Thorsteinsson's proposal has been most notably adopted and advanced by Matthew Thiessen and Rafael Rodríguez. For a brief history of the reception of and outline of Thorsteinsson's work, see Runar M. Thorsteinsson, Matthew Thiessen, and Rafael Rodríguez, "Paul's Interlocutor in Romans: The Problem of Identification" in Rodríguez and Thiessen, *The So-Called Jew*, 1–37. See also the other essays in *The So-Called Jew* for how this identification impacts various aspects of interpreting Romans. For a critique of this identification of the interlocutor, see Paul T. Sloan, "Paul's Jewish Addressee in Rom 2–4: Revisiting Recent Conversations," *JTS* (forthcoming). While I disagree with Sloan's conclusions regarding the identity of Paul's interlocutor, he demonstrates that it is possible to identify Paul's interlocutor as a Jew without creating a supersessionist or anti-Jewish Paul. For a similar non-supersessionist reading of this passage, see Stephen L. Young, "Ethnic Ethics: Paul's Eschatological Myth of Jewish Sin," *NTS* (forthcoming).

believe that circumcision could turn a non-Jew into a Jew, nor that it offers the non-Jew any benefit. Paul argues similarly in Romans, which calls into question the value of the interlocutor's circumcision (2:25–29). This revisionist identification reframes Paul's discussion of circumcision, foreskin, and Jewish identity in this passage, and problematizes the standard reading of this text.

5.2.1 Identifying the So-Called Jew

Following his indictment of the gentile world for its panoply of vices—which are rooted in the veneration of cultic images (1:18–32)—Paul condemns a hypocritical gentile who judges his fellow non-Jew, yet is guilty of doing the same things (2:1–5).[25] Paul then turns to discuss how God will judge the world—both Jews and gentiles—according to works (2:6–16). After this brief aside—which elaborates on the theme of judgement in 2:1–5—Paul then returns to his indictment of an interlocutor in 2:17.[26] This time, however, Paul identifies the one he is apostrophizing with more specificity: "But if you call yourself a Jew..." or "But if you are called a Jew..." (Εἰ δὲ σὺ Ἰουδαῖος ἐπονομάζῃ). There is considerable debate surrounding how this interlocutor relates to the one in 2:1–5 and if Paul is imagining the same individual in both sections. While I am inclined to believe that Paul is conjuring the same interlocutor in both passages[27]—and throughout Romans more

---

[25] In 1:18–32, Paul employs a fairly standard Jewish critique of gentiles and establishes that gentile impiety (ἀσέβεια) and wickedness (ἀδικία) are rooted in their worship of idols and failure to worship the God of Israel. On this point, see Dale B. Martin, "Heterosexism and the Interpretation of Romans 1:18–32," *BibInt* 3 (2007): 332–55. That non-Jews were idolatrous is a commonplace amongst ancient Jewish thinkers (e.g., Philo, *Decalogue* 52–63; *Special Laws* 1.13–28; 2.166; Let. Aris. 137; Bel 1:3–7; Wis 11–15; 1 Pet 4:3) and linking gentiles with idolatry is also not uncommon for Paul. In 1 Thess, Paul comments that the Thessalonians have turned away from idols to serve the living and true God (1:9), which results in their ability control their desires (πάθει ἐπιθυμίας; 4:3–5). Similarly, in 1 Cor 12:2 Paul speaks about his ex-pagan gentiles' former worship of idols which led them astray. Further, Paul's vice lists in Gal 5:19–21 and 1 Cor 6:9–10 also position the worship of idols alongside vices similar to those found in Rom 1:18–32.
[26] Thorsteinsson, *Paul's Interlocutor*, 158–59, 161–63; Thorsteinsson, Thiessen, and Rodríguez, "Paul's Interlocutor," 23–24; Mortensen, *Paul Among the Gentiles*, 121–23.
[27] The most comprehensive argument for this perspective is Thorsteinsson, *Paul's Interlocutor*, 151–242, esp. 152–64. See also, Garroway, *Paul's Gentile-Jews*, 89–95; King, *Speech-in-Character*, 248–51; Mortensen, *Paul Among the Gentiles*, 123–25.

broadly[28]—for the sake of space I will focus primarily on identifying the individual in 2:17 based on what Paul says about him in 2:17–29.[29]

As noted above, the identification of this individual as one who calls himself a Jew or one who is called a Jew brings his Jewishness into question. The verb ἐπονομάζω is a NT *hapax legomenon*, and the inflected form Paul uses here (ἐπονομάζῃ) can either be interpreted as a middle ("you call yourself") or a passive verb ("you are called"). Lionel Windsor argues that ancient usage of the word only attests to the passive form—not middle—which typically occurs in passages related to the naming of places (e.g., Exod 15:23 [ἐπωνομάσθη]; Josephus, *Ant.* 2.1 [ἐπωνομάζετο]).[30] The passive form also occurs when individuals receive names, however, as far as I can tell, this always occurs in the third person (e.g., Dionysius of Halicarnassus, *Ant. rom.* 30.50.3 [ἐπωνομάσθη]; Diodorus Siculus, *Bib. hist.* 11.47.2 [ἐπωνομάσθη]).[31] In the second person, ἐπονομάζῃ appears to be a unique inflection only used in Rom 2:17 and in references to this text, so other usage may not be entirely decisive for interpreting Paul.[32]

---

[28] Both Rodríguez (*If You Call Yourself*) and Mortensen (*Paul among the Gentiles*) have offered full-scale readings of Romans in which the interlocutor from 2:17 remains Paul's dialogue partner throughout the letter. Cf. Fredriksen, *Pagans' Apostle*, 156.
[29] The majority of scholars believe that the interlocutor is the same throughout chapter 2, although they either identify him as a "typical" Jew (e.g., Cranfield, *Romans*, 1:137–39; Dunn, *Romans 1–8*, 108; Thomas R. Schreiner, *Romans*, BECNT [Grand Rapids: Baker Academic, 1998], 102–3) or an unrepentant Jew (Simon J. Gathercole, *Where Is Boasting? Early Jewish Soteriology and Paul's Response in Romans 1–5* [Grand Rapids: Eerdmans, 2002], 206–15). There is a small minority of scholars who identify a gentile interlocutor in 2:1–5 and a Jewish interlocutor in 2:17–29 (e.g., Neil Elliott, *The Rhetoric of Romans: Argumentative Constraint and Strategy and Paul's Dialogue with Judaism*, JSNTSup 45 [Sheffield: JSOT Press, 1990], 127; Stowers, *Rereading*, 100–4, 150–53). There is also a small minority of scholars who understand there to be two different gentile interlocutors in 2:1–5 and 2:17–29; a gentile moralist and a judaized gentile proselyte (e.g., Rodríguez, *If You Call Yourself*, 38–40, 48–53; Thiessen, *Gentile Problem*, 52–59). King (*Speech-in-Character*, 248) takes the peculiar view that the interlocutor is "religiously Jewish" throughout chapter 2, and that his ethnicity is ambiguous.
[30] Windsor, *Paul and the Vocation*, 148.
[31] Cf. ὠνομάσθη in Rom 15:20.
[32] The non-contracted form ἐπονομάζει can be either a second- or third-person form, but it seems to exclusively appears as a third-person verb. The non-prefixed cognate ὀνομάζῃ appears in the second-person passive form a handful of times (e.g., Dio Cassius, *Hist. rom.* 78.8.2 [τίς δὲ ὀνομάζῃ]), and I have not found any instances where it clearly functions as a middle. The closest example to our current text that features σύ as the subject of a second-person middle/passive naming verb is found in a spurious text attributed to John Chrysostom, which, referencing Abraham, says, "…And neither are you called 'father'" (*Theatr.* 6 [*PG* 56:552; καὶ οὔτε σὺ ὀνομάζῃ πατήρ]). Here, the context indicates that it is functioning as a passive. Additionally, I have not found any instances of ὀνομάζῃ or ἐπονομάζῃ with a reflexive second-person pronoun, though instances of third-person forms of

Since this inflected form of ἐπονομάζω is unique to Paul, we have to rely on context for understanding how it is being used. Given the emphatic σὺ[33] that functions as the subject of the verbs in 2:17–18 (ἐπαναπαύῃ, καυχᾶσαι, γινώσκεις, δοκιμάζεις), Paul is placing emphasis on what the interlocutor *does*. "You rest... boast...know...determine." It is conceivable, then, that Paul is also highlighting what the interlocutor does with the verb ἐπονομάζῃ: *"you* call yourself a Jew," which is different than actually *being* a Jew. As Paul will go on to argue in the rest of chapter two, the interlocutor's behavior does not match with his self-designation, nor does it align with the description Paul provides of Jews elsewhere in Rom 9–11.[34] It is worth noting that Paul's identification of the interlocutor is unique amongst his epistles. Elsewhere in Paul's writings, Jews are always *Jews* and never *those who call themselves Jews*.[35] This is adjacent to what I noted in the chapter on Galatians regarding "the circumcision" (ἡ περιτομή) and "those who have themselves circumcised" or "those who receive circumcision" (οἱ περιτεμνόμενοι). The former are always Jews, and the latter are always gentile proselytes. Even when Paul speaks negatively against his own countrymen, he does not call into question their ethnic bona fides. For example, in 2 Cor 11:22 Paul castigates the *pseudapostoloi*, yet still grants them their ethnic status as Hebrews, Israelites, and the seed of Abraham (cf. Gal 2:14–15).

There is additional evidence that supports the idea that the interlocutor may not be what he says he is. Looking elsewhere in the Pauline corpus, 1 Cor 5:11 offers some insights about individuals who bear a name that does not accurately reflect reality. There, Paul urges the Corinthians to not associate or eat with someone who calls himself a brother (ἀδελφὸς ὀνομαζόμενος)[36] and lives a life marked by vice. They are to remove the so-called brother from their midst because he is not what

---

these verbs with third-person reflective pronouns are extant (e.g., Themistius, *Or.* 31.354b [ἑαυτοῦ plus ἐπονομάζει]).
33 Thorsteinsson, *Paul's Interlocutor*, 163; Jewett, *Romans*, 221–22; Longenecker, *Romans* 299.
34 This point is the subject of Novenson's essay, "The Self-Styled Jew." In this essay he points out the incongruity between the "Jew" of Rom 2 with the actual Jews of Rom 9–11. As Novenson mentions, this incongruity has not gone unnoticed by Pauline scholars. For example, E. P. Sanders says that "the description of Jewish behavior in 2:17–24 is unparalleled" (*Paul, the Law*, 124). Similarly, Lloyd Gaston notes the "puzzling" nature of Rom 2:17–29 and the striking difference in what is said about Jews there and in Rom 9:4–5 (*Paul and the Torah*, 138).
35 Rom 1:16; 2:9, 10, 28, 29; 3:1, 9, 29; 9:24; 10:12; 1 Cor 1:22, 23, 24; 9:20; 10:32; 12:13; 2 Cor 11:24; Gal 2:13, 14, 15; 3:28; 1 Thess 2:14.
36 The participle ὀνομαζόμενος suffers from the same ambiguity as ἐπονομάζῃ and could either be translated as a middle or a passive. Either way, the supposed identity of the individual does not align with reality.

he says he is (1 Cor 5:13). He calls himself a brother, but in actuality he is a fraud.[37] Like the one who calls himself a Jew in Rom 2:17–29, his actions do not align with his supposed identity and serve to demonstrate his erroneous self-identification. Similarly, in Revelation 2:9 and 3:9, John writes about individuals that "say they are Jews, but are not." These verses are in themselves quite controversial and interpretation regarding them is varied, but what is clear is that—in John's eyes— there are individuals who are claiming to be Jews but—by his definition—are not.[38] Outside of the New Testament, Epictetus frequently indicts those who say they are one thing, but act as though they are not. For example, he critiques someone who calls himself a Stoic (*Diatr.* 3.24.41; Στωικὸν σεαυτῷ εἶναι λέγεις), but whose actions indicate that his self-identification as a Stoic is a false ascription.[39]

One question remains: Is the category of "non-Jew who identifies as a Jew" a plausible category in the ancient world? As Novenson comments, "the assumption of the name 'Jew' by non-Jews is relatively well-attested in sources from the early Roman period."[40] For example, Epictetus states that there are some who act the part of a Jew and are actually Greeks, but after full commitment to the Jewish way of life they should in fact be called Jews (καλεῖται Ἰουδαῖος, *Diatr.* 2.9.20–22).[41] The argument that the interlocutor is a gentile proselyte is, therefore, tenable. This hypothetical individual has taken on Torah, undergone circumcision, and now believes that he has become a Jew. Unlike Epictetus, however, Paul does not believe that his interlocutor is worthy of the name Jew.

5.2.2 Indicting the So-Called Jew

In 2:17–18, Paul notes that the so-called Jew rests in the law, boasts in God, knows the will [of God], and is able to determine what is advantageous since he has been catechized from the law. Here, none of these behaviors are portrayed negatively;

---

37 Novenson, "The Self-Styled Jew," 141.
38 On the identity of these individuals as judaizing gentiles, see Murray, *Playing a Jewish Game*, 76–80. Cf. David Frankfurter, "Jews or Not? Reconstructing the 'Other' in Rev 2:9 and 3:9," *HTR* 94 (2001): 403–25, at 416–22.
39 Cf. Epictetus, *Diatr.* 2.19.19, 28; 3.7.17.
40 Novenson, "The Self-Styled Jew," 142. Here, Novenson points the reader to Cohen (*Beginnings of Jewishness*, 25–68) for evidence.
41 For discussions of this text in the context of Rom 2:17, see Thorsteinsson, *Paul's Interlocutor*, 199–201; Rodríguez, *If You Call Yourself*, 51–53; Novenson, "The Self-Styled Jew," 142–43. Relatedly, this text lends credibility to the idea that the interlocutor is a gentile proselyte regardless of how one interprets ἐπονομάζῃ. The focus is on being called something, rather than actually being that thing.

these are simply the things that pious Jews do and the privileges that they have been given as God's people.⁴² In 2:19–20, Paul shifts his focus to the fact that the interlocutor has convinced himself that he is an instructor of those in need of instruction from the law: a guide to the blind, a light to those in darkness, an instructor of the ignorant, and a teacher of children (cf. Isa 42:6–7).⁴³ Once again, this behavior is not necessarily portrayed negatively. Only when the interlocutor is exposed in the remainder of the chapter as a gentile poseur whose actions are far from his adopted persona does 2:17–20 take on negative connotations.

Paul's problem with the interlocutor's behavior begins to manifest itself in 2:21–22:⁴⁴ "You, then, who teaches another do not teach yourself. You who proclaim, "Do not steal," steals. You who says, "Do not commit adultery," commits adultery. You who abhor idols commits sacrilege."⁴⁵ The problem with the interlocutor is

---

42 Schreiner, *Romans*, 129–30. Windsor (*Paul and the Vocation*, 153–54) and Rodríguez (*If You Call Yourself*, 86) rightly note that boasting is often perceived to have negative connotations in the English-speaking world, but that ancient thinkers often use it positively to mean "to take pride in" or "to glory in." For Paul, boasting in God is a positive thing as long as the boast is legitimate. See also my comments on Paul and boasting in §3.7.2. Cf. Barclay, *Paul and the Gift*, 469.

43 Stowers (*Rereading*, 150–53) argues that this indicates that the interlocutor is a Jewish teacher who instructs gentiles in Torah. As Novenson ("The Self-Styled Jew," 145) notes, the category of Jewish missionary teacher of gentiles is not widely attested in antiquity. The identification of the interlocutor as an instructor of gentiles does not confirm or deny his identity as a Jew or a non-Jew, but if my identification of the agitators in Galatians (and Philippians) is correct, Paul was aware of judaizing gentiles that encouraged other gentiles to judaize as well.

44 These verses are almost universally rendered as questions, but it is also equally possible that they should simply be rendered as declarative statements. See e.g., Origen, *Comm. Rom.* 2.11.5; Vulg.; Matthew Thiessen, "Paul's So-Called Jew and Lawless Lawkeeping," in Rodríguez and Thiessen, *The So-Called Jew*, 76; cf. Stowers, *Diatribe*, 219n78; Dunn, *Romans 1–8*, 113.

45 Various attempts have been made to understand how these accusations could apply to Jews en masse or a particular segment of Jews (e.g., Cranfield, *Romans*, 1:168; Douglas J. Moo, *The Epistle to the Romans*, NICNT [Grand Rapids: Eerdmans, 1996], 164–65; Gathercole, *Where is Boasting*, 211–12; Windsor, *Paul and the Vocation*, 164–68; Sloan, "Paul's Jewish Addressee"; Young, "Ethnic Ethics"). If, however, we understand that the interlocutor is portrayed as a judaizing gentile, then these charges make sense in light of Paul's language elsewhere about his understanding of the situation of Jews (esp. Rom 9–11; on the situation of Jews in Rom 9–11, see Young, "Ethnic Ethics"). As Thiessen (*Gentile Problem*, 60–63) points out, the vices that occur here also occur in Wis 14:23–27 and refer specifically to the transgressions of gentiles, not Jews (cf. 1 Cor 6:9–11). While Sloan ("Paul's Jewish Addressee") successfully demonstrates that there is substantial ancient evidence that preserves accounts of Jews indicting other Jews for various transgressions, that does not necessarily lead to the conclusion that Paul has a Jewish interlocutor in view in this passage. It should also be mentioned that given the fictitious nature of the interlocutor, Paul is not necessarily concerned with historical instances of these three vices, rather, he is constructing the image of a type of hypocritical individual whose actions do not align with their teaching. Mortensen (*Paul Among the Gentiles*, 130n58) notes that the charge of robbing temples/sacrilege (ἱεροσυλέω) is specifically men-

that he does not practice what he preaches.⁴⁶ Like the judge who does the same things as those whom he judges (2:1–5), he instructs others in the law, but does not heed his own instruction. His self-designated status as a Jew does not align with the way he conducts himself.⁴⁷ Many interpreters who understand that the interlocutor is a gentile proselyte have highlighted the fact that this kind of argument was a common Hellenistic rhetorical move that was used to critique the stereotypical pretentious person.⁴⁸ Stowers argues that from an ancient rhetorical perspective, the individual in 2:17–29 clearly belongs to this well know type.⁴⁹ "The pretentious person is above all a boaster and someone who pretends to be what he is not….Desire for praise and honor motivates the pretender."⁵⁰ In regard to the incongruity between the individual's name and deeds, J. Christiaan Beker points out that the purpose of 2:21–29 is to "paganize" Paul's interlocutor.⁵¹ If the interlocutor is a gentile proselyte then this "paganization" serves to undermine his self-identification as a Jew. Similarly, Friedrich Wilhelm Horn rightly comments that Paul uses 2:21–24 to confront the interlocutor's self-understanding in 2:17–20.⁵² This is not because Paul redefines what it means to be a Jew in 2:28–29, but because the interlocutor was never an ethnically Jewish individual in the first place.

---

tioned by Theon (*Progymnasmata* 106, 108) when he discusses examples of how to construct a *topos* to amplify the wrongdoings of an individual. It is possible that Paul is drawing on some past rhetorical training and awareness of this trope when constructing the amplified image of a wrongdoer. On the perplexing charge of ἱεροσυλέω, see Novenson ("The Self-Styled Jew," 145–47), who argues that it could signify the violation of sacred space by foreigners (cf. Acts 19:37; 21:28; b. Pesaḥ 3b).

46 Contra Rodríguez (*If You Call Yourself*, 54–56) who notes that if these are to be taken as questions, Paul's use of οὐ in the first question would indicate a positive response: "Yes, I do teach myself." This, however, would have a knock-on effect to the following questions and would indicate that the interlocutor does *not* do these things. For Rodríguez, the true indictment of the interlocutor comes in 2:23–27 when Paul exposes his law-breaking circumcision (56–61). On law-breaking circumcision, see §5.4.1 below.
47 Cf. Timothy W. Berkley, *From a Broken Covenant to Circumcision of the Heart: Pauline Intertextual Exegesis in Romans 2:17–29*, SBLDS 175 (Atlanta: Society of Biblical Literature, 2000), 133.
48 E.g., Garroway, *Paul's Gentile-Jews*, 92; Thiessen, *Gentile Problem*, 53–54, 62–63.
49 While Stowers believes this interlocutor is a Jewish teacher of gentiles, his exposition of the motif of the pretentious person is groundbreaking (*Rereading*, 144–50).
50 Stowers, *Rereading*, 145. Cf. Theophrastus, *Char.* 23.1; Xenophon, *Cyr.* 2.2.12.
51 J. Christiaan Beker, *Paul the Apostle: The Triumph of God in Life and Thought* (Philadelphia: Fortress, 1980), 88. Beker, however, follows the traditional interpretation that this individual is actually an ethnic Jew.
52 Friedrich Wilhelm Horn, "Götzendiener, Tempelräuber und Betrüger. Polemik gegen Heiden, Juden und Judenchristen im Römerbrief" in *Polemik in der frühchristlichen Literatur*, ed. Oda Wischmeyer and Lorenzo Scornaienchi, BZNW 170 (Berlin: de Gruyter, 2011), 209–32, at 217.

Paul's fullest condemnation of the so-called Jew comes in 2:23–24: "You who boast in the law—through the transgression of the law—dishonor God. As it is written, *For because of you, the name of God is being blasphemed among the nations*" (2:23–24).[53] The so-called Jew who boasts in the law is actually a transgressor of the law and because of his transgression, the name of God is blasphemed among the nations. Rodríguez, Thiessen, and Novenson all comment that the interlocutor's transgression of the law could be a charge that his assumption of Torah itself is a transgression of Torah, since it did not belong to non-Jews in the first place.[54] The presentation of the interlocutor thus far has served to call into question his Jewish bona fides. Paul continues to challenge the interlocutor's claim to a Jewish identity in 2:25–29 when he challenges the validity and efficacy of the interlocutor's circumcision.

5.3 Circumcision and the So-Called Jew: Romans 2:25–29

After condemning the so-called Jew for his hypocrisy, Paul turns to discuss his circumcision.[55]

---

53 On Paul's usage of OG Isa 52:5, see Thorsteinsson, *Paul's Interlocutor*, 218–21; Thiessen, *Gentile Problem*, 63–64; Sloan, "Paul's Jewish Addressee." While Thorsteinsson, Thiessen, and Sloan each argue for a specific interpretation of Isa 52:5 that reinforces their understanding of who Paul's interlocutor is, Paul's use of sacred Jewish texts does not always align with the interpretations of modern historical-critical scholars. Regardless of how one reads Isa 52:5, that does not mean that Paul read and used it the same way. On Paul's use of sacred Jewish texts, see Sharp, *Divination and Philosophy*, 133–62.
54 Rodríguez, *If You Call Yourself*, 56–57; Thiessen, "Lawless Lawkeeping," 76–83; Novenson, "The Self-Styled Jew," 147. Further, Thiessen argues that some ancient Jews could—and did—classify a non-Jew's wrongful assumption of Torah as constituting committing the sins that Paul just accused his interlocutor of committing: theft, adultery, and sacrilege. On this point, Thiessen draws on texts from Baruch, 4Q372, and Jubilees that discuss that the Torah belongs to Israel alone. "In Rom 2:17–29, Paul argues that, in the very process of adopting the law, the gentile who judaizes becomes guilty of theft, adultery, and sacrilege, and is, therefore, no better off than the pagan gentiles whose condemnation he agrees with in Rom 1:18–32" ("Lawless Lawkeeping," 83).
55 Marcus A. Mininger (*Uncovering the Theme of Revelation in Romans 1:16–3:26*, WUNT 2/445 [Tübingen: Mohr Siebeck, 2017], 224–35) argues that Paul introduces the interlocutor's circumcision in 2:20 when he refers to his possession of "the form of knowledge and truth in the law" (τὴν μόρφωσιν τῆς γνώσεως καὶ τῆς ἀληθείας ἐν τῷ νόμῳ, 2:20). On this reading, the interlocutor has made the knowledge and truth of the law physically manifest in the form of his circumcised penis. While this interpretation is novel and well-argued by Mininger, I do not find it convincing. Since Paul highlights the circumcision of the interlocutor in the ensuing verses, it is improbable that he would refer to circumcision here with an opaque circumlocution. The general context of 2:17–24

For circumcision indeed has benefit if you keep the law, but if you are a transgressor of the law, your circumcision has become a foreskin. Therefore, if the foreskin observes the just commandments of the law, will not his foreskin be counted as circumcision? Then, the foreskin from nature who completes the law will condemn you, who through the letter and circumcision are a transgressor of the law. For it is not the Jew on display, nor the circumcision on display in the flesh, but the Jew in secret, and the circumcision of the heart in *pneuma*, not letter, whose praise is not from humans, but from God (2:25–29).

Due to the persistent identification of Paul's interlocutor as a Jew—or as a representative of Israel or Jews more broadly[56]—the majority reading of this passage asserts that Paul is indicting Jews for their inability to follow Torah, despite their boast in Torah (2:17–24). Since they were unable to faultlessly follow Torah, their circumcisions have become null and void and are of no value (2:25–27).[57] God has since replaced or redefined what counts as circumcision and what constitutes Jewish identity with the circumcision of the heart and the "true," "ultimate," or "eschatological" Jew (2:28–29).[58] Thus, the reading offered by John Barclay, "…what [Paul] argues in 2.25–9 thoroughly redefines the terms 'Jew' and 'circumcision' in a way which preserves their honorific status but cancels their normal denotation."[59] Andreas Blaschke comments that, "In 2:17–29, Paul redefines who actually is a Jew and what circumcision actually is."[60] Similarly, Nina Livesey notes, "With such [metaphorical] definitions, Paul provides a means by which a foreskinned Gentile can be both a 'Jew' and 'circumcised.'"[61] Thus—for

---

that focuses on the law, teaching the law, and transgressing the law also speaks against this interpretation.
56 Berkley, *From a Broken Covenant*, 117; Gathercole, *Where is Boasting*, 199; Windsor, *Paul and the Vocation*, 162–63.
57 Käsemann, *Römer*, 67–69; Blaschke, *Beschneidung*, 410–11, 414; Moo, *Romans*, 168–69; Horn, "Der Verzicht," 502; Schreiner, *Romans*, 138; Mimouni, *La circoncision*, 225; Livesey, *Circumcision*, 108.
58 Anton Fridrichsen, "Der wahre Jude und sein Lob: Röm 2,28f.," *SO* 1 (1922): 39–49, esp. 43–45; Barclay, "Paul and Philo," 544–46; Berkley, *From a Broken Covenant*, 151–55; Wolter, *Paulus*, 382; Wright, *Paul*, 1146; Kyle B. Wells, *Grace and Agency in Paul and Second Temple Judaism: Interpreting the Transformation of the Heart*, NovTSup 157 (Leiden: Brill, 2015), 217; Smit, "Real Circumcision," 90–91. On the concrete impact of this line of interpretation and how it influenced Nazi ideology, see Boyarin, *A Radical Jew*, 209–24.
59 Barclay, "Paul and Philo," 546. Barclay's comments on this text in *Paul and the Gift* are more nuanced: "Paul by no means wishes to exclude Jews in favor of Gentiles, and there is no reason to think that he here applies the label "Jew" to all believers, Gentiles as well as Jews. Rather, he is asking how, in the sight of God, Jewish identity is received and recognized" (469).
60 Blaschke, *Beschneidung*, 414 (my translation). "Paulus definiert in 2,17–29 neu, wer eigentlich Jude und was eigentlich Beschneidung ist."
61 Livesey, *Malleable Symbol*, 111.

some interpreters—this text serves as a concrete attack on the core of Judaism[62] and constitutes a hostile attitude toward (physical) circumcision.[63] Stowers rightly remarks, "Many interpreters have been certain that Paul effectively annuls Judaism in vv. 25–29."[64] The goal of this section is to point out the flaws with this predominant perspective and to propose a more nuanced reading of this passage.

5.3.1 Circumcision as Foreskin and Foreskin as Circumcision

In 2:25–27, Paul makes some remarkable and perplexing claims that generate a number of questions for the interpreter. How does the transgression of the law render an individual's circumcision as foreskin? How does observance of the law by a foreskin from nature (i.e., a non-Jew)[65] result in their foreskin being reckoned as circumcision? What type of law observance does Paul have in mind, and what is the benefit of circumcision that is in view? Further, how does the identity of Paul's interlocutor as a judaizing gentile—on the hypothesis I have proposed in this chapter—impact how one interprets this text?

Paul begins his exposé of the interlocutor's circumcision by stating that circumcision benefits those who keep the law, but for those who are transgressors of the law, their circumcisions have become foreskins (2:25). The benefit of circumcision that Paul has in mind is likely the covenantal privileges and relationship with God that Israel enjoys.[66] How, then, does the transgression of the law cause

---

62 E.g., Käsemann, *Römer*, 68.
63 Mimouni, *La circoncision*, 226.
64 Stowers, *Rereading*, 154.
65 To modern readers, saying that someone is "the foreskin from nature" or "was born foreskinned" is simply an empirical truth that applies to all infant males—barring some kind of physical anomaly or divine intrauterine circumcision. For Paul, however, the natural state of being "the foreskin" applies only to non-Jews. Jews on the other hand, are Jews by nature and are thus naturally circumcised. On this, see Eisenbaum, "Is Paul the Father," 517. There exists a tradition in ancient Judaism in which some individuals are born circumcised. On this, see Isaac Kalimi, "'He Was Born Circumcised': Some Midrashic Sources, Their Concept, Roots and Presumably Historical Context," *ZNW* 93 (2002): 1–12.
66 Some interpreters assume the benefit of circumcision in the eyes of many Jews would be a soteriological benefit—that is—having a circumcised penis would assure Jews of their future salvation (e.g., Fitzmyer, *Romans*, 321; Moo, *Romans* 167; Blaschke, *Beschneidung*, 410–11; Schreiner, *Romans*, 138; Horn, "Der Verzicht," 502). When Paul conditions the benefit of this circumcision upon proper law observance (ἐὰν νόμον πράσσῃς), these interpreters conclude that Paul is undermining the supposed soteriological benefit of circumcision, since—on their reading—this kind of law observance was an impossibility and Paul has already charged the interlocutor with not keeping the law.

one's circumcision to not bestow benefit and become a foreskin? A predominant position is that if a Jew cannot perfectly keep the law, then the covenant sign of circumcision is worthless.[67] On this reading, Paul dismantles the privileges of Jews.[68] Based on Paul's positive discussions of circumcision and law observance for Jews elsewhere (1 Cor 7:17–18; Phil 3:3–6), it seems unlikely that Paul would be arguing that a single transgression of the Torah would invalidate a Jew's circumcision and its concomitant covenantal benefits.[69] The glaring problem with this perspective is that Paul invalidates it just a few verses later in 3:1–2 where he states that circumcision does have benefit for Jews.[70] Presumably, all Jews did not perfectly keep the law, which is why the law contained the methods and means of atonement for transgressing it.

Another option interpreters have proposed is that Paul is focusing more on patterns of behavior as it pertains to the covenant and law observance. Boyarin, Barclay, and Nanos all note that the benefits of circumcision were rooted within the covenant and living according to the norms of Torah.[71] On this reading, circumcision can confer benefit to those who faithfully live within the covenant (i.e., the majority of Jews; Rom 3:1–2), and thus Paul is charging his interlocutor with behaving in a way that is not fitting of covenantal status. For example, Gathercole focuses on the seemingly "unrepentant" nature of the interlocutor,[72] whereas Longenecker argues that the focus here is on nominal Jews who are "professing but not practicing."[73] Similarly, Jewett emphasizes that to become a transgressor of the law, one's violations of the law must be "more than occasional or accidental."[74] Jewett's reading is somewhat akin to a view attributed to Rabbi Levi in Gen. Rab. 48:8.[75] In this text, Abraham is depicted as sitting at the gates of Gehenna ensuring that no circumcised Israelite enters. But when Israelites who sinned too much (שחטאו יותר מדיי) appear at the gates, Abraham performs foreskin transplants upon them by covering their circumcisions with the foreskins of infants who died before they

---

67 E.g., Moo, *Romans*, 168–69; Schreiner, *Romans*, 138; cf. Windsor, *Paul and the Vocation*, 175.
68 Eduard Lohse, *Der Brief an die Römer*, KEK 4 (Göttingen: Vandenhoeck & Ruprecht, 2003) 112–13.
69 So Matthew Thiessen, "Paul's Argument against Gentile Circumcision in Romans 2:17–29," *NovT* 56 (2014): 384–85; Rodríguez, *If You Call Yourself*, 57–58; Thiessen, *Gentile Problem*, 64.
70 In 2:25 Paul uses the verbal form ὠφελέω (ὠφελεῖ) and in 3:1 he uses the nominal form ὠφέλεια (ὠφέλεια) to discuss the relative benefits of circumcision. Stowers (*Rereading*, 154) notes that both 2:25 and 3:1–2 attest to the idea that circumcision has value for Jews. See also, Neutel, "Circumcision Gone Wrong," 387; Longenecker, *Romans*, 314.
71 Boyarin, *A Radical Jew*, 92–93; Barclay, "Paul and Philo," 545; Nanos, "Paul's Non-Jews," 44–45.
72 Gathercole, *Where is Boasting*, 201–2. See also Stowers, *Rereading*, 226.
73 Longenecker, *Romans*, 314.
74 Jewett, *Romans*, 232.
75 Thiessen, *Gentile Problem*, 65.

were circumcised. Like the so-called Jew of Rom 2:25, their circumcisions have thus become foreskins. Thiessen, however, rightly notes that Paul does not say that the interlocutor sins too much, only that he is a transgressor of the law.[76] While the covenantal perspective is a more plausible framework than the view regarding perfect law observance—and is confirmed to by Paul's statements in 3:1–2—it is a framework that applies to Jews, which this interlocutor may not actually be.

In 2:27 the interlocutor's transgression of the law comes into sharp focus—as does his identity as a gentile proselyte. Paul states that it is "through the letter and circumcision" (διὰ γράμματος καὶ περιτομῆς) that he is a transgressor of the law. This prepositional phrase is generally understood as indicating attendant circumstances and is translated disjunctively: "despite having the letter and circumcision."[77] On this reading, Paul is arguing that though he possesses the law and has a circumcised penis, the interlocutor is still unable to keep the law. A more natural reading, however, is that the διά-plus-genitive construction should be taken in its standard sense where it indicates instrumentality.[78] How is it, then, that one can become a transgressor of the law "through the letter and circumcision"? As I discussed previously, for some ancient Jews—Paul included—circumcisions had to be performed properly in order for them to be valid.[79] That is, for circumcision to be covenantally efficacious, it needed to be performed on a descendant of Abraham on the eighth-day after birth. So, on Paul's understanding of the function and performance of circumcision, it was never the means by which a non-Jew can become a Jew, and attempting to use it in this way constitutes a transgression of the laws pertaining to circumcision.[80]

---

[76] Thiessen, *Gentile Problem*, 65. Like the other uses in the NT, παραβάτης likely refers to the transgression of a single law (Luke 6:4 [Codex Bezae]; Gal 2:18; Jas 2:9, 11).

[77] Cranfield, *Romans*, 1:174; Fitzmyer, *Romans*, 322; Moo, *Romans*, 173n38; Schreiner, *Romans*, 139; Thorsteinsson, *Paul's Interlocutor*, 228n232; Jewett, *Romans*, 234; Mortensen, *Paul among the Gentiles*, 132.

[78] Gottlob Schrenk, "γράφω, γραφή, κτλ," *TDNT*, 1:765; Dunn, *Romans 1–8*, 122–23; Rodríguez, *If You Call Yourself*, 59; Thiessen, *Gentile Problem*, 65–66; Novenson, "The Self-Styled Jew," 148; Mininger, *Uncovering*, 247–48. Despite their identification of this prepositional phrase as functioning instrumentally, Schrenk, Dunn, and Mininger each provide unsatisfactory explanations for how the interlocutor becomes a transgressor through the letter and circumcision. Both Schrenk and Mininger fail to actually comment on how this works, and their interpretations are effectively the same as those who argue that this phrase indicates attendant circumstances. Dunn, on the other hand, argues that the interlocutor's emphasis on the law and circumcision as ethnic signifiers is what causes him to be a transgressor.

[79] See discussion in §3.4.2.

[80] Thiessen, "Paul's Argument," 387–88.

In 2:25–27, then, Paul argues that the interlocutor's circumcision has failed to bring about the expected result of conferring benefit upon him because his circumcision *itself* was a transgression of the γράμμα of the law.⁸¹ The ritual fails to bring about the desired result and status because it was not carried out in accordance with the laws pertaining to circumcision—i.e., it was performed on a non-descendant of Abraham and not on the eighth-day after birth. Thus, the transgression of the law that invalidates a circumcision does not refer to a transgression of any of the laws of Torah or to a broader pattern of living as a transgressor, but rather to the specific law pertaining to circumcision.⁸² Additionally—according to Paul, the Hebrew Bible, and Jubilees—circumcision never functioned as the means through which a non-Jew became a Jew. As both Neutel and Smit have put forth, Paul's discussion of the interlocutor's circumcision in Rom 2:25–27 constitutes a textbook example of "ritual disruption" or "ritual failure."⁸³ The ritual does not have efficacy because it was not properly performed. And in the case of the interlocutor, the result which he desired—becoming a Jew—was never intended to be a function of the ritual. This interpretation also helps us make sense of Paul's claim that the transgression of the law of circumcision makes one's circumcision into a foreskin (ἡ περιτομή σου ἀκροβυστία γέγονεν, 2:25). While γέγονεν is universally translated in its basic sense to demonstrate something becoming something else ("has become a foreskin"), it is also possible—and preferable in this case—to translate it resultantly ("has proven to be") or generatively ("has produced a foreskin").⁸⁴ While this is not to say that the interlocutor's foreskin physically regenerates to cover his glans, but that his false circumcision demonstrates the true, naturally foreskinned (2:27) state of his penis (cf. Jer 9:25–26).⁸⁵

This reading also provides an explanation for Paul's surprising claim that the foreskin who observes the law has his foreskin reckoned (or considered) as cir-

---

81 Here, γράμμα refers to the letter of the law or the prescription of the law. Cf. Thorsteinsson, *Paul's Interlocutor,* 228–29.
82 Thiessen, "Paul's Argument," 385.
83 Neutel, "Circumcision Gone Wrong," 386–88; Smit, "Real Circumcision," 89–92. Neither Neutel nor Smit, however, argue that the ritual fails due to its improper performance.
84 Both of these translations are well within the standard range of meanings attested to by ancient usage of γίνομαι. See BDAG, s.v. "γίνομαι"; LSJ, s.v. "γίγνομαι." Elsewhere, Paul uses γέγονεν resultantly in 1 Thess 2:1: "For you yourselves know, brothers, that our coming to you did not prove to be empty (οὐ κενὴ γέγονεν)." Cf. Christine Hayes, "Thiessen and Kaden on Paul and the Gentiles," *JSPL* 7 (2017): 68–79, at 78.
85 Cf. Garroway, "The Circumcision of Christ," 318; Livesey, *Malleable Symbol,* 108. See also, Garroway, *Paul's Gentile-Jews,* 131.

cumcision (ἡ ἀκροβυστία αὐτοῦ εἰς περιτομὴν λογισθήσεται, 2:26).⁸⁶ Like many interpretations of 1 Cor 7:19, some scholars highlight the fact that circumcision was a part of the law and, therefore, by not undergoing it, the foreskin would be breaking the law.⁸⁷ This, however, is an overly simplistic understanding of the law of circumcision and the purpose of circumcision in many expressions of ancient Judaism—especially as it pertains to non-Jews and circumcision. On the reading I am proposing, the foreskin who remains in his naturally foreskinned state (ἐκ φύσεως ἀκροβυστία, 2:27)⁸⁸ actually observes and upholds the requirements of the law pertaining to circumcision.⁸⁹ For Paul, this qualifies as completing the law of circumcision (τὸν νόμον τελοῦσα, 2:27). Based on an inference from the converse (οὖν), Paul can make the puzzling assertion that foreskin will be reckoned (λογισθήσεται) as circumcision.⁹⁰

The reckoning of one's foreskin as circumcision has not been sufficiently considered by interpreters who argue for a gentile interlocutor in this text, but Thorsteinsson and Garroway constitute the exceptions.⁹¹ Thorsteinsson correctly notes that Paul does not have actual physical circumcision in mind here—after all, Paul is adamant that gentiles in his assemblies should not be circumcised (e. g., Gal 5:2).⁹² Rather, Thorsteinsson argues that this reckoned circumcision likely refers

---

86 On this text, Barclay ("Paul and Philo," 545) notes that Paul's claim that law observance is not just *necessary* for circumcision to have value but also that it is *sufficient* to count as circumcision is "astonishing" (cf. Livesey, *Malleable Symbol*, 108–9). Adjacently, Nanos ("Paul's Non-Jews," 45–46) comments that this hypothetical individual's law observance constitutes legitimate Jewish behavior —in contrast to the interlocutor—and, therefore, his dedication to keep the law mirrors that of what a circumcised individual should do. Thus, he can be "valued/regarded" as circumcised. Against Barclay's reading, see Windsor, *Paul and the Vocation*, 179 (cf. Josephus, *Ant*. 20.34–50; Philo, *QE* 2.2).
87 Moo, *Romans*, 171; Cf. Stowers, *Rereading*, 157; Boyarin, *Radical Jew*, 96; Wright, *Paul*, 922; Wells, *Grace and Agency*, 212. For my reading of 1 Cor 7:19, see §2.5.
88 As I noted in §4.4, Paul conceives of gentiles as naturally foreskinned and Jews as being naturally circumcised (Rom 2:27; 1 Cor 7:17–19; Gal 2:15; Phil 3:2–3; cf. m. Ned. 3.11).
89 Thus rightly Novenson, "Self-Style Jew," 149. Contra Räisänen (*Paul and the Law*, 103) who asserts that this "refers unequivocally to the totality of the law." Thiessen (*Gentile Problem*, 69) incorrectly notes that the gentile audience of Romans would not be able to keep the law of circumcision. While they may not be able to properly undergo circumcision, by refraining from doing so they actually observe the law.
90 Windsor, *Paul and the Vocation*, 179.
91 A discussion of how λογισθήσεται is functioning in 2:26 is absent from the accounts given by Thiessen, Rodríguez, Novenson, and Mortensen.
92 Thorsteinsson, *Paul's Interlocutor*, 227.

more broadly to eschatological covenantal status and to heart circumcision.[93] Garroway, too, contends that heart-circumcision is in view here, but he takes his reading one step further. He argues that in Rom 2:25–29, Paul's point "is not that circumcision of the heart matters while circumcision of the penis does not. In fact, circumcision of the penis is of paramount importance. What has changed is what counts for genital circumcision."[94] On Garroway's reading, the metaphorical circumcision of heart also brings about an "ontologically transformative circumcision of the penis"[95] which renders foreskinned gentiles as if they were physically circumcised(!). This visually imperceptible removal of the foreskin is performed on the individual by the Messiah (Rom 15:8)[96] and confers upon them the circumcision that is required for entry into the family of Abraham.[97] While Garroway's reading creatively deals with multiple interpretive and conceptual problems within the text, I find it unconvincing for numerous reasons. Most notably, Paul's language regarding this reckoned circumcision is terse and does not offer the reader much in the way of explanation of what this entails or how it occurs.[98] Garroway's assertion that this reckoned circumcision refers to a circumcision of the heart (2:29) that imperceptibly modifies fleshly gentile foreskins goes well beyond Paul's brief mention of reckoned circumcision and ancient Jewish discussions of the relationship between physical and heart-circumcision.[99] Garroway's reading also undoes the important binary of circumcision and foreskin that Paul continues to uphold throughout Romans and his other epistles (e.g., Rom 3:29–30).[100] As Nanos comments, "Within the contrast being developed, as well as the rest of the letter and Paul's arguments against Christ-following non-Jews undertaking lit-

---

93 Thorsteinsson, *Paul's Interlocutor*, 227–29. See also, Wright, *Paul*, 501; Barclay, *Paul and the Gift*, 470.
94 Garroway, *Paul's Gentile-Jews*, 131. See also, Garroway, "The Circumcision of Christ," 318–19.
95 Garroway, *Paul's Gentile-Jews*, 131.
96 Here, Garroway translates διάκονος as "agent" rather than "servant" or "messenger." For my discussion of this text and Garroway's reading of it, see §5.8.
97 Garroway, *Paul's Gentile-Jews*, 132.
98 So Longenecker, *Romans*, 315–16.
99 The assumption that this reckoned circumcision refers to heart-circumcision is misguided. As discussed below, Paul does not argue that heart circumcision applies to gentiles, nor does he apply the category of "circumcision" to non-Jews. On this point, Garroway's misreading and conflation of Phil 3:3 with Rom 2:25–29 leads to some of the shortcomings of his interpretation of this text ("The Circumcision of Christ," 317–19; *Paul's Gentile-Jews*, 129–32).
100 Nanos, *Mystery of Romans*, 176; Thiessen, *Gentile Problem*, 55–57; Tucker, *After Supersessionism*, 100.

eral circumcision, it is illogical to suppose that Paul means that the non-Jew actually becomes circumcised."[101]

It should be noted that Paul's statement about reckoned circumcision is an inference (οὖν) based on his conclusions about the interlocutor's law-breaking circumcision in 2:25. Here, Paul appears to be adopting or assuming the interlocutor's premise that a circumcision would be desirable for a foreskinned person. Paul, however, indicates that the status the interlocutor is seeking through his circumcision is available to him (i.e., Abrahamic sonship), but not on the terms he is proposing. Based on Paul's argument that an incorrectly performed circumcision on a non-Jew actually proves to be (or produces) a foreskin, Paul infers the opposite; that a non-Jew who remains in his naturally foreskinned state—and thus completes the law of circumcision—can hypothetically have his foreskin reckoned as a circumcision.[102] This is not to say that his foreskinned penis *actually* becomes a circumcised one—perceptible or not—but that through his completion of the law of circumcision (2:27), he has more claim to the status represented by circumcision than the interlocutor does.[103] This fictive reckoning does not function as the actual means through which non-Jews are able to become children of Abraham, as Garroway asserts, rather, it serves a polemical purpose for Paul.[104] Since the interlocutor attempts to achieve a proper standing before God through circumcision and fails, Paul argues that a foreskinned gentile who does nothing and simply remains in foreskin has a better claim to the status of circumcision than those who are incorrectly circumcised.[105] Indeed, the foreskin from nature who remains as such will condemn the foreskin from nature who wrongfully undergoes circumcision (2:27). This is not to say that he functions as some type of eschatological judge,

---

[101] Nanos, "Paul's Non-Jews," 46.
[102] Cf. Thorsteinsson, *Paul's Interlocutor*, 227.
[103] Stowers, *Rereading*, 141; Hayes, "Paul and the Gentiles," 78; cf. Dunn, *Romans 1–8*, 122; Windsor, *Paul and the Vocation*, 179.
[104] Garroway, *Paul's Gentile-Jews*, 83–86.
[105] This reading also accounts for the different verbs Paul uses in 2:25 and 26 to discuss the circumcision proving to be (γίνομαι) a foreskin and the foreskin being reckoned (λογίζομαι) as a circumcision. In 2:25, Paul is referring to a something he deems to be a demonstrable reality: circumcision is unable to make a naturally foreskinned non-Jew into a naturally circumcised Jew, and the foreskin who undergoes circumcision demonstrates that. Whereas in 2:26, Paul affirms the converse through the hypothetical fictive reckoning of the status of circumcision upon non-Jews who do not modify their foreskins. Contra Berkley, *From a Broken Covenant*, 146n109. Like Berkley, Garroway conflates Paul's use of γίνομαι and λογίζομαι, even referring to 2:25 as speaking of "reckoned epispasm" (*Paul's Gentile-Jews*, 198n37).

but, rather, it should be understood in the sense that through his completion of the law, he effectively condemns those who transgress it.¹⁰⁶

5.3.2 Heart Circumcision and the Jew in Secret

In 2:28–29, Paul briefly discusses the idea of the circumcision of the heart (περιτομὴ καρδίας) alongside the Jew in secret (ὁ ἐν τῷ κρυπτῷ Ἰουδαῖος). Despite the fact that this is the *only* place where circumcision of the heart is mentioned in Paul's extant writings—not to mention the entire New Testament—interpreters have latched onto this text to argue that in it Paul redefines what circumcision is and what constitutes true Jewish identity.¹⁰⁷ In so doing—they argue—Paul makes the categories of "circumcision" and "Jew" applicable to all Messiah-followers, irrespective of ethnic background or the presence or lack of a foreskin. While the early Christian interpretive tradition makes heart-circumcision (or "true circumcision") an essential Christian symbol and doctrine, heart-circumcision is at its core an ancient Jewish symbol.¹⁰⁸ Given the scarcity of evidence for this theme in Paul and the New Testament, it is possible that Paul's interpreters—both ancient and

---

106 Thus rightly Novenson, "The Self-Styled Jew," 149. See also, Cranfield, *Romans*, 1:174; Moo, *Romans*, 171–72; Mininger, *Uncovering*, 247n75.

107 In Stephen's speech in Acts 7, he accuses some of his fellow Jews as having "uncircumcised hearts" (ἀπερίτμητοι καρδίαις; Acts 7:51)—like the prophet Jeremiah—as a critique of their failure to recognize Jesus as the Righteous One. Some also find a reference or allusion to heart-circumcision in Phil 3:3 and Col 2:11. See my discussion on why heart-circumcision is not in view in Phil 3:3 in chapter 3. I do not think heart circumcision is in view in Col 2:11 either. There I think the author's logic follows Paul's understanding of pneumatic union and participation with the Messiah. By the virtue of their pneumatic union with the Messiah, they participate in his own circumcision.

108 The earliest Christian and patristic references to circumcision of the heart or spiritual circumcision make their appeals to the Hebrew Bible and the prophet Jeremiah, not Paul or Rom 2:29 (Barn. 9; Justin, *Dial.* 15.7; 19.3; 41.4; cf. 11.5; 12.3; 18.2; 23.3; 24.1; 28.4; 43.2; 92.4; 113.7; 114.4; 137.1). While Justin and the author of Barnabas do not directly reference Paul or his epistles, the reasons for their lack of appeal to Paul are complex but can partially be attributed to their anti-Jewish rhetoric. Rather than appeal to Paul—a "Christian"— they may only appeal to the Hebrew Bible to discredit their rhetorical Jewish foes. On this, see James Carleton Paget, "Paul and the Epistle of Barnabas," *NovT* 38 (1996): 359–81. On the possibility that Justin was familiar with Paul's epistles, see Rodney Werline, "The Transformation of Pauline Arguments in Justin Martyr's Dialogue with Trypho," *HTR* 92 (1999): 79–93. Irenaeus (*Haer.* 4.16.1) appeals to Col 2:11 and Jer 4:4 when discussing heart circumcision. Clement (*Strom.* 7.9) mentions Paul and heart-circumcision in a discussion of 1 Cor 9 and Pauline accommodation, but makes no reference to Rom 2:29. As far as I can tell, the earliest direct appeal to Rom 2:29 in a discussion of heart-circumcision is Tertullian, *Marc.* 5.13. On spiritual circumcision in early Christian texts, see Everett Ferguson, "Spiritual Circumcision in Early Christianity," *SJT* 41 (1988): 485–97.

modern—have overemphasized the centrality of this theme in his thought. Or to state it differently, Paul's interpreters have made a theological mountain out of a cardiological mohel.

For example, Daniel Boyarin comments that in Rom 2:28–29, "Paul introduces his major concern throughout his ministry: producing a new, single human essence, one of 'true Jews' whose 'circumcision' does not mark off their bodies as ethnically distinct from any other human bodies."[109] Barclay summarizes Boyarin's understanding of Paul and his religion as being a "radically Hellenized Judaism [that takes] its spiritualizing tendencies to their reductive conclusions."[110] While Barclay's essay on Paul, Philo, and circumcision was written as a corrective to Boyarin's position—which he successfully accomplishes through a clear dismantling of Boyarin's thoroughly Hellenized and Platonized portrayal of Paul—he too concludes that Paul offers a radical redefinition of circumcision and Jewish identity.[111] Similarly, Dunn emphasizes the supposed collapse of distinction between Jew and gentile in 2:28–29, commenting that since both Jew and gentile have access to the spirit of God, old boundary markers like ethnicity and circumcision have become redundant, and thus, "the eschatological Jew is Gentile as well as Jew!"[112]

One of the crucial problems with these readings is how Paul uses the terms Jew and circumcision elsewhere in his writings. Every other instance of Ἰουδαῖος in Paul's epistles refers only to ethnic Jews and nowhere is the category of περιτομή applied to non-Jews.[113] Similarly, Paul affirms the ongoing validity and practice of circumcision for ethnic Jews (Rom 3:1–2; 1 Cor 7:17–19). While it is not impossible that Paul could be redefining these terms to include non-Jews, this would be startlingly novel in the ancient world.[114] As far as I am aware, no

---

[109] Boyarin, *A Radical Jew*, 94. See also, *A Radical Jew*, 25–29, 77–82, 92–97.
[110] Barclay, "Paul and Philo," 537.
[111] Barclay, "Paul and Philo," 543–56.
[112] Dunn, *Romans 1–8*, 125; cf. idem, *Theology of Paul*, 149, 424; idem, *New Perspective on Paul*, 472.
[113] Rom 1:16; 2:9–10, 17; 3:1, 9, 29–30; 4:9, 12; 9:24; 10:12; 1 Cor 1:22–24; 7:19; 9:20; 10:32; 12:13; 2 Cor 11:24; Gal 2:7–9, 12–15; 3:28; 1 Thess 2:14; cf. Eph 2:11, Col 3:11; 4:11. The only instance where this may be the case is Phil 3:3, but as I have argued in my discussion of that text, Paul uses περιτομή in his typical way to refer to Jews—himself and Timothy.
[114] Thus rightly Windsor, *Paul and the Vocation*, 183; cf. J. M. F. Heath, *Paul's Visual Piety: The Metamorphosis of the Beholder* (Oxford: Oxford University Press, 2013), 136. While Windsor does not offer a wholesale redefinition of these categories—and who they can apply to—in such a way that they are entirely divorced from their historical referents, he does redefine these categories in a way that allows them to be applied to foreskinned gentile synagogue adherents (181–91). For Windsor, Paul is arguing that "true" Jewish identity is not found in the mainstream synagogue, rather, it is to be found within Christ-following communities. Thus, "true" Jewish identity is contingent upon one's fidelity to the Messiah. While Paul would agree that Jews should show fidelity to

5.3 Circumcision and the So-Called Jew: Romans 2:25–29 — 171

other ancient Jewish source applies the categories of *circumcision* and *Jew* to foreskinned gentiles.[115] Furthermore, if Paul is decoupling heart circumcision from physical penile-circumcision in 2:28–29, this would constitute a departure from all ancient Jewish sources.[116] While it is possible that Paul is offering an innovative take on these categories, we should not rush to try and see him as innovating at every turn. Through a reconsideration of the syntax of 2:28–29, I believe we can establish that this is not what Paul is saying.

The most damning piece of evidence against this line of interpretation is the text of Rom 2:28–29 itself. One of the major issues all interpreters face when looking at 2:28–29 is its "strikingly concise and elliptic" form.[117] In the NA[28], the text is rendered:

οὐ γὰρ ὁ ἐν τῷ φανερῷ Ἰουδαῖός ἐστιν οὐδὲ ἡ ἐν τῷ φανερῷ ἐν σαρκὶ περιτομή, ἀλλ' ὁ ἐν τῷ κρυπτῷ Ἰουδαῖος, καὶ περιτομὴ καρδίας ἐν πνεύματι οὐ γράμματι, οὗ ὁ ἔπαινος οὐκ ἐξ ἀνθρώπων ἀλλ' ἐκ τοῦ θεοῦ.

In order to make sense of this difficult text, it is often supplemented with various additions in translations to help clarify Paul's thought, but I will demonstrate that this practice actually obscures Paul's thought. On this, Stowers comments, "The highly elliptical language of 2:28–29 makes it easy to read and translate, as traditional Christian treatments have, in a manner that spiritualizes circumcision and Judaism to the point that they vanish."[118] For example, this is how Cranfield has chosen to render this text, with his additions in brackets:[119]

Jesus as the Messiah (Rom 9–11), their status as "Jews" or the "circumcision" is not contingent upon this fidelity. As discussed below, the importation and imposition of the category of the "true Jew" drastically changes the meaning of the text and misleads interpreters. For other interpreters who argue that Paul is restricting "true" Jewishness to Jews who have circumcised hearts, see Fitzmyer, *Romans*, 323; John Goldingay, "The Significance of Circumcision," *JSOT* 88 (2000): 3–18, at 15.

115 M. Ned. 3:11 actually does the opposite and treats circumcised *goyim* as if they are still foreskinned, and foreskinned Jews as if they are circumcised.

116 The lone exception may be the allegorists Philo mentions in *Migration* 89–93. Circumcision of the heart, however, is not mentioned in this account, only the internal excision of pleasure and passions that external circumcision represents. On the interconnectedness between physical and heart-circumcision, see the discussion below.

117 Cranfield, *Romans*, 1:175.

118 Stowers, *Rereading*, 155. Similarly, Novenson ("The Self-Style Jew," 149) notes how much "theological mileage" interpreters have gotten out of translations that emphasize redefinition.

119 Similarly, see also the additions added by Jewett, *Romans*, 219.

> οὐ γὰρ ὁ ἐν τῷ φανερῷ [Ἰουδαῖος] Ἰουδαῖός ἐστιν οὐδὲ ἡ ἐν τῷ φανερῷ ἐν σαρκὶ [περιτομή] περιτομή [ἐστιν] ἀλλ' ὁ ἐν τῷ κρυπτῷ Ἰουδαῖος [Ἰουδαῖός ἐστιν], καὶ περιτομὴ καρδίας ἐν πνεύματι οὐ γράμματι [περιτομή ἐστιν], οὗ ὁ ἔπαινος οὐκ ἐξ ἀνθρώπων [ἐστιν] ἀλλ' ἐκ τοῦ θεοῦ.[120]

> For the Jew on display is not [a Jew], nor [is] the circumcision on display in the flesh [circumcision], but the Jew in secret [is a Jew], and the circumcision of the heart by the *pneuma*, not the letter, [is circumcision]; the praise for such a person [is] not from people, but from God.[121]

While such additions make for an easier text to translate, they drastically change the meaning of the text.[122] Both Matthew Thiessen and Matthew Novenson have offered a much more straightforward way to render and translate this perplexing text that does not rely on excessive additions:[123]

> For it is not the Jew on display, nor the circumcision on display in the flesh, but the Jew in secret, and the circumcision of the heart in *pneuma*, not letter, whose praise [is] not from man, but from God.

On this translation of the text, the traditional interpretation is left without legs to stand on.[124] The purpose of this text is not to redefine the concepts of "Jew" and "circumcision,"[125] but to demonstrate to the interlocutor that not all Jews and not all circumcisions receive praise from God.[126] His attempt to receive praise from

---

120 Cranfield, *Romans*, 1:175.
121 My translation of Cranfield's reconstruction.
122 Wells (*Grace and Agency*, 217)—noting the terseness of Paul's language in 2:28–29—erroneously comments that reconstructing it with additions "has little consequence on the sense of the verses."
123 Thiessen, "Paul's Argument," 377; idem, *Gentile Problem*, 58; Novenson, "The Self-Styled Jew," 138. See also the similar translation in Witherington and Hyatt, *Paul's Letter to the Romans*, 86, 91–92.
124 As Novenson ("The Self-Styled Jew," 138) notes, regardless of one's interpretation of Rom 2:28–29, this translation (or a version of it) should become the standard. Translations that rely on numerous additions, especially the adjectives "true," "real," "ultimate," or "eschatological," which are foreign to the Greek text, should be abandoned.
125 For example, Berkley states that the purpose of Rom 2:28–29 is to provide an answer to one main question: "Who, in fact, is a Jew?" (*From a Broken Covenant*, 152). Similarly, Ralph Bisschops ("Metaphor in Religious Transformation") utilizes cognitive linguistics to interpret the supposed shift in Paul's thought regarding the identification of who is a Jew and what counts as circumcision. While Bisschops' study employs a cutting edge methodological approach to evaluate Paul's reference to circumcision of the heart, his overall conclusions regarding Paul and circumcision of the heart follow the standard scholarly consensus.
126 Novenson, "The Self-Styled Jew," 150; Thiessen, *Gentile Problem*, 69–70; cf. Heath, *Paul's Visual Piety*, 159.

God through Jewishness and circumcision on display will only garner him praise from men (cf. Matt 6:1–18).[127] The praise that comes from God is given to the Jew in secret,[128] whose physical, penile-circumcision is accompanied by circumcision of the heart (cf. Jer 9:25–26).[129] This reading helps make sense of the questions that the interlocutor asks in 3:1: "What then is the advantage of the Jew? Or what is the benefit of circumcision?" If Paul has just stated that not all Jews and circumcisions receive praise from God (2:28–29), then it is logical for the interlocutor to ask if there is any value in being a circumcised Jew.

The distinction between what is on display (φανερός) and what is in secret (or "hidden"; κρυπτός) frames the discussion of the Jew who receives praise from men and who receives it from God.[130] As Barclay has correctly pointed out, Paul is not employing a Platonic contrast between what is visible and invisible, rather, "What is 'hidden' for Paul is not what is, by constitution, invisible and incorruptible, but simply what is not (presently) accessible to human eyes."[131] The Jew on display who is circumcised in his flesh also needs be a Jew in secret whose heart is circumcised to receive praise from God. This does not imply that heart-circumcision is in-

---

127 For a traditional assessment of this theme, see Eduard Schweizer, ""Der Jude im Verborgenen..., dessen Lob nicht von Menschen, sondern von Gott kommt": Zu Röm 2,28f und Mt 6,1–18," in *Neues Testament und Kirche: Für Rudolf Schnackenburg*, ed. Joachim Gnilka (Freiburg: Herder, 1974), 115–124. See also Fridrichsen, "Der wahre Jude."
128 While the reference to the "Jew in secret" is likely analogous to the pattern of hidden piety encouraged by Jesus in Matt 6, this identification could also indicate a special status beyond simply being Jewish. Carmen Palmer (*Converts*, 129–57, esp. 153–54) argues that in the DSS Serekh tradition, circumcision of the heart turned a normal Judean into a "supra-Judean." Notably, this special status is closed off from gentile converts, since this tradition rejects gentile converts due to their perceived genealogical impurity (see Palmer's [116–21, 127] discussion of 4QpNah Frags. 3–4, II, 7–10 and 4QFlor Frag. 1, I, 1–4).
129 Like the "neither/nor" texts in 1 Cor 7:19 and Gal 5:6 and 6:15, Paul is not negating the importance of being an external Jew or circumcision in the flesh, but is employing the "not/but" contrast to make his point about what receives praise from God.
130 Some have argued that Paul is retrieving the language of φανερός and κρυπτός from LXX Deut 29:28, which is the only place where this word-pair occurs in the LXX: "The secret things (τὰ κρυπτὰ) belong to the Lord our God, but the evident things (τὰ φανερὰ) belong to us and to our children into the age, to do all of the words of this law." On this, see Berkley, *From a Broken Covenant*, 99–100; Heath, *Paul's Visual Piety*, 159–62; Wells, *Grace and Agency*, 217–21. While Berkley and Wells take this to amount to an unfavorable view of circumcision, Heath is more cautious and notes that there is nothing in this possible reference that denigrates circumcision. Given the emphasis on doing the law, if Paul is retrieving this language from this text—which is a claim I am skeptical of—this would not amount to a negative evaluation of physical circumcision for Jews.
131 Barclay, "Paul and Philo," 554. See also Mininger, *Uncovering*, 248–54. Like Barclay, Mininger emphasizes that the φανερός-κρυπτός distinction refers to what is presently visible or hidden to human eyes, not what is external or internal.

visible or immaterial for Paul, rather that it is only visible to God, who sees the heart (1 Kgdms 16:7; 3 Kgdms 8:39; Prov 15:11; 1 Thess 2:4).[132]

Paul makes the distinction that circumcision of the heart is ἐν πνεύματι, and not [ἐν] γράμματι.[133] That is, the agent that performs the circumcision of the heart is the divine *pneuma*. The letter, by contrast, is unable to bring about heart-circumcision since it only prescribes how to modify foreskins.[134] Many interpreters often miss this point and put forth the interpretation that πνεύματι and γράμματι refer to two different types of circumcision—of heart and of foreskin[135]—but since the prepositional phrase ἐν πνεύματι οὐ γράμματι modifies περιτομὴ καρδίας, they should be understood as referring to the instruments that can and cannot bring about heart-circumcision. It is possible that Paul highlights that it is performed by the *pneuma*, not God or the Messiah, because—for some ancient thinkers, including Paul—the heart is one of the main places where *pneuma* was located within an individual (Rom 8:15; 2 Cor 1:22; Gal 4:6; Cf. Ezek 36:26; Philo, *Spec. Laws* 1.6; QG 2.59; Aetius, *Placit.* 4.5.6).[136] Thus, the divine *pneuma* may be performing this circumcision upon the human *pneuma* within the heart of the individual.[137] While in ancient Jewish texts the Israelites themselves (Deut 10:16; Jer 4:4; cf. Lev 26:41) and God (Deut 30:6; Jub. 1:23) are both given as possible agents of heart-circumcision, Paul credits the *pneuma* with this role (cf. Odes Sol. 11.1–3).[138]

It is important to note that Paul is not unique in his emphasis on the importance of heart-circumcision. Like many ancient Jewish thinkers, Paul notes that circumcision of the foreskin should be accompanied by circumcision of the heart[139]

---

132 On ancient Jewish visuality and how it impacts the interconnectedness between physical penile-circumcision and heart-circumcision, see Heath, *Paul's Visual Piety*, 132–37, 158–62.
133 The πνεῦμα-γράμμα contrast is often interpreted through the lenses of Rom 7:6 and 2 Cor 3:6. As Mininger (*Uncovering*, 255–57) notes, the contexts of these passages are quite different and should not be conflated so as to present one singular understanding of how the word-pair is functioning for Paul. Contra Wright, *Paul*, 323–24.
134 On this point, see Mininger (*Uncovering*, 259), who notes that ἐν πνεύματι and [ἐν] γράμματι represent the instrumentalities that are and are not able to circumcise the heart. Cf. Longenecker, *Romans*, 317.
135 E.g., Fitzmyer, *Romans*, 323; Dunn, *Romans 1–8*, 124; Thorsteinsson, *Paul's Interlocutor*, 229.
136 I am indebted to Matthew Sharp and Isaac Soon on this point.
137 As Stowers (*Rereading*, 155) notes, it is not immediately clear if this *pneuma* refers to the divine *pneuma* or the individual's *pneuma*.
138 In the Odes of Solomon (11.1–3), the Most High uses his holy spirit as the tool with which he circumcises the heart. The author of Jubilees (1:23) makes a similar connection between circumcision of the heart and a holy spirit, although there a holy spirit is given to the Israelites by God after he circumcises their hearts.
139 In some strands of modern Pauline scholarship there is a penchant for attempting to decipher which texts from the Hebrew Bible Paul may be interpreting in order to understand his reference

(Deut 10:16; 30:6; Lev 26:41; Jer 4:4; 9:25–26; Ezek 44:7, 9; 1QpHab 11.13; 4Q434 Frag. 1, 1.4; Jub. 1:23; Odes Sol. 11.1–3 Philo, *Spec. Laws* 1.304–5; *QG* 3.46; cf. 1QS 5.5).[140] In all of these texts,[141] circumcision of the heart is never divorced from physical circumcision of the foreskin, nor is there any privileging of the former over the latter.[142] It is incorrect to assume that by emphasizing the circumcision of the heart Paul is in any way denigrating penile-circumcision or claiming that is no longer necessary for Jews.[143] Similarly, both Jeremiah and Jubilees are exceedingly stringent regard-

---

to the circumcision of the heart. While Paul is undoubtedly drawing on a fairly standard tradition of heart-circumcision in ancient Judaism, the attempts by some to reverse-engineer a complicated web of allusions and intertextual references underlying 2:28–29 are fundamentally misguided. See, for example, Berkley, *From a Broken Covenant*; Wells, *Grace and Agency*, esp. 209–23. For an incisive critique of this methodological approach, see Paul Foster, "Echoes without Resonance: Critiquing Certain Aspects of Recent Scholarly Trends in the Study of the Jewish Scriptures in the New Testament," *JSNT* 38 (2015): 96–111.

140 On heart-circumcision in the Hebrew Bible and ancient Judaism, see Hans-Jürgen Hermisson, *Sprache und Ritus im altisraelischen Kult: zur "Spiritualisierung" der Kultbegriffe im Alten Testament*, WMANT 19 (Neukirchen-Vluyn: Neukirchener, 1965), 72–76; Roger Le Déaut, "Le thème de la circoncision du coeur (Dt. XXX 6; Jér. IV 4) dans les versions anciennes (LXX et Targum) et à Qumrân," in *Congress Volume: Vienna 1980*, ed. J. A. Emerton, VTSup 32 (Leiden: Brill, 1981), 178–205; Werner E. Lemke, "Circumcision of the Heart: The Journey of a Biblical Metaphor," in *God So Near: Essays on Old Testament Theology in Honor of Patrick D. Miller*, ed. Brent A. Strawn and Nancy R. Bowen (Winona Lake, IN: Eisenbrauns, 2003), 299–319; Heath, *Paul's Visual Piety*, 132–37; Palmer, *Converts*, 148–52. See also the discussion of the relevant heart-circumcision texts in Blaschke, *Beschneidung*.

141 It must be noted that many of these texts do not explicitly discuss circumcision of the foreskin alongside heart-circumcision. This fact, however, does not indicate that their employment of heart-circumcision functions as a replacement of or polemic against physical circumcision, which none of these texts gesture toward.

142 Hermisson, *Sprache und Ritus*, 76; Stowers, *Rereading*, 155; Bernat, *Sign of the Covenant*, 104; Livesey, *Malleable Symbol*, 111; Heath, *Paul's Visual Piety*, 136; Bisschops, "Metaphor," 322. Contra Peter C. Craigie, Page H. Kelley, and Joel F. Drinkard Jr., *Jeremiah 1–25*, WBC 26 (Dallas: Word, 1991), 154. Craigie, Kelley, and Drinkard Jr. incorrectly argue that Deuteronomy and Jeremiah do not advocate for physical circumcision and, therefore, only view the circumcision of the heart as being important. Lemke ("Circumcision of the Heart," 311–12) makes the puzzling claim that Ezek 44:6–9 argues the opposite, and that by intimately connecting physical and heart-circumcision, Ezekiel seeks to reverse circumcision's spiritualization and solely emphasize the importance of the fleshly rite. On the role of circumcision in Ezek 44:6–9, see Thiessen, *Contesting Conversion*, 46–47.

143 For example, Barclay comments that the circumcision of the heart is "the only sort that matters" ("Paul and Philo," 552). Similarly, Le Déaut ("Le théme," 203–4) says Paul follows the pattern of the Hebrew Bible in which the theme of spiritual circumcision prevails over material circumcision. Dunn goes one step further and argues that Paul's contrast between penile and heart-circumcision "has a clearly pejorative overtone" (*Romans 1–8*, 124). Commenting on Philo's insistence on continuing to practice physical circumcision alongside an allegorical understanding of it, John J.

ing the proper implementation of circumcision while also maintaining the importance of the circumcision of the heart (Jer 9:25–26; Jub. 1:23; 15:14, 25–26).[144]

Given Paul's remark about heart-circumcision being ἐν πνεύματι, this text is almost universally interpreted as saying that heart-circumcision is performed on *all* who receive the *pneuma* and, thus, applies to both Jews and gentiles who are in the Messiah.[145] This, however, is incorrect. As Nanos notes, since circumcision of the penis does not apply to non-Jews, neither does the circumcision of the heart.[146] While it is possible that Paul may be departing from Jewish tradition on this point, there is nothing explicit or implicit in this text that would include non-Jews amongst those who receive heart-circumcision.[147] As the translation and interpretation above indicate, Paul's mention of heart-circumcision is not employed to redefine who is a Jew or what counts for circumcision, but to demonstrate that not all Jews and circumcisions receive praise from God. Paul's emphasis on heart-circumcision may also have a polemical edge to it since it would exclude the judaizing gentile interlocutor from receiving praise from God as a "so-called Jew." This is not to say that Paul is a speaking polemically against Jewish identity or circumcision, but against an interlocutor who thinks that judaizing and circumcision are able to garner him praise from God deliver him from being under sin (3:9). Due to his status as non-Jew, he is—for Paul—by definition excluded from participating in the identities of Jew and circumcision, and is therefore unable to receive praise from God as a Jew in secret whose heart is circumcised.

Collins writes that "Philo's allegorical understanding of the significance of circumcision inevitably detracts from the importance of the physical rite, even though he defends that too" ("A Symbol of Otherness: Circumcision and Salvation in the First Century," in *Seers, Sibyls and Sages in Hellenistic-Roman Judaism*, JSJSup 54 [Leiden: Brill, 1997]; 221). See also, Berkley, *From a Broken Covenant*, 97–98; Bisschops, "Metaphor."

144 See Thiessen, *Gentile Problem*, 68–70.

145 Both Thiessen (*Gentile Problem*, 69–70) and Fredriksen (*Pagans' Apostle*, 157) comment that heart-circumcision is available to foreskinned non-Jews. Moo (*Romans*, 175) represents the standard Christian interpretation that ignores ethnic distinction in this text and argues that Paul is discussing or alluding to "Christians" when he speaks of heart-circumcision in Rom 2:29. See the helpful corrective by Mininger (*Uncovering*, 256n99) who takes a minimalist approach to this text—though he does argue from a standard translation that emphasizes how Jews are to be "properly defined."

146 Nanos, "Paul's Non-Jews," 51. See also the comments from Lemke ("Circumcision of the Heart," 311–12) on Ezek 44:6–9. He notes that for the author of Ezekiel, "all foreigners who are uncircumcised in flesh are, by definition, also uncircumcised in heart."

147 The supposed universalization of heart-circumcision fits within the general tendency of Pauline scholarship toward universalization and the mitigation of difference. Against this tendency, see Runesson, "Particularistic Judaism and Universalistic Christianity?"

5.4 The Benefit of Circumcision: Romans 3:1–2

Following in the wake of Paul's introduction of his judaizing gentile interlocutor and his claim that not all Jews and circumcisions receive praise from God, we hear the voice of the interlocutor for the first time: "What then is the advantage of the Jew? Or what is the benefit of circumcision?" (Rom 3:1).[148] As noted in the previous section, this question logically follows from what Paul says about who receives praise from God in 2:28–29. If not all Jews and circumcisions receive praise from God, is there any advantage or benefit to being a circumcised Jew? Paul responds in the affirmative: "Much in every way! First, that they[149] were entrusted with the oracles of God (τὰ λόγια τοῦ θεοῦ) …" (3:2).[150] Before Paul can list any other benefits, the interlocutor interjects and interrupts his explanation of Jewish privilege (3:3, 5, 7). Paul will go on to discuss the full advantage of Jews in Rom 9–11 (esp. 9:4–5; 11:26, 28–29),[151] but in the immediate passage he engages his hypothetical interlocutor to clear up some potential objections and questions that arise from his comments regarding the advantage and benefits afforded to circumcised Jews.[152]

---

[148] While there is debate surrounding who says what in 3:1–9, of the scholars that highlight the dialogical nature of this text, there is near universal agreement that Paul puts the words of 3:1 into the mouth of his imagined interlocutor. Stowers, *Rereading*, 165–66; Thorsteinsson, *Paul's Interlocutor*, 237; Rodríguez, *If You Call Yourself*, 64–65; Mortensen, *Paul Among the Gentiles*, 140–41; contra Elliott, *Rhetoric of Romans*, 139–41; King, *Speech-in-Character*, 269–70. For a full discussion of the history of interpretation of 3:1–9, see King, *Speech-in-Character*, 165–218.
[149] Paul's reference to Jews in the third person further demonstrates that his interlocutor is not one. It seems improbable that two Jews would talk about Jews in the third person. Paul's employment of the third person does not indicate that he no longer considers himself to be a Jew (cf. Mortensen, *Paul among the Gentiles*, 138n11), but logically follows from the interlocutor's inquiry. On this, see Joshua D. Garroway, "Paul's Gentile Interlocutor in Romans 3:1–20," in Rodríguez and Thiessen, *The So-Called Jew*, 85–100, at 91–92.
[150] While τὰ λόγια τοῦ θεοῦ can most broadly be understood as referring to the Torah or the whole of the Jewish scriptures (e.g., Fitzmyer, *Romans*, 326; Dunn, *Romans 1–8*, 130–31; Nanos, *Mystery of Romans*, 22; Windsor, *Paul and the Vocation*, 155), some have argued for a more specific referent. For example, Sam K. Williams ("The 'Righteousness of God' in Romans," *JBL* 99 [1980]: 241–90; 266–69) argues that it specifically refers to the promises given to Abraham. Williams' proposal is followed by Stowers (*Rereading*, 166–68) and Jewett (*Romans*, 243). Rodríguez (*If You Call Yourself*, 63; citing Jewett, Williams, and Stowers) offers a middle reading between these two proposals, noting that τὰ λόγια τοῦ θεοῦ is synonymous with the Torah, which includes the promises to Abraham regarding Israel and the nations.
[151] Fitzmyer, *Romans*, 326; Barclay, *Paul and the Gift*, 454; Fredriksen, *Pagans' Apostle*, 107; Longenecker, *Romans*, 181–82.
[152] In 3:3–4, the interlocutor inquires about the unfaithfulness of some Jews (ἡ ἀπιστία αὐτῶν) and if it nullifies God's faithfulness. Paul responds emphatically with μὴ γένοιτο. Following on

After Paul responds to the interlocutor's questions regarding Jewish privilege in light of Jewish ἀπιστία—and if that impacts God's judgement of gentile ἀδικία—the interlocutor asks if Jewish advantage leads to gentile disadvantage. "What then? Are we [non-Jews] disadvantaged (προεχόμεθα)?" (3:9a). The form and meaning of προεχόμεθα has continually vexed interpreters, leading to a variety of readings of this passage.[153] The general debate revolves around how the voice of προεχόμεθα should be understood (active, middle, or passive) and who "we" refers to.[154] Given that the majority of interpreters have understood that "we" refers to Jews, translating προεχόμεθα as a passive ("Are we disadvantaged?") proves to pose a contradiction with 3:1–2 where Jews are said to have an advantage. This contradiction has led many interpreters to attempt to justify strained translations that treat it as middle form or as a middle with active force ("What do we put forward on our behalf?" or "Are we at an advantage?").[155] If, however, the individual posing the question in 3:9a is a gentile, then this contradiction disappears and the verb can be translated as a passive, which is the most natural translation of this

---

Paul's claim that God is faithful to Jews in spite of some being unfaithful, the interlocutor turns to ask about the status of non-Jews, which is indicated by his shift from the third person to the first. "But If *our* unrighteous (ἡ ἀδικία ἡμῶν) confirms the righteousness of God, what should we say? Is not God unjust in inflicting wrath [on us]?" (Rom 5:5; cf. 1:18–32). Since God remains faithful to Jews despite the unfaithfulness of some, the interlocutor asks if God is unjust to judge and inflict wrath upon the ἀδικία of non-Jews. Again, Paul responds with μὴ γένοιτο, insisting that God is the judge of the κόσμος. In 3:7–8a, the interlocutor asks a similar question to 3:5, but focuses on his specific situation: "But if the truth of God abounds to his glory in *my* falsehood, why am I still being judged as a sinner? And why not say—as some slander us and say that we say—'Let us do evil in order that good might come'?" (cf. Rom 5:20–6:2). Paul does not even entertain this logic and dismisses it, saying that the condemnation of those who say such things is just (3:8b). The interlocutor's objections and questions arise out of his understanding of what Jewish ἀπιστία and non-Jewish ἀδικία mean for Jewish advantage. This reading of 3:1–8 is indebted to the insights from Garroway ("Paul's Gentile Interlocutor," 91–94) on the importance of understandings Paul's usage of pronouns in this passage. See also Mortensen, *Paul among the Gentiles*, 138–40.

153 The NRSV, for example, provides conflicting translations for this verb. The main text reads, "Are we any better off?" while an explanatory footnote supplies the information that this may also be translated as, "Are we at any disadvantage?" Similarly, BDAG (s.v. "προέχω") offers both renderings as possible, despite the fact that they are opposite in meaning and interpret the voice of the verb as being either passive or active.

154 For an overview of how προεχόμεθα has been interpreted, see Cranfield, *Romans*, 1:187–90; Nils Alstrup Dahl, "Romans 3.9: Text and Meaning," in Hooker and Wilson, *Paul and Paulinism*, 184–204; Moo, *Romans*, 199–201; Joshua D. Garroway, "Paul's Gentile Interlocutor in Romans 3:1–20," in Rodríguez and Thiessen, *The So-Called Jew*, 87–91.

155 E.g., Cranfield, *Romans*, 1:189–90; Dahl, "Romans 3.9"; Dunn, *Romans 1–8*, 146–48; Gaston, *Paul and the Torah*," 121. Cf. Rodríguez, *If You Call Yourself*, 67–68.

form.¹⁵⁶ Paul's response to this question is, "Not altogether" or "Not at all" (οὐ πάντως).¹⁵⁷ Jewish advantage does not lead to the complete disadvantage of gentiles, "for we have already charged (προητιασάμεθα)¹⁵⁸ that all, both Jews and Greeks, are under sin" (3:9b). As Paul will go on to discuss in 3:21–31, both Jews and gentiles—the circumcision and the foreskin—have sinned, and in this respect, there is no distinction between the two groups (3:22–23; cf. 10:12)—both are rightwised via *pistis* (3:26, 28, 30).

---

156 On translating προεχόμεθα as a passive, see Fitzmyer, *Romans*, 331; Stowers, *Rereading*, 173–74; Jewett, *Romans*, 256–57; Windsor, *Paul and the Vocation*, 155; Garroway, "Paul's Gentile Interlocutor," 87–91; cf. Mortensen, *Paul among the Gentiles*, 141.

157 Either translation of οὐ πάντως is possible, though I am inclined to agree with Cranfield (*Romans*, 1:190) that "not altogether" or "not in every respect" is the likely meaning of this phrase. Paul affirms the advantage and primacy of the Jews (1:16; 3:1–2), but this does not mean that gentiles are entirely at a disadvantage or are completely surpassed because both groups are under sin (ὑφ' ἁμαρτίαν, 3:9). On translating οὐ πάντως, see BDF §433.2; Moo, *Romans*, 200n16; Garroway, "Paul's Gentile Interlocutor," 94–95; Siebenthal, *Ancient Greek Grammar*, §269c; cf. 1 Cor 5:10.

158 Traditionally, interpreters argue that Paul has demonstrated the sinfulness of Jews in 1:18–32 —taken as an indictment of all humanity—and 2:1–29—taken as targeting Jews specifically. According to the reading I have proposed so far, Paul has not charged Jews of being under sin, only gentiles. The only thing that Paul—on the lips of his interlocutor—has charged some Jews with is ἀπιστία (3:3). I am persuaded by the proposal of Thorsteinsson (*Paul's Interlocutor*, 235–36) and Novenson ("The Self-Styled Jew," 152), which understands that προητιασάμεθα does not refer to what Paul has already stated previously in this letter, but to what the Jewish scriptures say about the sinfulness of Jews. This is indicated by the catena of citations Paul lists in 3:10–18, which he follows up by saying, "And we know that what the law says, it says to those who are in the law, so that every mouth would be shut and the whole cosmos be accountable to God" (3:19). The catena of scriptures speaks to "those in the law" (i.e., Jews) to indict them of being under sin. As Novenson comments, "That the gentiles are under sin is empirically demonstrable, which is the point not only of Rom 1:18–32, but also of 2:1–29. That the Jews are under sin is known from the testimony of the law—that is to say, from scripture rather than experience" ("The Self-Styled Jew," 152). Though it is unlikely to be original, the presence of the variant reading of ητιασαμεθα for προητιασάμεθα in some manuscripts (D* G 104. 1505 latt) indicates that some early interpreters of this text may have understood that Paul is pointing to the catena of scriptures in 3:10–18 by his use of προητιασάμεθα. Garroway ("Paul's Gentile Interlocutor," 95–97) takes a different approach to this problem and argues that προητιασάμεθα refers not to what Paul has already in Romans, but what he has said in other contexts and writings, especially Gal 3:22: "[S]cripture has imprisoned everything under sin."

5.5 The God of the Circumcision and the Foreskin: Romans 3:29–30

Based on the current state of both Jews and non-Jews being under sin (3:9), Paul turns to discuss how the righteousness of God (cf. Rom 1:16–17) has now been revealed through the faithfulness of the Messiah, Jesus (3:21–26).[159] This faithfulness —Paul argues—reveals God's righteousness to all who trust (3:22), makes those who trust right (3:24), is the means through which God deals with gentile sin (3:25),[160] demonstrates God's righteousness (3:26), and becomes the means that God uses to rightwise the one who is from the faithfulness of Jesus (τὸν ἐκ πίστεως Ἰησοῦ; 3:26).[161] Paul's announcement of the revelation of the righteousness of God and of the faithfulness of Jesus frames the discussion of how God rightwises both the circumcision and foreskin (3:27–31), and the discussion regarding the paternity of Abraham of both the circumcision and foreskin (4:1–25).

5.5.1 The One God of Jews and the Nations

After explaining the present revelation of the righteousness of God through the faithfulness of Jesus, Paul once again has his interlocutor raise his voice in 3:27: "Where, then, is boasting?"[162] Paul replies, "It is excluded." If Paul has just argued that all—both Jew and gentile—are under sin and all are rightwised via *pistis*, then what becomes of boasting? While boasting is most commonly understood here as

---

[159] On the meaning of the "righteousness of God" (δικαιοσύνη θεοῦ) in Rom 3, I am inclined to agree with the proposal put forth by Williams, "The 'Righteousness of God'." He argues that the righteousness of God in Romans refers primarily to "God's faithfulness in keeping his promise to Abraham" (265). Cf. George Howard, "Romans 3:21–31 and the Inclusion of the Gentiles," *HTR* 63 (1970): 223–33. See, however, Barclay's (*Paul and the Gift*, 475n64) caution against ascribing δικαιοσύνη θεοῦ any singular meaning.
[160] On the idea that "previously committed sins" (τῶν προγεγονότων ἁμαρτημάτων) refers specifically to those of gentiles, see Sam. K. Williams, *Jesus' Death as Saving Event: The Background and Origin of a Concept*, HDR 2 (Missoula, MT: Scholars Press, 1975), 32–34; Stowers, *Rereading*, 204–5; Rodríguez, *If You Call Yourself*, 85.
[161] On this phrase, see Johnson Hodge, *If Sons, Then Heirs*, 79–91, esp. 90–91. See also, Stowers, *Rereading*, 237–41; Pamela Eisenbaum, "A Remedy for Having Been Born of Woman: Jesus, Gentiles, and Genealogy in Romans," *JBL* 123 (2004): 671–702; Joshua W. Jipp, "Rereading the Story of Abraham, Isaac, and 'Us' in Romans 4," *JSNT* 32 (2009): 217–42; Young, "Paul's Ethnic Discourse," 30–51.
[162] The resumption of the dialogue between Paul and his interlocutor in 3:27 is generally agreed upon; e.g., Stowers, *Rereading*, 231–34; Dunn, *Romans 1–8*, 185–86; Jewett, *Romans*, 295–96; Rodríguez, *If You Call Yourself*, 86.

referring to either an individual's boasting in their works[163] or the supposed ethno-national boast of Jews,[164] the identity of the interlocutor as a circumcised, judaizing gentile should not be forgotten.[165] In the context of the ongoing dialogue between Paul and his interlocutor, this mention of boasting likely recalls the interlocutor's boast in God and the law mentioned in 2:17 and 2:23.[166] He glories in the relationship and standing he believes he has established with God through his adoption of the law and circumcision. As Paul has just shown, however, this is not a viable path to *dikaiosynē* (3:20). Paul continues by saying that people are rightwised by faithfulness (or "trust") apart from works of the law (χωρὶς ἔργων νόμου, Rom 3:28). Not even Abraham himself had this type of boast, since his rightwising was not from works (ἐξ ἔργων; Rom 4:2–3). For Paul, it is a dikaiological fact that no one ever was nor ever would be rightwised from works of the law (cf. Gal 2:15–16).[167] The law (i.e., Torah) always excluded this type of boasting since it attests that *dikaiosynē* comes from *pistis* and not from works (3:27b; cf. 9:30–10:4).[168] This is why Paul can respond to the interlocutor's question about invalidating the law through *pistis* by saying, "May it never be! Rather, we validate the law" (3:31).[169]

Following Paul's claim that people are rightwised by faithfulness and not works of the law (3:28), he turns to ask his interlocutor a question: "Or is God [the God] of Jews only?" (3:29a).[170] To which the interlocutor replies, "No, he is also God of the nations" (3:29b).[171] Paul affirms the interlocutor's statement:

---

[163] E.g., Cranfield, *Romans*, 1:219; Moo, *Romans*, 246; Fitzmyer, *Romans*, 362–63; Jewett, *Romans*, 295–96.
[164] E.g., Sanders, *Paul and the Law*, 32–33; Dunn, *Romans 1–8*, 185; Gathercole, *Where is Boasting*, 225–26. See also, Gaston, *Paul and the Torah*, 122–23 (citing Pss. Sol. 9:9).
[165] Rodríguez, *If You Call Yourself*, 86.
[166] Esler, *Conflict and Identity*, 168; Jewett, *Romans*, 295; cf. Rodríguez, *If You Call Yourself*, 86.
[167] Cf. Richard B. Hays, "'Have We Found Abraham to Be Our Forefather According to the Flesh?' A Reconsideration of Rom 4:1," *NovT* 27 (1985): 76–98, at 85.
[168] Cranfield, *Romans*, 1:220; Rodríguez, *If You Call Yourself*, 87–88. On the connection between Rom 3:27–28 and 9:30–10:4, see Gathercole, *Where is Boasting*, 226–30.
[169] Williams, "The Righteousness of God," 280; Jipp, "Rereading the Story," 225–26; Young, "Paul's Ethnic Discourse," 41. See also, Cranfield, *Romans*, 1:224; Stowers, *Rereading*, 240; Jewett, *Romans*, 303; Rodríguez, *If You Call Yourself*, 88; contra Dunn, *Romans 1–8*, 190–91; Schreiner, *Romans*, 207–8.
[170] Stowers (*Rereading*, 236) notes that Paul going on the offensive and asking questions of the interlocutor is typical of the diatribe. This strategy is used to push the interlocutor toward particular conclusions.
[171] Here, I follow Rodríguez (*If You Call Yourself*, 85) in placing these words in the mouth of the interlocutor and rendering it as a statement rather than a question. This translation also has the benefit of rendering οὐχὶ the same in both 3:27 and 3:29.

"Yes, he is also God of the nations, since (εἴπερ) God, who will rightwise the circumcision from faithfulness (ἐκ πίστεως) and the foreskin through the same faithfulness (διὰ τῆς πίστεως),[172] is one" (3:29c–30; cf. Deut 6:4).[173] The implication of this logic is that if God were to only rightwise individuals from works of the law, then he would only be the God of the Jews, but since God is one, he is the God of both Jews and non-Jews—the circumcision and foreskin—and thus, something else (i.e., *pistis*) is the grounds for God's rightwising.[174]

As Pamela Eisenbaum and Mark Nanos point out, some may be tempted to argue that since God is one, humanity is one—neither Jewish nor gentile, neither circumcision nor foreskin—but this is not the argument Paul makes, neither here nor elsewhere (Gal 3:28 notwithstanding).[175] For the God of Israel to be one—Paul argues—he must be the God of both Jews and non-Jews as distinct entities. For if Jews cease to be Jews, or non-Jews become Jews in order to be rightwised, God's oneness would be compromised.[176] This rightwising, therefore, does not subvert the distinction between the circumcision and foreskin, but rather upholds it.[177]

---

172 Here, I understand that the additional article refers anaphorically back to the *pistis* that immediately precedes it and functions like a demonstrative adjective. On this, see Nigel Turner, *Grammatical Insights into the New Testament* (Edinburgh: T&T Clark, 1965), 108–9.

173 Alternatively, one could also render this passage in this manner: "Yes, of Gentiles also. If indeed God, who will rightwise the circumcision from faithfulness, is one, he will also rightwise the foreskin through the faithfulness." This translation follows Hays ("Have We Found," 84–85), who argues that καὶ ἀκροβυστίαν διὰ τῆς πίστεως is "the elliptical apodosis of a conditional sentence whose protasis is introduced by εἴπερ." The translation above takes εἴπερ as establishing the grounds for the preceding statement (Donaldson, *Paul and the Gentiles*, 82; Jewett, *Romans*, 300). The difference between these translations is subtle, but each utilizes the oneness of God to imply something different; one indicates that God's oneness means he is God of both the circumcision and foreskin, whereas the other indicates that God's oneness means he will rightwise both the circumcision and foreskin on the same basis (*pistis*). Based on what Paul says in 3:28–29 (esp. 3:29a), the implication that God rightwises the circumcision and the foreskin on the same basis is indicated by the fact that he is the one God of both groups.

174 Williams, "The Righteousness of God," 278.

175 Eisenbaum, "Is Paul the Father," 521–22; Mark D. Nanos, "Paul and the Jewish Tradition: The Ideology of the Shema," in *Celebrating Paul: Festschrift in Honor of Jerome Murphy-O'Connor, O.P. and Joseph A. Fitzmyer, S.J.*, ed. Peter Spitaler, CBQMS 48 (Washington, DC: Catholic Biblical Association of America, 2012), 66–67. See also, idem, *Mystery of Romans*, 181–85.

176 Nanos, *Mystery*, 184. The idea of a persisting distinction between Jews and non-Jews in the assembly is attested to by 1 Cor 7:17–19, Gal 2:7–14, and Acts 15. For the idea that non-Jews would be included amongst the eschatological people of God as non-Jews alongside Jews, see Fredriksen, "Judaism, the Circumcision of Gentiles," 544–48; cf. Williams, "The Righteousness of God."

177 See Origen, *Comm. Rom.* 3.10.1–2; contra Baur, *Paul*, 1:351; Dunn, *Romans 1–8*, 189; Barclay, *Paul and the Gift*, 482; cf. Käsemann, *Römer*, 98.

This distinction is also attested to by the different prepositions Paul uses to describe how God rightwises both the circumcision and foreskin via *pistis*.[178]

5.6 Abraham's Faithful Foreskin: Romans 4:9–12

In many ways, the discussion of circumcision and foreskin in Romans culminates in Rom 4:9–12 where Paul comments on the foreskin and circumcision of Abraham in the context of his paternity and *pistis*.[179] Throughout Rom 2 and 3, Paul's discussion of circumcision (and foreskin) with his imagined judaizing gen-

---

178 The majority of modern interpreters follow Augustine (*Spir. et litt.* 29.50) in treating the variation between ἐκ πίστεως and διὰ τῆς πίστεως as simply being a stylistic differentiation. Stowers, however, proposes—following Origen and Theodore of Mopsuestia—that Paul was indicating a distinction between the two groups with this variation. Stanley K. Stowers, "ἐκ πίστεως and διὰ τῆς πίστεως in Romans 3:30," *JBL* 108 (1989): 665–74; idem, *Rereading*, 237–41. See also Christopher Bryan, *A Preface to Romans: Notes on the Epistle in Its Literary and Cultural Setting* (New York: Oxford University Press, 2000), 113–14. Stowers offers a strict systematization of these two prepositional phrases, arguing that Paul uses ἐκ πίστεως when the rightwising of Jews and/or gentiles is in view (Rom 1:17; 3:26, 30; 4:16; 5:1; 9:30, 32; 10:6; 14:23; Gal 2:16; 3:7–9, 11–12, 22, 24; 5:5), and διὰ [τῆς] πίστεως when *only* the rightwising of gentiles is in view (Rom 3:22, 25, 30–31; Gal 2:16; 3:14, 26; Phil 3:9; cf. Eph 3:12, 17; Col 2:12). For Stowers, the idiom διὰ [τῆς] πίστεως specifically refers to Jesus' conciliatory death (3:25) wherever it occurs. While Stowers is right to seek an explanation as to why Paul modifies his wording from phrase to phrase in 3:30, the extension of his reading to all the occurrences of these idioms is an overreach. The application of his reading to texts like Phil 3:9 (and possibly Gal 2:16)—where Paul says that he himself needs the *dikaiosynē* that is διὰ πίστεως Χριστοῦ—is particularly problematic. One of the crucial insights of Stowers' proposal, however, is his point that ἐκ and διά were used in ancient genealogical and procreative discourse as ways of speaking of primary, generative sources (ἐκ) and secondary, instrumental means of procreation (διά) (see, e.g., Origen, *Comm. Rom.* 3.10.2–3, citing 1 Cor 11:12). Taking this ancient usage into account—as well as the following section in Rom 4 that focuses on Abraham's paternity—Paul may be highlighting that Jewish participation in *pistis* is "more ancient and deeply rooted than gentile" since they are natural seed of Abraham (Bryan, *Preface to Romans*, 114). For gentiles, however, *pistis* comes from outside of them and is the means through which they are rightwised and incorporated into Abraham's lineage (cf. Käsemann, *Römer*, 98). Perhaps if one were to describe how this works with an arboreal metaphor, the grafting of a wild branch onto an existing, well-established tree would be apt (Rom 11:17–24). The subtle distinction that Paul makes with these prepositions indicates the same sentiment that he clearly states elsewhere regarding the priority of the Jews vis-à-vis his gospel and the righteousness of God; it is "to the Jew first, and *also* to the Greek" (Rom 1:16).

179 For an overview of how Abraham's circumcision is interpreted in Paul, early Christian texts, and Genesis Rabbah, see Malka Z. Simkovich, "Interpretations of Abraham's Circumcision in Early Christianity and Genesis Rabbah," in *New Vistas on Early Judaism and Christianity*, ed. Lorenzo DiTommaso and Gerbern S. Oegema, JCT 22 (London: T&T Clark, 2016), 249–68.

tile interlocutor has focused on the importance and value of proper circumcision for ethnic Jews and has denied any positive value to circumcision for naturally foreskinned gentiles. After declaring *pistis* as the mode of rightwising for both the circumcision and foreskin (3:28–30), Paul affirms that this *pistis* is compatible with and validates the law (3:31). Drawing on Paul's confirmation of the law, the interlocutor raises another question in 4:1: "What then? Shall we say we have found Abraham to be our forefather according to the flesh?"[180]

While the majority of interpreters who follow this translation understand that a Jewish voice is speaking—either Paul[181] or a Jewish interlocutor[182]—the judaizing gentile interlocutor remains in view.[183] Here, his reference to σάρξ should be understood as referring to the circumcised flesh of his foreskin. As Thiessen and Jipp observe, the Abraham narrative in Gen 17 consistently uses σάρξ to refer to the flesh of the foreskin that is to be circumcised (Gen 17:11, 13–14, 24–26; cf. Sir 44:19–20).[184] Thus the interlocutor is asking if his circumcision has made him—and judaized non-Jews more broadly—a descendant of Abraham.[185] Rather than answer this question with his typical μὴ γένοιτο (Rom 3:4, 6, 31; 6:2, 15; 7:7, 13; 9:14; 11:1, 11), Paul responds in 4:2–25 by demonstrating why gentiles can be considered Abraham's seed in their foreskinned state apart from circumcision, with this theme coming to its climax in 4:9–12.[186] The argument Paul

---

180 My understanding of the syntax of Rom 4:1 follows the work of Richard Hays ("Have We Found," 81), though I follow Rodríguez (*If You Call Yourself*, 89, 90n51) in placing the first question mark after Τί οὖν, not ἐροῦμεν. Prior to Hays, this was proposed by Theodor Zahn, *Der Brief des Paulus an die Römer* (Leipzig: Deichert, 1910), 215. Here, I understand that Ἀβραάμ is the direct object of εὑρηκέναι, not its subject. The "we" from ἐροῦμεν is also the subject of εὑρηκέναι (on this construction, see BDF §396). Contra Dunn, *Romans 1–8*, 199; Jewett, *Romans*, 307; Benjamin Schliesser, *Abraham's Faith in Romans 4: Paul's Concept of Faith in Light of the History of Reception of Genesis 15:6*, WUNT 2/224 (Tübingen: Mohr Siebeck, 2007), 323–25.
181 Hays, "Have We Found," 87, 93; Michael Cranford, "Abraham in Romans 4: The Father of All Who Believe," *NTS* 41 (1995): 73–76; N. T. Wright, "Paul and the Patriarch: The Role of Abraham in Romans 4," *JSNT* 35 (2013): 226–28; Young, "Paul's Ethnic Discourse."
182 Stowers, *Rereading*, 234, 242–43; Jipp, "Rereading the Story," 218n3. Jipp has since adopted the view that a judaizing gentile interlocutor is in view; Joshua W. Jipp, "What are the Implications of the Ethnic Identity of Paul's Interlocutor? Continuing the Conversation," in Rodríguez and Thiessen, *The So-Called Jew*, 189.
183 Garroway, *Paul's Gentile-Jews*, 10–11, 83–86; Mortensen, *Paul Among the Gentiles*, 153–55.
184 Thiessen, *Gentile Problem*, 206n34; Jipp, "What are the Implications," 189. See also, Cranford, "Abraham in Romans 4," 75; Wright, "Paul and the Patriarch," 227.
185 On this point, see the discussion on Abrahamic sonship and circumcision in Gal 3 and 4 in §3.4–5
186 For how this motif functions in Rom 4:2–8, see Cranford, "Abraham in Romans 4," 73–83; Wright, "Paul and the Patriarch," 232–36; Young, "Paul's Ethnic Discourse," 42.

makes in Rom 4 does not center around Abraham as simply an example of "justification by faith" that others are to follow—as many interpreters posit[187]—rather, it centers around Abraham as the reason why foreskinned gentiles can be blessed alongside the circumcised, physical descendants of Abraham (4:9, 11–12, 16), and also have him as their father.[188]

5.6.1 Reckoning *Dikaiosynē* to Abraham: Not "When?" but "How?"

Karin Neutel has recently demonstrated that when one surveys the scholarly literature on Rom 4:9–12 a rare consensus emerges amongst Paulinists.[189] The consensus perspective argues that the central issue Paul is highlighting in this passage is the timing of Abraham's rightwising in Gen 15: was it before he was circumcised or was it after he was circumcised?[190] As the chronology of Gen 15 and 17 attest, Abraham was indeed reckoned right prior to undergoing circumcision. This chronological fact is what Krister Stendahl referred to as "Paul's exegetical find."[191] Stendahl writes, "This is Paul's wonderful discovery, that Abraham believed *before* he was circumcised. The circumcision did not come from that passage, but it came *after*. Thus, we are justified by faith on the model of Abraham, without circumcision."[192]

Paul, however, does not appeal to this chronological fact in Rom 4:9–12. To be fair, the fact that Abraham was reckoned right *prior* to his circumcision is not an

---

[187] William Sanday and Arthur C. Headlam, *A Critical and Exegetical Commentary on the Epistle to the Romans*, 5th ed., ICC (Edinburgh: T&T Clark, 1977), 107; Cranfield, *Romans*, 224–25; Fitzmyer, *Romans*, 369–71; Thomas H. Tobin, "What Shall We Say That Abraham Found? The Controversy Behind Romans 4." *HTR* 88 (1995): 437–52; Moo, *Romans*, 255–64; Schreiner, *Romans*, 210. Jewett, *Romans*, 306, 309; Wolter, *Paulus*, 393–95.
[188] Surely, Paul does view Abraham as an example of *pistis* that individuals should emulate (4:11–12, 24), but that is not the main point he is trying to make in Rom 4. On this, see the discussions in Gaston, *Paul and the Torah*, 122–24; Cranford, "Abraham in Romans 4"; Eisenbaum, "A Remedy," 687–89; Jipp, "Rereading the Story"; Young, "Paul's Ethnic Discourse."
[189] Neutel, "Restoring Abraham's Foreskin," 53–54. Much of my understanding of Rom 4:9–12 has been shaped by Neutel's pioneering work on this text.
[190] See, e.g., Sanday and Headlam, *Romans*, 106; Cranfield, *Romans*, 236; Dunn, *Romans 1–8*, 209; Fitzmyer, *Romans*, 381; Stowers, *Rereading*, 243; Blaschke, *Beschneidung*, 416; Schliesser, *Abraham's Faith*, 357; Johnson Hodge, *If Sons, Then Heirs*, 82–83; Jipp, "Rereading the Story," 224–25; Garroway, *Paul's Gentile-Jews*, 83–84; Rodríguez, *If You Call Yourself*, 91–92; Wright, "Paul and the Patriarch," 224; Wolter, *Paulus*, 394; Barclay, *Paul and the Gift*, 486–87; Mortensen, *Paul Among the Gentiles*, 155–57.
[191] Krister Stendahl, *Final Account: Paul's Letter to the Romans* (Minneapolis: Fortress, 1995), 14, 21–32.
[192] Stendahl, *Final Account*, 14; emphasis added.

incorrect assertion—reading Genesis confirms this.¹⁹³ And while one can deduce this sequence of events from Paul's language vis-à-vis an awareness of the Abraham narrative, this sequence of events is not found in this text. Neutel perceptively notes that the language of chronology is absent from the Greek text of 4:9–12. Translators, however, have added it due to the common mistranslation of ἀκροβυστία as "uncircumcision" or "uncircumcised" and not "foreskin." Despite the common (mis)translation of ἀκροβυστία as "uncircumcision," the Greek word for uncircumcision (ἀπερίτμητος) appears nowhere in Paul's letters.¹⁹⁴ When Paul writes about gentile genitals he does not focus on their lack of circumcision (ἀπερίτμητος) but highlights the presence of their foreskin (ἀκροβυστία). Thus, when one examines the ways in which Rom 4:9–12 is typically translated, the emphasis is not on what Abraham had—a foreskin—but on what he lacked—circumcision.¹⁹⁵ It is worth looking at the NRSV translation of this passage—which is broadly representative of the majority of translations—to see the results of this translatorial tendency:

> Is this blessedness, then, pronounced only on the circumcised, or also on the uncircumcised (τὴν ἀκροβυστίαν)? We say, "Faith was reckoned to Abraham as righteousness." How then was it reckoned to him? Was it before or after he had been circumcised (ἐν περιτομῇ ὄντι ἢ ἐν ἀκροβυστίᾳ)? It was not after, but before he was circumcised (οὐκ ἐν περιτομῇ ἀλλ' ἐν ἀκροβυστίᾳ). He received the sign of circumcision as a seal of the righteousness that he had by faith while he was still uncircumcised (ἐν τῇ ἀκροβυστίᾳ). The purpose was to make him the ancestor of all who believe without being circumcised (τῶν πιστευόντων δι' ἀκροβυστίας) and who thus have righteousness reckoned to them, and likewise the ancestor of the circumcised who are not only circumcised but who also follow the example of the faith that our ancestor Abraham had before he was circumcised (ἐν ἀκροβυστίᾳ).

Rather than translate ἐν ἀκροβυστίᾳ as "in foreskin," or δι' ἀκροβυστίας as "through foreskin," the translators render it as "before he was circumcised," "while he was still uncircumcised," or "without being circumcised."¹⁹⁶ This translation not only misinterprets the language of ἀκροβυστία, but it also sidesteps the

---

193 Fitzmyer (*Romans*, 379), however, notes that the different sources for Gen 15 (J/E) and 17 (P) may obscure the actual chronology of Abraham's *pistis*, rightwising, and reception of circumcision.
194 In the New Testament, ἀπερίτμητος only occurs in Acts 7:51. In the LXX/OG, however, ἀπερίτμητος occurs as a gloss for ערל (Gen 17:14; Exod 12:48; Lev 26:41; Josh 5:7; Jer 9:25; Ezek 44:7, 9).
195 Neutel, "Restoring Abraham's Foreskin," 62–63.
196 Notably, there are a few scholars who do render ἀκροβυστία as "foreskin" in their discussions of Rom 4: Blaschke, *Beschneidung*, 416–17; Livesey, *Malleable Symbol*, 114–120; Økland, "Pauline Letters," 320–21. Interestingly, Jewett (*Romans*, 301, 304, 320) offers "uncircumcised foreskin" as a gloss of ἀκροβυστία, defining the presence of foreskin by the fact that it has not be circumcised. Here, Jewett draws on the work of Marcus, "Circumcision and Uncircumcision."

question Paul asks in 4:10: "How, then, was it reckoned?" (πῶς οὖν ἐλογίσθη). Instead, this reading answers "When, then, was it reckoned?" (as if: πότε οὖν ἐλογίσθη). Jipp even goes so far as modifying the question in his translation, saying that the question Paul asks *is* "When was it reckoned?"[197] In order to properly assess this text, a new translation is needed.

5.6.2 Foregrounding the Forefather's Foreskin: An Epispasmic Reading of Romans 4:9–12

> Therefore, is this blessing upon the circumcision or also upon the foreskin? For we say, *"Pistis* was reckoned to Abraham for *dikaiosynē."* How, then, was it reckoned? Being in circumcision or in foreskin? **Not in circumcision, but in foreskin.**[198] And he received the sign of circumcision, a seal of the *dikaiosynē* of the *pistis* which (was) in the foreskin, so that he would be the father of all the ones who trust through foreskin—so that *dikaiosynē* would be reckoned to them—and the father of the circumcision; (the father) to those not from the circumcision only, but also to those who follow in the footsteps of the in-foreskin *pistis* of our father Abraham.

Returning to what was noted above, the translation I have offered highlights not what Abraham lacked—circumcision—but what he possessed—a foreskin. While the difference between foreskin and uncircumcision may seem trivial at first glance, in actuality they convey two different messages. As Neutel demonstrates, by focusing on what Abraham lacked, interpreters assume that what Paul is saying in this passage is that since Abraham was uncircumcised when he was reckoned right, circumcision is not necessary. Paul's point changes, however, when we restore Abraham's foreskin to the text and bring it to the forefront of the discussion: since Abraham was in foreskin when he was reckoned right, foreskin does not prove to be a problem.[199] Given that foreskin—either of the penis or metaphorically ascribed to other body parts—is consistently portrayed negatively in ancient Jewish sources, Paul is highlighting the surprising nature of Abraham's *pistis*; it is "in foreskin" *pistis* and it is by this "in foreskin" *pistis* that Abraham is reckoned right.

With this epispasmic translation and framework in mind, we can now examine the rest of the passage with fresh eyes. After establishing that Abraham was in foreskin when his *pistis* was reckoned for *dikaiosynē*, Paul turns to discuss the re-

---

197 Jipp, "Rereading the Story," 224. See also, Hays, "Have We Found," 89.
198 Here, I follow Rodríguez (*If You Call Yourself*, 89) in placing the answer to the question on the lips of Paul's interlocutor.
199 Neutel, "Restoring Abraham's Foreskin," 68.

lationship between Abraham's circumcision and his paternity in 4:11. Here, Paul gestures toward Gen 17:11 where circumcision is declared by God to be "a sign of the covenant between me and you" (אות ברית/σημεῖον διαθήκης). Instead of noting that circumcision was a sign of the covenant,²⁰⁰ Paul refers to Abraham as receiving "the sign of circumcision, a seal of the *dikaiosynē* of the *pistis* which (was) in the foreskin" (σφραγῖδα τῆς δικαιοσύνης τῆς πίστεως τῆς ἐν τῇ ἀκροβυστίᾳ).²⁰¹ Since the majority of interpreters overlook ἀκροβυστία, they generally describe Paul as referring to circumcision simply in terms of "righteousness by faith,"²⁰² failing to acknowledge that Paul defines this *pistis* with the prepositional phrase τῆς ἐν τῇ ἀκροβυστίᾳ, "which (was) in the foreskin" as he also does in 4:12 (τῆς ἐν ἀκροβυστίᾳ πίστεως).²⁰³ Dunn even goes as far as completely ignoring this phrase in his commentary, moving from "the righteousness of faith" directly to the following purpose clause, "in order that..."²⁰⁴ When one acknowledges this prepositional phrase, Paul's reference to the sign of circumcision as a seal takes on a new meaning; circumcision is a seal on Abraham's foreskin of the *dikaiosynē* of the *pistis* which was in the foreskin. Thus, Abraham's circumcision is a sign that points positively to his foreskin. Foreskin was not a hindrance for Abraham's *pistis*, and it is through the seal of circumcision that he guarantees that foreskin is not a problem for those who trust through foreskin (4:11b, 12b; cf. 3:22; 4:16). Instead of circumcision serving primarily as a procedure that removes a problematic foreskin, here, Abraham's circumcision functions positively to include those who also trust in and through foreskin amongst his seed.

---

200 The lack of covenantal language is highlighted by many interpreters, e.g., Fitzmyer, *Romans*, 381; Cranford, "Abraham in Romans 4," 84; Blaschke, *Beschneidung*, 417; Livesey, *Malleable Symbol*, 116; Neutel, "Restoring Abraham's Foreskin," 68–69.
201 Paul uses σφραγίς in the same way in 1 Cor 9:2 to show that the seal demonstrates and guarantees a particular reality. While some interpreters assert that Paul is the first written source to describe circumcision as being a seal, Aramaic Levi 3:1 refers to circumcision as a seal a few hundred years before: "[C]ircumcise the foreskin of flesh...and you will be sealed." For a discussion of this text, see Jonas C. Greenfield, Michael E. Stone, and Ester Eschel, *The Aramaic Levi Document: Edition, Translation, Commentary*, SVTP 19 (Leiden: Brill, 2004), 113–16. Though he does not cite Aramaic Levi, Cranfield (*Romans*, 1:236) notes that referring to circumcision as a seal was likely well established in the Judaism of Paul's day. For other ancient texts that make this connection, see Barn. 9:6; John Chrysostom, *Hom. Eph.* 2; b. Šabb. 137b; TgSong 3:8; cf. *Pirke de Rabbi Eliezer* 10:9.
202 E.g., Fitzmyer, *Romans*, 381; Dunn, *Romans 1–8*, 209–10; Jewett, *Romans*, 319; Jipp, "Rereading the Story," 225; Livesey, *Malleable Symbol*, 117–18.
203 Neutel, "Restoring Abraham's Foreskin," 69–70. Young gets close to this interpretation but relies on the language of uncircumcision: "the righteousness of his uncircumcised-trust" ("Paul's Ethnic Discourse," 42).
204 Dunn, *Romans 1–8*, 210.

While some scholars have placed considerable emphasis on Paul's failure to refer to circumcision as a sign of the covenant, one should not read too much into this absence since Paul's primary goal in this section is to explicate how Abraham's circumcision positively relates to his paternity of foreskinned gentiles. That Abraham's circumcision has benefit and value for the circumcision is assumed by Paul throughout 4:9–12 (cf. 3:1–2; 4:16; 9:4–5; 11:25–26).[205] While overt covenantal language *is* missing from this passage, the purpose Paul provides for Abraham's reception of circumcision aligns with the covenantal blessing of Gen 17:4–7 to make Abraham the father of many nations: "He received the sign of circumcision…so that he would be the father of all those who trust through foreskin… and the father of the circumcision…"[206] So while Paul does not refer explicitly to the covenant—he rarely does in his epistles—the blessing and promise of the covenant are still in view here and throughout the remainder of chapter.

The last interpretive hurdle to bound in this passage relates to the number of groups mentioned in 4:12: καὶ πατέρα περιτομῆς τοῖς οὐκ ἐκ περιτομῆς μόνον ἀλλὰ καὶ τοῖς στοιχοῦσιν τοῖς ἴχνεσιν τῆς ἐν ἀκροβυστίᾳ πίστεως τοῦ πατρὸς ἡμῶν Ἀβραάμ. Traditionally, this verse is taken to only describe one group of individuals composed of circumcised Jews who are not only circumcised, but also follow in Abraham's example of faith. The key problem with this interpretation is the presence of the second τοῖς following the second καί. Scholars who argue that only one group is in view here either ignore the second τοῖς altogether,[207] or argue that it is a mistake in the text in need of emendation.[208] There is, however, no manuscript evidence that speaks against the inclusion of the second τοῖς, and it is almost certainly original. Based on this, 4:12 should be understood as having two groups in

---

205 Notably, in 4:9 the positive situation of the circumcision vis-à-vis the blessing of 4:6–8 (OG Ps 31:1–2) is taken for granted. On this, see e.g., Dunn, *Romans 1–8*, 208; Tobin, "What Shall We Say," 446. In Codex Bezae, μόνον is inserted in 4:9 after τὴν περιτομήν to clarify this point. Longenecker notes that while the omission of μόνον is likely the original reading, "the logic of the sentence suggests that an adverbial use of 'only' should be understood" (*Romans*, 472).
206 Cf. Rom 4:16–17. Here, I follow Thiessen (*Gentile Problem*, 83, 207n35) and Neutel ("Restoring Abraham's Foreskin," 71) in treating the διά in δι' ἀκροβυστίας as functioning instrumentally (see also Dunn, *Romans 1–8*, 210). We disagree, however, on what this prepositional phrase modifies in this verse. While I apply it to "all the ones who trust," they both apply it to Abraham: "so that he would be through foreskin the father of all who trust." Most scholars translate διά as "while" or "when", but—as in 2:27—the διά-plus-genitive construction indicates instrumentality or means (e.g., Fitzmyer, *Romans*, 381; Tobin, "What Shall We Say," 446; Jewett, *Romans*, 304; Young, "Paul's Ethnic Discourse," 42).
207 E.g., Esler, *Conflict and Identity*, 189–90; Rodríguez, *If You Call Yourself*, 89; Wright, "Paul and the Patriarch," 225; Thiessen, *Gentile Problem*, 83.
208 E.g., Sanday and Headlam, *Romans*, 108; Cranfield, *Romans*, 1:237; Dunn, *Romans 1–8*, 210–11.

view: the ones from the circumcision (Jews) and the ones who follow in the footsteps of the in-foreskin *pistis* of our father Abraham (non-Jews).[209] This reading is confirmed by the similar statement in 4:16b: "not to those from the law only, but also to those from the faithfulness of Abraham, who is the father of us all."[210]

To understand how Abraham's paternity is portrayed in 4:11b–12, it is helpful to lay out the text chiastically:[211]

- (A) the father of the ones who believe through foreskin—so that *dikaiosynē* would be reckoned to them
  - (B) and the father of the circumcision;
  - (B') (the father) to those not from the circumcision only,
- (A') but also to those who follow in the footsteps of the in-foreskin *pistis* of our father Abraham.

As both Gaston and Tobin note, the lines that refer to the foreskin are more developed.[212] This is because—unlike the circumcision—the foreskin are not natural, fleshly descendants of Abraham, and the logic of his paternity of them needs to be explained (cf. Rom 3:30). Thus, in response the question the interlocutor raises in 4:1, Paul answers with a resounding no: "You have not found Abraham to be your forefather through your judaizing circumcision. For Abraham is the father of non-Jews who trust through their foreskin, not those who remove their foreskin."

5.7 The Messiah as Agent of the Circumcision: Romans 15:8

The final mention of circumcision in Romans is found in 15:8, where Paul refers to the Messiah as having become an agent of the circumcision (Χριστὸν διάκονον

---

[209] Gaston, *Paul and the Torah*, 61, 124; Tobin, "What Shall We Say," 446–47; Jewett, *Romans*, 320–21; Livesey, *Malleable Symbol*, 118–19; Neutel, "Restoring Abraham's Foreskin," 71–73. Cf. Windsor, *Paul and the Vocation*, 83; Tucker, *After Supersessionism*, 70. There is a small minority of scholars who understand that Paul has two groups in view here, but that Paul does so by appealing to two different types of circumcision—spiritual and physical. On this reading, the reference to Abraham as the father of the circumcision indicates spiritual circumcision, and the reference to the ones from the circumcision indicates physical circumcision. See Lucien Cerfaux, "Abraham 'père en circoncision' des Gentils," in *Recueil Lucien Cerfaux*, 3 vols. (Gembloux: J. Duculot, 1954–1962), 2:333–38; James Swetnam, "The Curious Crux at Romans 4,12," *Bib* 61 (1980): 110–15.
[210] Tobin, "What Shall We Say," 448; cf. Stowers, *Rereading*, 246.
[211] Gaston, *Paul and the Torah*, 124; Tobin, "What Shall We Say," 446–447. See also Livesey, *Malleable Symbol*, 118–19.
[212] Gaston, *Paul and the Torah*, 124; Tobin, "What Shall We Say," 447.

γεγενῆσθαι περιτομῆς). In this passage, Paul offers a condensed summary of the message of Romans (cf. Rom 1:1–6) by bringing together the important themes of God's truthfulness (Rom 3:1–7), God's promise to Abraham (Rom 4), the inclusion of the nations (Rom 3–4; 9–11), and the Davidic Messiah (Rom 1:3; cf. 9–11).[213] Following his exhortation in 15:7 for those in Rome to receive one another as the Messiah has received them, Paul states, "For I say the Messiah has become an agent of the circumcision for the sake of the truthfulness of God (ὑπὲρ ἀληθείας θεοῦ), in order to confirm the promises to the fathers (εἰς τὸ βεβαιῶσαι τὰς ἐπαγγελίας τῶν πατέρων), and in order that the nations would glorify God for his mercy (τὰ δὲ ἔθνη ὑπὲρ ἐλέους δοξάσαι τὸν θεόν)" (15:8–9).[214] To substantiate this claim about the Messiah, Paul cites four passages of scripture that highlight a future in which the nations are found worshiping God alongside Israel and being under the rule of the Messiah (Ps 18:50; Deut 32:43; Ps 117:1; Isa 11:10).[215] As numerous interpreters note, the emphasis in this section is the inclusion of the nations within the people of God as a result of the work of the Messiah.[216]

When approaching the subject of circumcision in this text, interpreters are nearly unanimous in their agreement that Paul uses circumcision here to refer metonymically to Jews.[217] On this reading, scholars typically treat περιτομῆς as an objective genitive, with the circumcision (i.e., the Jews) being the object of the Messiah's service: "a servant to the circumcision."[218] The most notable exception to this understanding was originally proposed by Origen and has recently

---

[213] On the conceptual link between these themes, see Williams, "The Righteousness of God."
[214] On the thorny syntax of 15:8–9, see the discussions in Williams, "The Righteousness of God," 285–89; J. Ross Wagner, "The Christ, Servant of Jew and Gentile: A Fresh Approach to Romans 15:8–9," *JBL* 116 (1997): 473–486; A. Andrew Das, "'Praise the Lord, All You Gentiles': The Encoded Audience of Romans 15.7–13," *JSNT* 34 (2011): 90–110. Here, my translation follows the typical understanding of the syntax of the verse where βεβαιῶσαι and δοξάσαι are governed by εἰς τό, which explains the Messiah's function as the διάκονον περιτομῆς.
[215] On Paul's use of these texts, see Novenson, *Christ Among the Messiahs*, 153–60; Sharp, *Divination and Philosophy*, 146–48.
[216] E.g., Williams, "The Righteousness of God" 286–89; Gaston, *Paul and the Torah*, 116–34, esp. 133–34; Donaldson, *Paul and the Gentiles*, 95–100; Rodríguez, *If You Call Yourself*, 281; See also, Barclay, *Paul and the Gift*, 460; Fredriksen, *Pagans' Apostle*, 155–64.
[217] E.g., Cranfield, *Romans*, 2:740; Fitzmyer, *Romans*, 706; Dunn, *Romans 9–16*, 846–47; Marcus, "Circumcision and Uncircumcision," 75–76; Stowers, *Rereading*, 132–33, 196; Wagner, "The Christ," 476; Blaschke, *Beschneidung*, 424–25; Jewett, *Romans*, 890; Das, "Praise the Lord."
[218] Here, some scholars have proposed that Paul may have in mind traditions about Jesus as a servant (Matt 20:28; Mark 10:43–45; cf. Matt 15:24); Cranfield, *Romans*, 2:741; Fitzmyer, *Romans*, 706; Dunn, *Romans 9–16*, 846; Jewett, *Romans*, 891.

been put forth by Garroway.²¹⁹ They propose a reading in which circumcision refers to circumcision of the heart that the Messiah performs, linking this text to their interpretations of Rom 2:25–29 and Col 2:11.²²⁰ Instead of translating διάκονος as "servant" or "minister," Garroway renders it as "agent," indicating that the Messiah is a performer of circumcisions—like a mohel²²¹—who circumcises the hearts of non-Jews in order that they are able to be counted as (genitally) circumcised descendants of Abraham.

Along with the vast majority of interpreters—against Origen and Garroway—I agree that circumcision here refers to the Jewish people: "the circumcision." While περιτομῆς is anarthrous, this does not necessarily indicate that Paul only has the procedure itself in mind. Paul does not use the article with circumcision in any consistent pattern to indicate that he is talking about the procedure or the collective body of circumcised individuals; only context can determine the word's refer-

---

219 There are a couple of other exceptions to the standard reading. Williams ("The Righteousness of God," 286) and Gaston (*Paul and the Torah*, 133) both take περιτομῆς as a genitive of origin, translating this phrase as, "a servant from the circumcision," indicating that the Messiah "comes from the Jews" and is "rooted firmly in Judaism." If this were the case, one could reasonably expect Paul to use ἐκ plus the genitive to denote origin as he consistently does elsewhere (e. g., Rom 3:26; 4:12, 16; 10:6 Gal 2:12; 3:6–9). Paul does, however, use διάκονος plus a genitive of origin to describe Phoebe in Rom 16:1. E. H. Gifford (*The Epistle of St. Paul to the Romans* [London: John Murray, 1886], 224), who is followed by Sanday and Headlam (*Romans*, 397–98), argues circumcision refers to the covenant of circumcision, indicating that the Messiah must "fulfill the covenant of circumcision both in His person and His work." They propose Paul has in mind that by virtue of being circumcised (Luke 2:21) and fulfilling the law (Rom 10:4; cf. Gal 4:4–5), Jesus is able to bring about the blessing to the nations assured in the covenant of circumcision. Thus, he is a "minister" working to fulfill the covenant of circumcision. While this reading has some merit in light of Gal 3:15–18 (cf. 2 Cor 3:6), covenantal language is broadly absent from Romans (9:4; 11:27 [Jer 31:33]) and Paul appears to distance circumcision from explicit covenantal language elsewhere in Romans (4:11). The reading I give below provides similar conclusions vis-à-vis the promises and inclusion of the nations, but within a more plausible understanding of how circumcision is functioning.
220 Origen, *Comm. Rom.* 10.8.3; Garroway, "The Circumcision of Christ," 305–13; idem, *Paul's Gentile-Jews*, 118–22. Mortensen (*Paul Among the Gentiles*, 335–36) follows Garroway on this point. See also the discussion in Patrick McMurray, *Sacrifice, Brotherhood and the Body: Abraham and the Nations in Romans* (Lanham, MD: Lexington Books/Fortress Academic, 2021). While Origen proposes a couple of possible interpretations, this appears to be the one he holds to be the most likely. Garroway seems to have come to his interpretation independently of Origen, as he is not referenced in either of his works on this text. In addition to Rom 2:25–29 and Col 2:11, Garroway also cites Rom 4:12, Phil 3:3, and Eph 2:11–13 as evidence for his reading.
221 Garroway, "The Circumcision of Christ," 306. In *Paul's Gentile-Jews*, however, Garroway avoids using "mohel" as a descriptor for the Messiah (119).

ent.²²² The interpretation proposed by Origen and Garroway that reads Paul's mention of circumcision here as a reference to the circumcision that the Messiah performs is grammatically possible, but based on my interpretation of Rom 2 and 4 it is to be rejected.²²³ There is no indication from the immediate context that would point to this special type of circumcision that only appears once (Rom 2:29) in the undisputed Pauline corpus.²²⁴

As noted above, for most interpreters who understand that circumcision here refers to the Jewish people, περιτομῆς functions as an objective genitive. Both Williams and Garroway point out that this common reading does not make sense of what follows.²²⁵ How does the Messiah being a servant *to* Jews—typically understood in the context of his earthly ministry—confirm the promises to the fathers and give the nations a reason to glorify God? Williams rightly comments that if this is what Paul intended to convey with this phrase, he has left a large gap for his readers to fill in.²²⁶ The nature of the Messiah's relationship to the circumcision as a διάκονος requires more clarification.

Another problem with the standard reading of this text is the translation of διάκονος as "servant." While this is among the possible translations for διάκονος, it does not adequately capture how Paul typically uses the word.²²⁷ Elsewhere, Paul commonly uses διάκονος to refer to individuals who are acting as intermediaries or agents on behalf of something or someone.²²⁸ For example, in Romans 13:4 the governing authorities are "God's agents" (θεοῦ διάκονός) who execute wrath on those who do wrong. In 1 Cor 3:5, Apollos and Paul are the agents used by the Lord through whom the Corinthians came to trust. In 2 Cor 3:6, Paul and Timothy

---

222 See the note in §3.8.2 for the grammatical discussion surrounding Paul's use of the article with circumcision. See also the brief discussion in Garroway, "Circumcision of Christ," 306n8. Notably, even Paul's usage of the article in Romans is inconsistent. Interpreters are unanimous in noting that in 3:1 Paul use an articular noun to refer to the practice (τῆς περιτομῆς) and in 3:30 he uses an anarthrous noun to refer to the collective group (περιτομήν).

223 The absence of Messiah language in Rom 2:25–29 and 4:9–12 works against Garroway's interpretation. His reading finds its strongest support in Col 2:11, where the author refers to individuals having been circumcised by a circumcision not performed by hands, that is, by the circumcision of Christ (ἐν τῇ περιτομῇ τοῦ Χριστοῦ).

224 Gifford, *Romans*, 224.

225 Williams, "The Righteousness of God," 285–86; Garroway, "The Circumcision of Christ," 305.

226 Williams, "The Righteousness of God," 285.

227 Paul does use the word in this sense in Rom 16:1 to describe Phoebe: "a servant of the assembly in Cenchreae."

228 LSJ, s.v. "διάκονος." On the range of meaning of διακονία and its cognates, see John N. Collins, *Diakonia: Re-Interpreting the Ancient Sources* (New York: Oxford University Press, 1990). For examples of this usage outside of Paul, see Philo, *On Joseph*, 241; Josephus, *J.W.* 4.388; *Ant.* 11.255; 4 Macc 9:17.

are agents of a new covenant (διακόνους καινῆς διαθήκης), not because they serve the covenant, but because they are intermediaries that represent it and advance it.²²⁹ In 2 Cor 6:4, they are agents of God (θεοῦ διάκονοι) through whom God makes his appeal for the Corinthians to be reconciled to himself (2 Cor 5:20). This sense is also used 2 Cor 11:15 and 11:23 where Paul refers to agents who are working on behalf of Satan, and his own superior behavior as an agent representing the Messiah. The only other place where Paul refers to the Messiah as a διάκονος—Gal 2:17—follows this pattern of usage. There, Paul emphatically denies the possibility that the Messiah is an agent of sin (ἁμαρτίας διάκονος), working on its behalf and promoting it.²³⁰

If we read Rom 15:8–9 in light of Paul's usage of διάκονος elsewhere, Paul is stating that the Messiah has become an agent of the circumcision (i.e., the Jewish people), working on their behalf for the sake of the truthfulness of God.²³¹ He did this in order to confirm God's promises to the fathers, and to cause the nations to glorify God. As Barclay comments, "[T]he actualization of those promises embraces the Gentiles, who are called to 'the obedience of faith' (1:5); although the syntax is difficult, the purpose of the 'servant of the circumcision' appears to include the Gentiles' 'glorifying God for his mercy' (15:9)."²³² While these promises have yet to be fulfilled, the appearance and work of the Messiah has confirmed their legitimacy and is demonstrated by the fact that the nations have begun to turn and worship the god of Israel as Abrahamic children (Rom 3:21–26; 4:9–25). The focus here is not on how the Messiah served the circumcision, but how the Messiah functions as an intermediary on their behalf for the sake of the truthfulness of God. The Messiah's work has confirmed the promises of God, and—as Paul sees it—it is now his task to carry out his commission from the Messiah to bring about the obedience of faithfulness amongst the nations (Rom 1:1–6; 11:13–14; 15:16–19).

---

229 Garroway, "The Circumcision of Christ," 305.
230 Gaston, *Paul and the Torah*, 133; Longenecker, *Galatians*, 90; Garroway, "The Circumcision of Christ," 305; Barclay, *Paul and the Gift*, 371, 384.
231 This reading takes περιτομῆς as a subjective genitive, as are the genitives that modify διάκονος in the examples above: θεοῦ, καινῆς διαθήκης, ἁμαρτίας. Contra Donaldson, *Paul and the Gentiles*, 328n53. Cf. Collins, *Diakonia*, 227–28.
232 Barclay, *Paul and the Gift*, 460. See also Novenson (*Christ Among the Messiahs*, 156–60), who notes that Paul's understanding of the messiahship of Jesus—specifically as it relates to his citation of Isa 11:10 in Rom 15:12—is connected to prophetic oracles of gentile inclusion, and thus is part of the impetus for Paul's gentile mission.

5.8 Conclusion

In this chapter, I have shown how Paul uses circumcision and foreskin in Romans within the context of his dialogue with an imagined interlocutor whom I have identified as a circumcised, judaizing gentile—a so-called Jew. Similar to Galatians, Paul utilizes his discussion of circumcision to demonstrate that circumcision does not effect a positive change for naturally foreskinned gentiles (Rom 2:25–27). While Paul's imagined interlocutor believes his circumcision and adoption of Torah has brought him into a proper relationship with God—perhaps even transforming him into an Abrahamic son according to the flesh (Rom 4:1)—Paul argues that his circumcision itself makes him a transgressor of the law. In fact, his circumcision proves to be a foreskin. The positive change the interlocutor is looking for can only be brought about through *pistis* (e. g., Rom 3:21–31; 4:9–12, 16). Paul's criticism of proselyte circumcision, however, is not to be confused with hostility towards Jewish circumcision, which he continues to affirm the benefit and value of (Rom 3:1–2). Further, the importance of circumcision as the marker par excellence of Jews is confirmed by Paul's reference to the Messiah as an agent of the circumcision, working on their behalf to confirm the promises made to the patriarchs (Rom 15:8).

Discussions of circumcision in Romans—and in Paul more generally—have placed a great deal of weight on what Paul says in Rom 2:28–29 since this is the only explicit reference to circumcision of the heart in his epistles. Here, it is traditionally argued that Paul redefines what it means to be a Jew and what counts as circumcision. Following the translations proposed by Thiessen and Novenson, I have suggested that Paul does not redefine these categories, rather, these verses serve to demonstrate that not all Jews and not all circumcisions receive praise from God. Like the prophet Jeremiah (9:25–26), Paul's reference to heart-circumcision does not constitute a rejection of the physical practice, but is used to highlight that Jews need to have circumcised hearts alongside circumcised penises in order to be pleasing to God. Within the context of Paul's critique of his imagined judaizing gentile interlocutor, this also has a polemical edge to it because it highlights the ineffectual nature of his attempts to be pleasing to God through Jewishness and circumcision on display.

After affirming the positive benefit of circumcision for Jews (Rom 3:1–2), and noting that both Jews and gentiles are under sin (3:9), Paul argues that both groups are made right via *pistis* (3:28–30). Here, Paul bases his argument on God's oneness; since God is one, the circumcision and the foreskin must be made right on the same basis. This does not collapse the distinction between these groups, rather, it upholds the distinction. For God to be one, he must be the God of all people, not just Jews. "As it is written, I have made you the father of many nations" (Rom 4:17).

Following the discussion of *pistis* in Rom 3, Paul turns to comment on Abraham's *pistis* and how it relates to his paternity of non-Jews (Rom 4:9–12). While translators have historically emphasized the idea that Abraham was "uncircumcised" when he exhibited *pistis* toward God, following the pioneering work of Karin Neutel, I offered an epispasmic translation of this passage that emphasizes the fact that Abraham was "in foreskin" when he trusted God. Rather than focusing on what Abraham lacked—a circumcision—Paul highlights what Abraham possessed—a foreskin. The presence of a foreskin was not a hindrance for Abraham, and Paul wants his foreskinned audience to know that it does not pose a hindrance to their trust either—or their status as Abraham's seed. Like Galatians, Paul rejects the possibility that non-Jews can become Abrahamic seed through fleshly means (κατὰ σάρκα, Rom 4:1), but unlike Galatians he does not appeal to the infusion of Christ's *pneuma* as accomplishing this feat. Rather, in Rom 4, Paul focuses on the central role *pistis* plays in connecting an individual to Abraham's lineage.

As is the case with Paul's other epistles, circumcision and foreskin are deployed in Romans in various ways to talk about Jews and non-Jews, and their relationship to Israel's God. Paul uses these terms metonymically, metaphorically, and concretely to refer to the state of an individual's penis. Despite the historical emphasis on Rom 2:25–29 as the pinnacle of Paul's thought on circumcision, I have demonstrated that the majority reading of heart-circumcision in Paul is not only misguided, but drastically overemphasized. Much more central to Paul's thought on circumcision are the promises to the patriarchs and the Messiah's role in confirming those promises (Rom 4:9–12; 15:8; Gal 3:6–14, 27–29; 4:21–31).

6 Conclusion
Paul: The Apostle to the Foreskin

But even the circumcision in which they trusted has been abolished. For he has said that circumcision is not a matter of the flesh. But they transgressed, because an evil angel instructed them. (Barn. 9.4 [modified from Ehrman])

Indeed the custom of circumcising the flesh, handed down from Abraham, was given to you as a distinguishing mark, to set you off from other nations and from us [Christians]. The purpose of this was that you and only you might suffer the afflictions that are now justly yours; that only your land be desolate, and your cities ruined by fire; that the fruits of your land be eaten by strangers before your very eyes; that not one of you be permitted to enter Jerusalem. (Justin, *Dial.* 16.2 [Falls])

Perhaps [circumcision] was given because of some angel hostile to the Jewish nation who had power to injure those of them who were not circumcised, but who was powerless against those circumcised...For Jesus destroyed [that angel] by an indescribable divine power. This is why his disciples are forbidden to be circumcised, and why they are told: "If you are circumcised, Christ shall profit you nothing." (Origen, *Cels.* 5.48 [Chadwick])

6.1 Re-reading Paul and Circumcision

This study began by briefly looking at the words attributed to Jesus in Gos. Thom. 53. Responding to his disciples' inquiry regarding the benefit of circumcision, Jesus says, "If [circumcision] were beneficial, their father would beget them already circumcised from their mother. Rather, the true circumcision in spirit has become completely profitable." I used this example to illustrate the similarity between Thomas' Jesus and the prominent claims made about Paul and circumcision: he devalues it, abrogates it, redefines it, and spiritualizes it. In this study of circumcision in Paul's epistles, I have argued this is not actually how Paul writes and thinks about circumcision. When Paul's statements about circumcision are read in their epistolary, rhetorical, and ethnic contexts, a different picture of circumcision emerges. Rather than summarize each of my chapters here, I will offer a brief synthesis of some of my findings in light of some early Christian polemics against the practice of circumcision.

Shortly after the turn of the second century CE, gentile Christian authors had begun to turn Jews and Judaism into the rhetorical foils of Christians and Christianity. While many of these authors acknowledged the connection between their faith and Judaism, this link generally served the sole purpose of demonstrating the supposed superiority of their own faith. Through creative interpretations of the Hebrew Bible—most often allegorical or typological—these gentile Christian authors delegitimized Judaism and appropriated its symbols for their rhetorical and theological advantage.[1] Given the centrality of circumcision as a marker of Jewish difference, it became an easy target for these non-Jewish authors to take aim at.

6.2 Early Christian Circumcision Polemics

In one of the earliest Christian polemics against circumcision, the author of the Epistle of Barnabas proposes that Israel misunderstood the practice of circumcision by maintaining its implementation as a physical rite.[2] While Abraham's enactment of circumcision is presented as being valid (Barn. 9.7–9), its continued practice post-Abraham is rejected (Barn. 9.4).[3] Appealing to the heart-circumcision texts in Deuteronomy and Jeremiah, and the repeated call for Israel to hear the voice of God and the prophets, the author contends that circumcision only applies to hearts and ears (Barn. 9.1–5; 10.12). "But even the circumcision in which they trusted has been abolished. For he has said that circumcision is not a matter of the flesh. But they transgressed because an evil angel instructed them" (Barn. 9.4 [modified from Ehrman]). Not only does Barnabas demonize the historic practice of circumcision by attributing it to the influence of an evil angel, its continued practice post-Abraham constituted a transgression against God.[4] Further, the author contends that the unremarkable nature of Jewish circumcision is demonstrated by the fact that Syrians, Arabs, and Egyptian are also known to practice it (Barn. 9.6).

Barnabas appropriates the rite of circumcision for the church by arguing that when Abraham received circumcision he did so with knowledge of Jesus, which is why he circumcised from his house "eighteen and three hundred men" (Barn. 9.8; cf. Gen 14:14; 17:23). For eighteen is composed of *iota* (ten) and *ēta* (eight), signifying

---

[1] Andrew Jacobs refers to this standard treatment of circumcision and other Jewish practices in early Christian polemics as "the twin notes of repudiation and appropriation" (*Christ Circumcised: A Study in Early Christian History and Difference* [Philadelphia: University of Pennsylvania Press, 2012], 35).
[2] For a recent treatment of circumcision in Barnabas, see Isaac T. Soon, "Satan and Circumcision: The Devil as the ἄγγελος πονηρός in Barn 9:4," *VC* (2021): 1–13.
[3] While the author justifies Abraham's implementation of circumcision allegorically and christologically, the logic undergirding its post-Abrahamic abolishment is unclear and a clear misreading of Gen 17.
[4] Soon, "Satan and Circumcision," 3–4, 6; cf. Carleton Paget, "Barnabas 9.4," 242–43.

Jesus (ιη), and *tau* (three hundred) represents the cross (τ).⁵ Circumcision was not given as a seal (Barn. 9.6, cf. Rom 4:11), but as a prediction of Jesus and the cross. Here, Barnabas' creative exegesis of two passages from Genesis strips off the significance attributed to circumcision by Jews—Paul included—and turns it into a symbol that foretold Christ and his cross.

Writing a few decades after Barnabas, Justin's *Dialogue with Trypho* attacks the practice of circumcision from a variety of angles.⁶ Justin argues that circumcision is a sign (σημεῖον; cf. Rom 4:11) that separates Jews from the other nations and Christians, and marks them out for suffering (*Dial.* 16.2; 19.2). He proposes that God set them apart with the mark of circumcision because he foreknew the evil they would commit, notably the murder of the Just One (ὁ δίκαιος [i.e., Jesus]) and the prophets that came before him (*Dial.* 16.4). Justin points to the suffering of Jews that occurred as a result of the Bar Kokhba revolt in 135 CE to demonstrate the validity of his interpretation; their land is desolate, their cities destroyed, and they are unable to enter into Jerusalem. In addition to this aspect of his polemic, Justin appeals to the men in the Hebrew Bible who were pleasing to God before circumcision was instituted as evidence that the practice was not necessary (*Dial.* 19). Similarly, the fact that women cannot be circumcised demonstrates that the practice holds no soteriological value (*Dial.* 23.5). Furthermore, like many Christian interpreters, Justin argues that since the rite of circumcision has been abolished, Jews need another circumcision, namely the true circumcision belonging to Christians (*Dial.* 12.3; 14.1; 19.3; 41.4). This circumcision is performed on the heart by the words of Jesus (*Dial.* 113.6–7; 114.4).

Similar to the proposal in Barnabas, Origen links the practice of circumcision to an angelic being. Though unlike Barnabas' evil angel that sows the idea of fleshly circumcision, Origen argues Jews practiced circumcision for apotropaic purposes in order to ward off a hostile angel that could hurt the uncircumcised but was powerless against the circumcised (*Cels.* 5.48). Instead of being a deceitful angel, Origen's angel is a destroyer (cf. Exod 4:24–26; 12:12–13, 21–23). While Origen affirms the practice of physical circumcision for ancient Jews (contra Barnabas), rather than it merely symbolizing the covenant of God with Abraham, it also served to keep a violent, hostile angel at bay (cf. Jub. 15:25–26). Origen then contends that through his own circumcision, Jesus destroyed (καθαιρέω) this angel

---

5 On the interpretive methods used by Barnabas in 9.8, see Reidar Hvalvik, "Barnabas 9. 7–9 and the Author's Supposed Use of *Gematria*," *NTS* 33 (1987): 276–82; Larry W. Hurtado, *The Earliest Christian Artifacts: Manuscripts and Christian Origins* (Grand Rapids: Eerdmans, 2006), 114, 147.
6 On circumcision in Justin, see Nina E. Livesey, "Theological Identity Making: Justin's Use of Circumcision to Create Jews and Christians," *JECS* 18 (2010): 51–79; eadem, *Malleable Symbol*, 124–30; Jacobs, *Christ Circumcised*, 36–38, 46–50.

and, consequently, abolished the need for physical circumcision. So while Jesus' physical circumcision affirms its historic practice by Jews, it simultaneously functions as the act that "renders it moot and past tense."[7] Since Jesus destroyed this angel—and thus the need for the protection circumcision provided—his disciples (i.e., Christians) are forbidden from being circumcised. Origen follows this up by quoting Gal 5:2 as a proof text for why circumcision is forbidden but without any clarification as to how this relates to his hypothesis about the hostile angel. Perhaps he simply quotes the words of Paul as an authoritative voice that makes a connection between the prohibition of circumcision and the work of Jesus.

In *Homilies on Genesis* 3.4–6, Origen turns to the spiritual and allegorical meaning of circumcision of the foreskin, which he argues was highlighted by Paul and overlooked by the fleshly interpretive practices of the Jews.[8] Citing Phil 3:2–3 and Rom 2:28–29, Origen proposes that Paul rightly perceived what the Jews before him missed; circumcision of the foreskin was to be taken allegorically, just as the various other types of circumcision in the Hebrew Bible were understood in a non-literal sense (e.g., ears, lips, and heart). In a similar way to how Philo argues that circumcision signified the excision of pleasure and sexual licentiousness (*Migr.* 92; *Spec. Laws* 1.1–11), Origen proposes that the true meaning of circumcision of the foreskin is chastity, whereas uncircumcision of the foreskin represents unbridled lust (*Hom. Gen.* 3.6). Expanding the metaphor, Origen writes, "But also each of our members must be said to be circumcised if they are devoted to the service of God's commands. But if they revel beyond the laws divinely prescribed for them, they are to be reckoned uncircumcised" (*Hom. Gen.* 3.6 [Heine]). He concludes his discussion of circumcision by engaging a hypothetical Jew and asking him to compare Jewish and Christian conceptions of circumcision. "Do not even you yourself perceive and understand that this circumcision of the Church is honorable, holy, worthy of God; that that of yours is unseemly, detestable, disgusting, presenting a thing vulgar both in condition and appearance" (*Hom. Gen.* 3.6 [Heine]). While Origen had linked Jewish circumcision with mutilation in a previous section (*Hom. Gen.* 3.4, citing Phil 3:2), here, his scathing critique of physical circumcision reaches its crescendo.

---

7 Jacobs, *Christ Circumcised*," 53.
8 On this text—and Origen and Judaism more broadly—see Susanna Drake, *Slandering the Jew: Sexuality and Difference in Early Christian Texts* (Philadelphia: University of Pennsylvania Press, 2013), 38–58. See also, Maren R. Niehoff, "Circumcision as a Marker of Identity: Philo, Origen and the Rabbis on Gen 17: 1–14," *JSQ* 10 (2003): 89–123, at 108–14.

6.3 Paul and the Polemicists

The way these authors and Paul speak about circumcision in their writings in markedly different.[9] If one reads Paul and these texts side by side, it becomes clear that they are participating in two different conversations. Unfortunately, however, many of Paul's interpreters have read him as if he was participating in a similar discourse as these early polemicists. Despite the fact that Paul and these authors all share the belief that Jesus was God's Messiah, their positions on circumcision—and Jews and Judaism more broadly—are at opposite ends of the spectrum. Paul takes his knowledge of the work of the Messiah and rethinks his convictions about how foreskinned non-Jews can relate to Israel's god (Gal 1:13–16; 5:11), whereas Barnabas, Justin, and Origen take their understanding of the Messiah and wield it as a hermeneutical weapon against Jews and circumcision. For Barnabas, Jewish circumcision was a misguided practice that had its roots in deception. For Paul, circumcision was given to Abraham by God as a seal of righteousness (Rom 4:11). For Justin, circumcision marked out Jews for suffering. For Paul, circumcision was valuable and set Jews apart as God's elect people (Rom 3:1–2; 9:4–5; 11:1). For Origen, the Messiah abolished the practice of circumcision. For Paul, the work of the Messiah confirms the promises made to Israel's circumcised patriarchs (Rom 15:8).

Paul's primary concern when it comes to circumcision is that non-Jews in the Jesus movement do not have themselves circumcised (Gal 5:2–4; 1 Cor 7:18; cf. Gal 2:3; Phil 3:2). This is not because circumcision is bad, outdated, or has been redefined, but because it is not for them as naturally foreskinned people (Rom 2:27; cf. m. Ned 3:11). When it is performed on naturally foreskinned bodies it constitutes a mutilation (Phil 3:2) and a transgression of the laws pertaining to circumcision (Rom 2:25, 27; Gal 6:13). Circumcision continued to hold a valuable place in Paul's thinking and it continued to be a mark that defined him (Phil 3:3) and his Jewish kinsmen (e.g., Rom 3:1, 3:30; 4:12; 15:8; Gal 2:7–9; cf. Acts 21:21–26). In the only instance where Paul speaks of the metaphorical circumcision of the heart, it does not constitute a replacement of the physical rite, but—like the prophets before him—he notes that a circumcised penis needs to be accompanied by a circumcised heart (Rom 2:28–29). There is no evidence in his epistles (or Acts) that Paul ever reconsidered his position on circumcision as central to Jewish identity and praxis;

---

[9] To be sure, there are marked differences amongst these three later authors as well, but Paul's treatment of circumcision is fundamentally different from these authors' approaches.

he does not engage in the "repudiation and appropriation"[10] that characterizes later (gentile) Christian treatments of circumcision.

6.4 Conclusion: The Apostle to the Foreskin

In the epigraph to this book, Jewish-American novelist Michael Chabon recounts his wife's words to him on the eve of their son's *bris*. "'Why are we doing this again?' my wife asked me, not for the first time, on the night of the seventh day of our second son's life."[11] In this short essay, Chabon discloses the anguish and discomfort he and his wife experienced concerning their decision to have their son circumcised. If one of a parent's main roles is to protect their children, why should they subject their son to a painful and bloody rite? Though Chabon never explicitly states why he and his wife still chose to have their son circumcised—despite their unease and negative evaluation of the practice—the answer can be found in the opening line of the essay: "If you are a Jew, eight days after your son is born...." This is what Jews do.

Despite their differing assessments of circumcision, Paul would undoubtedly agree with Chabon on this point: circumcision is what Jews do. For Paul, it—quite literally—defines them. From the second century CE onward, however, the Christian interpretive tradition had taken Paul's statements about circumcision and gentiles, and universalized them out of their epistolary, rhetorical, and ethnic contexts. Paul's harsh words about the circumcision of non-Jews were taken as a rejection of circumcision tout court. The Jewish Paul's repudiation of circumcision for gentiles became the Christian Paul's repudiation of circumcision for everyone.

---

10 Jacobs, *Christ Circumcised*, 35.
11 Michael Chabon, "The Cut," in *Manhood for Amateurs: The Pleasures and Regrets of a Husband, Father, and Son* (New York: HarperCollins, 2009), 21–27, at 22.

Bibliography

Primary Sources

Aland, Barbara, Kurt Aland, Johannes Karavidopoulos, Carlo M. Martini, and Bruce M. Metzger, eds. *Novum Testamentum Graece.* 28th ed. Stuttgart: Deutsche Bibelgesellschaft, 2012.
Aquinas, Thomas. *Commentaires de Saint Thomas d'Aquin Sur Tout Les Épitres de S. Paul.* Translated by Abbé Bralé. 6 vols. Paris: Vivès, 1869.
Aristophanes. Edited and translated by Jeffrey Henderson. 5 vols. LCL. Cambridge: Harvard University Press, 1998–2008.
Aristotle. Translated by H. Rackham et al. 23 vols. LCL. Cambridge: Harvard University Press, 2020.
Arnim, Hans Friedrich August von, ed. *Stoicorum Veterum Fragmenta.* 4 vols. Stuttgart: Teubner, 1903–1924.
Calogeras, Nicephorus. *Euthymii Zigabeni Commentarius in XIV Epistolas Sancti Pauli et VII catholicas.* Vol. 1. Athens, 1887.
Celsus. *On Medicine.* Translated by W. G. Spencer. 3 vols. LCL. Cambridge: Harvard University Press, 1935–1938.
Charlesworth, James H., ed. *The Old Testament Pseudepigrapha.* 2 vols. New York: Doubleday, 1983–1985.
Chrysostom. *Discourses against Judaizing Christians.* Translated by Paul W. Harkins. FC 68. Washington, DC: Catholic University of America Press, 1979.
Danker, Frederick W., Walter Baur, William F. Arndt, and F. Wilbur Gingrich. *Greek-English Lexicon of the New Testament and Other Early Christian Literature.* 3rd ed. Chicago: University of Chicago Press, 2000.
Diels, Hermann, ed. *Doxographi Graeci.* Berlin: Reimer, 1879.
Dio Cassius. *Roman History.* Translated by Earnest Carey and Herbert B. Foster. 9 vols. LCL. Cambridge: Harvard University Press, 1914–1927.
Diodorus Siculus. *Library of History.* Translated by C. H. Oldfather et al. 12 vols. LCL. Cambridge: Harvard University Press, 1933–1967.
Dionysius of Halicarnassus. *Roman Antiquities.* Translated by Earnest Carey. 7 vols. LCL. Cambridge: Harvard University Press, 1937–1950.
Downey, G., A. F. Norman, and H. Schenkl, eds. *Themistii orationes quae supersunt.* 3 vols. Leipzig: Teubner, 1965–1974.
Elliger, Karl, and Wilhelm Rudolph, eds. *Biblia Hebraica Stuttgartensia.* 5th ed. Stuttgart: Deutsche Bibelgesellschaft, 1997.
Epictetus. Translated by W. A. Oldfather. 2 vols. LCL. Cambridge: Harvard University Press, 1925–1928.
Freedman, H., and Maurice Simon. *Midrash Rabbah.* 10 vols. London: Soncino, 1939.
Gaisford, T. *Etymologicum Magnum.* Oxford, 1848.
Galen. *On the Doctrines of Hippocrates and Plato.* Edited by Phillip De Lacy. 3 vols. CMG V 4,1,2. Berlin: Akademie, 1978–1984.
Galen. *On Semen.* Edited by Phillip De Lacy. CMG V 3,1. Berlin: Akademie, 1992.
Galen. *Method of Medicine.* Edited and translated by Ian Johnston and G. H. R. Horsley. 3 vols. LCL. Cambridge: Harvard University Press, 2011.
García Martínez, Florentino, and Eibert J. C. Tigchelaar, eds. *The Dead Sea Scrolls Study Edition.* 2 vols. Leiden: Brill, 1997.

Herodotus. *The Persian Wars*. Translated by A. D. Godley. 4 vols. LCL. Cambridge: Harvard University Press, 1920–1925.
Hesychii Alexandrini. *Lexicon*. Edited by Kurt Latte. 2 vols. Copenhagen: Munksgaard, 1953–1966.
Josephus. Edited by H. St. J. Thackeray et al. 10 vols. LCL. Cambridge: Harvard University Press, 1926–1965.
Justin Martyr. *Dialogue with Trypho*. Edited by Michael Slusser. Translated by Thomas B. Falls. SFC 3. Washington, DC: Catholic University of America Press, 2003.
Juvenal and Persius. Edited and translated by Susanna Morton Braund. LCL 91. Cambridge: Harvard University Press, 2004.
Kennedy, George A., ed. *Progymnasmata: Greek Textbooks of Prose Composition and Rhetoric*. Translated by George A. Kennedy. WGRW 10. Atlanta: Society of Biblical Literature, 2003.
Liddell, Henry George, Robert Scott, and Henry Stuart Jones. *A Greek-English Lexicon*. 9th ed. Oxford: Clarendon, 1996.
Magie, David, ed. *Historia Augusta*. 3 vols. LCL. Cambridge: Harvard University Press, 1921–1932.
Martial. *Epigrams*. Edited and translated by D. R. Shackleton Bailey. 3 vols. LCL. Cambridge: Harvard University Press, 1993.
Maimonides, Moses. *The Guide for the Perplexed*. Translated by Michael Friedländer. 2nd ed. London: Routledge, 1904.
Neusner, Jacob, ed. *The Talmud of the Land of Israel*. Translated by Jacob Neusner. 35 vols. Chicago: University of Chicago Press, 1982–1993.
Oribasius. *Collectionum Medicarum Reliquiae*. Edited by Ioannes Raeder. 4 vols. CMG VI 1,1–2,2. Leipzig: Teubner, 1928–1933.
Origen. *Contra Celsum*. Edited and translated by Henry Chadwick. Cambridge: Cambridge University Press, 1965.
Origen. *Homilies on Genesis and Exodus*. Translated by Ronald E. Heine. FC 71. Washington, DC: Catholic University of America Press, 1982.
Origen. *Commentary on the Epistle to the Romans, Books 1–5*. Translated by Thomas P. Scheck. FC 103. Washington, DC: Catholic University of America Press, 2001.
Origen. *Commentary on the Epistle to the Romans, Books 6–10*. Translated by Thomas P. Scheck. FC 104. Washington, DC: Catholic University of America Press, 2002.
Patrologia Graeca. Edited by J.-P. Migne. 162 vols. Paris, 1857–1886.
Petronius, and Seneca. *Satyricon. Apocolocyntosis*. Translated by Michael Heseltine and W. H. D. Rouse. LCL 15. Cambridge: Harvard University Press, 1913.
Philo. Translated by F. H. Colson et al. 12 vols. LCL. Cambridge: Harvard University Press, 1929–1962.
Phrynichus. *Sophistae Praeparatio Sophistica*. Edited by J. de Borries. Leipzig, 1911.
Quintilian. *The Orator's Education*. Edited and translated by Donald A. Russell. 5 vols. LCL. Cambridge: Harvard University Press, 2002.
Robinson, James M., ed. *The Nag Hammadi Library in English*. 4th rev. ed. Leiden: Brill, 1996.
Soranus. *Gynecology*. Translated by Owsei Temkin. Baltimore: Johns Hopkins University Press, 1956.
Stern, Menahem, ed. *Greek and Latin Authors on Jews and Judaism*. 3 vols. Jerusalem: Israel Academy of Sciences and Humanities, 1974–1984.
Storey, Ian C., ed. *Fragments of Old Comedy*. Translated by Ian C. Storey. 3 vols. LCL. Cambridge: Harvard University Press, 2011.
Strabo. *Geography*. Translated by Horace Leonard. 8 vols. LCL. Cambridge: Harvard University Press, 1917–1932.

Tacitus. *The Histories and The Annals*. Translated by Clifford H. Moore and John Jackson. 4 vols. LCL. Cambridge: Harvard University Press, 1937.
Taillardat, Jean. *Suétone: ΠΕΡΙ ΒΛΑΣΦΗΜΙΩΝ. ΠΕΡΙ ΠΑΙΔΙΩΝ (Extraits Byzantins)*. Paris: Les Belles Lettres, 1967.
The Ante-Nicene Fathers. Edited by Alexander Roberts and James Donaldson. 1885–1887. 10 vols. Repr., Peabody, MA: Hendrickson, 1994.
The Apostolic Fathers. Edited and translated by Bart Ehrman. 2 vols. LCL. Cambridge: Harvard University Press, 2003.
The Nicene and Post-Nicene Fathers. Edited by Philip Schaff. Series 1. 1886–1889. 14 vols. Repr., Peabody, MA: Hendrickson, 1994.
Theophrastus, and Herodas. *Characters. Mimes. Sophron and Other Mime Fragments*. Edited and translated by Jeffrey Rusten and I. C. Cunningham. LCL 225. Cambridge: Harvard University Press, 2003.
Xenophon. Translated by Walter Miller et al. 7 vols. LCL. Cambridge: Harvard University Press, 1914–2013.
The Holy Bible: New Revised Standard Version. Nashville: Thomas Nelson, 1989.

Secondary Sources

Abusch, Ra'anan. "Negotiating Difference: Genital Mutilation in Roman Slave Law and the History of the Bar Kokhba Revolt." Pages 71–91 in *The Bar Kokhba War Reconsidered: New Perspectives on the Second Jewish Revolt against Rome*. Edited by Peter Schäfer. TSAJ 100. Tübingen: Mohr Siebeck, 2003.
Adams, James N. *The Latin Sexual Vocabulary*. London: Duckworth, 1982.
Albertz, Rainer. "From Aliens to Proselytes: Non-Priestly and Priestly Legislation Concerning Strangers." Pages 53–69 in *The Foreigner and the Law: Perspectives from the Hebrew Bible and the Ancient Near East*. Edited by Reinhard Achenbach, Rainer Albertz, and Jakob Wöhrle. BZABR 16. Wiesbaden: Harrassowitz, 2011.
Amir, Yehoshua. "The Term Ἰουδαϊσμός (*IOUDAISMOS*), A Study in Jewish-Hellenistic Self-Identification." *Imm* 14 (1982): 34–41.
Barclay, John M. G. "Mirror-Reading a Polemical Letter: Galatians as a Test Case." *JSNT* 31 (1987): 73–93.
Barclay, John M. G. "Paul And Philo on Circumcision: Romans 2.25–9 in Social and Cultural Context." *NTS* 44 (2009): 536.
Barclay, John M. G. "Paul, the Gift and the Battle Over Gentile Circumcision: Revisiting the Logic of Galatians." *ABR* 58 (2010): 36–56.
Barclay, John M. G. *Paul and the Gift*. Grand Rapids: Eerdmans, 2015.
Barclay, John M. G. "An Identity Received from God: The Theological Configuration of Paul's Kinship Discourse." *EC* 8.3 (2017): 354–72.
Barrett, C. K. *The First Epistle to the Corinthians*. BNTC. London: Black, 1968.
Barrett, C. K. "The Allegory of Abraham, Sarah, and Hagar." Pages 154–70 in *Essays on Paul*. Philadelphia: Westminster, 1982.
Barrier, Jeremy W. "Jesus' Breath: A Physiological Analysis of πνεῦμα Within Paul's Letter to the Galatians." *JSNT* 2 (2014): 115–38.

Bartchy, S. Scott. *MAΛΛON XPHΣAI: First-Century Slavery and the Interpretation of I Corinthians 7:21.* SBLDS 11. Missoula, MT: Scholars Press, 1973.

Bartelt, Andrew H. "Dialectical Negation: An Exegetical Both/And." Pages 57–66 in *"Hear the Word of Yahweh": Essays on Scripture and Archaeology in Honor of Horace D. Hummel.* Edited by Dean O. Wenthe, Paul L. Schrieber, and Lee A. Maxwell. St. Louis: Concordia, 2002.

Batement IV, Herbert W. "Were the Opponents at Philippi Necessarily Jewish?" *BSac* 155 (1998): 39–61.

Baumgarten, Albert I. "The Name of the Pharisees." *JBL* 102 (1983): 411–28.

Baur, Ferdinand Christian. *Paul the Apostle of Jesus Christ.* 2 vols. London: Williams & Norgate, 1873.

Beker, J. Christiaan. *Paul the Apostle: The Triumph of God in Life and Thought.* Philadelphia: Fortress, 1980.

Berkley, Timothy W. *From a Broken Covenant to Circumcision of the Heart: Pauline Intertextual Exegesis in Romans 2:17–29.* SBLDS 175. Atlanta: Society of Biblical Literature, 2000.

Bernat, David A. *Sign of the Covenant: Circumcision in the Priestly Tradition.* AIL 3. Atlanta: Society of Biblical Literature, 2009.

Bernier, Jonathan. *Rethinking the Dates of the New Testament: The Evidence for Early Composition.* Grand Rapids: Baker Academic, 2022.

Betz, Hans Dieter. *Galatians: A Commentary on Paul's Letter to the Churches in Galatia.* Hermeneia. Philadelphia: Fortress, 1979.

Bickerman, Elias J. *The God of the Maccabees: Studies on the Meaning and Origin of the Maccabean Revolt.* Translated by Horst R. Moehring. SJLA 32. Leiden: Brill, 1979.

Bird, Michael F. *An Anomalous Jew: Paul among Jews, Greeks, and Romans.* Grand Rapids: Eerdmans, 2016.

Bisschops, Ralph. "Metaphor in Religious Transformation: 'Circumcision of the Heart' in Paul of Tarsus." Pages 294–329 in *Religion, Language, and the Human Mind.* Edited by Paul Chilton and Monika Kopytowska. New York: Oxford University Press, 2018.

Blanton IV, Thomas R. "The Expressive Prepuce: Philo's Defense of Judaic Circumcision in Greek and Roman Contexts." *SPhiloA* 31 (2019): 127–61.

Blanton IV, Thomas R. "Circumcision in the Early Jesus Movement: The Contributions of Simon Claude Mimouni, 'Paul within Judaism' and 'Lived Ancient Religion.'" *JJMJS* 8 (2021): 131–57.

Blaschke, Andreas. *Beschneidung: Zeugnisse der Bibel und verwandter Texte.* TANZ 28. Tübingen: Francke, 1998.

Blass, Friedrich, Albert Debrunner, and Robert W. Funk. *A Greek Grammar of the New Testament and Other Early Christian Literature.* Chicago: University of Chicago Press, 1961.

Bockmuehl, Markus. *Revelation and Mystery in Ancient Judaism and Pauline Christianity.* WUNT 2/36. Tübingen: Mohr Siebeck, 1990.

Bockmuehl, Markus. *The Epistle to the Philippians.* BNTC. London: Black, 1997.

Bockmuehl, Markus. *Jewish Law in Gentile Churches: Halakhah and the Beginning of Christian Public Ethics.* Grand Rapids: Baker Academic, 2000.

Boer, Martinus C. de. "The Meaning of the Phrase τὰ στοιχεῖα τοῦ κόσμου in Galatians." *NTS* 53 (2007): 204–24.

Boer, Martinus C. de. *Galatians: A Commentary.* NTL. Louisville: Westminster John Knox, 2011.

Bokovoy, David E. "Did Eve Acquire, Create, or Procreate with Yahweh? A Grammatical and Contextual Reassessment Of קנה in Genesis 4:1." *VT* 63 (2013): 19–35.

Bonnard, Pierre. *L'épître de saint Paul aux Philippiens.* CNT 10. Neuchatel: Delachaux & Niestle, 1973.

Borgen, Peder. "Paul Preaches Circumcision and Pleases Men." Pages 37–46 in *Paul and Paulinism: Essays in Honour of C. K. Barrett*. Edited by Morna D. Hooker and Stephen G. Wilson. London: SPCK, 1982.

Borgen, Peder. *Philo, John and Paul: New Perspectives on Judaism and Christianity*. BJS 131. Atlanta: Scholars Press, 1987.

Boyarin, Daniel. *A Radical Jew: Paul and the Politics of Identity*. Berkeley: University of California Press, 1994.

Boyarin, Daniel. "*Ioudaismos* within Paul: A Modified Reading of Gal 1:13–14." Pages 167–78 in *The Message of Paul the Apostle within Second Temple Judaism*. Edited by František Ábel. Lanham, MD: Lexington Books/Fortress Academic, 2020.

Boylan, Michael. "Galen: On Blood, the Pulse, and the Arteries." *Journal of the History of Biology* 40 (2007): 207–30.

Braxton, Brad Ronnell. *The Tyranny of Resolution: I Corinthians 7:17–24*. SBLDS 181. Atlanta: SBL Press, 2000.

Bremmer, Jan M. "Spartans and Jews: Abrahamic Cousins?" Pages 47–59 in *Abraham, the Nations, and the Hagarites: Jewish, Christian, and Islamic Perspectives on Kinship with Abraham*. Edited by Martin Goodman, George H. van Kooten, and Jacques T.A.G.M. van Ruiten. TBN 13. Leiden: Brill, 2010.

Bruce, F. F. *The Epistle to the Galatians*. NIGTC. Grand Rapids: Eerdmans, 1982.

Bryan, Christopher. "A Further Look at Acts 16:1–3." *JBL* 107 (1988): 292–94.

Bryan, Christopher. *A Preface to Romans: Notes on the Epistle in Its Literary and Cultural Setting*. New York: Oxford University Press, 2000.

Buell, Denise Kimber. *Why This New Race: Ethnic Reasoning in Early Christianity*. New York: Columbia University Press, 2005.

Bultmann, Rudolf. *Der Stil der paulinischen Predigt und die kynisch-stoische Diatribe*. FRLANT 13. Göttingen: Vandenhoeck & Ruprecht, 1910.

Bultmann, Rudolf. *Theology of the New Testament*. Translated by Kendrick Grobel. 2 vols. New York: Scribner's Sons, 1951.

Burkitt, F. C. *Christian Beginnings: Three Lectures*. London: University of London Press, 1924.

Burnett, David A. "A Neglected Deuteronomic Scriptural Matrix for the Nature of the Resurrection Body in 1 Corinthians 15:39–42." Pages 187–211 in *Scripture, Texts, and Tracings in 1 Corinthians*. Edited by Linda L. Belleville and B. J. Oropeza. Lanham, MD: Lexington Books/Fortress Academic, 2019.

Burton, Ernest de Witt. *A Critical and Exegetical Commentary on the Epistle to the Galatians*. ICC. Edinburgh: T&T Clark, 1921.

Butticaz, Simon. *La crise galate ou l'anthropologie en question*. BZNW 229. Berlin: de Gruyter, 2018.

Campbell, Douglas A. "Galatians 5.11: Evidence of an Early Law-Observant Mission by Paul?" *NTS* 57 (2011): 325–47.

Campbell, Douglas A. *Framing Paul: An Epistolary Biography*. Grand Rapids: Eerdmans, 2014.

Campbell, William S. *Paul and the Creation of Christian Identity*. LNTS 322. London: T&T Clark, 2006.

Campbell, William S. *Unity and Diversity in Christ: Interpreting Paul in Context*. Eugene, OR: Cascade, 2013.

Campbell, William S. *The Nations in the Divine Economy: Paul's Covenantal Hermeneutics and Participation in Christ*. Lanham, MD: Lexington Books/Fortress Academic, 2018.

Carleton Paget, James. "Barnabas 9:4: A Peculiar Verse on Circumcision." *VC* 45 (1991): 242–54.

Carleton Paget, James. "Paul and the Epistle of Barnabas." *NovT* 38 (1996): 359–81.

Cerfaux, Lucien. "Abraham 'père en circoncision' des Gentils." *Recueil Lucien Cerfaux*. 3 vols. Gembloux: J. Duculot, 1954–1962.

Chabon, Michael. "The Cut." Pages 21–27 in *Manhood for Amateurs: The Pleasures and Regrets of a Husband, Father, and Son*. New York: HarperCollins, 2009.

Charles, R. H. *The Book of Jubilees or The Little Genesis*. London: Black, 1902.

Choi, Hung-Sik. "ΠΙΣΤΙΣ in Galatians 5:5–6: Neglected Evidence for the Faithfulness of Chris." *JBL* 124 (2005): 467–90.

Christiansen, Ellen Juhl. *The Covenant in Judaism and Paul: A Study of Ritual Boundaries as Identity Markers*. AGJU 27. Leiden: Brill, 1995.

Ciampa, Roy E., and Brian S. Rosner. *The First Letter to the Corinthians*. PilNTC. Grand Rapids: Eerdmans, 2010.

Cohen, Shaye J. D. "Conversion to Judaism in Historical Perspective: From Biblical Israel to Post-Biblical Judaism." *CJud* 36.4 (1983): 31–45.

Cohen, Shaye J. D. "Was Timothy Jewish (Acts 16:1–3)? Patristic Exegesis, Rabbinic Law, and Matrilineal Descent." *JBL* 105 (1986): 251–68.

Cohen, Shaye J. D. *The Beginnings of Jewishness: Boundaries, Varieties, Uncertainties*. HCS 31. Berkeley: University of California Press, 1999.

Cohen, Shaye J. D. *Why Aren't Jewish Women Circumcised? Gender and Covenant in Judaism*. Berkeley: University of California Press, 2005.

Collange, Jean-François. *The Epistle of Saint Paul to the Philippians*. Translated by A. W. Heathcote. London: Epworth, 1979.

Collins, John J. *Seers, Sibyls, and Sages in Hellenistic-Roman Judaism*. JSJSup 54. Leiden: Brill, 1997.

Collins, John N. *Diakonia: Re-Interpreting the Ancient Sources*. New York: Oxford University Press, 1990.

Collman, Ryan D. "Beware the Dogs! The Phallic Epithet in Phil 3.2." *NTS* 67 (2021): 105–20.

Concannon, Cavan W. *"When You Were Gentiles": Specters of Ethnicity in Roman Corinth and Paul's Corinthian Correspondence*. New Haven: Yale University Press, 2014.

Craigie, Peter C., Page H. Kelley, and Joel F. Drinkard Jr. *Jeremiah 1–25*. WBC 26. Dallas: Word, 1991.

Cranfield, C. E. B. *A Critical and Exegetical Commentary on the Epistle to the Romans*. 2 vols. ICC. Edinburgh: T&T Clark, 1975–1979.

Cranford, Michael. "The Possibility of Perfect Obedience: Paul and an Implied Premise in Galatians 3:10 and 5:3." *NovT* 36 (1994): 242–58.

Cranford, Michael. "Abraham in Romans 4: The Father of All Who Believe." *NTS* 41 (1995): 71–88.

Dahl, Nils Alstrup. "Romans 3.9: Text and Meaning." Pages 184–204 in *Paul and Paulinism: Essays in Honour of C. K. Barrett*. Edited by Morna D. Hooker and Stephen G. Wilson. London: SPCK, 1982.

Das, A. Andrew. *Solving the Romans Debate*. Minneapolis: Fortress, 2007.

Das, A. Andrew. "'Praise the Lord, All You Gentiles': The Encoded Audience of Romans 15.7–13:" *JSNT* 34 (2011): 90–110.

Das, A. Andrew. "The Gentile-Encoded Audience of Romans: The Church Outside the Synagogue." Pages 29–46 in *Reading Paul's Letter to the Romans*. Edited by Jerry L. Sumney. RBS 73. Atlanta: Society of Biblical Literature, 2012.

Dawes, Gregory W. "'But If You Can Gain Your Freedom' (1 Corinthians 7:17–24)." *CBQ* 52 (1990): 681–97.

Debouxhtay, Pierre. "Le sens se ἀποκόπτομαι (Gal, V, 12)." *REG* 39 (1926): 323–26.

Deming, Will. "Paul and Indifferent Things." Pages 384–403 in *Paul in the Greco-Roman World: A Handbook*. Edited by J. Paul Sampley. Harrisburg, PA: Trinity, 2003.

deSilva, David A. *The Letter to the Galatians*. NICNT. Grand Rapids: Eerdmans, 2018.
Di Mattei, Steven. "Paul's Allegory of the Two Covenants (Gal 4.21–31) in Light of First-Century Hellenistic Rhetoric and Jewish Hermeneutics." *NTS* 52 (2006): 102–22.
Dingwall, Eric John. *Male Infibulation*. London: Bale, Sons & Danielsson, 1925.
Donaldson, Terence L. *Paul and the Gentiles: Remapping the Apostle's Convictional World*. Minneapolis: Fortress, 1997.
Donaldson, Terence L. *Judaism and the Gentiles: Jewish Patterns of Universalism (to 135 CE)*. Waco, TX: Baylor University Press, 2007.
Donaldson, Terence L. "Paul Within Judaism: A Critical Evaluation from a 'New Perspective' Perspective." Pages 277–301 in *Paul Within Judaism: Restoring the First-Century Context to the Apostle*. Minneapolis: Fortress, 2015.
Donaldson, Terence L. "Paul, Abraham's Gentile 'Offspring,' and the Torah." Pages 135–50 in *Torah Ethics and Early Christian Identity*. Edited by Susan J. Wendel and David M. Miller. Grand Rapids: Eerdmans, 2016.
Donfried, Karl P. "Justification and Last Judgment in Paul." *Int* 30 (1976): 140–52.
Donfried, Karl P. ed. *The Romans Debate*. Rev. and exp. ed. Edinburgh: T&T Clark, 1991.
Dover, K. J. *Greek Homosexuality*. Rev. ed. Cambridge: Harvard University Press, 1989.
Drake, Susanna. *Slandering the Jew: Sexuality and Difference in Early Christian Texts*. Philadelphia: University of Pennsylvania Press, 2013.
Dunn, James D. G. "The Incident at Antioch (Gal. 2:11–18)." *JSNT* 18 (1983): 3–57.
Dunn, James D. G. *Romans 1–8*. WBC 38A. Waco, TX: Word, 1988.
Dunn, James D. G. *Romans 9–16*. WBC 38B. Waco, TX: Word, 1988.
Dunn, James D. G. *A Commentary on the Epistle to the Galatians*. BNTC. London: Black, 1993.
Dunn, James D. G. *The Theology of Paul the Apostle*. Grand Rapids: Eerdmans, 1998.
Dunn, James D. G. *The Parting of the Ways: Between Christianity and Judaism and Their Significance for the Character of Christianity*. Rev. ed. London: SCM, 2006.
Dunn, James D. G. *The New Perspective on Paul*. Rev. ed. Grand Rapids: Eerdmans, 2008.
Dunn, James D. G. *Beginning from Jerusalem*. Christianity in the Making 2. Grand Rapids: Eerdmans, 2009.
Dunne, John Anthony. *Persecution and Participation in Galatians*. WUNT 2/454. Tübingen: Mohr Siebeck, 2017.
Eastman, Susan G. "'Cast Out the Slave Woman and Her Son': The Dynamics of Exclusion and Inclusion in Galatians 4.30:" *JSNT* 28 (2006): 309–36.
Eastman, Susan G. *Recovering Paul's Mother Tongue: Language and Theology in Galatians*. Grand Rapids: Eerdmans, 2007.
Eastman, Susan G. "Israel and the Mercy of God: A Re-Reading of Galatians 6.16 and Romans 9–11." *NTS* 56 (2010): 367–95.
Edwards, James R. "Galatians 5:12: Circumcision, the Mother Goddess, and the Scandal of the Cross." *NovT* 53 (2011): 319–37.
Ehrensperger, Kathy. "Die ›Paul within Judaism‹-Perspektive. Eine Übersicht." *EvT* 80 (2020): 455–64.
Ehrensperger, Kathy. "Trouble in Galatia: What Should Be Cut? (On Gal 5:12)." Pages 179–94 in *The Message of Paul the Apostle within Second Temple Judaism*. Edited by František Ábel. Lanham, MD: Lexington Books/Fortress Academic, 2020.
Eisenbaum, Pamela. "Is Paul the Father of Misogyny and Antisemitism?" *CrossCur* 50 (2000): 506–24.

Eisenbaum, Pamela. "A Remedy for Having Been Born of Woman: Jesus, Gentiles, and Genealogy in Romans." *JBL* 123 (2004): 671–702.

Eisenbaum, Pamela. *Paul Was Not a Christian: The Original Message of a Misunderstood Apostle.* New York: HarperOne, 2009.

Elliott, Neil. *The Rhetoric of Romans: Argumentative Constraint and Strategy and Paul's Dialogue with Judaism.* JSNTSup 45. Sheffield: JSOT Press, 1990.

Elliott, Susan. *Cutting Too Close for Comfort: Paul's Letter to the Galatians in Its Anatolian Cultic Context.* JSNTSup 248. London: T&T Clark, 2003.

Emmett, Grace. "Becoming a Man: Un/Manly Self-Presentation in the Pauline Epistles." PhD diss., Kings College London, 2020.

Emmett, Grace. "The Apostle Paul's Maternal Masculinity." *JECH* (2021): 1–23.

Engberg-Pedersen, Troels. *Cosmology and Self in the Apostle Paul: The Material Spirit.* Oxford: Oxford University Press, 2010.

Esler, Philip F. *Galatians.* London: Routledge, 1998.

Esler, Philip F. *Conflict and Identity in Romans: The Social Setting of Paul's Letter.* Minneapolis: Fortress, 2003.

Eyl, Jennifer. "Semantic Voids, New Testament Translation, and Anachronism: The Case of Paul's Use of Ekklēsia." *MTSR* 26 (2014): 315–39.

Eyl, Jennifer. "'I Myself Am an Israelite': Paul, Authenticity and Authority." *JSNT* 40 (2017): 148–68.

Fee, Gordon D. *The First Epistle to the Corinthians.* NICNT. Grand Rapids: Eerdmans, 1987.

Fee, Gordon D. *Paul's Letter to the Philippians.* NICNT. Grand Rapids: Eerdmans, 1995.

Feldman, Louis H. *Jew and Gentile in the Ancient World: Attitudes and Interactions from Alexander to Justinian.* Princeton: Princeton University Press, 1993.

Ferguson, Everett. "Spiritual Circumcision in Early Christianity." *SJT* 41 (1988): 485–97.

Fitzmyer, Joseph A. *Romans: A New Translation with Introduction and Commentary.* AB 33. New York: Doubleday, 1993.

Fitzmyer, Joseph A. *First Corinthians: A New Translation with Introduction and Commentary.* AB 32. New Haven: Yale University Press, 2008.

Foster, Paul. "Echoes without Resonance: Critiquing Certain Aspects of Recent Scholarly Trends in the Study of the Jewish Scriptures in the New Testament." *JSNT* 38 (2015): 96–111.

Franco, Cristiana. *Shameless: The Canine and the Feminine in Ancient Greece.* Translated by Matthew Fox. Joan Palevsky Imprint in Classical Literature. Berkeley: University of California Press, 2014.

Frankfurter, David. "Jews or Not? Reconstructing the 'Other' in Rev 2:9 and 3:9." *HTR* 94 (2001): 403–25.

Fredriksen, Paula. "Judaism, the Circumcision of Gentiles, and Apocalyptic Hope: Another Look at Galatians 1 and 2." *JTS* 42 (1991): 532–64.

Fredriksen, Paula. "Historical Integrity, Interpretive Freedom: The Philosopher's Paul and the Problem of Anachronism." Pages 61–73 in *St. Paul Among the Philosophers.* Edited by John D. Caputo and Linda Martin Alcoff. ISPR. Bloomington, IN: Indiana University Press, 2009.

Fredriksen, Paula. "Judaizing the Nations: The Ritual Demands of Paul's Gospel." *NTS* 56 (2010): 232–52.

Fredriksen, Paula. *Paul: The Pagans' Apostle.* New Haven: Yale University Press, 2017.

Fredriksen, Paula. "How Jewish Is God? Divine Ethnicity in Paul's Theology." *JBL* 137 (2018): 193–212.

Fredriksen, Paula. "God Is Jewish, but Gentiles Don't Have to Be: Ethnicity and Eschatology in Paul's Gospel." Pages 3–19 in *The Message of Paul the Apostle within Second Temple Judaism.* Edited by František Ábel. Lanham, MD: Lexington Books/Fortress Academic, 2020.

Fredriksen, Paula. "Paul the 'Convert'?" Pages 31–53 in *The Oxford Handbook of Pauline Studies*. Edited by Matthew V. Novenson and R. Barry Matlock. Oxford: Oxford University Press, 2022.

Fredriksen, Paula. "What Does It Mean to See Paul 'within Judaism'?" *JBL* 141 (2022): 359–80.

Fridrichsen, Anton. "Der wahre Jude und sein Lob: Röm 2,28f." *SO* 1 (1922): 39–49.

Funk, Robert W. *A Beginning-Intermediate Grammar of Hellenistic Greek*. 2nd ed. Missoula, MT: Scholars Press, 1973.

Gallas, Sven. "Fünfmal vierzig weniger einen ...". Die an Paulus vollzogenen Synagogalstrafen nach 2Kor 11,24." *ZNW* 81 (1990): 178–191.

Garland, David E. "The Composition and Unity of Philippians: Some Neglected Literary Factors." *NovT* 27 (1985): 141–73.

Garland, David E. *1 Corinthians*. BECNT. Grand Rapids: Baker Academic, 2003.

Garroway, Joshua D. *Paul's Gentile-Jews: Neither Jew nor Gentile, but Both*. New York: Palgrave Macmillan, 2012.

Garroway, Joshua D. "The Circumcision of Christ: Romans 15.7–13." *JSNT* 34 (2012): 303–22.

Garroway, Joshua D. "The Pharisee Heresy: Circumcision for Gentiles in the Acts of the Apostles." *NTS* 60 (2013): 20–36.

Garroway, Joshua D. "Paul's Gentile Interlocutor in Romans 3:1–20." Pages 85–100 in *The So-Called Jew in Paul's Letter to the Romans*. Edited by Rafael Rodríguez and Matthew Thiessen. Minneapolis: Fortress, 2016.

Garroway, Joshua D. *The Beginning of the Gospel: Paul, Philippi, and the Origins of Christianity*. Cham: Palgrave Macmillan, 2018.

Gaston, Lloyd. *Paul and the Torah*. Vancouver: University of British Columbia Press, 1987.

Gathercole, Simon J. *Where Is Boasting? Early Jewish Soteriology and Paul's Response in Romans 1–5*. Grand Rapids: Eerdmans, 2002.

Gathercole, Simon J. *The Gospel of Thomas: Introduction and Commentary*. TENTS 11. Leiden: Brill, 2014.

Gaventa, Beverly R. "The Maternity of Paul: An Exegetical Study of Galatians 4:19." Pages 189–201 in *The Conversation Continues: Studies in Paul and John In Honor of J. Louis Martyn*. Edited by Robert T. Fortna and Beverly R. Gaventa. Nashville: Abingdon, 1990.

Gaventa, Beverly R. *Our Mother Saint Paul*. Louisville: Westminster John Knox, 2007.

Gifford, E. H. *The Epistle of St. Paul to the Romans*. London: John Murray, 1886.

Goldingay, John. "The Significance of Circumcision:" *JSOT* 88 (2000): 3–18.

Goodman, Martin. *Mission and Conversion: Proselytizing in the Religious History of the Roman Empire*. Oxford: Clarendon, 1996.

Goodman, Martin. "The Politics of Judaea in the 50s CE: The Use of the New Testament." *JJS* 70 (2019): 225–36.

Grayston, Kenneth. "The Opponents in Philippians 3." *ExpTim* 97 (1986): 170–72.

Greenfield, Jonas C., Michael E. Stone, and Ester Eschel. *The Aramaic Levi Document: Edition, Translation, Commentary*. SVTP 19. Leiden: Brill, 2004.

Gregerman, Adam. "Response to Papers Presented at the American Academy of Religion Conference." *SCJR* 5 (2010): 1–10.

Gunther, John J. *St. Paul's Opponents and Their Background: A Study of Apocalyptic and Jewish Sectarian Teachings*. NovTSup 35. Leiden: Brill, 1973.

Hahm, David E. *The Origins of Stoic Cosmology*. Columbus: Ohio State University Press, 1977.

Hall, Robert G. "Epispasm and the Dating of Ancient Jewish Writings." *JSP* 2 (1988): 71–86.

Hall, Robert G. "Epispasm: Circumcision in Reverse." *BRev* 8.4 (1992): 52–57.

Hansen, G. Walter. *Abraham in Galatians: Epistolary and Rhetorical Contexts.* JSNTSup 29. Sheffield: JSOT Press, 1989.
Hardin, Justin K. *Galatians and the Imperial Cult.* WUNT 2/237. Tübingen: Mohr Siebeck, 2008.
Hardin, Justin K. "'If I Still Proclaim Circumcision' (Galatians 5:11a): Paul, The Law, and Gentile Circumcision." *JSPL* 3 (2013): 145–63.
Hardin, Justin K. "Galatians 1–2 Without a Mirror: Reflections on Paul's Conflict with the Agitators." *TynBul* 65 (2014): 275–303.
Harnack, Adolf von. *The Date of the Acts and of the Synoptic Gospels.* Translated by J. R. Wilkinson. London: Williams & Norgate, 1911.
Haworth, Marina. "The Wolfish Lover: The Dog as a Comic Metaphor in Homoerotic Symposium Pottery." *Archimédé* 5 (2018): 7–23.
Hayes, Christine E. *Gentile Impurities and Jewish Identities.* New York: Oxford University Press, 2002.
Hayes, Christine E. *What's Divine about Divine Law? Early Perspectives.* Princeton: Princeton University Press, 2015.
Hayes, Christine E. "Thiessen and Kaden on Paul and the Gentiles." *JSPL* 7 (2017): 68–79.
Hays, Richard B. "'Have We Found Abraham to Be Our Forefather According to the Flesh?' A Reconsideration of Rom 4:1." *NovT* 27 (1985): 76–98.
Hays, Richard B. *Echoes of Scripture in the Letters of Paul.* New Haven: Yale University Press, 1989.
Hays, Richard B. *The Faith of Jesus Christ: The Narrative Substructure of Galatians 3:1–4:11.* 2nd ed. Grand Rapids: Eerdmans, 2002.
Hays, Richard B. *The Conversion of the Imagination: Paul as Interpreter of Israel's Scripture.* Grand Rapids: Eerdmans, 2005.
Heath, J. M. F. *Paul's Visual Piety: The Metamorphosis of the Beholder.* Oxford: Oxford University Press, 2013.
Heil, John Paul. *Philippians: Let Us Rejoice in Being Conformed to Christ.* ECL 3. Atlanta: Society of Biblical Literature, 2010.
Henderson, Jeffrey. *The Maculate Muse: Obscene Language in Attic Comedy.* Oxford: Oxford University Press, 1991.
Hermisson, Hans-Jürgen. *Sprache und Ritus im altisraelischen Kult: zur "Spiritualisierung" der Kultbegriffe im Alten Testament.* WMANT 19. Neukirchen-Vluyn: Neukirchener Verlag, 1965.
Hewitt, J. Thomas. "Πνεῦμα, Genealogical Descent and Things That Do Not Exist According to Paul." *NTS* 68 (2022): 239–52.
Hezser, Catherine. *Jewish Slavery in Antiquity.* Oxford: Oxford University Press, 2005.
Hirsch, Emanuel. "Zwei Fragen zu Galater 6." *ZNW* 29 (1930): 192–97.
Hodges, Frederick M. "The Ideal Prepuce in Ancient Greece and Rome: Male Genital Aesthetics and Their Relation to *Lipodermos*, Circumcision, Foreskin Restoration, and the *Kynodesmē*." *Bulletin of the History of Medicine* 75 (2001): 375–405.
Holloway, Paul A. *Philippians: A Commentary.* Hermeneia. Minneapolis: Fortress, 2017.
Holmberg, Bengt. "Jewish *Versus* Christian Identity in the Early Church?" *RB* 105 (1998): 397–425.
Horn, Friedrich Wilhelm. *Das Angeld des Geistes: Studien zur paulinischen Pneumatologie.* FRLANT 154. Göttingen: Vandenhoeck & Ruprecht, 1992.
Horn, Friedrich Wilhelm. "Der Verzicht auf die Beschneidung im frühen Christentum." *NTS* 42 (1996): 479–505.
Horn, Friedrich Wilhelm. "Götzendiener, Tempelräuber und Betrüger. Polemik gegen Heiden, Juden und Judenchristen im Römerbrief." Pages 209–32 in *Polemik in der frühchristlichen Literatur.* Edited by Oda Wischmeyer and Lorenzo Scornaiench. BZNW 170. Berlin: de Gruyter, 2011.

Horrell, David. *Solidarity and Difference: A Contemporary Reading of Paul's Ethics.* London: T&T Clark, 2005.
Horsley, Richard A. *1 Corinthians.* ANTC. Nashville: Abingdon, 1998.
Houten, Christiana van. *The Alien in Israelite Law.* JSOTSup 107. Sheffield: JSOT Press, 1991.
Howard, George. "Romans 3:21–31 and the Inclusion of the Gentiles." *HTR* 63 (1970): 223–33.
Hubing, Jeff. *Crucifixion and New Creation: The Strategic Purpose of Galatians 6:11–17.* LNTS 508. London: T&T Clark, 2015.
Hübner, Hans. "Gal 3,10 und die Herkunft des Paulus." *KD* 19 (1973): 215–31.
Hultin, Jeremy F. *The Ethics of Obscene Speech in Early Christianity and Its Environment.* NovTSup 128. Leiden: Brill, 2008.
Hurtado, Larry W. *The Earliest Christian Artifacts: Manuscripts and Christian Origins.* Grand Rapids: Eerdmans, 2006.
Huttunen, Niko. *Paul and Epictetus on Law: A Comparison.* LNTS 405. London: T&T Clark, 2009.
Hvalvik, Reidar. "Barnabas 9. 7–9 and the Author's Supposed Use of *Gematria*." *NTS* 33 (1987): 276–82.
Isaac, Benjamin. *The Invention of Racism in Classical Antiquity.* Princeton: Princeton University Press, 2004.
Jackson-McCabe, Matt. *Jewish Christianity: The Making of the Christianity-Judaism Divide.* AYBRL. New Haven: Yale University Press, 2020.
Jacobs, Andrew S. *Christ Circumcised: A Study in Early Christian History and Difference.* Philadelphia: University of Pennsylvania Press, 2012.
Jewett, Robert. "Conflicting Movements in the Early Church as Reflected in Philippians." *NovT* 12 (1970): 362–90.
Jewett, Robert. "The Agitators and the Galatian Congregation." *New Testament Studies* 17 (1971): 198–212.
Jewett, Robert. *Romans: A Commentary.* Hermeneia. Minneapolis: Fortress, 2007.
Jipp, Joshua W. "Rereading the Story of Abraham, Isaac, and 'Us' in Romans 4." *JSNT* 32 (2009): 217–42.
Jipp, Joshua W. "What Are the Implications of the Ethnic Identity of Paul's Interlocutor? Continuing the Conversation." Pages 183–203 in *The So-Called Jew in Paul's Letter to the Romans.* Edited by Rafael Rodríguez and Matthew Thiessen. Minneapolis: Fortress, 2016.
Jipp, Joshua W., and Michael J. Thate. "*Dating* Thomas: Logion 53 as a Test Case for Dating the Gospel of Thomas within an Early Christian Trajectory." *BBR* 20 (2010): 237–56.
Johnson Hodge, Caroline. *If Sons, Then Heirs: A Study of Kinship and Ethnicity in the Letters of Paul.* New York: Oxford University Press, 2007.
Jonckheere, Frans. "La circonsion [sic] des anciens Egyptiens." *Centaurus* 1 (1951): 212–34.
Jónsson, Jakob. *Humour and Irony in the New Testament.* BZRGG 28. Leiden: Brill, 1985.
Kapparis, Konstantinos K. "The Terminology of Prostitution in the Ancient Greek World." Pages 222–55 in *Greek Prostitutes in the Ancient Mediterranean 800 BCE–200 CE.* Edited by Allison Glazebrook and Madeleine M. Henry. Madison: University of Wisconsin Press, 2011.
Käsemann, Ernst. *An die Römer.* 4th ed. HNT 8a. Tübingen: Mohr Siebeck, 1980.
Keener, Craig S. *Galatians.* NCBC. Cambridge: Cambridge University Press, 2018.
King, Justin. *Speech-in-Character, Diatribe, and Romans 3:1–9: Who's Speaking When and Why It Matters.* BibInt 163. Leiden: Brill, 2018.
Kitchell Jr., Kenneth F. *Animals in the Ancient World from A to Z.* New York: Routledge, 2014.

Kittel, Gerhard, and Gerhard Friedrich, eds. *Theological Dictionary of the New Testament.* Translated by Geoffrey W. Bromiley. 10 vols. Grand Rapids: Eerdmans, 1964–1976.
Klijn, A. F. J. "Paul's Opponents in Philippians III." *NovT* 7 (1965): 278–84.
Klinghardt, Matthias. "Himmlische Körper. Hintergrund und arguemtative Funktion von 1Kor 15,40 f." *ZNW* 106 (2015): 216–44.
Kobel, Esther. *Paulus als interkultureller Vermittler: Eine Studie zur kulturellen Positionierung des Apostels der Völker.* SCCB 1. Paderborn: Schöningh, 2019.
Koester, Helmut. "The Purpose of the Polemic of a Pauline Fragment." *NTS* 8 (1962): 317–32.
Kruse, Heinz. "Die 'dialektische Negation' als semitisches Idiom." *VT* 4 (1954): 385–400.
Kuefler, Mathew. *The Manly Eunuch: Masculinity, Gender Ambiguity, and Christian Ideology in Late Antiquity.* Chicago: University of Chicago Press, 2001.
Laato, Timo. *Paul and Judaism: An Anthropological Approach.* SFSHJ 115. Atlanta: Scholars Press, 1995.
Le Déaut, Roger. "Le thème de la circoncision du coeur (Deut. XXX 6; Jér. IV 4) dans les versions anciennes (LXX et Targum) et à Qumrân." Pages 178–205 in *Congress Volume, Vienna, 1980.* Edited by J. A. Emerton. VTSup 32. Leiden: Brill, 1981.
Lemke, Werner E. "Circumcision of the Heart: The Journey of a Biblical Metaphor." Pages 299–319 in *A God So Near: Essays on Old Testament Theology in Honor of Patrick D. Miller.* Edited by Brent A. Strawn and Nancy R. Bowen. Winona Lake, IN: Eisenbrauns, 2003.
Levison, John R. *The Spirit in First Century Judaism.* AGJU 29. Leiden: Brill, 1997.
Lightfoot, J. B. *Notes on Epistles of St Paul from Unpublished Commentaries.* London: Macmillan and Co., 1895.
Lightfoot, J. B. *Saint Paul's Epistle to the Galatians.* London: Macmillan & Co., 1896.
Linebaugh, Jonathan A. *God, Grace, and Righteousness in Wisdom of Solomon and Paul's Letter to the Romans: Texts in Conversation.* NovTSup 152. Leiden: Brill, 2013.
Livesey, Nina E. *Circumcision as a Malleable Symbol.* WUNT 2/295. Tübingen: Mohr Siebeck, 2010.
Livesey, Nina E. "Theological Identity Making: Justin's Use of Circumcision to Create Jews and Christians." *JECS* 18 (2010): 51–79.
Longenecker, Richard N. *Galatians.* WBC 41. Waco, TX: Word, 1990.
Longenecker, Richard N. *The Epistle to the Romans.* NIGTC. Grand Rapids: Eerdmans, 2016.
Lüdemann, Gerd. *Jesus After 2000 Years: What He Really Said and Did.* Translated by John Bowden. London: SCM, 2000.
Luther, Martin. *A Commentary on the Galatians.* Chester: Jones & Crane, 1796.
Maccoby, Hyam. "Paul and Circumcision: A Rejoinder." *JQR* 82 (1991): 177–80.
Marchal, Joseph A. *Appalling Bodies: Queer Figures Before and After Paul's Letters.* New York: Oxford University Press, 2020.
Marcus, Joel. "The Circumcision and the Uncircumcision in Rome." *NTS* 35 (1989): 67–81.
Martin, Dale B. *Slavery as Salvation: The Metaphor of Slavery in Pauline Christianity.* New Haven: Yale University Press, 1990.
Martin, Dale B. *The Corinthian Body.* New Haven: Yale University Press, 1999.
Martin, Dale B. "Heterosexism and the Interpretation of Romans 1:18–32." *BibInt* 3 (2007): 332–55.
Martin, Dale B. *Biblical Truths: The Meaning of Scripture in the Twenty-First Century.* New Haven: Yale University Press, 2017.
Martin, Ralph P., and Gerald F. Hawthorne. *Philippians.* Red. ed. Word Biblical Commentary 43. Nashville: Nelson, 2004.
Martin, Troy. "Apostasy to Paganism: The Rhetorical Stasis of the Galatian Controversy." *JBL* 114 (1995): 437–61.

Martin, Troy. "Pagan and Judeo-Christian Time-Keeping Schemes in Gal 4.10 and Col 2.16." *NTS* 42 (1996): 105–19.
Martin, Troy. "Paul's Pneumatological Statements and Ancient Medical Texts." Pages 105–26 in *The New Testament and Early Christian Literature in Greco-Roman Context: Studies in Honor of David E. Aune.* Edited by John Fotopoulos. NovTSup 122. Leiden: Brill, 2006.
Martyn, J. Louis. "The Covenants of Hagar and Sarah." Pages 160–92 in *Faith and History: Essays in Honor of Paul W. Meyer.* Edited by John T. Carroll, Charles H. Cosgrove, and E. Elizabeth Johnson. Atlanta: Scholars Press, 1990.
Martyn, J. Louis. *Galatians: A New Translation with Introduction and Commentary.* AB 33 A. New York: Doubleday, 1997.
Mason, Steve. "Jews, Judaeans, Judaizing, Judaism: Problems of Categorization in Ancient History." *JSJ* 38 (2007): 457–512.
Matera, Frank J. *Galatians.* SP 9. Collegeville, MN: Liturgical Press, 1992.
Matlock, R. Barry. "Helping Paul's Argument Work? The Curse of Galatians 3:10–14." Pages 154–79 in *The Torah in the New Testament.* Edited by Peter Oakes and Michael Tait. LNTS 401. London: T&T Clark, 2009.
Matlock, R. Barry. "'Jews By Nature': Paul, Ethnicity, and Galatians." Pages 304–15 in *Far From Minimal: Celebrating the Work and Influence of Philip R. Davies.* Edited by Duncan Burns and John W. Rogerson. London: T&T Clark, 2012.
McKnight, Scot. *A Light Among the Gentiles: Jewish Missionary Activity in the Second Temple Period.* Minneapolis: Fortress, 1991.
McMurray, Patrick. *Sacrifice, Brotherhood and the Body: Abraham and the Nations in Romans.* Lanham, MD: Lexington Books/Fortress Academic, 2021.
Mearns, Chris. "The Identity of Paul's Opponents at Philippi." *NTS* 33 (1987): 194–204.
Meiser, Martin. *Galater.* NTP 9. Göttingen: Vandenhoeck & Ruprecht, 2007.
Miller, Geoffrey David. "Attitudes toward Dogs in Ancient Israel: A Reassessment." *JSOT* 32 (2008): 487–500.
Mimouni, Simon Claude. *La circoncision dans le monde judéen aux époques grecque et romaine: Histoire d'un conflit interne au judaïsme.* CREJ 42. Paris-Louvain: Peeters, 2007.
Mininger, Marcus A. *Uncovering the Theme of Revelation in Romans 1:16–3:26: Discovering a New Approach to Paul's Argument.* WUNT 2/445. Tübingen: Mohr Siebeck, 2017.
Mitchell, Margaret M. "Paul and Judaism Now, Quo vadimus?" *JJMJS* 5 (2018): 55–78.
Montefiore, C. G. *Judaism and St. Paul: Two Essays.* London: Goschen, 1914.
Moo, Douglas J. *The Epistle to the Romans.* NICNT. Grand Rapids: Eerdmans, 1996.
Moo, Douglas J. *Galatians.* BECNT. Grand Rapids: Baker Academic, 2013.
Moore, George Foot. "Christian Writers on Judaism." *HTR* 14 (1921): 197–254.
Moorthy, Asha K. "A Seal of Faith: Rereading Paul on Circumcision, Torah, and the Gentiles." PhD diss., Columbia University, 2014.
Mortensen, Jacob P. B. *Paul Among the Gentiles: A "Radical" Reading of Romans.* NET 28. Tübingen: Narr, 2018.
Munck, Johannes. *Paul and the Salvation of Mankind.* Translated by Frank Clarke. London: SCM, 1959.
Murphy, James G. *A Critical and Exegetical Commentary on the Book of Exodus.* ICC. New York: I.K. Funk & Co., 1881.
Murray, Michele. *Playing a Jewish Game: Gentile Christian Judaizing in the First and Second Centuries CE.* Studies in Christianity and Judaism 13. Ontario: Wilfrid Laurier University Press, 2004.

Murray, Michele. "Romans 2 Within the Broader Context of Gentile Judaizing in Early Christianity." Pages 163–82 in *The So-Called Jew in Paul's Letter to the Romans*. Edited by Rafael Rodríguez and Matthew Thiessen. Minneapolis: Fortress, 2016.

Mußner, Franz. *Der Galaterbrief*. 5th ed. HThKNT 9. Freiburg: Herder, 1988.

Myers, Alicia D. *Blessed Among Women? Mothers and Motherhood in the New Testament*. New York: Oxford University Press, 2017.

Nanos, Mark D. *The Mystery of Romans: The Jewish Context of Paul's Letter*. Minneapolis: Fortress, 1996.

Nanos, Mark D. *The Irony of Galatians: Paul's Letter in First-Century Context*. Minneapolis: Fortress, 2002.

Nanos, Mark D. "Paul's Reversal of Jews Calling Gentiles 'Dogs' (Philippians 3:2): 1600 Years of an Ideological Tale Wagging an Exegetical Dog?" *BibInt* 17 (2009): 448–82.

Nanos, Mark D. "The Myth of the 'Law-Free' Paul Standing Between Christians and Jews." *SCJR* 4 (2009): 1–22.

Nanos, Mark D. "Paul and the Jewish Tradition: The Ideology of the Shema." Pages 62–80 in *Celebrating Paul: Festschrift in Honor of Jerome Murphy-O'Connor, O.P., and Joseph A. Fitzmyer, S.J.* Edited by Peter Spitaler. CBQMS 48. Washington, DC: Catholic Biblical Association of America, 2012.

Nanos, Mark D. "Paul's Polemic in Philippians 3 as Jewish-Subgroup Vilification of Local Non-Jewish Cultic and Philosophical Alternatives." *JSPL* 3 (2013): 47–91.

Nanos, Mark D. "Paul's Non-Jews Do Not Become 'Jews,' But Do They Become 'Jewish'?: Reading Romans 2:25–29 Within Judaism, Alongside Josephus." *JJMJS* 1 (2014): 26–53.

Nanos, Mark D. "Introduction." Pages 1–29 in *Paul within Judaism: Restoring the First-Century Context to the Apostle*. Edited by Mark D. Nanos and Magnus Zetterholm. Minneapolis: Fortress, 2015.

Nanos, Mark D. "How Could Paul Accuse Peter of 'Living *Ethné*-ishly' in Antioch (Gal 2:11–21) If Peter Was Eating According to Jewish Dietary Norms?" *JSPL* 6 (2016): 199–223.

Mark D. Nanos and Magnus Zetterholm, eds., *Paul within Judaism: Restoring the First-Century Context to the Apostle* (Minneapolis: Fortress, 2015).

Nasrallah, Laura Salah. *Archaeology and the Letters of Paul*. Oxford: Oxford University Press, 2018.

Neander, August. *Geschichte der Pflanzung und Leitung der christlichen Kirche durch die Apostel*. 4th ed. 2 vols. Hamburg: Perthes, 1847.

Neutel, Karin B. *A Cosmopolitan Ideal: Paul's Declaration "Neither Jew Nor Greek, Neither Slave Nor Free, Nor Male and Female" in the Context of First Century Thought*. LNTS 513. London: T&T Clark, 2015.

Neutel, Karin B. "Circumcision Gone Wrong: Paul's Message as a Case of Ritual Disruption." *Neot* 50 (2016): 373–96.

Neutel, Karin B. "Restoring Abraham's Foreskin: The Significance of ἀκροβυστία for Paul's Argument about Circumcision in Romans 4:9–12." *JJMJS* 8 (2021): 53–74.

Niehoff, Maren R. "Circumcision as a Marker of Identity: Philo, Origen and the Rabbis on Gen 17: 1–14." *JSQ* 10 (2003): 89–123.

Nongbri, Brent. *Before Religion: A History of a Modern Concept*. New Haven: Yale University Press, 2013.

Novenson, Matthew V. *Christ among the Messiahs: Christ Language in Paul and Messiah Language in Ancient Judaism*. New York: Oxford University Press, 2012.

Novenson, Matthew V. "Paul's Former Occupation in *Ioudaismos*." Pages 24–39 in *Galatians and Christian Theology: Justification, the Gospel, and Ethics in Paul's Letters*. Edited by Mark W. Elliot, Scott J. Hafemann, N. T. Wright, and John Frederick. Grand Rapids: Baker Academic, 2014.

Novenson, Matthew V. "The Self-Styled Jew of Romans 2 and the Actual Jews of Romans 9–11." Pages 133–62 in *The So-Called Jew in Paul's Letter to the Romans*. Edited by Rafael Rodríguez and Matthew Thiessen. Minneapolis: Fortress, 2016.

Novenson, Matthew V. "Whither the Paul within Judaism Schule?" *JJMJS* 5 (2018): 79–88.

Novenson, Matthew V. "Did Paul Abandon Either Judaism or Monotheism?" Pages 239–59 in *The New Cambridge Companion to St Paul*. Edited by Bruce W. Longenecker. Cambridge: Cambridge University Press, 2020.

Novenson, Matthew V. "What Eschatological Pilgrimage of the Gentiles?" Pages 61–73 in *Israel and the Nations: Paul's Gospel in the Context of Jewish Expectation*. Edited by František Ábel. Lanham, MD: Lexington Books/Fortress Academic, 2021.

Oakes, Peter. *Galatians*. PCNT. Grand Rapids: Baker Academic, 2015.

Oepke, Albrecht. *Der Brief Des Paulus an Die Galater*. THKNT 9. Berlin: Evangelische Verlagsanstalt, 1960.

Økland, Jorunn. "Pauline Letters." Pages 314–32 in *The Oxford Handbook of New Testament, Gender, and Sexuality*. Edited by Benjamin H. Dunning. New York: Oxford University Press, 2019.

Olyan, Saul M. *Rites and Rank: Hierarchy in Biblical Representations of Cult*. Princeton: Princeton University Press, 2000.

Ophir, Adi, and Ishay Rosen-Zvi. *Goy: Israel's Multiple Others and the Birth of the Gentile*. Oxford: Oxford University Press, 2018.

Paige, Terence. "Who Believes in 'Spirit'? πνεῦμα in Pagan Usage and Implications for the Gentile Christian Mission." *HTR* 95 (2002): 417–36.

Palmer, Carmen. *Converts in the Dead Sea Scrolls: The Gēr and Mutable Ethnicity*. STDJ 126. Leiden: Brill, 2018.

Parkin, Harry. "Romans i. 13–15." *ExpTim* 79 (1967): 95.

Parks, Sara. "When a Hat Isn't a Hat: Continuing the Tradition of Hebrew Penis Euphemisms in a Hellenistic Anti-Hellenistic Text." Paper presented at the Sheffield Institute for Interdisciplinary Biblical Studies Research Seminar. Sheffield, UK, February 2021.

Petrey, Taylor G. "Semen Stains: Seminal Procreation and the Patrilineal Genealogy of Salvation in Tertullian." *JECS* 22 (2014): 343–72.

Pilhofer, Peter. *Philippi: Band 2, Katalog der Inschriften von Philippi*. 2nd ed. WUNT 119. Tübingen: Mohr Siebeck, 2009.

Punch, John David. "Σκυβαλα Happens: Edification from a Four-Letter Word in the Word of God?" *BT* 65 (2015): 369–84.

Rabello, Alfredo Mordechai. "The Ban on Circumcision as a Cause of Bar Kokhba's Rebellion." *IsLR* 29 (1995): 176–214.

Rabens, Volker. *The Holy Spirit and Ethics in Paul*. WUNT 2/283. Tübingen: Mohr Siebeck, 2010.

Räisänen, Heikki. *Paul and the Law*. WUNT 29. Tübingen: Mohr Siebeck, 1983.

Räisänen, Heikki. "Galatians 2.16 and Paul's Break with Judaism." *NTS* 31 (1985): 543–53.

Ramsaran, Rollin A. "Paul and Maxims." Pages 429–56 in *Paul in the Greco-Roman World: A Handbook*. Edited by J. Paul Sampley. Harrisburg, PA: Trinity, 2003.

Reumann, John Henry Paul. *Philippians: A New Translation with Introduction and Commentary*. AB 33B. New Haven: Yale University Press, 2008.

Rhoads, David. "Children of Abraham, Children of God: Metaphorical Kinship in Paul's Letter to the Galatians." *CurTM* 31 (2004): 282–97.

Richardson, Peter. *Israel in the Apostolic Church*. SNTSMS 10. Cambridge: Cambridge University Press, 1969.

Ringe, Sharon R. "A Gentile Woman's Story." Pages 65–72 in *Feminist Interpretation of the Bible*. Edited by Letty M. Russell. Oxford: Blackwell, 1985.

Robertson, Paul. "De-Spiritualizing *Pneuma*: Modernity, Religion, and Anachronism in the Study of Paul." *MTSR* 26 (2014): 365–83.

Robinson, D. W. B. "The Circumcision of Titus, and Paul's 'Liberty.'" *ABR* 12 (1964): 24–42.

Robinson, D. W. B. "We Are the Circumcision." *ABR* 15 (1967): 28–35.

Rodríguez, Rafael. *If You Call Yourself a Jew: Reappraising Paul's Letter to the Romans*. Eugene, OR: Cascade, 2014.

Rodríguez, Rafael, and Matthew Thiessen, eds. *The So-Called Jew in Paul's Letter to the Romans*. Minneapolis: Fortress, 2016.

Rosen-Zvi, Ishay, and Adi Ophir. "Paul and the Invention of the Gentiles." *JQR* 105 (2015): 1–41.

Rudolph, David J. "Paul's 'Rule in All the Churches' (1 Cor 7:17–24) and Torah-Defined Ecclesiological Variegation." *SCJR* 5 (2010): 1–24.

Rudolph, David J. *A Jew to the Jews: Jewish Contours of Pauline Flexibility in 1 Corinthians 9:19–23*. 2nd ed. Eugene, OR: Pickwick, 2016.

Runesson, Anders. "Particularistic Judaism and Universalistic Christianity? Some Critical Remarks on Terminology and Theology." *ST* 53 (2000): 55–75.

Runesson, Anders. "Inventing Christian Identity: Paul, Ignatius, and Theodosius I." Pages 59–92 in *Exploring Early Christian Identity*. Edited by Bengt Holmberg. WUNT 226. Tübingen: Mohr Siebeck, 2008.

Runesson, Anders. "Paul's Rule in All the *Ekklēsiai*." Pages 214–23 in *Introduction to Messianic Judaism: Its Ecclesial Context and Biblical Foundations*. Edited by David Rudolph and Joel Willits. Grand Rapids: Zondervan, 2013.

Runesson, Anders. "The Question of Terminology: The Architecture of Contemporary Discussions on Paul." Pages 53–77 in *Paul within Judaism: Restoring the First-Century Context to the Apostle*. Edited by Mark D. Nanos and Magnus Zetterholm. Minneapolis: Fortress, 2015.

Runesson, Anders. "Entering a Synagogue with Paul: First-Century Torah Observance." Pages 11–26 in *Torah Ethics and Early Christian Identity*. Edited by Susan J. Wendel and David M. Miller. Grand Rapids: Eerdmans, 2016.

Runesson, Anders, and Daniel M. Gurtner, eds. *Matthew within Judaism: Israel and the Nations in the First Gospel*. ECL 27. Atlanta: SBL Press, 2020.

Sambursky, Samuel. *Physics of the Stoics*. London: Routledge & Kegan Paul, 1959.

Sanday, William, and Arthur C. Headlam. *A Critical and Exegetical Commentary on the Epistle to the Romans*. 5th ed. ICC. Edinburgh: T&T Clark, 1977.

Sanders, E. P. *Paul and Palestinian Judaism: A Comparison of Patterns of Religion*. Philadelphia: Fortress, 1977.

Sanders, E. P. *Paul, the Law, and the Jewish People*. Philadelphia: Fortress, 1983.

Sanders, E. P. *Jesus and Judaism*. Philadelphia: Fortress, 1985.

Sanders, E. P. "Jewish Associations with Gentiles and Galatians 2:11–14." Pages 170–88 in *The Conversation Continues: Studies in Paul & John in Honor of J. Louis Martyn*. Edited by Robert T. Fortna and Beverly R. Gaventa. Nashville: Abingdon, 1990.

Sanders, E. P. *Jewish Law from Jesus to the Mishnah: Five Studies*. London: SCM, 1990.

Sanders, E. P. *Paul: The Apostle's Life, Letters, and Thought*. Minneapolis: Fortress, 2015.

Sandnes, Karl Olav. *Belly and Body in the Pauline Epistles*. SNTSMS 120. Cambridge: Cambridge University Press, 2002.

Sanfridson, Martin. "Paul and Sacrifice in Corinth: Rethinking Paul's Views on Gentile Cults in 1 Corinthians 8 and 10." PhD diss., McMaster University, 2022.

Sasson, Jack M. "Circumcision in the Ancient Near East." *JBL* 5 (1966): 473–76.

Schliesser, Benjamin. *Abraham's Faith in Romans 4: Paul's Concept of Faith in Light of the History of Reception of Genesis 15:6*. WUNT 2/224. Tübingen: Mohr Siebeck, 2007.

Schreiner, Thomas R. "Circumcision: An Entrée into 'Newness' in Pauline Thought." PhD diss., Fuller Theological Seminary, 1983.

Schreiner, Thomas R. "Paul and Perfect Obedience to the Law: An Evaluation of the View of E. P. Sanders." *WTJ* 47 (1985): 246–78.

Schreiner, Thomas R. "The Abolition and Fulfillment of the Law in Paul." *JSNT* 35 (1989): 47–74.

Schreiner, Thomas R. *Romans*. BECNT. Grand Rapids: Baker Academic, 1998.

Schreiner, Thomas R. *Galatians*. ZECNT. Grand Rapids: Zondervan, 2010.

Schüssler Fiorenza, Elisabeth. *In Memory of Her: A Feminist Theological Reconstruction of Christian Origins*. London: SCM, 1983.

Schwartz, Daniel R. "Ends Meet: Qumran and Paul on Circumcision." Pages 295–307 in *The Dead Sea Scrolls And Pauline Literature*. Edited by Jean-Sébastien Rey. STDJ 102. Leiden: Brill, 2013.

Schwartz, Joshua. "Dogs in Jewish Society in the Second Temple Period and in the Time of the Mishnah and Talmud." *Journal of Jewish Studies* 55 (2004): 246–77.

Schweitzer, Albert. *Die Mystik des Apostels Paulus*. Tübingen: Mohr Siebeck, 1954.

Schweitzer, Albert. *The Mysticism of Paul the Apostle*. Translated by William Montgomery. Baltimore: Johns Hopkins University Press, 1998.

Schweizer, Eduard. ""Der Jude im Verborgenen…, dessen Lob nicht von Menschen, sondern von Gott kommt": Zu Röm 2,28f und Mt 6,1–18." Pages 115–24 in *Neues Testament und Kirche: Für Rudolf Schnackenburg*. Edited by Joachim Gnilka. Freiburg: Herder, 1974.

Sechrest, Love L. *A Former Jew: Paul and the Dialectics of Race*. LNTS 410. London: T&T Clark, 2009.

Segal, Alan F. *Paul the Convert: The Apostolate and Apostasy of Saul the Pharisee*. New Haven: Yale University Press, 1990.

Seifrid, Mark A. *Justification by Faith: The Origin and Development of a Central Pauline Theme*. NovTSup 68. Leiden: Brill, 1992.

Sharp, Matthew T. *Divination and Philosophy in the Letters of Paul*. Edinburgh Studies in Religion in Antiquity. Edinburgh: Edinburgh University Press, 2022.

Sharp, Matthew T. "Courting Daimons in Corinth: Daimonic Partnerships, Cosmic Hierarchies and Divine Jealousy in Paul." Pages 112–29 in *Demons in Judaism and Christianity: Characters, Characteristics, and Demonic Exegesis*. Edited by Hector M. Patmore and Josef Lössl. AGJU 113. Leiden: Brill, 2022.

Siebenthal, Heinrich von. *Ancient Greek Grammar for the Study of the New Testament*. Oxford: Peter Lang, 2019.

Silva, Moisés. *Philippians*. 2nd ed. BECNT. Grand Rapids: Baker Academic, 2005.

Simkovich, Malka Z. "Interpretations of Abraham's Circumcision in Early Christianity and Genesis Rabbah." Pages 249–68 in *New Vistas on Early Judaism and Christianity: From Enoch to Montréal and Back*. Edited by Lorenzo DiTommaso and Gerbern S. Oegema. London: Bloomsbury T&T Clark, 2016.

Skoda, Françoise. *Médecine ancienne et métaphore: Le vocabulaire de l'anatomie et de la pathologie en grec ancien*. Paris: Peeters/Selaf, 1988.

Sloan, Paul T. "Paul's Jewish Addressee in Rom 2–4: Revisiting Recent Conversations." *JTS* (forthcoming).

Smallwood, E. Mary. *The Jews under Roman Rule: From Pompey to Diocletian.* SJLA 20. Leiden: Brill, 1976.
Smit, Peter-Ben. "In Search of Real Circumcision: Ritual Failure and Circumcision in Paul." *JSNT* 40 (2017): 73–100.
Smith, David Raymond. *Hand This Man Over to Satan: Curse, Exclusion, and Salvation in 1 Corinthians 5.* LNTS 386. London: T&T Clark, 2009.
Soon, Isaac T. "'In Strength' Not 'by Force': Re-Reading the Circumcision of the Uncircumcised ἐν ἰσχύι in 1 Macc 2:46." *JSP* 29 (2020): 149–67.
Soon, Isaac T. "Satan and Circumcision: The Devil as the ἄγγελος πονηρός in Barn 9:4." *VC* (2021): 1–13.
Staden, Heinrich von. *Herophilus: The Art of Medicine in Early Alexandria.* Cambridge: Cambridge University Press, 1989.
Steiner, Richard C. "Incomplete Circumcision in Egypt and Edom: Jeremiah (9:24–25) in the Light of Josephus and Jonckheere." *JBL* 118 (1999): 497–505.
Stendahl, Krister. *Paul Among Jews and Gentiles, and Other Essays.* Philadelphia: Fortress, 1976.
Stendahl, Krister. *Final Account: Paul's Letter to the Romans.* Minneapolis: Fortress, 1995.
Stern, Josef. "Maimonides on the Covenant of Circumcision and the Unity of God." Pages 131–54 in *The Midrashic Imagination: Jewish Exegesis, Thought, and History.* Edited by Michael Fishbane. Albany: State University of New York Press, 1993.
Still, Todd D. "(Im)Perfection: Reading Philippians 3.5–6 in Light of the Number Seven." *NTS* 60 (2014): 139–48.
Stowers, Stanley K. *The Diatribe and Paul's Letter to the Romans.* SBLDS 57. Chico, CA: Scholars Press, 1981.
Stowers, Stanley K. "ἐκ πίστεως and διὰ τῆς πίστεως in Romans 3:30." *JBL* 108 (1989): 665–74.
Stowers, Stanley K. *A Rereading of Romans: Justice, Jews, and Gentiles.* New Haven: Yale University Press, 1994.
Stowers, Stanley K. "What Is 'Pauline Participation in Christ'?" Pages 352–71 in *Redefining First-Century Jewish and Christian Identities: Essays in Honor of Ed Parish Sanders.* Edited by Fabian E. Udoh, Susannah Heschel, Mark Chancey, and Gregory Tatum. CJAn 16. Notre Dame: University of Notre Dame Press, 2008.
Stowers, Stanley K. "The Dilemma of Paul's Physics: Features Stoic-Platonist or Platonist-Stoic?" Pages 231–53 in *From Stoicism to Platonism: The Development of Philosophy, 100 BCE–100 CE.* Edited by Troels Engberg-Pedersen. Cambridge: Cambridge University Press, 2017.
Suh, Michael K. W. "τὸ πνεῦμα 1 Corinthians 5:5: A Reconsideration of Patristic Exegesis." *VC* 72 (2018): 121–41.
Sumney, Jerry L. *"Servants of Satan", "False Brothers" and Other Opponents of Paul.* JSNTSup 188. Sheffield: Sheffield Academic, 1999.
Sumney, Jerry L. ed. *Reading Paul's Letter to the Romans.* RBS 73. Atlanta: Society of Biblical Literature, 2012.
Sweet, Waldo E. *Sport and Recreation in Ancient Greece: A Sourcebook with Translations.* Oxford: Oxford University Press, 1987.
Tatum, Gregory. *New Chapters in the Life of Paul: The Relative Chronology of His Career.* CBQMS 41. Washington, DC: Catholic Biblical Association of America, 2006.
Temkin, Owsei. *The Double Face of Janus and Other Essays in the History of Medicine.* Baltimore: Johns Hopkins University Press, 1977.
Thiessen, Matthew. "The Text of Genesis 17:14." *JBL* 128 (2009): 625–42.

Thiessen, Matthew. *Contesting Conversion: Genealogy, Circumcision, and Identity in Ancient Judaism and Christianity.* New York: Oxford University Press, 2011.
Thiessen, Matthew. "Gentiles as Impure Animals in the Writings of Early Christ Followers." Pages 19–32 in *Perceiving the Other in Ancient Judaism and Early Christianity.* Edited by Michal Bar-Asher Siegal, Wolfgang Grünstäudl, and Matthew Thiessen. WUNT 394. Tübingen: Mohr Siebeck, 2017.
Thiessen, Matthew. *Paul and the Gentile Problem.* New York: Oxford University Press, 2016.
Thiessen, Matthew. "Paul's So-Called Jew and Lawless Lawkeeping." Pages 59–83 in *The So-Called Jew in Paul's Letter to the Romans.* Edited by Rafael Rodríguez and Matthew Thiessen. Minneapolis: Fortress, 2016.
Thiessen, Matthew. "Paul, Essentialism, and the Jewish Law: In Conversation with Christine Hayes." *JSPL* 7 (2018): 80–85.
Thiselton, Anthony C. *The First Epistle to the Corinthians.* NIGNT. Grand Rapids: Eerdmans, 2000.
Thorsteinsson, Runar M. "Paul's Missionary Duty Towards Gentiles in Rome: A Note on the Punctuation and Syntax of Rom 1.13–15." *NTS* 48 (2002): 531–47.
Thorsteinsson, Runar M. *Paul's Interlocutor in Romans 2: Function and Identity in the Context of Ancient Epistolography.* ConBNT 40. Stockholm: Almqvist & Wiksell, 2003.
Thorsteinsson, Runar M., Matthew Thiessen, and Rafael Rodríguez. "Paul's Interlocutor in Romans: The Problem of Identification." Pages 1–37 in *The So-Called Jew in Paul's Letter to the Romans.* Edited by Rafael Rodríguez and Matthew Thiessen. Minneapolis: Fortress, 2016.
Tobin, Thomas H. "What Shall We Say That Abraham Found? The Controversy behind Romans 4." *HTR* 88 (1995): 437–52.
Tomson, Peter J. *Paul and the Jewish Law: Halakha in the Letters of the Apostle to the Gentiles.* CRINT 1. Assen: Van Gorcum, 1990.
Tomson, Peter J. "Halakhah in the New Testament: A Research Overview." Pages 135–206 in *The New Testament and Rabbinic Literature.* Edited by Reimund Bieringer, Florentino García Martínez, Didier Pollefeyt, and Peter J. Tomson. JSJSup 136. Leiden: Brill, 2010.
Tong, M Adryael. *Difference and Circumcision: Bodily Discourse and the Parting of the Ways.* Oxford: Oxford University Press, forthcoming.
Townsend, Philippa. "Who Were the First Christians? Jews, Gentiles and the *Christianoi.*" Pages 212–30 in *Heresy and Identity in Late Antiquity.* Edited by Eduard Iricinschi and Holger M. Zellentin. TSAJ 119. Tübingen: Mohr Siebeck, 2008.
Tucker, J. Brian. *Remain in Your Calling: Paul and the Continuation of Social Identities in 1 Corinthians.* Eugene, OR: Pickwick, 2011.
Tucker, J. Brian. *Reading Romans After Supersessionism: The Continuation of Jewish Covenantal Identity.* NTAS 6. Eugene, OR: Cascade, 2018.
Turner, Nigel. *Grammatical Insights into the New Testament.* Edinburgh: T&T Clark, 1965.
Tutrone, Fabio. "Barking at the Threshold: Cicero, Lucretius, and the Ambiguous Status of Dogs in Roman Culture." Pages 73–102 in *Impious Dogs, Haughty Foxes and Exquisite Fish: Evaluative Perception and Interpretation of Animals in Ancient and Medieval Mediterranean Thought.* Edited by Tristan Schmidt and Johannes Pahlitzsch. Berlin: de Gruyter, 2019.
Van Zile, Matthew P. "The Sons of Noah and the Sons of Abraham: The Origins of Noahide Law." *JSJ* 48 (2017): 386–417.
Vincent, Marvin R. *A Critical and Exegetical Commentary on the Epistles to the Philippians and to Philemon.* ICC. Edinburgh: T&T Clark, 1897.

Wagner, J. Ross. "The Christ, Servant of Jew and Gentile: A Fresh Approach to Romans 15:8–9." *JBL* 116 (1997): 473–85.
Walker Jr., William O. "Why Paul Went to Jerusalem: The Interpretation of Galatians 2:1–5." *CBQ* 54 (1992): 503–10.
Wasserman, Emma. *Apocalypse as Holy War: Divine Politics and Polemics in the Letters of Paul.* AYBRL. New Haven: Yale University Press, 2018.
Watson, Francis. *Paul, Judaism and the Gentiles.* SNTSMS 56. Cambridge: Cambridge University Press, 1986.
Watson, Francis. *Paul and the Hermeneutics of Faith.* London: T&T Clark, 2004.
Weiss, Daniel H. "Born into Covenantal Salvation? Baptism and Birth in Early Christianity and Classical Rabbinic Judaism." *JSQ* 24 (2017): 318–38.
Wells, Kyle B. *Grace and Agency in Paul and Second Temple Judaism: Interpreting the Transformation of the Heart.* NovTSup 157. Leiden: Brill, 2015.
Werline, Rodney. "The Transformation of Pauline Arguments in Justin Martyr's *Dialogue with Trypho*." *HTR* 92 (1999): 79–93.
White, Benjamin L. *Remembering Paul: Ancient and Modern Contests over the Image of the Apostle.* New York: Oxford University Press, 2014.
Williams, Demetrius K. *Enemies of the Cross of Christ: There Terminology of the Cross and Conflict in Philippians.* JSNTSup 223. Sheffield: Sheffield Academic, 2002.
Williams, Sam K. *Jesus' Death as Saving Event: The Background and Origin of a Concept.* HDR 2. Missoula, MT: Scholars Press, 1975.
Williams, Sam K. "The 'Righteousness of God' in Romans." *JBL* 99 (1980): 241–90.
Windsor, Lionel J. *Paul and the Vocation of Israel: How Paul's Jewish Identity Informs His Apostolic Ministry, with Special Reference to Romans.* BZNW 205. Berlin: de Gruyter, 2014.
Winer, G. B. *A Grammar of the NT Diction.* Translated by Edward Masson. Edinburgh: T&T Clark, 1860.
Winter, Bruce W. *Seek the Welfare of the City: Christians as Benefactors and Citizens.* Grand Rapids: Eerdmans, 1994.
Witherington III, Ben. *Grace in Galatia: A Commentary on St. Paul's Letter to the Galatians.* Grand Rapids: Eerdmans, 1998.
Witherington III, Ben, and Darlene Hyatt. *Paul's Letter to the Romans: A Socio-Rhetorical Commentary.* Grand Rapids: Eerdmans, 2004.
Wöhrle, Jakob. "The Integrative Function of the Law of Circumcision." Pages 71–87 in *The Foreigner and the Law: Perspectives from the Hebrew Bible and the Ancient Near East.* Edited by Reinhard Achenbach, Rainer Albertz, and Jakob Wöhrle. BZABR 16. Wiesbaden: Harrassowitz, 2011.
Wolter, Michael. *Paulus: Ein Grundriss seiner Theologie.* Neukirchen-Vluyn: Neukirchener Verlag, 2011.
Wright, N. T. *Paul and the Faithfulness of God.* 2 vols. Minneapolis: Fortress, 2013.
Wright, N. T. "Paul and the Patriarch: The Role of Abraham in Romans 4." *JSNT* 35 (2013): 207–41.
Wyschogrod, Michael. "A Jewish Postscript." Pages 179–87 in *Encountering Jesus: A Debate on Christology.* Edited by Stephen T. Davis. Atlanta: John Knox, 1988.
Yarbro Collins, Adela. *Mark: A Commentary.* Hermeneia. Minneapolis: Fortress, 2007.
Yates, John W. *The Spirit and Creation in Paul.* WUNT 2/251. Tübingen: Mohr Siebeck, 2008.
Yoshiko Reed, Annette. *Jewish-Christianity and the History of Judaism.* TSAJ 171. Tübingen: Mohr Siebeck, 2018.
Young, Stephen L. "Paul's Ethnic Discourse on 'Faith': Christ's Faithfulness and Gentile Access to the Judean God in Romans 3:21–5:1." *HTR* 108 (2015): 30–51.
Young, Stephen L. "Ethnic Ethics: Paul's Eschatological Myth of Jewish Sin." *NTS* (forthcoming).

Zahn, Theodor. *Der Brief des Paulus an die Römer.* Leipzig: Deichert, 1910.
Zetterholm, Karin H. "The Question of Assumptions: Torah Observance in the First Century." Pages 79–103 in *Paul within Judaism: Restoring the First-Century Context to the Apostle.* Edited by Mark D. Nanos and Magnus Zetterholm. Minneapolis: Fortress, 2015.
Zetterholm, Magnus. *The Formation of Christianity in Antioch: A Social-Scientific Approach to the Separation Between Judaism and Christianity.* London: Routledge, 2003.
Zetterholm, Magnus. *Approaches to Paul: A Student's Guide to Recent Scholarship.* Minneapolis: Fortress, 2009.
Zetterholm, Magnus. "Paul within Judaism: The State of the Questions." Pages 31–51 in *Paul within Judaism: Restoring the First-Century Context to the Apostle.* Edited by Mark D. Nanos and Magnus Zetterholm. Minneapolis: Fortress, 2015.

Index of Names

Abusch, Ra'anan 114 f.
Adams, James N. 32
Albertz, Rainer 72
Amir, Yehoshua 107

Barclay, John M. G. 6, 8, 10, 48, 56 f., 59, 61 f., 71, 79, 84, 86 f., 93, 122, 153, 158, 161, 163, 166 f., 170, 173, 175, 177, 180, 182, 185, 191, 194
Barrett, C. K. 23 f., 27, 36, 41 f., 63 f.
Barrier, Jeremy W. 77
Bartchy, S. Scott 25
Bartelt, Andrew H. 38
Batement IV, Herbert W. 127, 131, 139, 141
Baumgarten, Albert I. 112
Baur, Ferdinand Christian 5, 7, 52, 63, 119, 126, 182
Beker, J. Christiaan 159
Berkley, Timothy W. 159, 161, 168, 172 f., 175 f.
Bernat, David A. 70–73, 175
Bernier, Jonathan 19
Betz, Hans Dieter 65, 69, 89, 94 f., 113, 119
Bickerman, Elias J. 111
Bird, Michael F. 40, 125
Bisschops, Ralph 8, 172, 175 f.
Blanton IV, Thomas R. 12, 31, 97, 114
Blaschke, Andreas 11 f., 15 f., 22, 27, 33, 72–74, 86, 100, 106, 113 f., 120, 125, 143, 161 f., 175, 185 f., 188, 191
Bockmuehl, Markus 42 f., 50, 125, 129, 134 f., 137 f., 140 f., 143, 145
Boer, Martinus C. de 40, 63, 85, 89, 93, 110, 118, 120 f.
Bokovoy, David E. 68
Bonnard, Pierre 127, 140, 145
Borgen, Peder 100–102
Boyarin, Daniel 6, 37, 111, 137, 161, 163, 166, 170
Boylan, Michael 86
Braxton, Brad Ronnell 24 f., 34
Bremmer, Jan M. 75
Bruce, F. F. 56, 79, 86, 89, 100
Bryan, Christopher 33, 144, 183

Buell, Denise Kimber 35, 75
Bultmann, Rudolf 5, 7, 59, 151
Burkitt, F. C. 51
Burnett, David A. 77
Burton, Ernest de Witt 51 f., 100, 106, 120
Butticaz, Simon 92

Campbell, Douglas A. 19, 100 f., 103–105, 109
Campbell, William S. 10, 23 f., 39 f., 57, 97 f.
Carleton Paget, James 113, 169, 198
Cerfaux, Lucien 190
Chabon, Michael V, 202
Charles, R. H. 70
Choi, Hung-Sik 40, 94 f.
Christiansen, Ellen Juhl 65, 71, 74, 109
Ciampa, Roy E. 36, 43
Cohen, Shaye J. D. 14, 17, 32 f., 74, 101, 107, 144, 157
Collange, Jean-François 125, 141
Collins, John J. 175 f.
Collins, John N. 193 f.
Collman, Ryan D. 127, 129
Concannon, Cavan W. 35
Craigie, Peter C. 175
Cranfield, C. E. B. 149, 151, 155, 158, 164, 169, 171 f., 178 f., 181, 185, 188 f., 191
Cranford, Michael 87, 184 f., 188

Dahl, Nils Alstrup 178
Das, A. Andrew 30, 89, 91, 149–151, 191
Dawes, Gregory W. 26
Debouxhtay, Pierre 116
Deming, Will 37
deSilva, David A. 64, 81, 87, 89, 110
Di Mattei, Steven 64
Dingwall, Eric John 133
Donaldson, Terence L. 50, 61, 64, 99 f., 106–109, 182, 191, 194
Donfried, Karl P. 83, 149
Dover, K. J. 31
Drake, Susanna 200
Drinkard Jr., Joel F. 175

Dunn, James D. G. 8, 24f., 36, 41, 43, 54, 56–58, 60f., 63, 93f., 96, 99–101, 110, 112f., 118, 121, 125, 127, 129, 137, 139, 143, 149, 151, 155, 158, 164, 168, 170, 174f., 177f., 180–182, 184f., 188f., 191
Dunne, John Anthony 91

Eastman, Susan G. 35, 67, 90f., 143
Edwards, James R. 113, 115
Ehrensperger, Kathy 9, 51f., 114, 116–118, 136
Eisenbaum, Pamela 9, 42–44, 139, 162, 180, 182, 185
Elliott, Neil 155, 177
Elliott, Susan 115
Emmett, Grace 66
Engberg-Pedersen, Troels 76–80, 82f.
Eschel, Ester 188
Esler, Philip F. 52–54, 71, 150f., 181, 189
Eyl, Jennifer 19, 145f.

Fee, Gordon D. 22, 24, 27f., 33f., 36, 125, 127, 129, 131, 134f., 137f., 140–143, 145
Feldman, Louis H. 32
Ferguson, Everett 169
Fitzmyer, Joseph A. 24, 27f., 34, 36, 151, 162, 164, 171, 174, 177, 179, 181f., 185f., 188f., 191
Foster, Paul 175
Franco, Cristiana 128, 131
Frankfurter, David 157
Fredriksen, Paula 9f., 18–20, 27, 34–36, 43, 48–50, 52, 54f., 86, 106, 110, 112, 122, 139, 150, 155, 176f., 182, 191
Fridrichsen, Anton 161, 173
Funk, Robert W. 121

Gallas, Sven 100
Garland, David E. 25, 36, 129, 135
Garroway, Joshua D. 50, 100, 104f., 125, 143, 150, 153f., 159, 165–168, 177–179, 184f., 192–194
Gaston, Lloyd 20, 156, 178, 181, 185, 190–192, 194
Gathercole, Simon J. 5, 155, 158, 161, 163, 181
Gaventa, Beverly R. 66
Gifford, E. H. 192f.
Goldingay, John 171

Goodman, Martin 106, 120, 122
Grayston, Kenneth 127, 139, 143
Greenfield, Jonas C. 188
Gregerman, Adam 24
Gunther, John J. 126, 140
Gurtner, Daniel M. 9

Hahm, David E. 78
Hall, Robert G. 27, 31f.
Hansen, G. Walter 90f.
Hardin, Justin K. 48, 99, 104–110, 122
Harnack, Adolf von 29
Haworth, Marina 132
Hayes, Christine E. 14, 18, 34, 41, 43, 74, 83, 153, 165, 168
Hays, Richard B. 35, 63–65, 71, 81, 90f., 133, 181f., 184, 187
Headlam, Arthur C. 185, 189, 192
Heath, J. M. F. 170, 172–175
Heil, John Paul 136
Henderson, Jeffrey 131–133
Hermisson, Hans-Jürgen 175
Hewitt, J. Thomas 76
Hezser, Catherine 71
Hirsch, Emanuel 120
Hodges, Frederick M. 16, 31, 97, 114, 132f.
Holloway, Paul A. 94, 127, 134, 140
Holmberg, Bengt 54
Horn, Friedrich Wilhelm 28, 40, 78, 113f., 122, 127, 129, 136, 159, 161f.
Horrell, David. 37
Horsley, Richard A. 33
Houten, Christiana van 72
Howard, George 180
Hubing, Jeff 96
Hübner, Hans 106
Hultin, Jeremy F. 113f., 133
Hurtado, Larry W. 199
Huttunen, Niko 25, 43
Hvalvik, Reidar 199

Isaac, Benjamin 25

Jackson-McCabe, Matt 10
Jacobs, Andrew S. 198–200, 202
Jewett, Robert 119, 140f., 143, 149, 156, 163f., 171, 177, 179–182, 184–186, 188–191

Index of Names

Jipp, Joshua W.   5 f., 180 f., 184 f., 187 f.
Johnson Hodge, Caroline   16 f., 27, 75 f., 79, 85, 94, 180, 185
Jonckheere, Frans   32
Jónsson, Jakob   133

Kapparis, Konstantinos K.   132
Käsemann, Ernst   6, 161 f., 182 f.
Keener, Craig S.   49 f., 52, 72, 89 f., 93, 99, 110, 113, 118, 120
Kelley, Page H.   175
King, Justin.   151 f., 154 f., 177
Kitchell Jr., Kenneth F.   128
Klijn, A. F. J.   127, 134, 140 f.
Klinghardt, Matthias   77
Kobel, Esther   112
Koester, Helmut   131, 134, 140 f.
Kruse, Heinz   38
Kuefler, Mathew   113, 115

Laato, Timo   101
Le Déaut, Roger   175
Lemke, Werner E.   175 f.
Levison, John R.   78
Lightfoot, J. B.   29, 53, 89, 120
Linebaugh, Jonathan A.   8
Livesey, Nina E.   6, 13, 15 f., 28, 143, 150, 161, 165 f., 175, 186, 188, 190, 199
Longenecker, Richard N.   49, 52, 87, 90, 100, 106, 113, 119–121, 149, 156, 163, 167, 174, 177, 189, 194
Lüdemann, Gerd   5
Luther, Martin   5

Maccoby, Hyam   136 f.
Marchal, Joseph A.   115
Marcus, Joel   16 f., 186, 191
Martin, Dale B.   31, 76, 78, 83, 154
Martin, Ralph P.   125, 127, 129, 134 f., 137, 140 f., 143, 145
Martin, Troy   69, 77, 87
Martyn, J. Louis   47, 56 f., 65–69, 79, 93, 95–97, 99 f., 103, 110, 113
Mason, Steve   107, 111
Matera, Frank J.   64
Matlock, R. Barry   15, 34, 87
McKnight, Scot   106

McMurray, Patrick   192
Mearns, Chris   140 f.
Meiser, Martin   117
Miller, Geoffrey David   128
Mimouni, Simon Claude   12 f., 15, 104, 114, 125, 134, 161 f.
Mininger, Marcus A.   160, 164, 169, 173 f., 176
Mitchell, Margaret M.   19
Montefiore, C. G.   7
Moo, Douglas J.   56 f., 81, 89, 158, 161–164, 166, 169, 176, 178 f., 181, 185
Moore, George Foot   7
Moorthy, Asha K.   13 f., 51
Mortensen, Jacob P. B.   152, 154 f., 158, 164, 166, 177–179, 184 f., 192
Munck, Johannes   7, 10, 27 f., 48, 51–53, 106, 120, 149 f.
Murphy, James G.   72
Murray, Michele   27 f., 107, 118–121, 126, 139, 153, 157
Mußner, Franz   87, 89, 103, 113
Myers, Alicia D.   82

Nanos, Mark D.   9, 24, 35, 43, 47, 52, 54 f., 65, 119 f., 126–129, 131, 133 f., 136, 138, 140 f., 150, 152, 163, 166–168, 176 f., 182
Nasrallah, Laura Salah   19, 24
Neander, August   120
Neutel, Karin B.   16 f., 84, 113 f., 163, 165, 185–190, 196
Niehoff, Maren R.   200
Nongbri, Brent.   35
Novenson, Matthew V.   9, 19, 50, 98, 107, 111 f., 153, 156–160, 164, 166, 169, 171 f., 179, 191, 194 f.

Oakes, Peter   65, 110, 119
Oepke, Albrecht   113
Økland, Jorunn   16 f., 186
Olyan, Saul M.   71 f., 118
Ophir, Adi   18, 72

Paige, Terence   78
Palmer, Carmen   74, 173, 175
Parkin, Harry   150
Parks, Sara.   30
Petrey, Taylor G.   83

Pilhofer, Peter. 142
Punch, John David 133

Rabello, Alfredo Mordechai 114 f.
Rabens, Volker 77
Räisänen, Heikki 6 f., 37, 40, 136, 143, 166
Ramsaran, Rollin A. 37
Reumann, John Henry Paul 94, 125, 127, 134, 142 f., 145
Rhoads, David 76
Richardson, Peter 5, 27 f., 35, 118–120, 125, 143
Ringe, Sharon R. 130
Robertson, Paul 76
Robinson, D. W. B. 51, 103, 145
Rodríguez, Rafael 150–155, 157–160, 163 f., 166, 177 f., 180 f., 184 f., 187, 189, 191
Rosen-Zvi, Ishay 18, 72
Rosner, Brian S. 36, 43
Rudolph, David J. 24, 33, 38 f., 42, 98, 108, 144
Runesson, Anders 7, 9, 19, 23, 26 f., 42 f., 61, 86, 176

Sambursky, Samuel 79
Sanday, William 185, 189, 192
Sanders, E. P. 6, 8, 19, 22, 24, 26, 41, 49 f., 53–55, 57, 60, 81, 86 f., 93, 100, 106, 143, 156, 181
Sandnes, Karl Olav 140
Sanfridson, Martin 83
Sasson, Jack M. 32
Schliesser, Benjamin 184 f.
Schreiner, Thomas R. 6, 11, 15, 86, 89, 134, 155, 158, 161–164, 181, 185
Schüssler Fiorenza, Elisabeth 37
Schwartz, Daniel R. 74
Schwartz, Joshua. 128 f.
Schweitzer, Albert 27–29, 77, 81 f., 84, 123
Schweizer, Eduard 173
Sechrest, Love L. 75
Segal, Alan F. 104
Seifrid, Mark A. 82
Sharp, Matthew T. 19, 85, 160, 174, 191
Siebenthal, Heinrich von 109, 179
Silva, Moisés 129, 141, 143
Simkovich, Malka Z. 183
Skoda, Françoise 131

Sloan, Paul T. 153, 158, 160
Smallwood, E. Mary. 114
Smit, Peter-Ben 81, 115, 127, 135, 139, 141 f., 145, 161, 165
Smith, David Raymond 83
Soon, Isaac T. 94, 111, 133, 174, 198
Staden, Heinrich von 86
Steiner, Richard C. 73
Stendahl, Krister 7, 10, 185
Stern, Josef 101
Still, Todd D. 146
Stone, Michael E. 188
Stowers, Stanley K. 76 f., 79, 149–152, 155, 158 f., 162 f., 166, 168, 171, 174 f., 177, 179–181, 183–185, 190 f.
Suh, Michael K. W. 83
Sumney, Jerry L. 119, 149 f.
Sweet, Waldo E. 133

Tatum, Gregory 19
Temkin, Owsei 27, 78
Thate, Michael J. 5 f.
Thiessen, Matthew 14 f., 18, 27 f., 32–34, 42–44, 64 f., 67 f., 70, 72–80, 88, 90, 94, 100, 102, 106–111, 119–121, 123, 130, 135, 139, 144–146, 150, 153–155, 158–160, 163–167, 172, 175–178, 184, 189, 195
Thiselton, Anthony C. 25, 27, 31, 36, 84, 141
Thorsteinsson, Runar M. 149–154, 156 f., 160, 164–168, 174, 177, 179
Tobin, Thomas H. 185, 189 f.
Tomson, Peter J. 23, 26, 42, 44, 54
Tong, M Adryael 17, 73
Townsend, Philippa 9
Tucker, J. Brian 22–24, 27, 39, 42, 150, 167, 190
Turner, Nigel 182
Tutrone, Fabio 128, 131

Van Zile, Matthew P. 43 f.
Vincent, Marvin R. 137

Wagner, J. Ross 191
Walker Jr., William O. 51
Wasserman, Emma 85
Watson, Francis 56–61, 63, 65, 89, 100 f., 109, 127, 134, 140–142

Weiss, Daniel H.   83
Wells, Kyle B.   161, 166, 172f., 175
Werline, Rodney   169
White, Benjamin L.   18
Williams, Demetrius K.   127, 143
Williams, Sam K.   177, 180–182, 191–193
Windsor, Lionel J.   111, 145, 155, 158, 161, 163, 166, 168, 170, 177, 179, 190
Winer, G. B.   38f.
Winter, Bruce W.   31
Witherington III, Ben   64, 106, 114, 149, 172
Wöhrle, Jakob   71
Wolter, Michael   125, 143, 161, 185

Wright, N. T.   8, 35, 37, 42, 77, 94, 125, 143, 161, 166f., 174, 184f., 189
Wyschogrod, Michael   44

Yarbro Collins, Adela   129
Yates, John W.   97
Yoshiko Reed, Annette.   9f.
Young, Stephen L.   75, 153, 158, 180f., 184f., 188f.

Zahn, Theodor   184
Zetterholm, Karin H.   86
Zetterholm, Magnus   7, 9, 31, 49f., 54

Index of Subjects

Abraham   21, 51, 63–72, 74–76, 79–81, 84f., 88, 90f., 110, 122–124, 136, 148, 155f., 163, 165, 167f., 177, 180f., 183–192, 198, 200f.
– circumcision of   13–15, 51, 69, 101, 103, 106–108, 122, 182–190, 198, 201
– promise to   21, 75, 84, 124, 177, 180, 191, 193f., 196
– seed of   63f., 75f., 79f., 85, 110, 122, 156, 183
Abrahamic sonship   48, 71, 81, 94, 97, 102, 109f., 122f., 168, 184
adiaphora   37
agitators   47–49, 55, 60f., 63–68, 85, 87, 90–92, 95–97, 99–103, 112–122, 126, 133, 135, 140, 158
– identity of   119–122
allegory   13, 63f., 66f., 69, 90f., 123
anti-ethnocentric readings of Paul   56–59, 60–61, 123f.
anti-legalist readings of Paul   11f., 56f., 60–62, 86, 123f.
Antioch incident   52–55
Apostolic Council   43f., 48–50, 144

boasting   40, 58, 60, 96–99, 122, 145, 158, 180f.

calling   10, 23–28, 33f., 38f., 43, 104, 112
castration   92, 113–118, 124
Christ
– being in   23, 29, 39, 51, 58, 64, 77, 80–84, 86, 93–95, 97f.
– body of   80, 82–85
circumcision
– and women   17, 199
– as metonym   13, 17, 23, 27f., 45, 97, 143, 191, 196
– as rite of conversion   14f., 33, 65, 71, 106–109
– as seal   13, 51f., 187f., 199, 201
– as sign of the covenant   5, 7, 13, 37, 64, 69–74, 143, 163, 186–189, 199
– ban   114

– benefit of   148, 154, 162f., 165, 173, 177–179, 189, 195, 197
– law of   88f., 112, 165f., 168
– marker of Jewish identity   17, 28–32, 37, 39, 58, 60f., 74, 102, 144, 161, 170, 176, 201
– metaphorical   5, 8, 13, 161, 167, 201
– non-covenantal   70–74, 85f., 118, 144
– of the heart   5f., 8, 11, 13f., 125 137f. 148, 161, 167, 169–176, 192, 195f., 198–201
– on the eighth-day   14f., 21, 22, 69, 71–74, 85, 88, 98, 108f., 112, 120, 123, 126, 137f., 146, 164f.
– power of   40, 92–95
– proselyte   27, 36, 47–49, 51, 58, 65, 68, 106, 108f., 117, 122–124, 126, 139, 142, 146f., 153, 155, 164, 195
– reappropriation of   8, 125
– redefinition of   5f., 8, 21, 37, 125f., 142f., 146 148, 161, 169f., 172, 176 197,
– spiritualization of   5, 8, 11, 13, 125, 171, 175, 197
– universalization of   8, 11, 13, 21, 176
– value of   6, 8, 12f., 21, 27, 40, 62, 71–73, 92–94, 97, 154, 161, 163, 173, 184, 189, 195
commandments of God   22f., 27, 29, 34, 36–39, 41–43, 45

daimonia   82–85, 123
deadly sins   81f., 123
de-familiarization   17, 19f.
diatribe   151f., 181
dick   113
dogs   21, 125–134, 138, 140, 145–147

enslavement   75, 80, 85, 87
epispasm   26f., 30–33, 168
eschatological gentiles   50
ethnic essentialism   14f., 17f., 34, 130
exclusion   56–62, 71, 81, 84f., 90–92, 116–118, 124

foreskin   16–18
– as metonym   17, 23, 27, 97, 148

– flesh of   69f., 96–99, 122, 184, 188
– metaphorical   16
– natural   18, 27, 133, 139, 147, 162, 165f., 168, 201
– of Abraham   183–187
– restoration of. See *epispasm*

genealogical purity   14f., 173

Hagar   63, 66–69, 71, 91, 123
halakhah   26, 44, 54, 88, 100, 108f., 144
heart-circumcision. See *circumcision of the heart*

interlocutor in the book of Romans   148, 151–168, 172f., 176–179, 180f., 184, 190
intermarriage   73f., 83
Ioudaismos   105–112
Isaac   53, 63, 66–72, 74f., 88, 91, 123
Ishmael   63, 66–69, 71f., 74f., 85, 123

judaization   33, 35, 54f., 87, 107, 111, 122, 131, 135, 158

krasis   79f., 85f.

law observance   41–45, 56f., 59–62, 68, 84, 86–89, 101, 104, 120, 122, 162–164, 166
leaven   83, 92, 118

maternal imagery   66
matrilineal principle   144
Messiah. See *Christ*
mutilation   113f., 126, 131, 135, 136–139, 142, 145–147, 200

new creation   40, 95–99
Noachide laws   43f.

Paul
– and Judaism   7–11
– apostle to the gentiles   6, 9f., 49, 100f., 104, 106, 149–151
– opponents of   119–122, 126–142
Paul within Judaism   9–11
penile aesthetics   12, 30f., 97, 114
Peter (Cephas)   18, 42, 48, 50, 52–55, 111, 135, 139
pneuma   20, 42, 63, 67f., 72, 74–87, 92–94, 97, 102f., 129, 174, 176
pneumatic transformation   42, 77, 80

resident alien   44, 72f.
rhetorical negation   38–41
ritual failure   81, 135, 165

Sarah   63, 66–69, 71, 90f.
semen   82
spirit. See *pneuma*
stoicheia   80, 85, 87, 124

table-fellowship   53f.
theory of the *status quo*   29
Timothy   33, 56, 101, 126, 143–147, 170, 193
Titus   50–52, 55

uncircumcision. See *foreskin*
union   48, 73, 80, 82–84
– incompatible   82–85, 123
– of spouses   82
– pneumatic   20, 48, 76f., 80, 82, 123f., 169
– with a prostitute   82–85

Ancient Sources

Hebrew Bible/Old Testament

Genesis
2:7   77
4:1   68
14:14   198
15   74, 185 f.
16   68
16–21   63, 65, 90
16:1–4   68
17   13 f., 41, 65, 71, 74, 123–24, 184–86, 198
17:1   68
17:4   75
17:4–7   189
17:10–14   22, 69
17:11   16, 184, 188
17:12   69
17:13   71
17:13–14   184
17:14   16, 69 f., 146, 186
17:15–21   69
17:19–21   72
17:23   198
17:23–25   16
17:23–27   69
17:24–26   184
21:1–2   68
21:1–7   69, 71
21:9   67
21:10   67, 90 f.
25:1–2   63
34   73 f.
34:14   16
45:27   79

Exodus
4:24–26   199
4:25   16
6:12   16
6:30   16
12:12–13   199
12:19   72
12:21–23   199
12:43–45   73
12:43–49   72
12:48   16, 186
12:49   72
15:23   155
20:26   141
31:3   79
35:31   79

Leviticus
8–12   44
12:3   16, 22, 41, 69 f., 146
17–26   44
18:6   141
18:8–16   72
19:28   136
21   44
21:5   136
23:42   72
24:16   72
24:22   72
25:45–46   72
26:41   16, 174 f., 186

Numbers
5:14   79
14:23   79
15:14–16   72

Deuteronomy
6:4   182
10:16   125, 174 f.
17:7   91
19:19   91
21:21   91, 110
22:21   91
22:24   91
23:2   116, 118
23:19   128, 130
24:7   91
24:8–9   88

25:12   116
27:26   89
28:4   141
28:11   141
28:18   141
28:53   141
29:28   173
30:6   125, 174f.
30:9   141
32:43   191
34:9   79

Joshua
5:3   16
5:7   16

Judges
1:6–7   116
5:7   186
7:5   128

1 Samuel (1 Kingdoms)
16:7   174
17:36   17
17:43   128
24:14   128
30:12   79

2 Samuel (2 Kingdoms)
1:20   17
3:8   128
7:12   141
9:8   128
10:4   116
16:9   128
16:11   141

1 Kings (3 Kingdoms)
8:39   174
14:11   128
16:4   128
18:28   136
21:19–24   128
22:22–23   79

2 Kings (4 Kingdoms)
8:13   128

1 Chronicles
17:11   141

Ezra   14

Nehemiah   14

Esther
8:17   33

Job
30:1   128

Psalms
18:50   191
22:16   128
31:1–2   189
59:6   128
76:9   116
117:1   191
131:11   141

Proverbs
15:11   174
26:11   128

Isaiah
11:2–3   78
11:10   191, 194
15:2   136
18:5   116
42:6–7   158
52:5   160
54:1   66
56:3–7   50
56:10–11   128

Jeremiah
4:4   125, 169, 174f.
6:10   16
9:25   16f., 186
9:25–26   72f., 125, 138, 165, 172, 175f., 195
31:33   192

Lamentations
1:10   118

Ezekiel
32:17–32   72
36:26   174
44:6–9   74, 175 f.
44:7   16, 118, 125, 175, 186
44:9   16, 118, 175, 186

Daniel
1:3–17   53

Hosea
6:6   38
7:14   136

Jonah
1:2   108

Zephaniah
3:8–13   50

Zechariah
8:20–23   50

Ancient Jewish Writers

Josephus
Against Apion
2.85   129

Jewish Antiquities
2.1   155
4.139   112
4.206   128
8.120   43
11.255   193
12.226   75
12.240–41   30
13.257–58   33, 74
13.318–19   33, 74
14.106   93
17.41   112
20.17–47   87
20.34–48   106
20.34–50   166
20.38–40   33, 74
20.43   106
20.100   112

Jewish War
1.110   112
2.160   116
2.403   116
2.454   33, 87, 135
4.388   193
5.512   116

The Life
191   112

Philo
Against Flaccus
53   116

Allegorical Interpretation
3.8   116
3.88–89   25
3.127   116
3.129   116
3.134   116
3.140   116

On the Cherubim
40–47   68

On the Confusion of Tongues
184–86   86

On the Decalogue
52–63   154

On Drunkenness
23   116

On the Embassy to Gaius
139   129

On the Life of Joseph
241   193

On the Life of Moses
1.130–31   130

On the Migration of Abraham
89–93   36, 102, 171
92   101, 200

On the Special Laws
1.1–11   200
1.6   174
1.9–11   101
1.13–28   154
1.304–5   175
1.305   101
2.13   112
2.109   139
2.166   154

3.137   25
4.91   129

On the Virtues
209–220   25

Questions and Answers on Exodus
2.2   166

Questions and Answers on Genesis
2.59   86, 174
3.18   68
3.46   175
3.46–52   101
3.52   70

That Every Good Person Is Free
89–91   129

Deuterocanonical Books

Tobit
1:11   53
6:2   128
11:4   128
14:6   50

Judith
10:5   53
11:19   128
12:17–19   53
14   33

Wisdom of Solomon
11–15   154

Sirach
23:6   141
32:23–24   43
44:19–20   184

Bel and the Dragon
1:3–7   154

1 Maccabees
1:11–15   30
2:27   112
2:46   111
12:21   75

2 Maccabees
2:21   111
4:12   30
6:1   112
7:1–2   53
7:2   112
7:37   112
8:1   111
14:38   111

1 Esdras   14

4 Maccabees
4:23   112
4:26   111
5:33   112
9:17   193

Old Testament Pseudepigrapha

Joseph and Aseneth
7:1 53

Jubilees 14
1:22 – 24 102
1:23 174 – 76
15:14 71, 146, 176
15:25 – 26 22, 70, 176, 199
15:33 88
16:14 70 f.
17:4 67
22:16 53
30 74
30:11 – 14 144

Letter of Aristeas
137 154
181 – 294 53

Odes of Solomon
11:1 – 3 174 f.
11:1 – 5 12

Psalms of Solomon
9:9 181

Testament of Moses
8:1 30
8:1 – 5 30
8:3 30
8:4 – 5 31

Dead Sea Scrolls

1QpHab
11:13 102, 175

1QS
5.5 175
5:5 – 6 102

4Q434
Frag. 1, 1.4 175

4QFlor
Frag. 1, I, 1 – 4 173

4QMMT 14

4QpNah
Frags. 3 – 4, II, 7 – 10 173

8QGen 70

New Testament

Matthew
5:13 94
6:1 – 18 172
10:10 134
10:27 108
15:21 – 28 129
15:24 129, 191
15:26 129

19:17 – 19 43
20:28 191

Mark
5:20 108
7:24 – 30 129
7:26 129
7:27 129
9:43 116

9:45   116
10:43–45   191

Luke
1:5   144
3:22   78
6:4   164
6:18   78
8:55   78
10:7   134
12:3   108

John
18:10   116
18:26   116

Acts
2:4   78
6:14   112
7   169
7:51   16, 169, 186
7:59   78
9:2   108
10   50
10:45   17, 52
11   49f.
11:2   17, 52
11:25–30   49
12:25   49
15   23, 32f., 44–46, 49f., 60, 182
15:1   50, 89, 108, 112
15:1–5   104
15:1–29   49
15:5   44, 50f., 89, 112
15:19–20   44
15:20–29   43
15:24   109
15:29   44
16:1–3   33, 56, 144
16:3   101
19:23   108
19:37   159
21   32
21:21   26, 144
21:21–26   201
21:28   159
22:3   112

24:5   108
24:14   108
24:22   108
26:5   112
27:28   116
28:17   112
28:22   108

Romans
1:1–6   191, 194
1:3   191
1:5   6, 194
1:5–6   150f.
1:6   150
1:10–13   149
1:13–15   150f.
1:15   105
1:16   18, 35, 156, 170, 179, 183
1:16–17   180
1:17   183
1:18–32   154, 178f.
2   183
2:1   152
2:1–5   154f., 159
2:1–29   179
2:3   152
2:6–16   154
2:9   156
2:9–10   18, 35, 170
2:10   156
2:17   21, 98, 148, 152, 153–60, 170, 181
2:17–18   156f.
2:17–20   158f.
2:17–24   160f.
2:17–29   30, 152, 155, 157, 159
2:19–20   158
2:20   160
2:21–22   158
2:21–24   159
2:21–29   159
2:23   98, 181
2:23–24   160
2:23–27   159
2:25   13, 148, 162, 164f., 168, 201
2:25–27   21, 133, 162, 195
2:25–29   5, 148, 153f., 160–76, 192f., 196
2:26   13, 148, 166, 168

2:27	13, 18, 133, 139, 146, 148, 164–166, 168, 189, 201
2:28	148, 156
2:28–29	6, 8, 11, 13, 35, 125, 143, 153, 159, 161, 169–176, 177, 195, 200 f.
2:28–3:2	148
2:29	21, 102, 148, 156, 167, 169, 193
3	180, 183, 196
3–4	191
3:1	13, 148, 152, 156, 170, 172, 177, 193, 201
3:1–2	6, 12, 21, 62, 137, 148, 163 f., 170, 177–79, 189, 195, 201
3:1–7	191
3:1–8	178
3:1–9	177
3:2	177
3:3	177, 179
3:3–4	177
3:4	152, 184
3:5	177 f.
3:6	152, 184
3:7	177
3:7–8	178
3:9	18, 35, 152, 156, 170, 176, 178–80
3:10–18	179
3:19	179
3:20	135, 181
3:21–26	180, 194
3:21–31	179, 195
3:22	35, 180, 183, 188
3:22–23	45, 179
3:24	180
3:25	180, 183
3:26	179 f., 183, 192
3:27	180 f.
3:27–28	181
3:27–31	180
3:28	135, 179, 181
3:28–29	182
3:28–30	45, 184, 195
3:29	18, 156, 181
3:29–30	21, 27 f., 35, 57, 167, 170, 180–83
3:30	13, 17, 27, 109, 121, 133, 148, 179, 183, 193, 201
3:30–31	183
3:31	60, 152, 181, 184
4	13, 51, 136, 183, 185, 191, 196
4:1	152, 184, 190, 195 f.
4:1–25	180
4:2	98
4:2–3	181
4:2–8	184
4:2–25	184
4:6–8	189
4:9	13, 109, 133, 148, 170, 185, 189
4:9–12	15, 17, 21, 27, 35, 149, 183–90, 193, 195 f.
4:9–25	194
4:10	13, 148, 187
4:11	13, 148, 188, 192, 199, 201
4:11–12	185, 190
4:12	13, 52, 121, 148, 170, 188 f., 192, 201
4:16	183, 185, 188–90, 192, 195
4:16–17	189
4:17	195
5:1	183
5:2–3	98
5:5	43, 178
5:11	98
5:20–6:2	178
6:1	152
6:2	152, 184
6:4	26
6:15	152, 184
7:6	174
7:7	152, 184
7:8–12	43
7:13	152, 184
8:4	26
8:15	174
8:31	152
9–11	62, 156, 158, 171, 177, 191
9:3	122
9:4	192
9:4–5	146, 177, 189, 201
9:14	152, 184
9:19	152
9:20	152
9:24	18, 35, 156, 170
9:30	152, 183
9:30–10:4	181
9:32	183
10:4	44
10:6	183, 192

10:12   10, 18, 35, 45, 156, 170, 179
11:1   152, 184, 201
11:8   98
11:11   152, 184
11:13   151
11:13–14   6, 194
11:13–24   10
11:16   82
11:17–24   35, 183
11:25–26   189
11:26   177
11:27   192
11:28–29   177
13:4   193
13:9   43
13:10   43
13:13   26
14–15   30
14:15   26
14:23   183
15:7   191
15:8   13, 15, 21, 27, 109, 121, 148 f., 151, 167, 190–94, 195 f., 201
15:8–9   191, 194
15:9   194
15:12   194
15:15–16   151
15:16–19   194
15:17   98
15:20   105, 155
16:1   193
16:3   134
16:9   134
16:21   134

1 Corinthians
1:2   25
1:17   105
1:22   18, 156
1:22–24   35, 170
1:23   18, 110, 156
1:24   18, 156
1:29   98
1:31   98
2:11   78
2:12   78
3:3   26

3:5   193
3:5–7   38
3:9   134
3:21   98
4:7   98
4:14–15   66
4:17   22
5:1–11   83
5:5–6   92, 118
5:6   83, 92, 98
5:9   92
5:10   179
5:11   156
5:13   91, 157
6:9–10   154
6:9–11   158
6:15   151
6:15–19   82 f., 123
6:17   80
7   23, 25 f., 33, 44
7:2   24
7:9   24
7:12–14   82
7:14   82
7:15   22
7:17   20, 22 f., 25, 27–29, 34, 39, 43, 45
7:17–18   38, 163
7:17–19   5 f., 27, 109, 166, 170, 182
7:17–20   20, 22, 31, 35, 101
7:18   26, 28, 57, 120, 148, 201
7:18–19   133
7:18–20   24
7:19   12 f., 20, 22, 27 f., 34, 37 f., 40, 42–45, 92, 95, 97 f., 124, 166, 170, 173
7:20   23 f., 25 f.
7:21   24, 26
7:21–24   24
7:22   26
7:24   23–26
7:26   24
7:29   24
7:31   24
7:36–38   24
8:1–13   44
8:6   122
9   169
9:15–16   98

9:16   105
9:18   105
9:19–22   28, 44
9:20   156, 170
9:20–21   100 f.
9:24   132
10:14–22   82 f., 123
10:14–33   44
10:16–22   151
10:21   84
10:32   18, 35, 156, 170
11:12   183
12:2   34–36, 154
12:13   18, 35, 80, 123, 156, 170
12:23   141
12:24   80
12:27   80, 123
13:3   98
14:14   78
14:37   43
15   80
15:1   105
15:2   105
15:31   98
15:35–58   76
15:38–41   77
15:42–54   24
15:44   76
15:45   77
15:47   80
15:47–49   77
15:50   77

2 Corinthians
1:22   80, 174
3:6   174, 192 f.
5:5   80
5:12   98
5:16   98
5:17   98
5:20   194
6:4   194
8:23   134
10:2–3   26
10:16   105
11   122
11:13   134

11:15   194
11:17   105
11:22   121 f., 156
11:23   194
11:24   100, 156, 170
12:11   38
12:18   26

Galatians
1:6   55
1:6–7   47, 52, 60
1:6–9   117
1:7   47, 105, 120
1:8   105
1:9   105
1:11   50, 105
1:11–12   104
1:11–2:10   105
1:12   108
1:13–14   106 f., 110 f., 124
1:13–16   201
1:14   112
1:15–16   6
1:16   50, 104 f., 108
1:23   104 f.
2   21, 48 f.
2:1–5   51
2:1–10   49
2:1–15   117
2:2   50, 132
2:3   13, 51, 55, 111, 135, 148, 201
2:3–5   33
2:4–5   51
2:5   55, 89
2:7   13, 17, 35, 51, 100
2:7–9   6, 27 f., 109, 120, 170, 201
2:7–12   28
2:7–14   182
2:9   13, 52, 57
2:11–13   52
2:11–14   135
2:12   13, 27, 109, 192
2:12–15   170
2:13   55, 156
2:13–15   120
2:14   35, 55, 111, 135, 156
2:14–15   18, 35, 156

2:15   18, 57, 139, 156, 166
2:15–16   112, 181
2:16   47, 95, 135, 183
2:17   151, 194
2:18   164
3   44, 63, 75, 184
3–4   63, 81, 136
3:2   47, 68, 95, 135
3:2–3   76, 79
3:2–7   79
3:2–14   94
3:3   68, 97, 102
3:3–5   58, 68
3:5   47, 68, 76, 79, 95, 135
3:6–7   75, 123
3:6–9   81, 192
3:6–14   196
3:7–9   68, 183
3:8–9   95, 135
3:10   57, 89, 135
3:10–11   95, 135
3:10–14   110
3:11   47, 57
3:11–12   95, 135, 183
3:13   110
3:14   58, 63, 68, 75 f., 79, 102, 123, 183
3:15–18   192
3:16   76, 79
3:16–19   85
3:18   47, 68
3:19–21   151
3:21   87
3:21–22   57
3:22   95, 135, 179, 183
3:23–4:5   87
3:24   95, 135, 183
3:26   183
3:27   76, 79
3:27–29   79, 196
3:28   10, 18, 35, 117, 120, 156, 170, 182
3:29   68, 75, 79 f., 97, 102, 123
4   63, 67, 75, 85, 184
4:3   87
4:5–7   85
4:6   63, 68, 76, 78 f., 97, 174
4:6–7   58, 75, 123
4:8   35, 69

4:8–9   85
4:10   56, 87
4:13   105
4:19   66
4:21   47, 65, 89 f., 122
4:21–22   74
4:21–31   66, 68 f., 94, 97, 196
4:21–5:1   48, 63, 80, 90
4:22–23   67
4:24   67
4:26   67
4:26–31   68
4:27   66
4:28–29   67, 102
4:29   67, 76, 79
4:30   90, 117 f.
4:31   67, 85
5   40, 56–58, 61 f., 81, 90, 142
5:1   69, 85
5:1–6   12
5:2   14, 27, 47 f., 55–60, 62, 69, 80 f., 84, 89, 91, 121, 148, 166, 200
5:2–3   47
5:2–4   13, 33, 48, 56, 68, 80, 82, 91, 93, 95, 117 f., 123, 135, 201
5:2–6   12
5:3   56–59, 86, 88 f., 91, 118, 120, 148
5:4   56, 62, 81, 87, 89, 93, 117
5:4–6   94
5:5   183
5:5–6   93
5:6   12 f., 15, 20, 37, 40, 48, 62, 92–95, 98, 120, 124, 133, 173
5:7   117, 132
5:9   118
5:10   47, 120
5:11   13, 20, 48, 58, 99–112, 201
5:12   7, 47 f., 68, 92, 112–18, 120, 124, 134
5:13   101
5:13–26   103
5:14   22
5:16   26, 101
5:17   101
5:19   101
5:19–21   154
5:24   101
6:4   98

6:11 97
6:12 55, 99, 110 f., 122, 135, 148
6:12–13 13, 47 f., 87, 95, 119–22
6:12–14 58
6:13 13, 28, 96–98, 108, 117 f., 120–22, 124, 136, 148, 201
6:14 96, 98, 110, 122
6:15 5, 12 f., 15, 20, 37, 40, 48, 92 f., 95–99, 120, 124, 133, 173
6:16 35, 99, 143

Ephesians
2:11 109, 121, 133, 143, 170
2:11–13 192
2:11–22 12

Philippians
1:1 6, 126, 143
1:12 130
1:19 78
1:26 98
2:7 85
2:12 130
2:16 98, 132
2:25 134
2:25–30 145
3 127
3:1 130
3:2 7, 21, 113, 126, 127–39, 140, 146, 200 f.
3:2–3 33, 141, 145, 166, 200
3:2–5 135
3:3 5 f., 8, 11, 13, 15, 21, 27, 35, 78, 98, 109, 121, 125 f., 133, 138, 142–47, 167, 169 f., 192, 201
3:3–6 146, 163
3:3–8 98
3:4 98, 138
3:4–6 144
3:5 13, 70, 88, 138
3:5–6 21, 60, 98, 112, 126, 146 f.
3:6 86
3:7–8 98
3:9 135, 183
3:12 183
3:13 130
3:13–14 132
3:17 130, 145, 183
3:18–19 126, 140–42, 146

3:19 142
4:1 130
4:3 134
4:8 130
4:13 40, 94
4:15 104
4:18 145
4:21 130

Colossians
2:11 169, 192 f.
2:12 183
3:11 10, 109, 121, 133, 170
4:11 52, 121, 143, 170

1 Thessalonians
1:9 35
2:1 165
2:4 174
2:12 26
2:14 156, 170
2:19 98
3:2 134
4:3–5 154

Titus
1:10 121, 143

Philemon
1 134
10 66
24 134

James
2:9 164
2:11 164
2:26 78
5:16 94

1 Peter
4:3 154

Revelation
2:9 157
3:9 157
5:2 108 f.
16:15 141

Early Christian Writings

Ambrosiaster
Commentary on Philippians
3:5   146

Augustine
Letters
40.4   28
40.6   28

The Spirit and the Letter
29.50   183

The Work of Monks
12   28

Clement of Alexandria
Stromateis
7.9   169

Epistle of Barnabas
9   169
9.1–5   198
9.1–9   12
9.4   196–98
9.6   33, 188, 198 f.
9.7–9   198
9.8   198
10.12   198

Epistle to Diognetus
4:1–4   12

Irenaeus
Against Heresies
4.16.1   169

John Chrysostom
Adversus Judaeos
1.2.1–2   127

Contra ludos et theatra
6   155

Homilies on Ephesians
2   188

Homilies on Galatians
5   5
5:3   88

Homilies on Philippians
10   146
11   127

Homilies on Romans
6   153

Justin Martyr
Dialogue with Trypho
10   70
11.5   169
12.3   169, 199
14.1   199
15.7   169
16.2   197, 199
16.4   199
18.2   169
18.2–19.3   125
19.2   199
19.3   5, 28, 169, 199
23   70
23.2   169
23.5   199
24.1   169
28.4   169
41.4   169, 199
43.2   169
92.3–4   5
92.4   169
113.6–7   199
113.7   169
114.4   169, 199
137.1   169

Origen
Against Celsus
5.48   197, 199

Commentary on Romans
2.11.4   153
2.11.5   158

2.13.11–12   65
2.13.11–17   72
2.13.16   72
3.10.1–2   182
3.10.2–3   183
10.8.3   192

Homilies on Genesis
3.4   200
3.4–6   200
3.6   101, 200

Tertullian
Against Marcion
5.2   47
5.4.8   68
5.13   169

Theodoret
Commentary on Philippians
3:5   146

New Testament Apocrypha and Pseudepigrapha

Epistle to the Apostles
31:1   146

Gospel of Philip
82:26–30   12

Gospel of Thomas
53   5, 12, 21, 197

Rabbinic Works

Mishnah
Avot
3:11   31

Bekhorot
5:6   129

Nedarim
3:11   17f., 139, 166, 171, 201
4:3   129

Shabbat
19:6   88

Tosefta
Avodah Zarah
8:4   43

Sanhedrin
13:2   106

Shabbat
16:6   31

Babylonian Talmud
Avodah Zarah
3b   106
27a   17, 139

Pesahim
3b   159

Shabbat
137b   188

Yevamot
24b   106

Targum Pseudo-Jonathan
Gen 21:10   68

Midrash Tanhuma
Tazria
7   5

Terumah
3   129

Genesis Rabbah
46:2   69
48:8   31, 163
53:11   67
55:4   67

Pesiqta Rabbati
161a   106

Pirke de Rabbi Eliezer
10:9   188
29   129

Sifra Kedoshim
8:3   88

Greco-Roman Literature

Aelius Theon
Progymnasmata
8   152
106   159
108   159

Aetius
De Placita Philosophorum
4.5.6   174

Alexander of Aphrodisias
On Mixture
216.14–218.6   79
252.1   86

Aristophanes
Lysistrata
158   132

Aristotle
Politics
1252a–1255b   25

Aulus Cornelius Celsus
On Medicine
7.25.1   26, 114

Comica Adespota
1057   132

Digesta
48.8.4.2   114f.
48.8.11   115

Dio Cassius
Historiae romanae
78.8.2   155
80.11   114

Diodorus Siculus
Bibliotheca historica
1.28.3   33
3.32.4   33
4.6.1–4   142
11.47.2   155
34.1.2   53

Dionysius of Halicarnassus
Antiquitates romanae
30.50.3   155

Epictetus
Diatribai
2.9.20–22   157
2.19.19   157
2.19.28   157
2.20.19   116
3.1.31   113
3.7.17   157
3.24.41   157

Etymologicum Magnum
549.27   133

Eustathius of Thessalonica
Commentary on the Odyssey
2.147   132

Ancient Sources

Galen
Method of Medicine
14.15   114

On the Doctrines of Hippocrates and Plato
7.3.30   86

On Semen
1.5.18   82

Herodotus
Histories
2.36–37   33, 72
2.104   33

Hesychius of Alexandria
κ 4573   132
κ 4594   133
κ 4762   133

Historia Augusta
Hadrian
14.2   114, 137

Julius Pollux
Onomastikon
2.4.171   133

Juvenal
Satires
14.96–106   32 f., 87

Martial
Epigrams
7.30   32
7.82   32

Oribasius
Collectionum Medicarum Reliquiae
50.3.1   133

Petronius
Poems
24   32

Satyricon
102.13   32

Plato
Laws
959b   112

Plato Comicus
174.16   132

Plutarch
Against the Stoics on Common Conceptions
1078B–E   79

Quintilian
Institutio oratoria
9.2.29–37   152

Soranus
Gynecology
2.9.14   114
2.16.34   27, 32, 114

Stobaeus
1.55.5–11   79, 86

Strabo
Geography
16.4.5   137
16.4.9   137
16.4.17   114, 137
17.2.5   33

Tacitus
Histories
4.1–5.2   32
5.5.2   53

Themistius
Orations
31.354b   156

Theophrastus
Characteres
23.1   159

Xenophon
Cyropaedia
2.2.12   159
8.4.4   108

Medieval Christian Writings

Euthymius Zigabenus
Commentary on Romans
2.17   153
2.28   153
2.29   153

Thomas Aquinas
Commentary on Romans
§240–45   5

www.ingramcontent.com/pod-product-compliance
Lightning Source LLC
Chambersburg PA
CBHW020227170426
43201CB00007B/343